An Introduction to Multiagent Systems

Michael Wooldridge
Department of Computer Science,
University of Liverpool, UK

JOHN WILEY & SONS, LTD

Library of Congress Cataloging-in-Publication Data

Wooldridge, Michael J., 1966–
     An introduction to multiagent systems / Michael Wooldridge.
         p. cm.
     Includes bibliographical references and index.
     ISBN 0-471-49691-X
     1. Intelligent agents (Computer software)   I. Title.

QA76.76.I58 W65 2001
006.3 — dc21
                                                2001055949

British Library Cataloguing in Publication Data

A catalogue record for this book is available from the British Library

ISBN 0 471 49691 X

Typeset in 9.5/12.5pt Lucida Bright by T&T Productions Ltd, London.
Printed and bound in Great Britain by Biddles Ltd, Guildford and Kings Lynn.
This book is printed on acid-free paper responsibly manufactured from sustainable forestry in which at least two trees are planted for each one used for paper production.

An Introduction to
Multiagent Systems

To my family:
Jean, John, Andrew,
Christopher, and of course Janine.

Contents

Preface

Multiagent systems are systems composed of multiple interacting computing elements, known as *agents*. Agents are computer systems with two important capabilities. First, they are at least to some extent capable of *autonomous action* – of deciding *for themselves* what they need to do in order to satisfy their design objectives. Second, they are capable of interacting with other agents – not simply by exchanging data, but by engaging in analogues of the kind of social activity that we all engage in every day of our lives: cooperation, coordination, negotiation, and the like.

Multiagent systems are a relatively new sub-field of computer science – they have only been studied since about 1980, and the field has only gained widespread recognition since about the mid-1990s. However, since then international interest in the field has grown enormously. This rapid growth has been spurred at least in part by the belief that agents are an appropriate software paradigm through which to exploit the possibilities presented by massive open distributed systems – such as the Internet. Although they will certainly have a pivotal role to play in exploiting the potential of the Internet, there is a lot more to multiagent systems than this. Multiagent systems seem to be a natural metaphor for understanding and building a wide range of what we might crudely call *artificial social systems*. The ideas of multiagent systems are not tied to a single application domain, but, like objects before them, seem to find currency in a host of different application domains.

My intention in writing this book is simple. I aim to introduce the main issues in the theory and practice of multiagent systems in a way that will be accessible to anyone with a basic background in computer science/IT. The book is deliberately intended to sit on the fence between science and engineering. Thus, as well as discussing the principles and issues in the theory of multiagent systems (i.e. the *science* of multiagent systems), I very much hope that I manage to communicate something of how to *build* such systems (i.e. multiagent systems *engineering*).

The multiagent systems field can be understood as consisting of two closely interwoven strands of work. The first is concerned with *individual* agents, while the second is concerned with *collections* of these agents. The structure of the book reflects this division. The first part of the book – Chapter 1 – sets the scene by discussing where the multiagent system field emerged from, and presenting some visions of where it is going. The second part – Chapters 2–5 inclusive – are concerned with individual agents. Following an introduction to the concept of agents, their environments, and the various ways in which we might tell agents what to do, I describe and contrast the main techniques that have been proposed in the literature for building agents. Thus I discuss agents that decide what to do via logical deduction, agents in which decision making resembles the process of practical reasoning in humans, agents that do not explicitly reason at all, and, finally, agents that make decisions by combining deductive and other decision-making mechanisms. In the third part of the book – Chapters 6–10 inclusive – I focus on collections of agents. Following a discussion on the various ways in which multi-agent encounters and interactions can be classified, I discuss the ways in which self-interested agents can reach agreements, communicate with one another, and work together. I also discuss some of the main approaches proposed for designing multiagent systems. The fourth and final part of the book presents two advanced supplemental chapters, on applications of agent systems, and formal methods for reasoning about agent systems, respectively.

I have assumed that the main audience for the book will be undergraduate students of computer science/IT – the book should be suitable for such students in their second or third year of study. However, I also hope that the book will be accessible to computing/IT professionals, who wish to know more about some of the ideas driving one of the major areas of research and development activity in computing today.

Prerequisites: what you need to know before you start

The book assumes a knowledge of computer science that would be gained in the first year or two of a computing or information technology degree course. In order of decreasing importance, the specific skills required in order to understand and make the most of the book are

- an understanding of the principles of programming in high level languages such as C or Java, the ability to make sense of pseudo-code descriptions of algorithms, and a nodding acquaintance with some of the issues in concurrent and distributed systems (e.g. threads in Java);
- familiarity with the basic concepts and issues of artificial intelligence (such as the role of search and knowledge representation);
- familiar with basic set and logic notation (e.g. an understanding of what is meant by such symbols as $\in, \subseteq, \cap, \cup, \wedge, \vee, \neg, \forall, \exists, \vdash, \models$).

However, in order to gain some value from the book, all that is really required is an appreciation of what computing is about. There is not much by way of abstract mathematics in the book, and wherever there is a quantity n of mathematics, I have tried to compensate by including at least $2n$ intuition to accompany and explain it.

Teaching with this book

I have written this book primarily with its use as a course text in mind. The book is specifically intended for middle to advanced undergraduates, or beginning graduates of computing/IT. The students at my University for whom this book is intended are either in the third year of an undergraduate computing degree, or else in the second semester of a three semester 'conversion' MSc course (i.e. an MSc course designed to equip graduates with non-computing degrees with basic computing skills).

The book contains somewhat more material than is likely to be taught in most one-semester undergraduate courses, but strong students should certainly be able to read and make sense of most of the material in a single semester. The 'core' of the book is Chapters 1–9 and 11 inclusive. This is the material that I would regard as being the 'core curriculum' of the multiagent systems field. This material is divided into four main parts:

- an introduction (Chapter 1), which sets the scene for the remainder of the book;

- an introduction to intelligent agents (Chapters 2–5 inclusive);

- an introduction to multiagent systems (Chapters 6–9 inclusive);

- a discussion of applications of multiagent systems (Chapter 11).

Although individual teachers may wish to spend larger or smaller amounts of time covering the different parts of the book, I would nevertheless expect most courses to at least touch on the material in all these chapters.

I have included three jokers in the pack.

- Chapter 10 (*Methodologies*) introduces techniques for the analysis and design of multiagent systems, some of the pitfalls associated with designing and deploying multiagent systems, and a discussion of mobile agents technology. Most of this material is, more than any other material in the book, not yet really at a stage where I believe it can form part of an undergraduate degree (at least in my opinion!). I would not therefore expect this material to be taught on most undergraduate courses; it is included because (i) I suspect it *will* be important in the near future; (ii) I wanted to provide pointers for those interested in finding out more; and most importantly (iii) I think its interesting, and it is my book.

- Chapter 12 (*Logics for Multiagent Systems*) focuses on logics for multiagent systems. Logics of agency form a significant part of the research literature on multiagent systems, but in my experience, many students view this material as being hard – perhaps because it seems so abstract. However, I strongly felt that omitting this material entirely would be doing the field a disservice, and again, I find it interesting. Hence Chapter 12. Students with courses on logic or semantics under their belt should find this chapter a breeze.

- Appendix A (*A History Lesson*) gives a (rather subjective!) history of the agents field. Nobody has yet attempted to do this, and so it seems to me to be a useful thing to do. Originally, this section was included in Chapter 1, but several reviewers of the draft manuscript felt that perhaps it included too much material to be really useful in an introductory chapter.

Lecture slides and other associated teaching material, as well as extensive Web links for this book are available at

`http://www.csc.liv.ac.uk/~mjw/pubs/imas/`

I welcome additional teaching materials (e.g. tutorial/discussion questions, exam papers and so on), which I will make available on an 'open source' basis – please email to

`M.J.Wooldridge@csc.liv.ac.uk`

Chapter structure

Every chapter of the book ends with three sections, which I hope will be of wider interest.

- A 'class reading' suggestion, which lists one or two key articles from the research literature that may be suitable for class reading in seminar-based courses.

- A 'notes and further reading' section, which provides additional technical comments on the chapter and extensive pointers into the literature for advanced reading. This section is aimed at those who wish to gain a deeper, research-level understanding of the material.

- An 'exercises' section, which might form the basis of homework to be set for students. Exercises are graded on a scale of one to four, with one being the easiest (a few minutes work), and four being the hardest (research projects). Exercises of difficulty three might be undertaken as projects over some weeks or months; exercises of level one or two should be feasible within a few hours at most, and might be undertaken as part of weekly homework or tutorials. Some exercises are suggested for class discussion.

What I left out and why

Part of the joy in working in the multiagent systems field is that it takes inspiration from, and in turn contributes to, a very wide range of other disciplines. The field is in part Artificial Intelligence (AI), part economics, part software engineering, part social sciences, and so on. But this poses a real problem for anyone writing a book on the subject, namely, what to put in and what to leave out. While there is a large research literature on agents, there are not too many models to look at with respect to textbooks on the subject, and so I have had to make some hard choices here. When deciding what to put in/leave out, I have been guided to a great extent by what the 'mainstream' multiagent systems literature regards as important, as evidenced by the volume of published papers on the subject. The second consideration was what might reasonably be (i) taught and (ii) understood in the context of a typical one-semester university course. This largely excluded most abstract theoretical material, which will probably make most students happy – if not their teachers.

I deliberately chose to omit some material as follows.

Learning. My view is that learning is an important agent capability, but is not central to agency. After some agonizing, I therefore decided not to cover learning. There are plenty of references to learning algorithms and techniques: see, for example, Kaelbling (1993), Weiß (1993, 1997), Weiß and Sen (1996) and Stone (2000).

Artificial life. Some sections of this book (in Chapter 5 particularly) are closely related to work carried out in the artificial life, or 'alife' community. However, the work of the alife community is carried out largely independently of that in the 'mainstream' multiagent systems community. By and large, the two communities do not interact with one another. For these reasons, I have chosen not to focus on alife in this book. (Of course, this should not be interpreted as in any way impugning the work of the alife community: it just is not what this book is about.) There are many easily available references to alife on the Web. A useful starting point is Langton (1989); another good reference is Mitchell (1996).

Mobility. There is something of a schism in the agents community between those that do mobility and those who do not – I mostly belong to the second group. Like learning, I believe mobility is an important agent capability, which is particularly valuable for some applications. But, like learning, I do not view it to be central to the multiagent systems curriculum. In fact, I do touch on mobility, in Chapter 10 – but only relatively briefly: the interested reader will find plenty of references in this chapter.

Markov decision problems. Markov decision problems (MDPs), together with their close relatives partially observable MDPs, are now the subject of much attention in the AI community, as they seem to provide a promising approach to the problem of making decisions under uncertainty. As we will see in much of the remainder of this book, this is a fundamental problem in the agent agent community also. To give a detailed introduction to MDPs, however, would be out of the question in a textbook on agents. See Blythe (1999) for pointers into the literature, and Kaelbling *et al.* (1998) for a detailed technical overview of the area and issues; Russell and Norvig (1995, pp. 498–522) give an overview in the context of an AI textbook.

In my opinion, the most important thing for students to understand are (i) the 'big picture' of multiagent systems (why it is important, where it came from, what the issues are, and where it is going), and (ii) what the key tools, techniques, and principles are. Students who understand these two things should be well equipped to make sense of the deeper research literature if they choose to.

Omissions and errors

In writing this book, I tried to set out the main threads of work that make up the multiagent systems field, and to critically assess their relative merits. In doing so, I have tried to be as open-minded and even-handed as time and space permit. However, I will no doubt have unconsciously made my own foolish and ignorant prejudices visible, by way of omissions, oversights, and the like. If you find yourself speechless with rage at something I have omitted – or included, for that matter – then all I can suggest is that you accept my apology, and take solace from the fact that someone else is almost certainly more annoyed with the book than you are.

> Little did I imagine as I looked upon the results of my labours where these sheets of paper might finally take me. Publication is a powerful thing. It can bring a man all manner of unlooked-for events, making friends and enemies of perfect strangers, and much more besides.
>
> Matthew Kneale (*English Passengers*)

Comments and corrections – and suggestions for a possible second edition – are welcome, and should be sent to the email address given above.

Web references

It would be very hard to write a book about Web-related issues without giving URLs as references. In many cases, the best possible reference to a subject is a Web site, and given the speed with which the computing field evolves, many important topics are only documented in the 'conventional' literature very late in the day. But citing Web pages as authorities can create big problems for the reader. Companies go bust, sites go dead, people move, research projects finish, and when these things happen, Web references become useless. For these reasons, I have therefore attempted to keep Web references to a minimum. I have preferred to cite the 'conventional' (i.e. printed), literature over Web pages when given a choice. In addition, I have tried to cite only Web pages that are likely to be stable and supported for the foreseeable future. The date associated with a Web page is the date at which I checked the reference was working. Many useful Web links are available from the book's Web page, listed earlier.

Acknowledgments

Several people gave invaluable feedback on the 'history of the field' section. In particular, Les Gasser and Victor Lesser were extremely helpful in sorting out my muddled view of the early days of distributed AI, and Jeff Rosenschein gave a lot of help in understanding how game-theoretic techniques entered the multi-agent systems literature. Keith Decker gave suggestions about material to cover on brokers and middle agents. Michael Fisher helped with examples to illustrate his Concurrent MetateM language in Chapter 3. Valentina Tamma set me straight on ontologies and DAML. Karen Mosman from Wiley was (and indeed is) an unspeakably cheerful, enthusiastic, and charming editor, and I suppose I should grudgingly admit that I very much enjoyed working with her. Simon Parsons and Peter McBurney were enormously helpful with the section on argumentation. Nick Jennings, as ever, gave encouragement, support, and sensible practical advice on contents and style.

Marie Devlin, Shaheen Fatima, Marc-Philippe Huget, Peter McBurney, Carmen Pardavila, and Valentina Tamma read drafts of the book and gave detailed, helpful comments. Marie saved me many hours and much tedium by checking and crosschecking the bibliography for me. I *hate* books with sloppy or incomplete references, and so Marie's help was particularly appreciated. We both made extensive use of the CITESEER autonomous citation system from NEC (see NEC, 2001), which, as well as helping to provide the definitive reference for many obscure articles, also helped to obtain the actual text in many instances. Despite all this help, many typos and more serious errors will surely remain, and these are of course my responsibility.

I have taught parts of this book in various guises at various locations since 1995. The comments and feedback from students and other participants at these venues has helped me to improve it significantly. So, thanks here to those at the 1996 German Spring School on AI (KIFS) in Günne am Möhnesee, the AgentLink summer schools in Utrecht (1999), Saarbrücken (2000), and Prague (2001), the ESSLLI course on agent theory in Saarbrücken (1998), tutorial participants at ICMAS in San Francisco (1995) and Paris (1998), tutorial participants at ECAI in Budapest (1996), Brighton (1998), and Berlin (2000), and AGENTS in Minneapolis (1998), Seattle (1999), Barcelona (2000), and Montreal (2001), as well as students in courses on agents that I have taught at Lausanne (1999), Barcelona (2000), Helsinki (1999 and 2001), and Liverpool (2001). Boi Faltings in Lausanne, Ulises Cortes and Carles Sierra in Barcelona, and Heimo Lammanen and Kimmo Raatikainen in Helsinki were all helpful and generous hosts during my visits to their respective institutions.

As ever, my heartfelt thanks go out to my colleagues and friends in the multiagent systems research community, who have made academia rewarding and enjoyable. You know who you are! Deserving of a special mention here are Carles Sierra and Carme: their kindness and hospitality has been astonishing.

I took over as Head of Department while I was completing this book, which nearly killed both the book and the Department stone dead. Fortunately – or not, depending on your point of view – Katrina Houghton fought hard to keep the University at bay, and thus bought me enough time to complete the job. For this

I am more grateful than she could imagine. Paul Leng was a beacon of common sense and good advice as I took over being Head of Department, without which I would have been *even more* clueless about the job than I am now.

A network of friends have helped me keep my feet firmly on the ground throughout the writing of this book, but more generally throughout my career. Special thanks here to Dave, Janet, Pangus, Addy, Josh, Ant, Emma, Greggy, Helen, Patrick, Bisto, Emma, Ellie, Mogsie, Houst, and the rest of the Herefordians.

My family have always been there, and writing this book has been made much easier for that. My parents, Jean and John Wooldridge, have always supported me in my career. Brothers Andrew and Christopher have done what all good brothers do: mercilessly tease at every opportunity, while simultaneously making their love abundantly clear. Janine, as ever, has been my world.

Finally, I hope everyone in the Department office will accept this finished book as definitive proof that when I said I was 'working at home', I really was. Well, sometimes at least.

Mike Wooldridge
Liverpool
Autumn 2001

1

Introduction

The history of computing to date has been marked by five important, and continuing, trends:

- *ubiquity*;
- *interconnection*;
- *intelligence*;
- *delegation*; and
- *human-orientation*.

By ubiquity, I simply mean that the continual reduction in cost of computing capability has made it possible to introduce processing power into places and devices that would hitherto have been uneconomic, and perhaps even unimaginable. This trend will inevitably continue, making processing capability, and hence intelligence of a sort, ubiquitous.

While the earliest computer systems were isolated entities, communicating only with their human operators, computer systems today are usually *interconnected*. They are *networked* into large *distributed* systems. The Internet is the obvious example; it is becoming increasingly rare to find computers in use in commercial or academic settings that do not have the capability to access the Internet. Until a comparatively short time ago, distributed and concurrent systems were seen by many as strange and difficult beasts, best avoided. The very visible and very rapid growth of the Internet has (I hope) dispelled this belief forever. Today, and for the future, distributed and concurrent systems are essentially the norm in commercial and industrial computing, leading some researchers and practitioners to revisit the very foundations of computer science, seeking theoretical models that better reflect the reality of computing as primarily a process of interaction.

The third trend is toward ever more *intelligent* systems. By this, I mean that the *complexity* of tasks that we are capable of automating and delegating to computers has also grown steadily. We are gaining a progressively better understanding of how to engineer computer systems to deal with tasks that would have been unthinkable only a short time ago.

The next trend is toward ever increasing delegation. For example, we routinely delegate to computer systems such safety critical tasks as piloting aircraft. Indeed, in fly-by-wire aircraft, the judgement of a computer program is frequently trusted over that of experienced pilots. Delegation implies that we *give control* to computer systems.

The fifth and final trend is the steady move away from machine-oriented views of programming toward concepts and metaphors that more closely reflect the way in which we ourselves understand the world. This trend is evident in every way that we interact with computers. For example, in the earliest days of computers, a user interacted with computer by setting switches on the panel of the machine. The internal operation of the device was in no way hidden from the user – in order to use it successfully, one had to fully understand the internal structure and operation of the device. Such primitive – and unproductive – interfaces gave way to command line interfaces, where one could interact with the device in terms of an ongoing dialogue, in which the user issued instructions that were then executed. Such interfaces dominated until the 1980s, when they gave way to graphical user interfaces, and the direct manipulation paradigm in which a user controls the device by directly manipulating graphical icons corresponding to objects such as files and programs. Similarly, in the earliest days of computing, programmers had no choice but to program their computers in terms of raw machine code, which implied a detailed understanding of the internal structure and operation of their machines. Subsequent programming paradigms have progressed away from such low-level views: witness the development of assembler languages, through procedural abstraction, to abstract data types, and most recently, objects. Each of these developments have allowed programmers to conceptualize and implement software in terms of higher-level – more human-oriented – abstractions.

These trends present major challenges for software developers. With respect to ubiquity and interconnection, we do not yet know what techniques might be used to develop systems to exploit ubiquitous processor power. Current software development models have proved woefully inadequate even when dealing with relatively small numbers of processors. What techniques might be needed to deal with systems composed of 10^{10} processors? The term *global computing* has been coined to describe such unimaginably large systems.

The trends to increasing delegation and intelligence imply the need to build computer systems that can act effectively on our behalf. This in turn implies two capabilities. The first is the ability of systems to operate *independently*, without our direct intervention. The second is the need for computer systems to be able to act in such a way as to *represent our best interests* while interacting with other humans or systems.

The trend toward interconnection and distribution has, in mainstream computer science, long been recognized as a key challenge, and much of the intellectual energy of the field throughout the last three decades has been directed toward developing software tools and mechanisms that allow us to build distributed systems with greater ease and reliability. However, when coupled with the need for systems that can represent our best interests, distribution poses other fundamental problems. When a computer system acting on our behalf must interact with another computer system that represents the interests of another, it may well be that (indeed, it is likely), that these interests are not the same. It becomes necessary to endow such systems with the ability to *cooperate* and *reach agreements* with other systems, in much the same way that we cooperate and reach agreements with others in everyday life. This type of capability was not studied in computer science until very recently.

Together, these trends have led to the emergence of a new field in computer science: *multiagent systems*. The idea of a multiagent system is very simple. An agent is a computer system that is capable of *independent* action on behalf of its user or owner. In other words, an agent can figure out for itself what it needs to do in order to satisfy its design objectives, rather than having to be told explicitly what to do at any given moment. A multiagent system is one that consists of a number of agents, which *interact* with one another, typically by exchanging messages through some computer network infrastructure. In the most general case, the agents in a multiagent system will be representing or acting on behalf of users or owners with very different goals and motivations. In order to successfully interact, these agents will thus require the ability to *cooperate*, *coordinate*, and *negotiate* with each other, in much the same way that we cooperate, coordinate, and negotiate with other people in our everyday lives.

This book is about multiagent systems. It addresses itself to the two key problems hinted at above.

- How do we build agents that are capable of independent, autonomous action in order to successfully carry out the tasks that we delegate to them?

- How do we build agents that are capable of interacting (cooperating, coordinating, negotiating) with other agents in order to successfully carry out the tasks that we delegate to them, particularly when the other agents cannot be assumed to share the same interests/goals?

The first problem is that of *agent design*, and the second problem is that of *society design*. The two problems are not orthogonal – for example, in order to build a society of agents that work together effectively, it may help if we give members of the society models of the other agents in it. The distinction between the two issues is often referred to as the *micro/macro* distinction. In the remainder of this book, I address both of these issues in detail.

Researchers in multiagent systems may be predominantly concerned with engineering systems, but this is by no means their only concern. As with its stable mate AI, the issues addressed by the multiagent systems field have profound implications for our understanding of ourselves. AI has been largely focused on the issues of intelligence in individuals. But surely a large part of what makes us unique as a species is our *social* ability. Not only can we communicate with one another in high-level languages, we can cooperate, coordinate, and negotiate with one another. While many other species have social ability of a kind – ants and other social insects being perhaps the best-known examples – no other species even begins to approach us in the sophistication of our social ability. In multiagent systems, we address ourselves to such questions as follow.

- How can cooperation emerge in societies of self-interested agents?

- What sorts of common languages can agents use to communicate their beliefs and aspirations, both to people and to other agents?

- How can self-interested agents recognize when their beliefs, goals, or actions conflict, and how can they reach agreements with one another on matters of self-interest, without resorting to conflict?

- How can autonomous agents coordinate their activities so as to cooperatively achieve goals?

While these questions are all addressed in part by other disciplines (notably economics and the social sciences), what makes the multiagent systems field unique and distinct is that it emphasizes that the agents in question are *computational*, *information processing* entities.

The remainder of this chapter

The purpose of this first chapter is to orient you for the remainder of the book. The chapter is structured as follows.

- I begin, in the following section, with some scenarios. The aim of these scenarios is to give you some feel for the long-term visions that are driving activity in the agents area.

- As with multiagent systems themselves, not everyone involved in the agent community shares a common purpose. I therefore summarize the different ways that people think about the 'multiagent systems project'.

- I then present and discuss some common objections to the multiagent systems field.

1.1 The Vision Thing

It is very often hard to understand what people are doing until you understand what their motivation is. The aim of this section is therefore to provide some motivation for what the agents community does. This motivation comes in the style of long-term future visions – ideas about how things might be. A word of caution: these visions are exactly that: visions. None is likely to be realized in the immediate future. But for each of the visions, work *is* underway in developing the kinds of technologies that might be required to realize them.

> Due to an unexpected system failure, a space probe approaching Saturn loses contact with its Earth-based ground crew and becomes disoriented. Rather than simply disappearing into the void, the probe recognizes that there has been a key system failure, diagnoses and isolates the fault, and correctly re-orients itself in order to make contact with its ground crew.

They key issue here is the ability of the space probe to act autonomously. First the probe needs to recognize that a fault has occurred, and must then figure out what needs to be done and how to do it. Finally, the probe must actually do the actions it has chosen, and must presumably monitor what happens in order to ensure that all goes well. If more things go wrong, the probe will be required to recognize this and respond appropriately. Notice that this is the kind of behaviour that we (humans) find easy: we do it every day, when we miss a flight or have a flat tyre while driving to work. But, as we shall see, it is *very* hard to design computer programs that exhibit this kind of behaviour.

NASA's Deep Space 1 (DS1) mission is an example of a system that is close to this kind of scenario. Launched from Cape Canaveral on 24 October 1998, DS1 was the first space probe to have an autonomous, agent-based control system (Muscettola *et al.*, 1998). Before DS1, space missions required a ground crew of up to 300 staff to continually monitor progress. This ground crew made all necessary control decisions on behalf of the probe, and painstakingly transmitted these decisions to the probe for subsequent execution. Given the length of typical planetary exploration missions, such a procedure was expensive and, if the decisions were ever required *quickly*, it was simply not practical. The autonomous control system in DS1 was capable of making many important decisions itself. This made the mission more robust, particularly against sudden unexpected problems, and also had the very desirable side effect of reducing overall mission costs.

The next scenario is not quite down-to-earth, but is at least closer to home.

> A key air-traffic control system at the main airport of Ruritania suddenly fails, leaving flights in the vicinity of the airport with no air-traffic control support. Fortunately, autonomous air-traffic control systems in nearby airports recognize the failure of their peer, and cooperate to track and deal with all affected flights. The potentially disastrous situation passes without incident.

There are several key issues in this scenario. The first is the ability of systems to take the initiative when circumstances dictate. The second is the ability of agents to *cooperate* to solve problems that are beyond the capabilities of any individual agents. The kind of cooperation required by this scenario was studied extensively in the Distributed Vehicle Monitoring Testbed (DVMT) project undertaken between 1981 and 1991 (see, for example, Durfee, 1988). The DVMT simulates a network of vehicle monitoring agents, where each agent is a problem solver that analyses sensed data in order to identify, locate, and track vehicles moving through space. Each agent is typically associated with a sensor, which has only a partial view of the entire space. The agents must therefore cooperate in order to track the progress of vehicles through the entire sensed space. Air-traffic control systems have been a standard application of agent research since the work of Cammarata and colleagues in the early 1980s (Cammarata *et al.*, 1983); a recent multiagent air-traffic control application is the OASIS system implemented for use at Sydney airport in Australia (Ljunberg and Lucas, 1992).

Well, most of us are neither involved in designing the control systems for NASA space probes, nor are we involved in the design of safety critical systems such as air-traffic controllers. So let us now consider a vision that is closer to most of our everyday lives.

> After the wettest and coldest UK winter on record, you are in desperate need of a last minute holiday somewhere warm and dry. After specifying your requirements to your personal digital assistant (PDA), it converses with a number of different Web sites, which sell services such as flights, hotel rooms, and hire cars. After hard negotiation on your behalf with a range of sites, your PDA presents you with a package holiday.

This example is perhaps the closest of all four scenarios to actually being realized. There are many Web sites that will allow you to search for last minute holidays, but at the time of writing, to the best of my knowledge, none of them engages in active real-time negotiation in order to assemble a package specifically for you from a range of service providers. There are many basic research problems that need to be solved in order to make such a scenario work; such as the examples that follow.

- How do you state your preferences to your agent?
- How can your agent compare different deals from different vendors?
- What algorithms can your agent use to negotiate with other agents (so as to ensure you are not 'ripped off')?

The ability to negotiate in the style implied by this scenario is potentially very valuable indeed. Every year, for example, the European Commission puts out thousands of contracts to public tender. The bureaucracy associated with managing this process has an enormous cost. The ability to automate the tendering and negotiation process would save enormous sums of money (*taxpayers'* money!). Similar situations arise in government organizations the world over – a good example is the US military. So the ability to automate the process of software agents reaching mutually acceptable agreements on matters of common interest is not just an abstract concern – it may affect our lives (the amount of tax we pay) in a significant way.

1.2　Some Views of the Field

The multiagent systems field is highly interdisciplinary: it takes inspiration from such diverse areas as economics, philosophy, logic, ecology, and the social sciences. It should come as no surprise that there are therefore many different views about what the 'multiagent systems project' is all about. In this section, I will summarize some of the main views.

Agents as a paradigm for software engineering

Software engineers have derived a progressively better understanding of the characteristics of complexity in software. It is now widely recognized that *interaction* is probably the most important single characteristic of complex software. Software architectures that contain many dynamically interacting components, each with their own thread of control and engaging in complex, coordinated protocols, are typically orders of magnitude more complex to engineer correctly and efficiently than those that simply compute a function of some input through a single thread of control. Unfortunately, it turns out that many (if not most) real-world applications have precisely these characteristics. As a consequence, a major research topic in computer science over at least the past two decades has been the development of tools and techniques to model, understand, and implement systems in which interaction is the norm. Indeed, many researchers now believe that in the future, computation itself will be understood chiefly as a process of interaction. Just as we can understand many systems as being composed of essentially passive objects, which have a state and upon which we can perform operations, so we can understand many others as being made up of interacting, semi-autonomous agents. This recognition has led to the growth of interest in agents as a new paradigm for software engineering.

As I noted at the start of this chapter, the trend in computing has been – and will continue to be – toward ever more ubiquitous, interconnected computer systems. The development of software paradigms that are capable of exploiting the potential of such systems is perhaps the greatest challenge in computing at the start of the 21st century. Agents seem a strong candidate for such a paradigm.

Agents as a tool for understanding human societies

In Isaac Asimov's popular *Foundation* science fiction trilogy, a character called Hari Seldon is credited with inventing a discipline that Asimov refers to as 'psychohistory'. The idea is that psychohistory is a combination of psychology, history, and economics, which allows Seldon to predict the behaviour of human societies hundreds of years into the future. In particular, psychohistory enables Seldon to predict the imminent collapse of society. Psychohistory is an interesting plot device, but it is firmly in the realms of science fiction. There are far too many variables and unknown quantities in human societies to do anything except predict very broad trends a short term into the future, and even then the process is notoriously prone to embarrassing errors. This situation is not likely to change in the foreseeable future. However, multiagent systems do provide an interesting and novel new tool for simulating societies, which may help shed some light on various kinds of social processes. A nice example of this work is the EOS project (Doran and Palmer, 1995). The aim of the EOS project was to use the tools of multiagent systems research to gain an insight into how and why social complexity emerged in a Palaeolithic culture in southern France at the time of the last ice age. The goal of the project was not to directly simulate these ancient societies, but to try to understand some of the factors involved in the emergence of social complexity in such societies. (The EOS project is described in more detail in Chapter 12.)

1.3 Objections to Multiagent Systems

No doubt some readers are already sceptical about multiagent systems, as indeed are some in the international computer science research community. In this section, therefore, I have attempted to anticipate and respond to the most commonly voiced objections to multiagent systems.

Is it not all just distributed/concurrent systems?

The concurrent systems community have for several decades been investigating the properties of systems that contain multiple interacting components, and have been developing theories, programming languages, and tools for explaining, modelling, and developing such systems (Ben-Ari, 1990; Holzmann, 1991; Magee and Kramer, 1999). Multiagent systems are – by definition – a subclass of concurrent systems, and there are some in the distributed systems community who question whether multiagent systems are sufficiently different to 'standard' distributed/concurrent systems to merit separate study. My view on this is as follows. First, it is important to understand that when designing or implementing a multiagent system, it is *essential* to draw on the wisdom of those with experience in distributed/concurrent systems. Failure to do so invariably leads to exactly the kind of problems that this community has been working for so long to overcome. Thus it is important to worry about such issues as mutual exclusion over shared resources, deadlock, and livelock when implementing a multiagent system.

In multiagent systems, however, there are two important twists to the concurrent systems story.

- First, because agents are assumed to be autonomous – capable of making independent decisions about what to do in order to satisfy their design objectives – it is generally assumed that the synchronization and coordination structures in a multiagent system are not hardwired in at design time, as they typically are in standard concurrent/distributed systems. We therefore need mechanisms that will allow agents to synchronize and coordinate their activities *at run time*.

- Second, the encounters that occur among computing elements in a multiagent system are *economic* encounters, in the sense that they are encounters between *self-interested* entities. In a classic distributed/concurrent system, all the computing elements are implicitly assumed to share a common goal (of making the overall system function correctly). In multiagent systems, it is assumed instead that agents are primarily concerned with their own welfare (although of course they will be acting on behalf of some user/owner).

For these reasons, the issues studied in the multiagent systems community have a rather different flavour to those studied in the distributed/concurrent systems community. We are concerned with issues such as how agents can reach agreement through negotiation on matters of common interest, and how agents can dynamically coordinate their activities with agents whose goals and motives are unknown. (It is worth pointing out, however, that I see these issues as a natural next step for distributed/concurrent systems research.)

Is it not all just artificial intelligence (AI)?

The multiagent systems field has enjoyed an intimate relationship with the artificial intelligence (AI) field over the years. Indeed, until relatively recently it was common to refer to multiagent systems as a subfield of AI; although multiagent systems researchers would indignantly – and perhaps accurately – respond that AI is more properly understood as a subfield of multiagent systems. More recently, it has become increasingly common practice to define the endeavour of AI itself as one of constructing an intelligent agent (see, for example, the enormously successful introductory textbook on AI by Stuart Russell and Peter Norvig (Russell and Norvig, 1995)). There are several important points to be made here:

- First, AI has largely (and, perhaps, mistakenly) been concerned with the *components* of intelligence: the ability to learn, plan, understand images, and so on. In contrast the agent field is concerned with entities that *integrate* these components, in order to provide a machine that is capable of making independent decisions. It may naively appear that in order to build an agent, we need to solve *all* the problems of AI itself: in order to build an agent, we need to solve the planning problem, the learning problem, and so on

use our agent will surely need to learn, plan, and so on). This is not the
As Oren Etzioni succinctly put it: 'Intelligent agents are ninety-nine per-
computer science and one percent AI' (Etzioni, 1996). When we build
ent to carry out a task in some environment, we will very likely draw
AI techniques of some sort – but most of what we do will be standard
computer science and software engineering. For the vast majority of applications, it is not necessary that an agent has all the capabilities studied in
AI – for some applications, capabilities such as learning may even be undesirable. In short, while we may draw upon AI techniques to build agents, we
do not need to solve all the problems of AI to build an agent.

- Secondly, classical AI has largely ignored the *social* aspects of agency. I hope
you will agree that part of what makes us unique as a species on Earth is not
simply our undoubted ability to learn and solve problems, but our ability to
communicate, cooperate, and reach agreements with our peers. These kinds
of social ability – which we use every day of our lives – are surely just as
important to intelligent behaviour as are components of intelligence such
as planning and learning, and yet they were not studied in AI until about
1980.

Is it not all just economics/game theory?

Game theory is a mathematical theory that studies interactions among self-
interested agents (Binmore, 1992). It is interesting to note that von Neumann,
one of the founders of computer science, was also one of the founders of game
theory (Neumann and Morgenstern, 1944); Alan Turing, arguably the other great
figure in the foundations of computing, was also interested in the formal study
of games, and it may be that it was this interest that ultimately led him to write
his classic paper *Computing Machinery and Intelligence*, which may be seen as the
foundation of AI as a discipline (Turing, 1963). However, since these beginnings,
game theory and computer science went their separate ways for some time. Game
theory was largely – though by no means solely – the preserve of economists, who
were interested in using it to study and understand interactions among economic
entities in the real world.

Recently, the tools and techniques of game theory have found many applications in computational multiagent systems research, particularly when applied
to problems such as negotiation (see Rosenschein and Zlotkin (1994), Sandholm
(1999) and Chapters 6 and 7). Indeed, at the time of writing, game theory seems
to be the predominant theoretical tool in use for the analysis of multiagent systems. An obvious question is therefore whether multiagent systems are properly
viewed as a subfield of economics/game theory. There are two points here.

- First, many of the solution concepts developed in game theory (such as Nash
equilibrium, discussed in Chapter 6), were developed without a view to computation. They tend to be *descriptive* concepts, telling us the properties of

an appropriate, optimal solution *without* telling us how to compute a solution. Moreover, it turns out that the problem of computing a solution is often computationally very hard (e.g. NP-complete or worse). Multiagent systems research highlights these problems, and allows us to bring the tools of computer science (e.g. computational complexity theory (Garey and Johnson, 1979; Papadimitriou, 1994)) to bear on them.

- Secondly, some researchers question the assumptions that game theory makes in order to reach its conclusions. In particular, debate has arisen in the multiagent systems community with respect to whether or not the notion of a rational agent, as modelled in game theory, is valid and/or useful for understanding human or artificial agent societies.

(Please note that all this should *not* be construed as a criticism of game theory, which is without doubt a valuable and important tool in multiagent systems, likely to become much more widespread in use over the coming years.)

Is it not all just social science?

The social sciences are primarily concerned with understanding the behaviour of human societies. Some social scientists are interested in (computational) multiagent systems because they provide an experimental tool with which to model human societies. In addition, an obvious approach to the design of multiagent systems – which are artificial societies – is to look at how a particular function works in human societies, and try to build the multiagent system in the same way. (An analogy may be drawn here with the methodology of AI, where it is quite common to study how humans achieve a particular kind of intelligent capability, and then to attempt to model this in a computer program.) Is the multiagent systems field therefore simply a subset of the social sciences?

Although we can usefully draw insights and analogies from human societies, it does not follow that we can build artificial societies in exactly the same way. It is notoriously hard to precisely model the behaviour of human societies, simply because they are dependent on so many different parameters. Moreover, although it is perfectly legitimate to design a multiagent system by drawing upon and making use of analogies and metaphors from human societies, it does not follow that this is going to be the *best* way to design a multiagent system: there are other tools that we can use equally well (such as game theory – see above).

It seems to me that multiagent systems and the social sciences have a lot to say to each other. Multiagent systems provide a powerful and novel tool for modelling and understanding societies, while the social sciences represent a rich repository of concepts for understanding and building multiagent systems – but they are quite distinct disciplines.

Notes and Further Reading

There are now many introductions to intelligent agents and multiagent systems. Ferber (1999) is an undergraduate textbook, although it was written in the early 1990s, and so (for example) does not mention any issues associated with the Web. A first-rate collection of articles introducing agent and multiagent systems is Weiß (1999). Many of these articles address issues in much more depth than is possible in this book. I would certainly recommend this volume for anyone with a serious interest in agents, and it would make an excellent companion to the present volume for more detailed reading.

Three collections of research articles provide a comprehensive introduction to the field of autonomous rational agents and multiagent systems: Bond and Gasser's 1988 collection, *Readings in Distributed Artificial Intelligence*, introduces almost all the basic problems in the multiagent systems field, and although some of the papers it contains are now rather dated, it remains essential reading (Bond and Gasser, 1988); Huhns and Singh's more recent collection sets itself the ambitious goal of providing a survey of the whole of the agent field, and succeeds in this respect very well (Huhns and Singh, 1998). Finally, Bradshaw (1997) is a collection of papers on software agents.

For a general introduction to the theory and practice of intelligent agents, see Wooldridge and Jennings (1995), which focuses primarily on the theory of agents, but also contains an extensive review of agent architectures and programming languages. A short but thorough roadmap of agent technology was published as Jennings *et al.* (1998).

Class reading: introduction to Bond and Gasser (1988).   This article is probably the best survey of the problems and issues associated with multiagent systems research yet published. Most of the issues it addresses are fundamentally still open, and it therefore makes a useful preliminary to the current volume. It may be worth revisiting when the course is complete.

Exercises

(1) **[Class discussion.]**

Moore's law – a well-known dictum in computing – tells us that the number of transistors that it is possible to place on an integrated circuit doubles every 18 months. This suggests that world's net processing capability is currently growing at an *exponential* rate. Within a few decades, it seems likely that computers will outnumber humans by several orders of magnitude – for every person on the planet there will be tens, hundreds, perhaps thousands or millions of processors, linked together by some far distant descendant of today's Internet. (This is not fanciful thinking: just extrapolate from the record of the past five decades.)

In light of this, discuss the following.

- What such systems might offer – what possibilities are there?
- What are the challenges to make this vision happen?

2

Intelligent Agents

The aim of this chapter is to give you an understanding of what agents are, and some of the issues associated with building them. In later chapters, we will see specific approaches to building agents.

An obvious way to open this chapter would be by presenting a definition of the term *agent*. After all, this is a book about multiagent systems – surely we must all agree on what an agent is? Sadly, there is no universally accepted definition of the term agent, and indeed there is much ongoing debate and controversy on this very subject. Essentially, while there is a general consensus that *autonomy* is central to the notion of agency, there is little agreement beyond this. Part of the difficulty is that various attributes associated with agency are of differing importance for different domains. Thus, for some applications, the ability of agents to *learn* from their experiences is of paramount importance; for other applications, learning is not only unimportant, it is undesirable[1].

Nevertheless, some sort of definition is important – otherwise, there is a danger that the term will lose all meaning. The definition presented here is adapted from Wooldridge and Jennings (1995).

> An *agent* is a computer system that is *situated* in some *environment*, and that is capable of *autonomous action* in this environment in order to meet its design objectives.

---

[1] Michael Georgeff, the main architect of the PRS agent system discussed in later chapters, gives the example of an air-traffic control system he developed; the clients of the system would have been horrified at the prospect of such a system modifying its behaviour at run time...

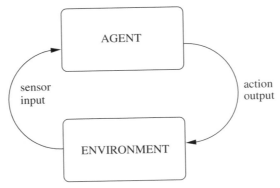

Figure 2.1   An agent in its environment. The agent takes sensory input from the environment, and produces as output actions that affect it. The interaction is usually an ongoing, non-terminating one.

Figure 2.1 gives an abstract view of an agent. In this diagram, we can see the action output generated by the agent in order to affect its environment. In most domains of reasonable complexity, an agent will not have *complete* control over its environment. It will have at best *partial* control, in that it can *influence* it. From the point of view of the agent, this means that the same action performed twice in apparently identical circumstances might appear to have entirely different effects, and in particular, it may *fail* to have the desired effect. Thus agents in all but the most trivial of environments must be prepared for the possibility of *failure*. We can sum this situation up formally by saying that environments are in general assumed to be *non-deterministic*.

Normally, an agent will have a repertoire of actions available to it. This set of possible actions represents the agents *effectoric capability*: its ability to modify its environments. Note that not all actions can be performed in all situations. For example, an action 'lift table' is only applicable in situations where the weight of the table is sufficiently small that the agent *can* lift it. Similarly, the action 'purchase a Ferrari' will fail if insufficient funds are available to do so. Actions therefore have *preconditions* associated with them, which define the possible situations in which they can be applied.

The key problem facing an agent is that of deciding *which* of its actions it should perform in order to best satisfy its design objectives. *Agent architectures*, of which we shall see many examples later in this book, are really software architectures for decision-making systems that are embedded in an environment. At this point, it is worth pausing to consider some examples of agents (though not, as yet, intelligent agents).

Control systems

First, any *control* system can be viewed as an agent. A simple (and overused) example of such a system is a thermostat. Thermostats have a sensor for detecting room temperature. This sensor is directly embedded within the environment (i.e. the room), and it produces as output one of two signals: one that indicates that the temperature is too low, another which indicates that the temperature is OK. The actions available to the thermostat are 'heating on' or 'heating off'. The action 'heating on' will generally have the effect of raising the room temperature, but this cannot be a *guaranteed* effect – if the door to the room is open, for example, switching on the heater may have no effect. The (extremely simple) decision-making component of the thermostat implements (usually in electro-mechanical hardware) the following rules:

$$\text{too cold} \longrightarrow \text{heating on,}$$
$$\text{temperature OK} \longrightarrow \text{heating off.}$$

More complex environment control systems, of course, have considerably richer decision structures. Examples include autonomous space probes, fly-by-wire aircraft, nuclear reactor control systems, and so on.

Software demons

Second, most software demons (such as background processes in the Unix operating system), which monitor a software environment and perform actions to modify it, can be viewed as agents. An example is the X Windows program xbiff. This utility continually monitors a user's incoming email, and indicates via a GUI icon whether or not they have unread messages. Whereas our thermostat agent in the previous example inhabited a *physical* environment – the physical world – the xbiff program inhabits a *software* environment. It obtains information about this environment by carrying out software functions (by executing system programs such as ls, for example), and the actions it performs are software actions (changing an icon on the screen, or executing a program). The decision-making component is just as simple as our thermostat example.

To summarize, agents are simply computer systems that are capable of autonomous action in some environment in order to meet their design objectives. An agent will typically sense its environment (by physical sensors in the case of agents situated in part of the real world, or by software sensors in the case of software agents), and will have available a repertoire of actions that can be executed to modify the environment, which may appear to respond non-deterministically to the execution of these actions.

2.1 Environments

Russell and Norvig suggest the following classification of environment properties (Russell and Norvig, 1995, p. 46).

Accessible versus inaccessible. An accessible environment is one in which the agent can obtain complete, accurate, up-to-date information about the environment's state. Most real-world environments (including, for example, the everyday physical world and the Internet) are not accessible in this sense.

Deterministic versus non-deterministic. A deterministic environment is one in which any action has a single guaranteed effect – there is no uncertainty about the state that will result from performing an action.

Static versus dynamic. A static environment is one that can be assumed to remain unchanged except by the performance of actions by the agent. In contrast, a dynamic environment is one that has other processes operating on it, and which hence changes in ways beyond the agent's control. The physical world is a highly dynamic environment, as is the Internet.

Discrete versus continuous. An environment is discrete if there are a fixed, finite number of actions and percepts in it.

We begin our discussion with accessibility. First, note that in extreme cases, the laws of physics prevent many environments from being completely accessible. For example, it may be that as I write, the surface temperature at the North Pole of Mars is $-100\,°$C, but the laws of physics will prevent me from knowing this fact for some time. This information is thus *inaccessible* to me. More mundanely, in almost any realistic environment uncertainty is inherently present.

The more accessible an environment is, the simpler it is to build agents that operate effectively within it. The reason for this should be self-evident. Ultimately, a 'good' agent is one that makes the 'right' decisions. The quality of decisions that an agent can make is clearly dependent on the quality of the information available to it. If little, or inaccurate information is available, then the agent's decision is uninformed, and is hence likely to be poor. As more complete and accurate information becomes available, the potential to make a good decision increases.

The next source of complexity we consider is *determinism*. An environment is deterministic if the outcome of any action performed is uniquely defined, and non-deterministic otherwise. Non-determinism can seem an unusual property to attribute to environments. For example, we usually imagine that software environments, governed as they are by precise rules, are paradigms of determinism. Non-determinism captures several important aspects of such environments as follows.

- Non-determinism captures the fact that agents have a limited 'sphere of influence' – they have at best partial control over their environment.

- Similarly, actions are typically performed by agents in order to bring about some desired state of affairs. Non-determinism captures the fact that actions can *fail* to have the desired result.

Clearly, deterministic environments are preferable from the point of view of the agent designer to non-deterministic environments. If there is never any uncertainty about the outcome of some particular action, then an agent need never stop to determine whether or not a particular action had a particular outcome, and thus whether or not it needs to reconsider its course of action. In particular, in a deterministic environment, an agent designer can assume that the actions performed by an agent will always succeed: they will never fail to bring about their intended effect.

Unfortunately, as Russell and Norvig (1995) point out, if an environment is sufficiently complex, then the fact that it is *actually* deterministic is not much help. To all intents and purposes, it may as well be non-deterministic. In practice, almost all realistic environments must be regarded as non-deterministic from an agent's perspective.

Non-determinism is closely related to *dynamism*. Early artificial intelligence research on action selection focused on planning algorithms – algorithms that, given a description of the initial state of the environment, the actions available to an agent and their effects, and a goal state, will generate a plan (i.e. a sequence of actions) such that when executed from the initial environment state, the plan will guarantee the achievement of the goal (Allen *et al.*, 1990). However, such planning algorithms implicitly assumed that the environment in which the plan was being executed was *static* – that it did not change except through the performance of actions by the agent. Clearly, many environments (including software environments such as computer operating systems, as well as physical environments such as the real world), do not enjoy this property – they are dynamic, with many processes operating concurrently to modify the environment in ways that an agent has no control over.

From an agent's point of view, dynamic environments have at least two important properties. The first is that if an agent performs no external action between times t_0 and t_1, then it cannot assume that the environment at t_1 will be the same as it was at time t_0. This means that in order for the agent to select an appropriate action to perform, it must perform *information gathering* actions to determine the state of the environment (Moore, 1990). In a static environment, there is no need for such actions. The second property is that other processes in the environment can 'interfere' with the actions it attempts to perform. The idea is essentially the concept of interference in concurrent systems theory (Ben-Ari, 1990). Thus if an agent checks that the environment has some property φ and then starts executing some action α on the basis of this information, it cannot in general guarantee that the environment will continue to have property φ while it is executing α.

These properties suggest that static environments will be inherently simpler to design agents for than dynamic ones. First, in a static environment, an agent need only ever perform information gathering actions *once*. Assuming the information it gathers correctly describes the environment, and that it correctly understands the effects of its actions, then it can accurately *predict* the effects of its actions on the environment, and hence how the state of the environment will evolve. (This is in fact how most artificial intelligence planning algorithms work (Lifschitz, 1986).) Second, in a static environment, an agent never needs to worry about *synchronizing* or *coordinating* its actions with those of other processes in the environment (Bond and Gasser, 1988).

The final distinction made in Russell and Norvig (1995) is between *discrete* and *continuous* environments. A discrete environment is one that can be guaranteed to only ever be in a finite number of discrete states; a continuous one may be in uncountably many states. Thus the game of chess is a discrete environment – there are only a finite (albeit very large) number of states of a chess game. Russell and Norvig (1995) give taxi driving as an example of a continuous environment.

Discrete environments are simpler to design agents for than continuous ones, for several reasons. Most obviously, digital computers are themselves discrete-state systems, and although they can simulate continuous systems to any desired degree of accuracy, there is inevitably a mismatch between the two types of systems. Some information must be lost in the mapping from continuous environment to discrete representation of that environment. Thus the information a discrete-state agent uses in order to select an action in a continuous environment will be made on the basis of information that is inherently approximate. Finally, with finite discrete state environments, it is in principle possible to enumerate all possible states of the environment and the optimal action to perform in each of these states. Such a lookup table approach to agent design is rarely possible in practice, but it is at least *in principle* possible for finite, discrete state environments.

In summary, the most complex general class of environments are those that are inaccessible, non-deterministic, dynamic, and continuous. Environments that have these properties are often referred to as *open* (Hewitt, 1986).

Environmental properties have a role in determining the complexity of the agent design process, but they are by no means the only factors that play a part. The second important property that plays a part is the nature of the *interaction* between agent and environment.

Originally, software engineering concerned itself with what are known as 'functional' systems. A functional system is one that simply takes some input, performs some computation over this input, and eventually produces some output. Such systems may formally be viewed as functions $f : I \rightarrow O$ from a set I of inputs to a set O of outputs. The classic example of such a system is a compiler, which can be viewed as a mapping from a set I of legal source programs to a set O of corresponding object or machine code programs.

One of the key attributes of such functional systems is that they *terminate*. This means that, formally, their properties can be understood in terms of preconditions and postconditions (Hoare, 1969). The idea is that a precondition φ represents what must be true of the program's environment in order for that program to operate correctly. A postcondition ψ represents what will be true of the program's environment after the program terminates, assuming that the precondition was satisfied when execution of the program commenced. A program is said to be completely correct with respect to precondition φ and postcondition ψ if it is guaranteed to terminate when it is executed from a state where the precondition is satisfied, and, upon termination, its postcondition is guaranteed to be satisfied. Crucially, it is assumed that the agent's environment, as characterized by its precondition φ, is *only* modified through the actions of the program itself. As we noted above, this assumption does not hold for many environments.

Although the internal complexity of a functional system may be great (e.g. in the case of a compiler for a complex programming language such as Ada), functional programs are, in general, comparatively simple to correctly and efficiently engineer. For example, functional systems lend themselves to design methods based on 'divide and conquer'. Top-down stepwise refinement (Jones, 1990) is an example of such a method. Semi-automatic refinement techniques are also available, which allow a designer to refine a high-level (formal) specification of a functional system down to an implementation (Morgan, 1994).

Unfortunately, many computer systems that we desire to build are not functional in this sense. Rather than simply computing a function of some input and then terminating, many computer systems are *reactive*, in the following sense:

> Reactive systems are systems that cannot adequately be described by the *relational* or *functional* view. The relational view regards programs as functions...from an initial state to a terminal state. Typically, the main role of reactive systems is to maintain an interaction with their environment, and therefore must be described (and specified) in terms of their on-going behaviour...[E]very concurrent system...must be studied by behavioural means. This is because each individual module in a concurrent system is a reactive subsystem, interacting with its own environment which consists of the other modules.
>
> (Pnueli, 1986)

There are at least three current usages of the term *reactive system* in computer science. The first, oldest, usage is that by Pnueli and followers (see, for example, Pnueli (1986), and the description above). Second, researchers in AI planning take a reactive system to be one that is capable of responding rapidly to changes in its environment – here the word 'reactive' is taken to be synonymous with 'responsive' (see, for example, Kaelbling, 1986). More recently, the term has been used to denote systems which respond directly to the world, rather than reason explicitly about it (see, for example, Connah and Wavish, 1990).

Reactive systems are harder to engineer than functional ones. Perhaps the most important reason for this is that an agent engaging in a (conceptually) non-terminating relationship with its environment must continually make *local* decisions that have *global* consequences. Consider a simple printer controller agent. The agent continually receives requests to have access to the printer, and is allowed to grant access to any agent that requests it, with the proviso that it is only allowed to grant access to one agent at a time. At some time, the agent reasons that it will give control of the printer to process p_1, rather than p_2, but that it will grant p_2 access at some later time point. This seems like a reasonable decision, when considered in isolation. But if the agent *always* reasons like this, it will *never* grant p_2 access. This issue is known as *fairness* (Francez, 1986). In other words, a decision that seems entirely reasonable in a local context can have undesirable effects when considered in the context of the system's entire history. This is a simple example of a complex problem. In general, the decisions made by an agent have long-term effects, and it is often difficult to understand such long-term effects.

One possible solution is to have the agent explicitly reason about and predict the behaviour of the system, and thus any temporally distant effects, at run-time. But it turns out that such prediction is extremely hard.

Russell and Subramanian (1995) discuss the essentially identical concept of *episodic* environments. In an episodic environment, the performance of an agent is dependent on a number of discrete episodes, with no link between the performance of the agent in different episodes. An example of an episodic environment would be a mail sorting system (Russell and Subramanian, 1995). As with reactive systems, episodic interactions are simpler from the agent developer's perspective because the agent can decide what action to perform based only on the current episode – it does not need to reason about the interactions between this and future episodes.

Another aspect of the interaction between agent and environment is the concept of *real time*. Put at its most abstract, a real-time interaction is simply one in which time plays a part in the evaluation of an agent's performance (Russell and Subramanian, 1995, p. 585). It is possible to identify several different types of real-time interactions:

- those in which a decision must be made about what action to perform within some specified time bound;

- those in which the agent must bring about some state of affairs as quickly as possible;

- those in which an agent is required to repeat some task, with the objective being to repeat the task as often as possible.

If time is not an issue, then an agent can deliberate for as long as required in order to select the 'best' course of action in any given scenario. Selecting the best course of action implies search over the space of all possible courses of action, in order to find the 'best'. Selecting the best action in this way will take time exponential in the number of actions available to the agent[2]. It goes without saying that for any

---

[2]If the agent has n actions available to it, then it has $n!$ courses of action available to it (assuming no duplicate actions).

realistic environment, such deliberation is not viable. Thus any realistic system must be regarded as real-time in some sense.

Some environments are real-time in a much stronger sense than this. For example, the PRS, one of the best-known agent systems, had fault diagnosis on NASA's Space Shuttle as its initial application domain (Georgeff and Lansky, 1987). In order to be of any use, decisions in such a system must be made in milliseconds.

2.2   Intelligent Agents

We are not used to thinking of thermostats or Unix demons as agents, and certainly not as *intelligent* agents. So, when do we consider an agent to be intelligent? The question, like the question '*what is intelligence?*' itself, is not an easy one to answer. One way of answering the question is to list the kinds of capabilities that we might expect an intelligent agent to have. The following list was suggested in Wooldridge and Jennings (1995).

Reactivity. Intelligent agents are able to perceive their environment, and respond in a timely fashion to changes that occur in it in order to satisfy their design objectives.

Proactiveness. Intelligent agents are able to exhibit goal-directed behaviour by *taking the initiative* in order to satisfy their design objectives.

Social ability. Intelligent agents are capable of interacting with other agents (and possibly humans) in order to satisfy their design objectives.

These properties are more demanding than they might at first appear. To see why, let us consider them in turn. First, consider *proactiveness*: goal-directed behaviour. It is not hard to build a system that exhibits goal-directed behaviour – we do it every time we write a procedure in Pascal, a function in C, or a method in Java. When we write such a procedure, we describe it in terms of the *assumptions* on which it relies (formally, its *precondition*) and the *effect* it has if the assumptions are valid (its *postcondition*). The effects of the procedure are its *goal*: what the author of the software intends the procedure to achieve. If the precondition holds when the procedure is invoked, then we expect that the procedure will execute *correctly*: that it will terminate, and that upon termination, the postcondition will be true, i.e. the goal will be achieved. This is goal-directed behaviour: the procedure is simply a plan or recipe for achieving the goal. This programming model is fine for many environments. For example, it works well when we consider functional systems, as discussed above.

But for non-functional systems, this simple model of goal-directed programming is not acceptable, as it makes some important limiting assumptions. In particular, it assumes that the environment *does not change* while the procedure is executing. If the environment does change, and, in particular, if the assumptions

(precondition) underlying the procedure become false while the procedure is executing, then the behaviour of the procedure may not be defined – often, it will simply crash. Also, it is assumed that the goal, that is, the reason for executing the procedure, remains valid at least until the procedure terminates. If the goal does *not* remain valid, then there is simply no reason to continue executing the procedure.

In many environments, neither of these assumptions are valid. In particular, in domains that are *too complex* for an agent to observe completely, that are *multiagent* (i.e. they are populated with more than one agent that can change the environment), or where there is *uncertainty* in the environment, these assumptions are not reasonable. In such environments, blindly executing a procedure without regard to whether the assumptions underpinning the procedure are valid is a poor strategy. In such dynamic environments, an agent must be *reactive*, in just the way that we described above. That is, it must be responsive to events that occur in its environment, where these events affect either the agent's goals or the assumptions which underpin the procedures that the agent is executing in order to achieve its goals.

As we have seen, building purely goal-directed systems is not hard. As we shall see later, building *purely reactive* systems – ones that *continually* respond to their environment – is also not difficult. However, what turns out to be hard is building a system that achieves an effective *balance* between goal-directed and reactive behaviour. We want agents that will attempt to achieve their goals systematically, perhaps by making use of complex procedure-like patterns of action. But we do not want our agents to continue blindly executing these procedures in an attempt to achieve a goal either when it is clear that the procedure will not work, or when the goal is for some reason no longer valid. In such circumstances, we want our agent to be able to react to the new situation, in time for the reaction to be of some use. However, we do not want our agent to be *continually* reacting, and hence never focusing on a goal long enough to actually achieve it.

On reflection, it should come as little surprise that achieving a good balance between goal-directed and reactive behaviour is hard. After all, it is comparatively rare to find humans that do this very well. This problem – of effectively integrating goal-directed and reactive behaviour – is one of the key problems facing the agent designer. As we shall see, a great many proposals have been made for how to build agents that can do this – but the problem is essentially still open.

Finally, let us say something about *social ability*, the final component of flexible autonomous action as defined here. In one sense, social ability is trivial: every day, millions of computers across the world routinely exchange information with both humans and other computers. But the ability to exchange bit streams is not really social ability. Consider that in the human world, comparatively few of our meaningful goals can be achieved without the *cooperation* of other people, who cannot be assumed to *share* our goals – in other words, they are themselves autonomous, with their own agenda to pursue. To achieve our goals in such situations, we must *negotiate* and *cooperate* with others. We may be required to understand and reason about the goals of others, and to perform actions (such as paying them money) that we would not otherwise choose to perform, in order to get them to cooperate with us, and achieve our goals. This type of social ability is much more complex, and much less well understood, than simply the ability to exchange binary information. Social ability in general (and topics such as negotiation and cooperation in particular) are dealt with elsewhere in this book, and will not therefore be considered here. In this chapter, we will be concerned with the decision making of *individual* intelligent agents in environments which may be dynamic, unpredictable, and uncertain, but do not contain other agents.

2.3   Agents and Objects

Programmers familiar with object-oriented languages such as Java, C++, or Smalltalk sometimes fail to see anything novel in the idea of agents. When one stops to consider the relative properties of agents and objects, this is perhaps not surprising.

> There is a tendency...to think of objects as 'actors' and endow them with human-like intentions and abilities. It's tempting to think about objects 'deciding' what to do about a situation, [and] 'asking' other objects for information. ... Objects are not passive containers for state and behaviour, but are said to be the agents of a program's activity.
>
> (NeXT Computer Inc., 1993, p. 7)

Objects are defined as computational entities that *encapsulate* some state, are able to perform actions, or *methods* on this state, and communicate by message passing. While there are obvious similarities, there are also significant differences between agents and objects. The first is in the degree to which agents and objects are autonomous. Recall that the defining characteristic of object-oriented programming is the principle of encapsulation – the idea that objects can have control over their own internal state. In programming languages like Java, we can declare instance variables (and methods) to be `private`, meaning they are only accessible from within the object. (We can of course also declare them `public`, meaning that they can be accessed from anywhere, and indeed we must do this for methods so that they can be used by other objects. But the use of `public` instance variables is usually considered poor programming style.) In this way, an object can be thought of as exhibiting autonomy over its state: it has control over it. But an object does not exhibit control over its *behaviour*. That is, if a method m is made available for other objects to invoke, then they can do so whenever they wish – once an object has made a method `public`, then it subsequently has no control over whether or not that method is executed. Of course, an object *must* make methods available to other objects, or else we would be unable to build a system out of them. This is not normally an issue, because if we build a system, then we design the objects that go in it, and they can thus be assumed to share a 'common goal'. But in many types of multiagent system (in particular, those that contain agents built by different organizations or individuals), no such common goal can be assumed. It cannot be taken for granted that an agent i will execute an action (method) a just because another agent j wants it to – a may not be in the best interests of i. We thus do not think of agents as invoking methods upon one another, but rather as *requesting* actions to be performed. If j requests i to perform a, then i may perform the action or it may not. The locus of control with respect to the decision about whether to execute an action is thus different in agent and object systems. In the object-oriented case, the decision lies with the object that invokes the method. In the agent case, the decision lies with the agent that receives the request. This distinction between objects and agents has been nicely summarized in the following slogan.

> Objects do it for free; agents do it because they want to.

Of course, there is nothing to stop us implementing agents using object-oriented techniques. For example, we can build some kind of decision making about whether to execute a method into the method itself, and in this way achieve a stronger kind of autonomy for our objects. The point is that autonomy of this kind is not a component of the basic object-oriented model.

The second important distinction between object and agent systems is with respect to the notion of flexible (reactive, proactive, social) autonomous behaviour. The standard object model has nothing whatsoever to say about how to build systems that integrate these types of behaviour. Again, one could object that we can build object-oriented programs that *do* integrate these types of behaviour. But this argument misses the point, which is that the standard object-oriented programming model has nothing to do with these types of behaviour.

The third important distinction between the standard object model and our view of agent systems is that agents are each considered to have their own thread of control – in the standard object model, there is a single thread of control in the system. Of course, a lot of work has recently been devoted to *concurrency* in object-oriented programming. For example, the Java language provides built-in constructs for multi-threaded programming. There are also many programming languages available (most of them admittedly prototypes) that were specifically designed to allow concurrent object-based programming. But such languages do not capture the idea of agents as *autonomous* entities. Perhaps the closest that the object-oriented community comes is in the idea of *active objects*.

> An active object is one that encompasses its own thread of control. . .. Active objects are generally autonomous, meaning that they can exhibit some behaviour without being operated upon by another object. Passive objects, on the other hand, can only undergo a state change when explicitly acted upon.

(Booch, 1994, p. 91)

Thus active objects are essentially agents that do not necessarily have the ability to exhibit flexible autonomous behaviour.

To summarize, the traditional view of an object and our view of an agent have at least three distinctions:

- agents embody a stronger notion of autonomy than objects, and, in particular, they decide for themselves whether or not to perform an action on request from another agent;

- agents are capable of flexible (reactive, proactive, social) behaviour, and the standard object model has nothing to say about such types of behaviour; and

- a multiagent system is inherently multi-threaded, in that each agent is assumed to have at least one thread of control.

2.4   Agents and Expert Systems

Expert systems were the most important AI technology of the 1980s (Hayes-Roth *et al.*, 1983). An expert system is one that is capable of solving problems or giving advice in some knowledge-rich domain (Jackson, 1986). A classic example of an expert system is MYCIN, which was intended to assist physicians in the treatment of blood infections in humans. MYCIN worked by a process of interacting with a user in order to present the system with a number of (symbolically represented) facts, which the system then used to derive some conclusion. MYCIN acted very much as a *consultant*: it did not operate directly on humans, or indeed any other environment. Thus perhaps the most important distinction between agents and expert systems is that expert systems like MYCIN are inherently *disembodied*. By this, I mean that they do not interact directly with any environment: they get their information not via sensors, but through a user acting as middle man. In the same way, they do not *act* on any environment, but rather give feedback or advice to a third party. In addition, expert systems are not generally capable of cooperating with other agents.

In summary, the main differences between agents and expert systems are as follows:

- 'classic' expert systems are disembodied – they are not coupled to any environment in which they act, but rather act through a user as a 'middleman';

- expert systems are not generally capable of reactive, proactive behaviour; and

- expert systems are not generally equipped with social ability, in the sense of cooperation, coordination, and negotiation.

Despite these differences, some expert systems (particularly those that perform real-time control tasks) look very much like agents. A good example is the ARCHON system, discussed in Chapter 9 (Jennings *et al.*, 1996a).

2.5 Agents as Intentional Systems

One common approach adopted when discussing agent systems is the *intentional stance*. With this approach, we 'endow' agents with *mental states*: beliefs, desires, wishes, hope, and so on. The rationale for this approach is as follows. When explaining human activity, it is often useful to make statements such as the following.

> Janine took her umbrella because she *believed* it was going to rain.
> Michael worked hard because he *wanted* to finish his book.

These statements make use of a *folk psychology*, by which human behaviour is predicted and explained through the attribution of *attitudes*, such as believing and wanting (as in the above examples), hoping, fearing, and so on (see, for example, Stich (1983, p. 1) for a discussion of folk psychology). This folk psychology is well established: most people reading the above statements would say they found their meaning entirely clear, and would not give them a second glance.

The attitudes employed in such folk psychological descriptions are called the *intentional* notions[3]. The philosopher Daniel Dennett has coined the term *intentional system* to describe entities 'whose behaviour can be predicted by the method of attributing belief, desires and rational acumen' (Dennett, 1978, 1987, p. 49). Dennett identifies different 'levels' of intentional system as follows.

> A *first-order* intentional system has beliefs and desires (etc.) but no beliefs and desires *about* beliefs and desires. ... A *second-order* intentional system is more sophisticated; it has beliefs and desires (and no doubt other intentional states) about beliefs and desires (and other intentional states) – both those of others and its own.
>
> (Dennett, 1987, p. 243)

One can carry on this hierarchy of intentionality as far as required.

Now we have been using phrases like belief, desire, intention to talk about computer programs. An obvious question is whether it is legitimate or useful to attribute beliefs, desires, and so on to artificial agents. Is this not just anthropomorphism? McCarthy, among others, has argued that there are occasions when the *intentional stance* is appropriate as follows.

---

[3]Unfortunately, the word 'intention' is used in several different ways in logic and the philosophy of mind. First, there is the BDI-like usage, as in 'I intended to kill him'. Second, an intentional notion is one of the attitudes, as above. Finally, in logic, the word intension (with an 's') means the internal content of a concept, as opposed to its extension. In what follows, the intended meaning should always be clear from context.

To ascribe *beliefs, free will, intentions, consciousness, abilities,* or *wants* to a machine is <u>legitimate</u> when such an ascription expresses the same information about the machine that it expresses about a person. It is <u>useful</u> when the ascription helps us understand the structure of the machine, its past or future behaviour, or how to repair or improve it. It is perhaps never <u>logically required</u> even for humans, but expressing reasonably briefly what is actually known about the state of the machine in a particular situation may require mental qualities or qualities isomorphic to them. Theories of belief, knowledge and wanting can be constructed for machines in a simpler setting than for humans, and later applied to humans. Ascription of mental qualities is <u>most straightforward</u> for machines of known structure such as thermostats and computer operating systems, but is <u>most useful</u> when applied to entities whose structure is incompletely known.

(McCarthy, 1978) (The underlining is from Shoham (1990).)

What objects can be described by the intentional stance? As it turns out, almost any automaton can. For example, consider a light switch as follows.

It is perfectly coherent to treat a light switch as a (very cooperative) agent with the capability of transmitting current at will, who invariably transmits current when it believes that we want it transmitted and not otherwise; flicking the switch is simply our way of communicating our desires.

(Shoham, 1990, p. 6)

And yet most adults in the modern world would find such a description absurd – perhaps even infantile. Why is this? The answer seems to be that while the intentional stance description is perfectly consistent with the observed behaviour of a light switch, and is internally consistent,

...it does not *buy us anything,* since we essentially understand the mechanism sufficiently to have a simpler, mechanistic description of its behaviour.

(Shoham, 1990, p. 6)

Put crudely, the more we know about a system, the less we need to rely on animistic, intentional explanations of its behaviour – Shoham observes that the move from an intentional stance to a technical description of behaviour correlates well with Piaget's model of child development, and with the scientific development of humankind generally (Shoham, 1990). Children will use animistic explanations of objects – such as light switches – until they grasp the more abstract technical concepts involved. Similarly, the evolution of science has been marked by a gradual move from theological/animistic explanations to mathematical ones. My own experiences of teaching computer programming suggest that, when faced with completely unknown phenomena, it is not only children who adopt animistic explanations. It is often easier to teach some computer concepts by using explanations such as 'the computer does not know...', than to try to teach abstract principles first.

An obvious question is then, if we have alternative, perhaps less contentious ways of explaining systems: why should we bother with the intentional stance? Consider the alternatives available to us. One possibility is to characterize the behaviour of a complex system by using the *physical stance* (Dennett, 1996, p. 36). The idea of the physical stance is to start with the original configuration of a system, and then use the laws of physics to predict how this system will behave.

> When I predict that a stone released from my hand will fall to the ground, I am using the physical stance. I don't attribute beliefs and desires to the stone; I attribute mass, or weight, to the stone, and rely on the law of gravity to yield my prediction.

> (Dennett, 1996, p. 37)

Another alternative is the *design stance*. With the design stance, we use knowledge of what purpose a system is supposed to fulfil in order to predict how it behaves. Dennett gives the example of an alarm clock (see pp. 37–39 of Dennett, 1996). When someone presents us with an alarm clock, we do not need to make use of physical laws in order to understand its behaviour. We can simply make use of the fact that all alarm clocks are designed to wake people up if we set them with a time. No understanding of the clock's mechanism is required to justify such an understanding – we know that *all* alarm clocks have this behaviour.

However, with very complex systems, even if a complete, accurate picture of the system's architecture and working *is* available, a physical or design stance explanation of its behaviour may not be practicable. Consider a computer. Although we might have a complete technical description of a computer available, it is hardly practicable to appeal to such a description when explaining why a menu appears when we click a mouse on an icon. In such situations, it may be more appropriate to adopt an intentional stance description, if that description is consistent, and simpler than the alternatives.

Note that the intentional stance is, in computer science terms, nothing more than an *abstraction tool*. It is a convenient shorthand for talking about complex systems, which allows us to succinctly predict and explain their behaviour without having to understand how they actually work. Now, much of computer science is concerned with looking for good abstraction mechanisms, since these allow system developers to *manage complexity* with greater ease. The history of programming languages illustrates a steady move away from low-level machine-oriented views of programming towards abstractions that are closer to human experience. Procedural abstraction, abstract data types, and, most recently, objects are examples of this progression. So, why not use the intentional stance as an abstraction tool in computing – to explain, understand, and, crucially, *program* complex computer systems?

For many researchers this idea of programming computer systems in terms of mentalistic notions such as belief, desire, and intention is a key component of agent-based systems.

2.6 Abstract Architectures for Intelligent Agents

We can easily formalize the abstract view of agents presented so far. First, let us assume that the environment may be in any of a finite set E of discrete, instantaneous states:

$$E = \{e, e', \dots\}.$$

Notice that whether or not the environment 'really is' discrete in this way is not too important for our purposes: it is a (fairly standard) modelling assumption, which we can justify by pointing out that any *continuous* environment can be modelled by a discrete environment to any desired degree of accuracy.

Agents are assumed to have a repertoire of possible actions available to them, which transform the state of the environment. Let

$$Ac = \{\alpha, \alpha', \dots\}$$

be the (finite) set of actions.

The basic model of agents interacting with their environments is as follows. The environment starts in some state, and the agent begins by choosing an action to perform on that state. As a result of this action, the environment can respond with a number of possible states. However, only one state will *actually* result – though of course, the agent does not know in advance which it will be. On the basis of this second state, the agent again chooses an action to perform. The environment responds with one of a set of possible states, the agent then chooses another action, and so on.

A *run*, r, of an agent in an environment is thus a sequence of interleaved environment states and actions:

$$r : e_0 \xrightarrow{\alpha_0} e_1 \xrightarrow{\alpha_1} e_2 \xrightarrow{\alpha_2} e_3 \xrightarrow{\alpha_3} \dots \xrightarrow{\alpha_{u-1}} e_u.$$

Let

- $\mathcal{R}$ be the set of all such possible finite sequences (over E and Ac);
- $\mathcal{R}^{Ac}$ be the subset of these that end with an action; and
- $\mathcal{R}^E$ be the subset of these that end with an environment state.

We will use $r, r', \dots$ to stand for members of $\mathcal{R}$.

In order to represent the effect that an agent's actions have on an environment, we introduce a *state transformer* function (cf. Fagin *et al.*, 1995, p. 154):

$$\tau : \mathcal{R}^{Ac} \to \wp(E).$$

Thus a state transformer function maps a run (assumed to end with the action of an agent) to a set of possible environment states – those that could result from performing the action.

There are two important points to note about this definition. First, environments are assumed to be *history dependent*. In other words, the next state of an environment is not solely determined by the action performed by the agent and the current state of the environment. The actions made *earlier* by the agent also play a part in determining the current state. Second, note that this definition allows for *non-determinism* in the environment. There is thus *uncertainty* about the result of performing an action in some state.

If $\tau(r) = \varnothing$ (where r is assumed to end with an action), then there are no possible successor states to r. In this case, we say that the system has *ended* its run. We will also assume that all runs eventually terminate.

Formally, we say an environment Env is a triple $Env = \langle E, e_0, \tau \rangle$, where E is a set of environment states, $e_0 \in E$ is an initial state, and τ is a state transformer function.

We now need to introduce a model of the agents that inhabit systems. We model agents as functions which map runs (assumed to end with an environment state) to actions (cf. Russell and Subramanian, 1995, pp. 580, 581):

$$Ag : \mathcal{R}^E \to Ac.$$

Thus an agent makes a decision about what action to perform based on the history of the system that it has witnessed to date.

Notice that while environments are implicitly non-deterministic, agents are assumed to be deterministic. Let $\mathcal{AG}$ be the set of all agents.

We say a *system* is a pair containing an agent and an environment. Any system will have associated with it a set of possible runs; we denote the set of runs of agent Ag in environment Env by $\mathcal{R}(Ag, Env)$. For simplicity, we will assume that $\mathcal{R}(Ag, Env)$ contains only *terminated* runs, i.e. runs r such that r has no possible successor states: $\tau(r) = \varnothing$. (We will thus not consider infinite runs for now.)

Formally, a sequence

$$(e_0, \alpha_0, e_1, \alpha_1, e_2, \dots)$$

represents a run of an agent Ag in environment $Env = \langle E, e_0, \tau \rangle$ if

(1) e_0 is the initial state of Env;

(2) $\alpha_0 = Ag(e_0)$; and

(3) for $u > 0$,

$$e_u \in \tau((e_0, \alpha_0, \dots, \alpha_{u-1})),$$

where

$$\alpha_u = Ag((e_0, \alpha_0, \dots, e_u)).$$

Two agents Ag_1 and Ag_2 are said to be *behaviourally equivalent* with respect to environment Env if and only if $\mathcal{R}(Ag_1, Env) = \mathcal{R}(Ag_2, Env)$, and simply behaviourally equivalent if and only if they are behaviourally equivalent with respect to all environments.

Notice that so far, I have said nothing at all about how agents are actually implemented; we will return to this issue later.

Purely reactive agents

Certain types of agents decide what to do without reference to their history. They base their decision making entirely on the present, with no reference at all to the past. We will call such agents *purely reactive*, since they simply respond directly to their environment. (Sometimes they are called *tropistic* agents (Genesereth and Nilsson, 1987): tropism is the tendency of plants or animals to react to certain stimulae.)

Formally, the behaviour of a purely reactive agent can be represented by a function

$$Ag : E \rightarrow Ac.$$

It should be easy to see that for every purely reactive agent, there is an equivalent 'standard' agent, as discussed above; the reverse, however, is not generally the case.

Our thermostat agent is an example of a purely reactive agent. Assume, without loss of generality, that the thermostat's environment can be in one of two states – either too cold, or temperature OK. Then the thermostat is simply defined as follows:

$$Ag(e) = \begin{cases} \text{heater off} & \text{if } e = \text{temperature OK,} \\ \text{heater on} & \text{otherwise.} \end{cases}$$

Perception

Viewing agents at this abstract level makes for a pleasantly simple analysis. However, it does not help us to construct them. For this reason, we will now begin to *refine* our abstract model of agents, by breaking it down into sub-systems in exactly the way that one does in standard software engineering. As we refine our view of agents, we find ourselves making *design choices* that mostly relate to the subsystems that go to make up an agent – what data and control structures will be present. An *agent architecture* is essentially a map of the internals of an agent – its data structures, the operations that may be performed on these data structures, and the control flow between these data structures. Later in this book, we will discuss a number of different types of agent architecture, with very different views on the data structures and algorithms that will be present within an agent. In the remainder of this section, however, we will survey some fairly high-level design decisions. The first of these is the separation of an agent's decision function into *perception* and *action* subsystems: see Figure 2.2.

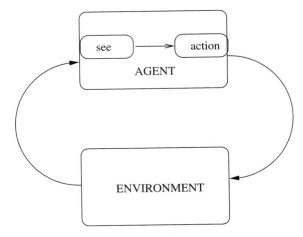

Figure 2.2   Perception and action subsystems.

The idea is that the function *see* captures the agent's ability to observe its environment, whereas the *action* function represents the agent's decision-making process. The *see* function might be implemented in hardware in the case of an agent situated in the physical world: for example, it might be a video camera or an infrared sensor on a mobile robot. For a software agent, the sensors might be system commands that obtain information about the software environment, such as ls, finger, or suchlike. The *output* of the *see* function is a *percept* – a perceptual input. Let *Per* be a (non-empty) set of percepts. Then *see* is a function

$$see : E \rightarrow Per$$

which maps environment states to percepts, and *action* is a function

$$action : Per^* \rightarrow Ac$$

which maps sequences of percepts to actions. An agent Ag is now considered to be a pair $Ag = \langle see, action \rangle$, consisting of a *see* function and an *action* function.

These simple definitions allow us to explore some interesting properties of agents and perception. Suppose that we have two environment states, $e_1 \in E$ and $e_2 \in E$, such that $e_1 \neq e_2$, but $see(e_1) = see(e_2)$. Then two *different* environment states are mapped to the *same* percept, and hence the agent would receive the same perceptual information from different environment states. As far as the agent is concerned, therefore, e_1 and e_2 are *indistinguishable*. To make this example concrete, let us return to the thermostat example. Let x represent the statement

'the room temperature is OK'

and let y represent the statement

'John Major is Prime Minister'.

If these are the only two facts about our environment that we are concerned with, then the set E of environment states contains exactly four elements:

$$E = \{\underbrace{\{\neg x, \neg y\}}_{e_1}, \underbrace{\{\neg x, y\}}_{e_2}, \underbrace{\{x, \neg y\}}_{e_3}, \underbrace{\{x, y\}}_{e_4}\}.$$

Thus in state e_1, the room temperature is not OK, and John Major is not Prime Minister; in state e_2, the room temperature is not OK, and John Major *is* Prime Minister. Now, our thermostat is sensitive *only* to temperatures in the room. This room temperature is not causally related to whether or not John Major is Prime Minister. Thus the states where John Major is and is not Prime Minister are literally *indistinguishable* to the thermostat. Formally, the *see* function for the thermostat would have two percepts in its range, p_1 and p_2, indicating that the temperature is too cold or OK, respectively. The *see* function for the thermostat would behave as follows:

$$see(e) = \begin{cases} p_1 & \text{if } e = e_1 \text{ or } e = e_2, \\ p_2 & \text{if } e = e_3 \text{ or } e = e_4. \end{cases}$$

Given two environment states $e \in E$ and $e' \in E$, let us write $e \sim e'$ if $see(e) = see(e')$. It is not hard to see that '$\sim$' is an *equivalence relation* over environment states, which partitions E into mutually indistinguishable sets of states. Intuitively, the coarser these equivalence classes are, the less effective is the agent's perception. If $|\sim| = |E|$ (i.e. the number of distinct percepts is equal to the number of different environment states), then the agent can distinguish *every* state – the agent has perfect perception in the environment; it is *omniscient*. At the other extreme, if $|\sim| = 1$, then the agent's perceptual ability is non-existent – it cannot distinguish between *any* different states. In this case, as far as the agent is concerned, all environment states are identical.

Agents with state

We have so far modelled an agent's decision function as from *sequences* of environment states or percepts to actions. This allows us to represent agents whose decision making is influenced by history. However, this is a somewhat unintuitive representation, and we shall now replace it by an equivalent, but somewhat more natural, scheme. The idea is that we now consider agents that *maintain state* – see Figure 2.3.

These agents have some internal data structure, which is typically used to record information about the environment state and history. Let I be the set of all internal states of the agent. An agent's decision-making process is then based, at least in part, on this information. The perception function *see* for a state-based agent is unchanged, mapping environment states to percepts as before:

$$see : E \rightarrow Per.$$

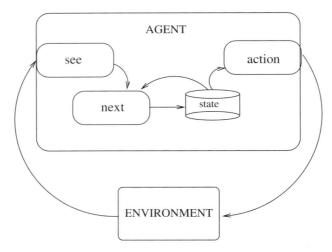

Figure 2.3   Agents that maintain state.

The action-selection function $action$ is defined as a mapping

$$action : I \rightarrow Ac$$

from internal states to actions. An additional function $next$ is introduced, which maps an internal state and percept to an internal state:

$$next : I \times Per \rightarrow I.$$

The behaviour of a state-based agent can be summarized in the following way. The agent starts in some initial internal state i_0. It then observes its environment state e, and generates a percept $see(e)$. The internal state of the agent is then updated via the $next$ function, becoming set to $next(i_0, see(e))$. The action selected by the agent is then $action(next(i_0, see(e)))$. This action is then performed, and the agent enters another cycle, perceiving the world via see, updating its state via $next$, and choosing an action to perform via $action$.

   It is worth observing that state-based agents as defined here are in fact no more powerful than the standard agents we introduced earlier. In fact, they are *identical* in their expressive power – every state-based agent can be transformed into a standard agent that is behaviourally equivalent.

2.7   How to Tell an Agent What to Do

We do not (usually) build agents for no reason. We build them in order to carry out *tasks* for us. In order to get the agent to do the task, we must somehow communicate the desired task to the agent. This implies that the task to be carried out must be *specified* by us in some way. An obvious question is how to specify these tasks: how to tell the agent what to do. One way to specify the task would be simply to write a program for the agent to execute. The obvious advantage of this approach is that we are left in no uncertainty about what the agent will do; it will do exactly what we told it to, and no more. But the very obvious disadvantage is that we have to think about exactly how the task will be carried out ourselves – if unforeseen circumstances arise, the agent executing the task will be unable to respond accordingly. So, more usually, we want to *tell our agent what to do without telling it how to do it*. One way of doing this is to define tasks *indirectly*, via some kind of *performance measure*. There are several ways in which such a performance measure can be defined. The first is to associate *utilities* with states of the environment.

Utility functions

A utility is a numeric value representing how 'good' the state is: the higher the utility, the better. The task of the agent is then to bring about states that maximize utility – we do not specify to the agent how this is to be done. In this approach, a task specification would simply be a function

$$u : E \to \mathbb{R}$$

which associates a real value with every environment state. Given such a performance measure, we can then define the overall utility of an agent in some particular environment in several different ways. One (pessimistic) way is to define the utility of the agent as the utility of the *worst* state that might be encountered by the agent; another might be to define the overall utility as the average utility of all states encountered. There is no right or wrong way: the measure depends upon the kind of task you want your agent to carry out.

The main disadvantage of this approach is that it assigns utilities to *local* states; it is difficult to specify a *long-term* view when assigning utilities to individual states. To get around this problem, we can specify a task as a function which assigns a utility not to individual states, but to runs themselves:

$$u : \mathcal{R} \to \mathbb{R}.$$

If we are concerned with agents that must operate independently over long periods of time, then this approach appears more appropriate to our purposes. One well-known example of the use of such a utility function is in the Tileworld (Pollack, 1990). The Tileworld was proposed primarily as an experimental environment for evaluating agent architectures. It is a simulated two-dimensional grid environment on which there are agents, tiles, obstacles, and holes. An agent can move in four directions, up, down, left, or right, and if it is located next to a tile, it can push it. An obstacle is a group of immovable grid cells: agents are not allowed to travel freely through obstacles. Holes have to be filled up with tiles by the agent. An agent scores points by filling holes with tiles, with the aim being to fill as many

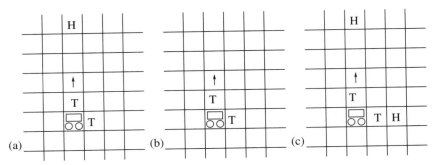

Figure 2.4   Three scenarios in the Tileworld are (a) the agent detects a hole ahead, and begins to push a tile towards it; (b) the tile disappears before the agent can get to it – the agent should recognize this change in the environment, and modify its behaviour appropriately; and (c) the agent was pushing a tile north, when a hole appeared to its right; it would do better to push the tile to the right, than to continue to head north.

holes as possible. The Tileworld is an example of a *dynamic* environment: starting in some randomly generated world state, based on parameters set by the experimenter, it changes over time in discrete steps, with the random appearance and disappearance of holes. The experimenter can set a number of Tileworld parameters, including the frequency of appearance and disappearance of tiles, obstacles, and holes; and the choice between hard bounds (instantaneous) or soft bounds (slow decrease in value) for the disappearance of holes. In the Tileworld, holes appear randomly and exist for as long as their *life expectancy*, unless they disappear because of the agent's actions. The interval between the appearance of successive holes is called the *hole gestation time*. The performance of an agent in the Tileworld is measured by running the Tileworld testbed for a predetermined number of time steps, and measuring the number of holes that the agent succeeds in filling. The performance of an agent on some particular run is then defined as

$$u(r) \mathrel{\hat{=}} \frac{\text{number of holes filled in } r}{\text{number of holes that appeared in } r}.$$

This gives a normalized performance measure in the range 0 (the agent did not succeed in filling even one hole) to 1 (the agent succeeded in filling every hole that appeared). Experimental error is eliminated by running the agent in the environment a number of times, and computing the average of the performance.

Despite its simplicity, the Tileworld allows us to examine several important capabilities of agents. Perhaps the most important of these is the ability of an agent to *react* to changes in the environment, and to *exploit opportunities* when they arise. For example, suppose an agent is pushing a tile to a hole (Figure 2.4(a)), when this tile disappears (Figure 2.4(b)). At this point, pursuing the original objective is pointless, and the agent would do best if it noticed this change, and as a consequence 'rethought' its original objective. To illustrate what I mean by recognizing opportunities, suppose that in the same situation, a hole appears to the right of the agent (Figure 2.4(c)). The agent is more likely to be able to fill this hole than its originally planned one, for the simple reason that it only has to push the tile one step, rather than four. All other things being equal, the chances of the hole on the right still being there when the agent arrives are four times greater.

Assuming that the utility function u has some upper bound to the utilities it assigns (i.e. that there exists a $k \in \mathbb{R}$ such that for all $r \in \mathcal{R}$, we have $u(r) \leqslant k$), then we can talk about *optimal* agents: the optimal agent is the one that maximizes expected utility.

Let us write $P(r \mid Ag, Env)$ to denote the probability that run r occurs when agent Ag is placed in environment Env. Clearly,

$$\sum_{r \in \mathcal{R}(Ag,Env)} P(r \mid Ag, Env) = 1.$$

Then the optimal agent Ag_{opt} in an environment Env is defined as the one that *maximizes expected utility*:

$$Ag_{\text{opt}} = \arg \max_{Ag \in \mathcal{AG}} \sum_{r \in \mathcal{R}(Ag,Env)} u(r)P(r \mid Ag, Env). \tag{2.1}$$

This idea is essentially identical to the notion of maximizing expected utility in *decision theory* (see Russell and Norvig, 1995, p. 472).

Notice that while (2.1) tells us the properties of the desired agent Ag_{opt}, it sadly does not give us any clues about how to *implement* this agent. Worse still, some agents cannot be implemented on some actual machines. To see this, simply note that agents as we have considered them so far are just abstract mathematical functions $Ag : \mathcal{R}^E \to Ac$. These definitions take no account of (for example) the amount of memory required to implement the function, or how complex the computation of this function is. It is quite easy to define functions that cannot actually be computed by any real computer, and so it is just as easy to define agent functions that cannot ever actually be implemented on a real computer.

Russell and Subramanian (1995) introduced the notion of *bounded optimal* agents in an attempt to try to address this issue. The idea is as follows. Suppose m is a particular computer – for the sake of argument, say it is the Dell Latitude L400 I am currently typing on: a laptop with 128 MB of RAM, 6 GB of disk space, and a 500 MHz Pentium III processor. There are only a certain set of programs that can run on this machine. For example, any program requiring more than 128 MB RAM clearly cannot run on it. In just the same way, only a certain subset of the set of all agents $\mathcal{AG}$ can be implemented on this machine. Again, any agent Ag that required more than 128 MB RAM would not run. Let us write $\mathcal{AG}_m$ to denote the subset of $\mathcal{AG}$ that can be implemented on m:

$$\mathcal{AG}_m = \{Ag \mid Ag \in \mathcal{AG} \text{ and } Ag \text{ can be implemented on } m\}.$$

Now, assume we have machine (i.e. computer) m, and we wish to place this machine in environment Env; the task we wish m to carry out is defined by utility function $u : \mathcal{R} \to \mathbb{R}$. Then we can replace Equation (2.1) with the following, which more precisely defines the properties of the desired agent Ag_{opt}:

$$Ag_{\mathrm{opt}} = \arg \max_{Ag \in \mathcal{AG}_m} \sum_{r \in \mathcal{R}(Ag, Env)} u(r) P(r \mid Ag, Env). \qquad (2.2)$$

The subtle change in (2.2) is that we are no longer looking for our agent from the set of all possible agents $\mathcal{AG}$, but from the set $\mathcal{AG}_m$ of agents that can actually be implemented on the machine that we have for the task.

Utility-based approaches to specifying tasks for agents have several disadvantages. The most important of these is that it is very often difficult to derive an appropriate utility function; the Tileworld is a useful environment in which to experiment with agents, but it represents a gross simplification of real-world scenarios. The second is that usually we find it more convenient to talk about tasks in terms of 'goals to be achieved' rather than utilities. This leads us to what I call *predicate* task specifications.

Predicate task specifications

Put simply, a predicate task specification is one where the utility function acts as a *predicate* over runs. Formally, we will say a utility function $u : \mathcal{R} \to \mathbb{R}$ is a predicate if the range of u is the set $\{0, 1\}$, that is, if u guarantees to assign a run either 1 ('true') or 0 ('false'). A run $r \in \mathcal{R}$ will be considered to satisfy the specification u if $u(r) = 1$, and fails to satisfy the specification otherwise.

We will use Ψ to denote a predicate specification, and write $\Psi(r)$ to indicate that run $r \in \mathcal{R}$ which satisfies Ψ. In other words, $\Psi(r)$ is true if and only if $u(r) = 1$. For the moment, we will leave aside the questions of what form a predicate task specification might take.

Task environments

A *task environment* is defined to be a pair $\langle Env, \Psi \rangle$, where Env is an environment, and

$$\Psi : \mathcal{R} \to \{0, 1\}$$

is a predicate over runs. Let $\mathcal{TE}$ be the set of all task environments. A task environment thus specifies:

- the properties of the system the agent will inhabit (i.e. the environment Env); and also
- the criteria by which an agent will be judged to have either failed or succeeded in its task (i.e. the specification Ψ).

Given a task environment $\langle Env, \Psi \rangle$, we write $\mathcal{R}_{\Psi}(Ag, Env)$ to denote the set of all runs of the agent Ag in the environment Env that satisfy Ψ. Formally,

$$\mathcal{R}_{\Psi}(Ag, Env) = \{r \mid r \in \mathcal{R}(Ag, Env) \text{ and } \Psi(r)\}.$$

We then say that an agent Ag succeeds in task environment $\langle Env, \Psi \rangle$ if

$$\mathcal{R}_\Psi(Ag, Env) = \mathcal{R}(Ag, Env).$$

In other words, Ag succeeds in $\langle Env, \Psi \rangle$ if every run of Ag in Env satisfies specification Ψ, i.e. if

$$\forall r \in \mathcal{R}(Ag, Env) \quad \text{we have } \Psi(r).$$

Notice that this is in one sense a *pessimistic* definition of success, as an agent is only deemed to succeed if every possible run of the agent in the environment satisfies the specification. An alternative, *optimistic* definition of success is that the agent succeeds if *at least one* run of the agent satisfies Ψ:

$$\exists r \in \mathcal{R}(Ag, Env) \quad \text{such that } \Psi(r).$$

If required, we could easily modify the definition of success by extending the state transformer function τ to include a probability distribution over possible outcomes, and hence induce a probability distribution over runs. We can then define the success of an agent as the probability that the specification Ψ is satisfied by the agent. As before, let $P(r \mid Ag, Env)$ denote the probability that run r occurs if agent Ag is placed in environment Env. Then the probability $P(\Psi \mid Ag, Env)$ that Ψ is satisfied by Ag in Env would simply be

$$P(\Psi \mid Ag, Env) = \sum_{r \in \mathcal{R}_\Psi(Ag, Env)} P(r \mid Ag, Env).$$

The notion of a predicate task specification may seem a rather abstract way of describing tasks for an agent to carry out. In fact, it is a generalization of certain very common forms of tasks. Perhaps the two most common types of tasks that we encounter are *achievement tasks* and *maintenance tasks*.

(1) Achievement tasks. Those of the form 'achieve state of affairs φ'.

(2) Maintenance tasks. Those of the form 'maintain state of affairs ψ'.

Intuitively, an achievement task is specified by a number of *goal states*; the agent is required to bring about one of these goal states (we do not care which one – all are considered equally good). Achievement tasks are probably the most commonly studied form of task in AI. Many well-known AI problems (e.g. the Blocks World) are achievement tasks. A task specified by a predicate Ψ is an achievement task if we can identify some subset G of environment states E such that $\Psi(r)$ is true just in case one or more of G occur in r; an agent is successful if it is guaranteed to bring about one of the states G, that is, if every run of the agent in the environment results in one of the states G.

Formally, the task environment $\langle Env, \Psi \rangle$ specifies an achievement task if and only if there is some set $G \subseteq E$ such that for all $r \in \mathcal{R}(Ag, Env)$, the predicate $\Psi(r)$ is true if and only if there exists some $e \in G$ such that $e \in r$. We refer to the set G of an achievement task environment as the *goal states* of the task; we use $\langle Env, G \rangle$ to denote an achievement task environment with goal states G and environment Env.

A useful way to think about achievement tasks is as the agent *playing a game* against the environment. In the terminology of game theory (Binmore, 1992), this is exactly what is meant by a 'game against nature'. The environment and agent both begin in some state; the agent takes a turn by executing an action, and the environment responds with some state; the agent then takes another turn, and so on. The agent 'wins' if it can *force* the environment into one of the goal states G.

Just as many tasks can be characterized as problems where an agent is required to bring about some state of affairs, so many others can be classified as problems where the agent is required to *avoid* some state of affairs. As an extreme example, consider a nuclear reactor agent, the purpose of which is to ensure that the reactor never enters a 'meltdown' state. Somewhat more mundanely, we can imagine a software agent, one of the tasks of which is to ensure that a particular file is never simultaneously open for both reading and writing. We refer to such task environments as *maintenance* task environments.

A task environment with specification Ψ is said to be a maintenance task environment if we can identify some subset B of environment states, such that $\Psi(r)$ is false if any member of B occurs in r, and true otherwise. Formally, $\langle Env, \Psi \rangle$ is a maintenance task environment if there is some $B \subseteq E$ such that $\Psi(r)$ if and only if for all $e \in B$, we have $e \notin r$ for all $r \in \mathcal{R}(Ag, Env)$. We refer to B as the *failure set*. As with achievement task environments, we write $\langle Env, B \rangle$ to denote a maintenance task environment with environment Env and failure set B.

It is again useful to think of maintenance tasks as games. This time, the agent wins if it manages to *avoid* all the states in B. The environment, in the role of opponent, is attempting to force the agent into B; the agent is successful if it has a winning strategy for avoiding B.

More complex tasks might be specified by *combinations* of achievement and maintenance tasks. A simple combination might be 'achieve any one of states G while avoiding all states B'. More complex combinations are of course also possible.

2.8 Synthesizing Agents

Knowing that there exists an agent which will succeed in a given task environment is helpful, but it would be more helpful if, knowing this, we also had such an agent to hand. How do we obtain such an agent? The obvious answer is to 'manually' implement the agent from the specification. However, there are at least two other possibilities (see Wooldridge (1997) for a discussion):

(1) we can try to develop an algorithm that will *automatically synthesize* such agents for us from task environment specifications; or

(2) we can try to develop an algorithm that will *directly execute* agent specifications in order to produce the appropriate behaviour.

In this section, I briefly consider these possibilities, focusing primarily on agent synthesis.

Agent synthesis is, in effect, automatic programming: the goal is to have a program that will take as input a task environment, and from this task environment automatically generate an agent that succeeds in this environment. Formally, an agent synthesis algorithm syn can be understood as a function

$$syn : \mathcal{TE} \to (\mathcal{AG} \cup \{\bot\}).$$

Note that the function syn can output an agent, or else output $\bot$ – think of $\bot$ as being like `null` in Java. Now, we will say a synthesis algorithm is

sound if, whenever it returns an agent, this agent succeeds in the task environment that is passed as input; and

complete if it is guaranteed to return an agent whenever there exists an agent that will succeed in the task environment given as input.

Thus a sound and complete synthesis algorithm will only output $\bot$ given input $\langle Env, \Psi \rangle$ when no agent exists that will succeed in $\langle Env, \Psi \rangle$.

Formally, a synthesis algorithm syn is sound if it satisfies the following condition:

$$syn(\langle Env, \Psi \rangle) = Ag \text{ implies } \mathcal{R}(Ag, Env) = \mathcal{R}_\Psi(Ag, Env).$$

Similarly, syn is complete if it satisfies the following condition:

$$\exists Ag \in \mathcal{AG} \text{ s.t. } \mathcal{R}(Ag, Env) = \mathcal{R}_\Psi(Ag, Env) \text{ implies } syn(\langle Env, \Psi \rangle) \neq \bot.$$

Intuitively, soundness ensures that a synthesis algorithm always delivers agents that do their job correctly, but may not always deliver agents, even where such agents are in principle possible. Completeness ensures that an agent will always be delivered where such an agent is possible, but does not guarantee that these agents will do their job correctly. Ideally, we seek synthesis algorithms that are both sound *and* complete. Of the two conditions, soundness is probably the more important: there is not much point in complete synthesis algorithms that deliver 'buggy' agents.

Notes and Further Reading

A view of artificial intelligence as the process of agent design is presented in Russell and Norvig (1995), and, in particular, Chapter 2 of Russell and Norvig

(1995) presents much useful material. The definition of agents presented here is based on Wooldridge and Jennings (1995), which also contains an extensive review of agent architectures and programming languages. The question of 'what is an agent' is one that continues to generate some debate; a collection of answers may be found in Müller *et al.* (1997). The relationship between agents and objects has not been widely discussed in the literature, but see Gasser and Briot (1992). Other interesting and readable introductions to the idea of intelligent agents include Kaelbling (1986) and Etzioni (1993).

The abstract model of agents presented here is based on that given in Genesereth and Nilsson (1987, Chapter 13), and also makes use of some ideas from Russell and Wefald (1991) and Russell and Subramanian (1995). The properties of perception as discussed in this section lead to *knowledge theory*, a formal analysis of the information implicit within the state of computer processes, which has had a profound effect in theoretical computer science: this issue is discussed in Chapter 12.

The relationship between artificially intelligent agents and software complexity has been discussed by several researchers: Simon (1981) was probably the first. More recently, Booch (1994) gives a good discussion of software complexity and the role that object-oriented development has to play in overcoming it. Russell and Norvig (1995) introduced the five-point classification of environments that we reviewed here, and distinguished between the 'easy' and 'hard' cases. Kaelbling (1986) touches on many of the issues discussed here, and Jennings (1999) also discusses the issues associated with complexity and agents.

The relationship between agent and environment, and, in particular, the problem of understanding how a given agent will perform in a given environment, has been studied empirically by several researchers. Pollack and Ringuette (1990) introduced the Tileworld, an environment for experimentally evaluating agents that allowed a user to experiment with various environmental parameters (such as the rate at which the environment changes – its *dynamism*). Building on this work, Kinny and Georgeff (1991) investigated how a specific class of agents, based on the *belief–desire–intention* model (Wooldridge, 2000b), could be tailored to perform well in environments with differing degrees of change and complexity. An attempt to prove some results corresponding to Kinny and Georgeff (1991) was Wooldridge and Parsons (1999); an experimental investigation of some of these relationships, building on Kinny and Georgeff (1991), was Schut and Wooldridge (2000). An informal discussion on the relationship between agent and environment is Müller (1999).

In artificial intelligence, the planning problem is most closely related to achievement-based task environments (Allen *et al.*, 1990). STRIPS was the archetypal planning system (Fikes and Nilsson, 1971). The STRIPS system is capable of taking a description of the initial environment state e_0, a specification of the goal to be achieved, E_{good}, and the actions Ac available to an agent, and generates a sequence of actions $\pi \in Ac^*$ such that when executed from e_0, π will achieve one of the states E_{good}. The initial state, goal state, and actions were characterized in STRIPS using a subset of first-order logic. Bylander showed that the (propositional) STRIPS decision problem (given e_0, Ac, and E_{good} specified in propositional logic, does there exist a $\pi \in Ac^*$ such that π achieves E_{good}?) is PSPACE-complete (Bylander, 1994).

More recently, there has been renewed interest by the artificial intelligence planning community in *decision theoretic* approaches to planning (Blythe, 1999). One popular approach involves representing agents and their environments as 'partially observable Markov decision processes' (POMDPs) (Kaelbling *et al.*, 1998). Put simply, the goal of solving a POMDP is to determine an optimal policy for acting in an environment in which there is uncertainty about the environment state (cf. our visibility function), and which is non-deterministic. Work on POMDP approaches to agent design are at an early stage, but show promise for the future.

The discussion on task specifications is adapted from Wooldridge (2000a) and Wooldridge and Dunne (2000).

Class reading: Franklin and Graesser (1997).   This paper informally discusses various different notions of agency. The focus of the discussion might be on a comparison with the discussion in this chapter.

Exercises

(1) **[Level 1.]**

Give other examples of agents (not necessarily intelligent) that you know of. For each, define as precisely as possible the following.

(1) The environment that the agent occupies (physical, software, etc.), the states that this environment can be in, and whether the environment is: accessible or inaccessible; deterministic or non-deterministic; episodic or non-episodic; static or dynamic; discrete or continuous.

(2) The action repertoire available to the agent, and any preconditions associated with these actions.

(3) The goal, or design objectives of the agent – what it is intended to achieve.

(2) **[Level 1.]**

Prove the following.

(1) For every purely reactive agent, there is a behaviourally equivalent standard agent.

(2) There exist standard agents that have no behaviourally equivalent purely reactive agent.

(3) **[Level 1.]**

Show that state-based agents are equivalent in expressive power to standard agents, i.e. that for every state-based agent there is a behaviourally equivalent standard agent and vice versa.

(4) **[Level 1.]**

There were two ways of specifying tasks by utility functions, by associating utilities with either states ($u : E \rightarrow \mathbb{R}$) or with runs ($u : \mathcal{R} \rightarrow \mathbb{R}$). The second type of utility function is strictly more expressive than the first. Give an example of a utility function over runs that cannot be defined simply by associating utilities with states.

(5) **[Level 4.]**

Read about traditional *control theory*, and compare the problems and techniques of control theory with what we are trying to accomplish in building intelligent agents. How are the techniques and problems of traditional control theory similar to those of intelligent agent work, and how do they differ?

(6) **[Class discussion.]**

Discuss the various different ways in which a task might be specified.

3

Deductive Reasoning Agents

The 'traditional' approach to building artificially intelligent systems, known as *symbolic AI*, suggests that intelligent behaviour can be generated in a system by giving that system a *symbolic* representation of its environment and its desired behaviour, and syntactically manipulating this representation. In this chapter, we focus on the apotheosis of this tradition, in which these symbolic representations are *logical formulae*, and the syntactic manipulation corresponds to *logical deduction*, or *theorem-proving*.

I will begin by giving an example to informally introduce the ideas behind deductive reasoning agents. Suppose we have some robotic agent, the purpose of which is to navigate around an office building picking up trash. There are many possible ways of implementing the control system for such a robot – we shall see several in the chapters that follow – but one way is to give it a description, or *representation* of the environment in which it is to operate. Figure 3.1 illustrates the idea (adapted from Konolige (1986, p. 15)).

RALPH is an autonomous robot agent that operates in a real-world environment of corridors and big blocks. Sensory input is from a video camera; a subsystem labelled 'interp' in Figure 3.1 translates the video feed into an internal representation format, based on first-order logic.

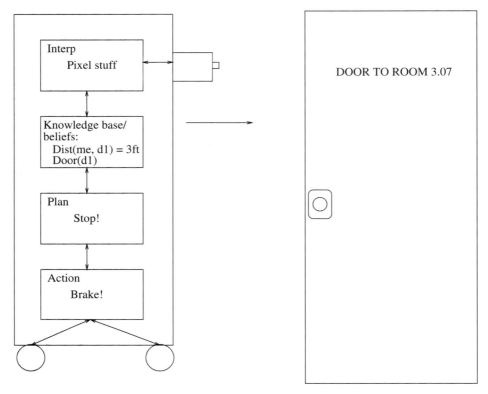

Figure 3.1   A robotic agent that contains a symbolic description of its environment.

The agent's information about the world is contained in a data structure which for historical reasons is labelled as a 'knowledge base' in Figure 3.1.

In order to build RALPH, it seems we must solve two key problems.

(1) The transduction problem. The problem of translating the real world into an accurate, adequate symbolic description of the world, in time for that description to be useful.

(2) The representation/reasoning problem. The problem of representing information symbolically, and getting agents to manipulate/reason with it, in time for the results to be useful.

The former problem has led to work on vision, speech understanding, learning, etc. The latter has led to work on knowledge representation, automated reasoning, automated planning, etc. Despite the immense volume of work that the problems have generated, many people would argue that neither problem is anywhere near solved. Even seemingly trivial problems, such as common sense reasoning, have turned out to be extremely difficult.

Despite these problems, the idea of agents as theorem provers is seductive. Suppose we have some theory of agency – some theory that explains how an intelligent agent should behave so as to optimize some performance measure (see Chapter 2). This theory might explain, for example, how an agent generates goals so as to satisfy its design objective, how it interleaves goal-directed and reactive behaviour in order to achieve these goals, and so on. Then this theory φ can be considered as a *specification* for how an agent should behave. The traditional approach to implementing a system that will satisfy this specification would involve *refining* the specification through a series of progressively more concrete stages, until finally an implementation was reached. In the view of agents as theorem provers, however, no such refinement takes place. Instead, φ is viewed as an *executable specification*: it is *directly executed* in order to produce the agent's behaviour.

3.1 Agents as Theorem Provers

To see how such an idea might work, we shall develop a simple model of logic-based agents, which we shall call *deliberate* agents (Genesereth and Nilsson, 1987, Chapter 13). In such agents, the internal state is assumed to be a database of formulae of classical first-order predicate logic. For example, the agent's database might contain formulae such as

$$Open(valve221)$$
$$Temperature(reactor4726, 321)$$
$$Pressure(tank776, 28).$$

It is not difficult to see how formulae such as these can be used to represent the properties of some environment. The database is the *information* that the agent has about its environment. An agent's database plays a somewhat analogous role to that of *belief* in humans. Thus a person might have a belief that valve 221 is open – the agent might have the predicate $Open(valve221)$ in its database. Of course, just like humans, agents can be wrong. Thus I might believe that valve 221 is open when it is in fact closed; the fact that an agent has $Open(valve221)$ in its database does not mean that valve 221 (or indeed any valve) is open. The agent's sensors may be faulty, its reasoning may be faulty, the information may be out of date, or the interpretation of the formula $Open(valve221)$ intended by the agent's designer may be something entirely different.

Let L be the set of sentences of classical first-order logic, and let $D = \wp(L)$ be the set of L *databases*, i.e. the set of sets of L-formulae. The internal state of an agent is then an element of D. We write $\Delta, \Delta_1, \ldots$ for members of D. The internal state of an agent is then simply a member of the set D. An agent's decision-making process is modelled through a set of *deduction rules*, ρ. These are simply rules of inference for the logic. We write $\Delta \vdash_\rho \varphi$ if the formula φ can be proved from the

```
Function: Action Selection as Theorem Proving
1.    function action(Δ : D) returns an action Ac
2.    begin
3.        for each α ∈ Ac do
4.            if Δ ⊢ρ Do(α) then
5.                return α
6.            end-if
7.        end-for
8.        for each α ∈ Ac do
9.            if Δ ⊬ρ ¬Do(α) then
10.               return α
11.           end-if
12.       end-for
13.       return null
14. end function action
```

Figure 3.2　Action selection as theorem-proving.

database Δ using only the deduction rules ρ. An agent's perception function *see* remains unchanged:

$$see : S \rightarrow Per.$$

Similarly, our *next* function has the form

$$next : D \times Per \rightarrow D.$$

It thus maps a database and a percept to a new database. However, an agent's action selection function, which has the signature

$$action : D \rightarrow Ac,$$

is defined in terms of its deduction rules. The pseudo-code definition of this function is given in Figure 3.2.

The idea is that the agent programmer will encode the deduction rules ρ and database Δ in such a way that if a formula $Do(\alpha)$ can be derived, where α is a term that denotes an action, then α is the best action to perform. Thus, in the first part of the function (lines (3)–(7)), the agent takes each of its possible actions α in turn, and attempts to prove the formula $Do(\alpha)$ from its database (passed as a parameter to the function) using its deduction rules ρ. If the agent succeeds in proving $Do(\alpha)$, then α is returned as the action to be performed.

What happens if the agent fails to prove $Do(\alpha)$, for all actions $a \in Ac$? In this case, it attempts to find an action that is *consistent* with the rules and database, i.e. one that is not explicitly forbidden. In lines (8)–(12), therefore, the agent attempts to find an action $a \in Ac$ such that $\neg Do(\alpha)$ cannot be derived from

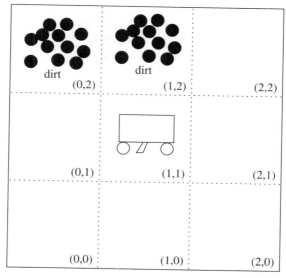

Figure 3.3 Vacuum world.

its database using its deduction rules. If it can find such an action, then this is returned as the action to be performed. If, however, the agent fails to find an action that is at least consistent, then it returns a special action *null* (or *noop*), indicating that no action has been selected.

In this way, the agent's behaviour is determined by the agent's deduction rules (its 'program') and its current database (representing the information the agent has about its environment).

To illustrate these ideas, let us consider a small example (based on the vacuum cleaning world example of Russell and Norvig (1995, p. 51)). The idea is that we have a small robotic agent that will clean up a house. The robot is equipped with a sensor that will tell it whether it is over any dirt, and a vacuum cleaner that can be used to suck up dirt. In addition, the robot always has a definite orientation (one of *north*, *south*, *east*, or *west*). In addition to being able to suck up dirt, the agent can move forward one 'step' or turn right 90°. The agent moves around a room, which is divided grid-like into a number of equally sized squares (conveniently corresponding to the unit of movement of the agent). We will assume that our agent does nothing but clean – it never leaves the room, and further, we will assume in the interests of simplicity that the room is a 3 × 3 grid, and the agent always starts in grid square (0, 0) facing north.

To summarize, our agent can receive a percept *dirt* (signifying that there is dirt beneath it), or *null* (indicating no special information). It can perform any one of three possible actions: *forward*, *suck*, or *turn*. The goal is to traverse the room continually searching for and removing dirt. See Figure 3.3 for an illustration of the vacuum world.

First, note that we make use of three simple *domain predicates* in this exercise:

$$In(x, y) \quad \text{agent is at } (x, y), \tag{3.1}$$

$$Dirt(x, y) \quad \text{there is dirt at } (x, y), \tag{3.2}$$

$$Facing(d) \quad \text{the agent is facing direction } d. \tag{3.3}$$

Now we specify our *next* function. This function must look at the perceptual information obtained from the environment (either *dirt* or *null*), and generate a new database which includes this information. But, in addition, it must *remove* old or irrelevant information, and also, it must try to figure out the new location and orientation of the agent. We will therefore specify the *next* function in several parts. First, let us write $old(\Delta)$ to denote the set of 'old' information in a database, which we want the update function *next* to remove:

$$old(\Delta) = \{P(t_1, \ldots, t_n) \mid P \in \{In, Dirt, Facing\} \text{ and } P(t_1, \ldots, t_n) \in \Delta\}.$$

Next, we require a function *new*, which gives the set of new predicates to add to the database. This function has the signature

$$new : D \times Per \to D.$$

The definition of this function is not difficult, but it is rather lengthy, and so we will leave it as an exercise. (It must generate the predicates $In(\ldots)$, describing the new position of the agent, $Facing(\ldots)$ describing the orientation of the agent, and $Dirt(\ldots)$ if dirt has been detected at the new position.) Given the *new* and *old* functions, the *next* function is defined as follows:

$$next(\Delta, p) = (\Delta \setminus old(\Delta)) \cup new(\Delta, p).$$

Now we can move on to the rules that govern our agent's behaviour. The deduction rules have the form

$$\varphi(\ldots) \longrightarrow \psi(\ldots),$$

where φ and ψ are predicates over some arbitrary list of constants and variables. The idea being that if φ matches against the agent's database, then ψ can be concluded, with any variables in ψ instantiated.

The first rule deals with the basic cleaning action of the agent: this rule will take priority over all other possible behaviours of the agent (such as navigation):

$$In(x, y) \wedge Dirt(x, y) \longrightarrow Do(suck). \tag{3.4}$$

Hence, if the agent is at location (x, y) and it perceives dirt, then the prescribed action will be to suck up dirt. Otherwise, the basic action of the agent will be to traverse the world. Taking advantage of the simplicity of our environment, we will hardwire the basic navigation algorithm, so that the robot will always move from $(0, 0)$ to $(0, 1)$ to $(0, 2)$ and then to $(1, 2)$, $(1, 1)$ and so on. Once the agent reaches

$(2, 2)$, it must head back to $(0, 0)$. The rules dealing with the traversal up to $(0, 2)$ are very simple:

$$In(0,0) \land Facing(north) \land \neg Dirt(0,0) \longrightarrow Do(forward), \qquad (3.5)$$

$$In(0,1) \land Facing(north) \land \neg Dirt(0,1) \longrightarrow Do(forward), \qquad (3.6)$$

$$In(0,2) \land Facing(north) \land \neg Dirt(0,2) \longrightarrow Do(turn), \qquad (3.7)$$

$$In(0,2) \land Facing(east) \longrightarrow Do(forward). \qquad (3.8)$$

Notice that in each rule, we must explicitly check whether the antecedent of rule (3.4) fires. This is to ensure that we only ever prescribe one action via the $Do(\ldots)$ predicate. Similar rules can easily be generated that will get the agent to $(2, 2)$, and once at $(2, 2)$ back to $(0, 0)$. It is not difficult to see that these rules, together with the *next* function, will generate the required behaviour of our agent.

At this point, it is worth stepping back and examining the pragmatics of the logic-based approach to building agents. Probably the most important point to make is that a literal, naive attempt to build agents in this way would be more or less entirely impractical. To see why, suppose we have designed out agent's rule set ρ such that for any database Δ, if we can prove $Do(\alpha)$, then α is an *optimal* action – that is, α is the best action that could be performed when the environment is as described in Δ. Then imagine we start running our agent. At time t_1, the agent has generated some database Δ_1, and begins to apply its rules ρ in order to find which action to perform. Some time later, at time t_2, it manages to establish $\Delta_1 \vdash_\rho Do(\alpha)$ for some $\alpha \in Ac$, and so α is the optimal action that the agent could perform at time t_1. But if the environment has *changed* between t_1 and t_2, then there is no guarantee that α will *still* be optimal. It could be far from optimal, particularly if much time has elapsed between t_1 and t_2. If $t_2 - t_1$ is infinitesimal – that is, if decision making is effectively instantaneous – then we could safely disregard this problem. But in fact, we know that reasoning of the kind that our logic-based agents use will be anything *but* instantaneous. (If our agent uses classical first-order predicate logic to represent the environment, and its rules are sound and complete, then there is no guarantee that the decision-making procedure will even *terminate*.) An agent is said to enjoy the property of *calculative rationality* if and only if its decision-making apparatus will suggest an action that was optimal *when the decision-making process began*. Calculative rationality is clearly not acceptable in environments that change faster than the agent can make decisions – we shall return to this point later.

One might argue that this problem is an artefact of the pure logic-based approach adopted here. There is an element of truth in this. By moving away from strictly logical representation languages and complete sets of deduction rules, one can build agents that enjoy respectable performance. But one also loses what is arguably the greatest advantage that the logical approach brings: a simple, elegant logical semantics.

There are several other problems associated with the logical approach to agency. First, the *see* function of an agent (its perception component) maps its environment to a percept. In the case of a logic-based agent, this percept is likely to be symbolic – typically, a set of formulae in the agent's representation language. But for many environments, it is not obvious how the mapping from environment to symbolic percept might be realized. For example, the problem of transforming an image to a set of declarative statements representing that image has been the object of study in AI for decades, and is still essentially open. Another problem is that actually *representing* properties of dynamic, real-world environments is extremely hard. As an example, representing and reasoning about *temporal information* – how a situation changes over time – turns out to be extraordinarily difficult. Finally, as the simple vacuum-world example illustrates, representing even rather simple *procedural* knowledge (i.e. knowledge about 'what to do') in traditional logic can be rather unintuitive and cumbersome.

To summarize, in logic-based approaches to building agents, decision making is viewed as deduction. An agent's 'program' – that is, its decision-making strategy – is encoded as a logical theory, and the process of selecting an action reduces to a problem of proof. Logic-based approaches are elegant, and have a clean (logical) semantics – wherein lies much of their long-lived appeal. But logic-based approaches have many disadvantages. In particular, the inherent computational complexity of theorem-proving makes it questionable whether agents as theorem provers can operate effectively in time-constrained environments. Decision making in such agents is predicated on the assumption of calculative rationality – the assumption that the world will not change in any significant way while the agent is deciding what to do, and that an action which is rational when decision making begins will be rational when it concludes. The problems associated with representing and reasoning about complex, dynamic, possibly physical environments are also essentially unsolved.

3.2   Agent-Oriented Programming

Yoav Shoham has proposed a 'new programming paradigm, based on a societal view of computation' which he calls *agent-oriented programming*. The key idea which informs AOP is that of directly programming agents in terms of *mentalistic* notions (such as belief, desire, and intention) that agent theorists have developed to represent the properties of agents. The motivation behind the proposal is that humans use such concepts as an *abstraction* mechanism for representing the properties of complex systems. In the same way that we use these mentalistic notions to describe and explain the behaviour of humans, so it might be useful to use them to program machines. The idea of programming computer systems in terms of mental states was articulated in Shoham (1993).

The first implementation of the agent-oriented programming paradigm was the AGENT0 programming language. In this language, an agent is specified in terms of a set of *capabilities* (things the agent can do), a set of initial *beliefs*, a set of initial *commitments*, and a set of *commitment rules*. The key component, which determines how the agent acts, is the commitment rule set. Each commitment rule contains a *message condition*, a *mental condition*, and an action. In order to determine whether such a rule fires, the message condition is matched against the messages the agent has received; the mental condition is matched against the beliefs of the agent. If the rule fires, then the agent becomes committed to the action.

Actions in Agent0 may be *private*, corresponding to an internally executed sub-routine, or *communicative*, i.e. sending messages. Messages are constrained to be one of three types: 'requests' or 'unrequests' to perform or refrain from actions, and 'inform' messages, which pass on information (in Chapter 8, we will see that this style of communication is very common in multiagent systems). Request and unrequest messages typically result in the agent's commitments being modified; inform messages result in a change to the agent's beliefs.

Here is an example of an Agent0 commitment rule:

```
COMMIT(
  ( agent, REQUEST, DO(time, action)
  ), ;;; msg condition
  ( B,
    [now, Friend agent] AND
    CAN(self, action) AND
    NOT [time, CMT(self, anyaction)]
  ), ;;; mental condition
  self,
  DO(time, action)  )
```

This rule may be paraphrased as follows:

> *if I receive a message from agent which requests me to do action at time, and I believe that*
>
> - *agent is currently a friend;*
> - *I can do the action;*
> - *at time, I am not committed to doing any other action,*
>
> *then commit to doing action at time.*

The operation of an agent can be described by the following loop (see Figure 3.4).

(1) Read all current messages, updating beliefs – and hence commitments – where necessary.

(2) Execute all commitments for the current cycle where the capability condition of the associated action is satisfied.

(3) Goto (1).

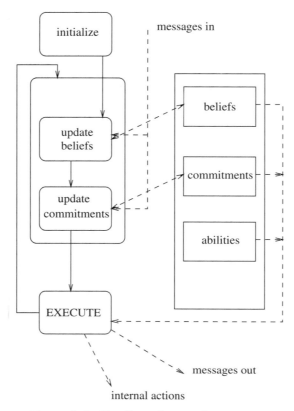

Figure 3.4   The flow of control in Agent0.

It should be clear how more complex agent behaviours can be designed and built in Agent0. However, it is important to note that this language is essentially a *prototype*, not intended for building anything like large-scale production systems. But it does at least give a feel for how such systems might be built.

3.3   Concurrent MetateM

The Concurrent MetateM language developed by Michael Fisher is based on the *direct execution* of logical formulae. In this sense, it comes very close to the 'ideal' of the agents as deductive theorem provers (Fisher, 1994). A Concurrent MetateM system contains a number of concurrently executing agents, each of which is able to communicate with its peers via asynchronous broadcast message passing. Each agent is programmed by giving it a *temporal logic* specification of the behaviour that it is intended the agent should exhibit. An agent's specification is executed directly to generate its behaviour. Execution of the agent program corresponds to iteratively building a logical model for the temporal agent specification. It is possible to prove that the procedure used to execute an agent specification is correct, in that if it is possible to satisfy the specification, then the agent will do so (Barringer *et al.*, 1989).

Agents in Concurrent MetateM are concurrently executing entities, able to communicate with each other through broadcast message passing. Each Concurrent MetateM agent has two main components:

- an *interface*, which defines how the agent may interact with its environment (i.e. other agents); and
- a *computational engine*, which defines how the agent will act – in Concurrent MetateM, the approach used is based on the MetateM paradigm of executable temporal logic (Barringer *et al.*, 1989).

An agent interface consists of three components:

- a unique *agent identifier* (or just agent id), which names the agent;
- a set of symbols defining which messages will be accepted by the agent – these are termed *environment propositions*; and
- a set of symbols defining messages that the agent may send – these are termed *component propositions*.

For example, the interface definition of a 'stack' agent might be

$$stack(pop, push)[popped, full].$$

Here, $stack$ is the agent id that names the agent, $\{pop, push\}$ is the set of environment propositions, and $\{popped, full\}$ is the set of component propositions. The intuition is that, whenever a message headed by the symbol pop is broadcast, the $stack$ agent will *accept* the message; we describe what this means below. If a message is broadcast that is not declared in the $stack$ agent's interface, then $stack$ ignores it. Similarly, the only messages that can be sent by the $stack$ agent are headed by the symbols $popped$ and $full$.

The computational engine of each agent in Concurrent MetateM is based on the MetateM paradigm of executable temporal logics (Barringer *et al.*, 1989). The idea is to directly execute an agent specification, where this specification is given as a set of *program rules*, which are temporal logic formulae of the form:

antecedent about past $\Rightarrow$ consequent about present and future.

The antecedent is a temporal logic formula referring to the past, whereas the consequent is a temporal logic formula referring to the present and future. The intuitive interpretation of such a rule is 'on the basis of the past, construct the future', which gives rise to the name of the paradigm: *declarative past and imperative future* (Gabbay, 1989). The rules that define an agent's behaviour can be animated by directly executing the temporal specification under a suitable operational model (Fisher, 1995).

Table 3.1   Temporal connectives for Concurrent MetateM rules.

Operator	Meaning
$\bigcirc \varphi$	φ is true 'tomorrow'
$\bullet \varphi$	φ was true 'yesterday'
$\Diamond \varphi$	at some time in the future, φ
$\Box \varphi$	always in the future, φ
$\blacklozenge \varphi$	at some time in the past, φ
$\blacksquare \varphi$	always in the past, φ
$\varphi \, \mathcal{U} \, \psi$	φ will be true until ψ
$\varphi \, \mathcal{S} \, \psi$	φ has been true since ψ
$\varphi \, \mathcal{W} \, \psi$	φ is true unless ψ
$\varphi \, \mathcal{Z} \, \psi$	φ is true zince ψ

To make the discussion more concrete, we introduce a propositional temporal logic, called Propositional MetateM Logic (PML), in which the temporal rules that are used to specify an agent's behaviour will be given. (A complete definition of PML is given in Barringer *et al.* (1989).) PML is essentially classical propositional logic augmented by a set of modal connectives for referring to the *temporal ordering* of events.

The meaning of the temporal connectives is quite straightforward: see Table 3.1 for a summary. Let φ and ψ be formulae of PML, then: $\bigcirc \varphi$ is satisfied at the current moment in time (i.e. now) if φ is satisfied at the next moment in time; $\Diamond \varphi$ is satisfied now if φ is satisfied either now or at some future moment in time; $\Box \varphi$ is satisfied now if φ is satisfied now and at all future moments; $\varphi \, \mathcal{U} \, \psi$ is satisfied now if ψ is satisfied at some future moment, and φ is satisfied until then – $\mathcal{W}$ is a binary connective similar to $\mathcal{U}$, allowing for the possibility that the second argument might never be satisfied.

The past-time connectives have similar meanings: $\bullet \varphi$ and $\bullet \varphi$ are satisfied now if φ was satisfied at the previous moment in time – the difference between them is that, since the model of time underlying the logic is bounded in the past, the beginning of time is treated as a special case in that, when interpreted at the beginning of time, $\bullet \varphi$ cannot be satisfied, whereas $\bullet \varphi$ will always be satisfied, regardless of φ; $\blacklozenge \varphi$ is satisfied now if φ was satisfied at some previous moment in time; $\blacksquare \varphi$ is satisfied now if φ was satisfied at all previous moments in time; $\varphi \, \mathcal{S} \, \psi$ is satisfied now if ψ was satisfied at some previous moment in time, and φ has been satisfied since then – $\mathcal{Z}$ is similar, but allows for the possibility that the second argument was never satisfied; finally, a nullary temporal operator can be defined, which is satisfied only at the beginning of time – this useful operator is called 'start'.

To illustrate the use of these temporal connectives, consider the following examples:

$$\Box important(agents)$$

means 'it is now, and will always be true that agents are important'.

$$\Diamond important(Janine)$$

means 'sometime in the future, Janine will be important'.

$$(\neg friends(us))\, \mathcal{U}\, apologize(you)$$

means 'we are not friends until you apologize'. And, finally,

$$\bigcirc apologize(you)$$

means 'tomorrow (in the next state), you apologize'.

The actual execution of an agent in Concurrent MetateM is, superficially at least, very simple to understand. Each agent obeys a cycle of trying to match the past-time antecedents of its rules against a *history*, and executing the consequents of those rules that 'fire'. More precisely, the computational engine for an agent continually executes the following cycle.

(1) Update the *history* of the agent by receiving messages (i.e. environment propositions) from other agents and adding them to its history.

(2) Check which rules *fire*, by comparing past-time antecedents of each rule against the current history to see which are satisfied.

(3) *Jointly execute* the fired rules together with any commitments carried over from previous cycles.

This involves first collecting together consequents of newly fired rules with old commitments – these become the *current constraints*. Now attempt to create the next state while satisfying these constraints. As the current constraints are represented by a disjunctive formula, the agent will have to choose between a number of execution possibilities.

Note that it may not be possible to satisfy *all* the relevant commitments on the current cycle, in which case unsatisfied commitments are carried over to the next cycle.

(4) Goto (1).

Clearly, step (3) is the heart of the execution process. Making the wrong choice at this step may mean that the agent specification cannot subsequently be satisfied.

When a proposition in an agent becomes *true*, it is compared against that agent's interface (see above); if it is one of the agent's *component propositions*, then that proposition is broadcast as a message to all other agents. On receipt of a message, each agent attempts to match the proposition against the environment propositions in their interface. If there is a match, then they add the proposition to their history.

$$rp(ask1, ask2)[give1, give2]:$$
$$\bullet\, ask1 \;\Rightarrow\; \Diamond give1;$$
$$\bullet\, ask2 \;\Rightarrow\; \Diamond give2;$$
$$\text{start} \;\Rightarrow\; \Box \neg(give1 \wedge give2).$$

$$rc1(give1)[ask1]:$$
$$\text{start} \;\Rightarrow\; ask1;$$
$$\bullet\, ask1 \;\Rightarrow\; ask1.$$

$$rc2(ask1, give2)[ask2]:$$
$$\bullet\, (ask1 \wedge \neg ask2) \;\Rightarrow\; ask2.$$

Figure 3.5 A simple Concurrent MetateM system.

Time	Agent		
	rp	$rc1$	$rc2$
0.		$ask1$	
1.	$ask1$	$ask1$	$ask2$
2.	$ask1, ask2, give1$	$ask1$	
3.	$ask1, give2$	$ask1, give1$	$ask2$
4.	$ask1, ask2, give1$	$ask1$	$give2$
5.	...	...	...

Figure 3.6 An example run of Concurrent MetateM.

Figure 3.5 shows a simple system containing three agents: rp, $rc1$, and $rc2$. The agent rp is a 'resource producer': it can '$give$' to only one agent at a time, and will commit to eventually $give$ to any agent that asks. Agent rp will only accept messages $ask1$ and $ask2$, and can only send $give1$ and $give2$ messages. The interface of agent $rc1$ states that it will only accept $give1$ messages, and can only send $ask1$ messages. The rules for agent $rc1$ ensure that an $ask1$ message is sent on every cycle – this is because start is satisfied at the beginning of time, thus firing the first rule, so $\bullet\, ask1$ will be satisfied on the next cycle, thus firing the second rule, and so on. Thus $rc1$ asks for the resource on every cycle, using an $ask1$ message. The interface for agent $rc2$ states that it will accept both $ask1$ and $give2$ messages, and can send $ask2$ messages. The single rule for agent $rc2$ ensures that an $ask2$ message is sent on every cycle where, on its previous cycle, it did not send an $ask2$ message, but received an $ask1$ message (from agent $rc1$). Figure 3.6 shows a fragment of an example run of the system in Figure 3.5.

Notes and Further Reading

My presentation of logic based agents draws heavily on the discussion of *deliberate agents* presented in Genesereth and Nilsson (1987, Chapter 13), which represents the logic-centric view of AI and agents very well. The discussion is also partly based on Konolige (1986). A number of more-or-less 'pure' logical approaches to agent programming have been developed. Well-known examples include the ConGolog system of Lespérance and colleagues (Lésperance *et al.*, 1996) (which is based on the *situation calculus* (McCarthy and Hayes, 1969)). Note that these architectures (and the discussion above) assume that if one adopts a logical approach to agent building, then this means agents are essentially theorem provers, employing explicit symbolic reasoning (theorem-proving) in order to make decisions. But just because we find logic a useful tool for conceptualizing or specifying agents, this does not mean that we must view decision making as logical manipulation. An alternative is to *compile* the logical specification of an agent into a form more amenable to efficient decision making. The difference is rather like the distinction between interpreted and compiled programming languages. The best-known example of this work is the *situated automata* paradigm of Rosenschein and Kaelbling (1996). A review of the role of logic in intelligent agents may be found in Wooldridge (1997). Finally, for a detailed discussion of calculative rationality and the way that it has affected thinking in AI (see Russell and Subramanian, 1995).

The main references to Agent0 are Shoham (1990, 1993). Shoham's AOP proposal has been enormously influential in the multiagent systems community. In addition to the reasons set out in the main text, there are other reasons for believing that an intentional stance will be useful for understanding and reasoning about computer programs (Huhns and Singh, 1998). First, and perhaps most importantly, the ability of heterogeneous, self-interested agents to communicate seems to imply the ability to talk about the beliefs, aspirations, and intentions of individual agents. For example, in order to *coordinate* their activities, agents must have information about the intentions of others (Jennings, 1993a). This idea is closely related to Newell's *knowledge level* (Newell, 1982). Later in this book, we will see how mental states such as beliefs, desires, and the like are used to give a semantics to *speech acts* (Searle, 1969; Cohen and Levesque, 1990a). Second, mentalistic models are a good candidate for representing information about end users. For example, imagine a tutoring system that works with students to teach them Java programming. One way to build such a system is to give it a *model* of the user. Beliefs, desires, intentions, and the like seem appropriate for the make-up of such models.

Michael Fisher's Concurrent MetateM language is described in Fisher (1994); the execution algorithm that underpins it is described in Barringer *et al.* (1989). Since Shoham's proposal, a number of languages have been proposed which claim to be agent oriented. Examples include Becky Thomas's Planning Communicating

Agents (PLACA) language (Thomas, 1993; Thomas, 1995), MAIL (Haugeneder *et al.*, 1994), and the AgentSpeak(L) language (Rao, 1996a).

Class reading: Shoham (1993).   This is the article that introduced agent-oriented programming and, throughout the late 1990s, was one of the most cited articles in the agent community. The main point about the article, as far as I am concerned, is that it explicitly articulates the idea of programming systems in terms of 'mental states'. Agent0, the actual language described in the article, is not a language that you would be likely to use for developing 'real' systems. A useful discussion might be had on (i) whether 'mental states' are really useful in programming systems; (ii) how one might go about proving or disproving the hypothesis that mental states are useful in programming systems, and (iii) how Agent0-like features might be incorporated in a language such as Java.

$$SnowWhite(ask)[give]:$$
$$\bullet\, ask(x) \Rightarrow \Diamond give(x)$$
$$give(x) \wedge give(y) \Rightarrow (x = y)$$

$$eager(give)[ask]:$$
$$start \Rightarrow ask(eager)$$
$$\bullet\, give(eager) \Rightarrow ask(eager)$$

$$greedy(give)[ask]:$$
$$start \Rightarrow \Box ask(greedy)$$

$$courteous(give)[ask]:$$
$$((\neg ask(courteous)\, S\, give(eager)) \wedge$$
$$(\neg ask(courteous)\, S\, give(greedy))) \Rightarrow ask(courteous)$$

$$shy(give)[ask]:$$
$$start \Rightarrow \Diamond ask(shy)$$
$$\bullet\, ask(x) \Rightarrow \neg ask(shy)$$
$$\bullet\, give(shy) \Rightarrow \Diamond ask(shy)$$

Figure 3.7   Snow White in Concurrent MetateM.

Exercises

(1) **[Level 2.]** (The following few questions refer to the vacuum-world example.)

Give the full definition (using pseudo-code if desired) of the *new* function, which defines the predicates to add to the agent's database.

(2) **[Level 2.]**

Complete the vacuum-world example, by filling in the missing rules. How intuitive do you think the solution is? How elegant is it? How compact is it?

(3) **[Level 2.]**

Try using your favourite (imperative) programming language to code a solution to the basic vacuum-world example. How do you think it compares with the logical solution? What does this tell you about trying to encode essentially *procedural* knowledge (i.e. knowledge about what action to perform) as purely logical rules?

(4) **[Level 2.]**

If you are familiar with Prolog, try encoding the vacuum-world example in this language and running it with randomly placed dirt. Make use of the `assert` and `retract` meta-level predicates provided by Prolog to simplify your system (allowing the program itself to achieve much of the operation of the *next* function).

(5) **[Level 2.]**

Try scaling the vacuum world up to a 10×10 grid size. Approximately how many rules would you need to encode this enlarged example, using the approach presented above? Try to generalize the rules, encoding a more general decision-making mechanism.

(6) **[Level 3.]**

Suppose that the vacuum world could also contain *obstacles*, which the agent needs to avoid. (Imagine it is equipped with a sensor to detect such obstacles.) Try to adapt the example to deal with obstacle detection and avoidance. Again, compare a logic-based solution with one implemented in a traditional (imperative) programming language.

(7) **[Level 3.]**

Suppose the agent's sphere of perception in the vacuum world is enlarged, so that it can see the *whole* of its world, and see *exactly* where the dirt lay. In this case, it would be possible to generate an *optimal* decision-making algorithm – one which cleared up the dirt in the smallest time possible. Try and think of such general algorithms, and try to code them both in first-order logic and a more traditional programming language. Investigate the effectiveness of these algorithms when there is the possibility of *noise* in the perceptual input the agent receives (i.e. there is a non-zero probability that the perceptual information is wrong), and try to develop decision-making algorithms that are robust in the presence of such noise. How do such algorithms perform as the level of perception is reduced?

(8) **[Level 2.]**

Consider the Concurrent MetateM program in Figure 3.7. Explain the behaviour of the agents in this system.

(9) **[Level 4.]**

Extend the Concurrent MetateM language by operators for referring to the beliefs and commitments of other agents, in the style of Shoham's Agent0.

(10) **[Level 4.]**

Give a formal semantics to Agent0 and Concurrent MetateM.

4

Practical Reasoning Agents

Whatever the merits of agents that decide what to do by proving theorems, it seems clear that *we* do not use purely logical reasoning in order to decide what to do. Certainly something like logical reasoning can play a part, but a moment's reflection should confirm that for most of the time, very different processes are taking place. In this chapter, I will focus on a model of agency that takes its inspiration from the processes that seem to take place as we decide what to do.

4.1 Practical Reasoning Equals Deliberation Plus Means–Ends Reasoning

The particular model of decision making is known as *practical reasoning*. Practical reasoning is reasoning directed towards actions – the process of figuring out what to do.

> Practical reasoning is a matter of weighing conflicting considerations for and against competing options, where the relevant considerations are provided by what the agent desires/values/cares about and what the agent believes.

> (Bratman, 1990, p. 17)

It is important to distinguish practical reasoning from *theoretical reasoning* (Eliasmith, 1999). Theoretical reasoning is directed towards beliefs. To use a rather tired example, if I believe that all men are mortal, and I believe that Socrates is a man, then I will usually conclude that Socrates is mortal. The process of concluding that Socrates is mortal is theoretical reasoning, since it affects only my beliefs about the world. The process of deciding to catch a bus instead of a train, however, is practical reasoning, since it is reasoning directed towards action.

Human practical reasoning appears to consist of at least two distinct activities. The first of these involves deciding *what* state of affairs we want to achieve; the second process involves deciding *how* we want to achieve these states of affairs. The former process – deciding what states of affairs to achieve – is known as *deliberation*. The latter process – deciding how to achieve these states of affairs – we call *means–ends reasoning*.

To better understand deliberation and means–ends reasoning, consider the following example. When a person graduates from university with a first degree, he or she is faced with some important choices. Typically, one proceeds in these choices by first deciding what sort of career to follow. For example, one might consider a career as an academic, or a career in industry. The process of deciding which career to aim for is deliberation. Once one has fixed upon a career, there are further choices to be made; in particular, how to bring about this career. Suppose that after deliberation, you choose to pursue a career as an academic. The next step is to decide *how to achieve* this state of affairs. This process is means–ends reasoning. The end result of means–ends reasoning is a *plan* or *recipe* of some kind for achieving the chosen state of affairs. For the career example, a plan might involve first applying to an appropriate university for a PhD place, and so on. After obtaining a plan, an agent will typically then attempt to carry out (or *execute*) the plan, in order to bring about the chosen state of affairs. If all goes well (the plan is sound, and the agent's environment cooperates sufficiently), then after the plan has been executed, the chosen state of affairs will be achieved.

Thus described, practical reasoning seems a straightforward process, and in an ideal world, it would be. But there are several complications. The first is that deliberation and means–ends reasoning are *computational* processes. In all real agents (and, in particular, artificial agents), such computational processes will take place under *resource bounds*. By this I mean that an agent will only have a fixed amount of memory and a fixed processor available to carry out its computations. Together, these resource bounds impose a limit on the size of computations that can be carried out in any given amount of time. No real agent will be able to carry out arbitrarily large computations in a finite amount of time. Since almost any real environment will also operate in the presence of *time constraints* of some kind, this means that means–ends reasoning and deliberation must be carried out in a fixed, finite number of processor cycles, with a fixed, finite amount of memory space. From this discussion, we can see that resource bounds have two important implications:

- Computation is a valuable resource for agents situated in real-time environ-ments. The ability to perform well will be determined at least in part by the ability to make efficient use of available computational resources. In other words, an agent must *control* its reasoning effectively if it is to perform well.

- Agents cannot deliberate indefinitely. They must clearly *stop* deliberating at some point, having chosen some state of affairs, and commit to achieving this state of affairs. It may well be that the state of affairs it has fixed upon is not optimal – further deliberation may have led it to fix upon an another state of affairs.

We refer to the states of affairs that an agent has chosen and committed to as its *intentions*.

Intentions in practical reasoning

First, notice that it is possible to distinguish several different types of intention. In ordinary speech, we use the term 'intention' to characterize both *actions* and *states of mind*. To adapt an example from Bratman (Bratman, 1987, p. 1), I might intentionally push someone under a train, and push them with the intention of killing them. Intention is here used to characterize an action – the action of push-ing someone under a train. Alternatively, I might have the intention this morning of pushing someone under a train this afternoon. Here, intention is used to char-acterize my state of mind. In this book, when I talk about intentions, I mean inten-tions as states of mind. In particular, I mean *future-directed intentions* – intentions that an agent has towards some future state of affairs.

The most obvious role of intentions is that they are *pro-attitudes* (Bratman, 1990, p. 23). By this, I mean that they tend to lead to action. Suppose I have an intention to write a book. If I truly have such an intention, then you would expect. me to make a *reasonable attempt* to achieve it. This would usually involve, at the very least, me initiating some plan of action that I believed would satisfy the intention. In this sense, intentions tend to play a primary role in the production of action. As time passes, and my intention about the future becomes my inten-tion about the present, then it plays a direct role in the production of action. Of course, having an intention does not necessarily lead to action. For example, I can have an intention now to attend a conference later in the year. I can be utterly sincere in this intention, and yet if I learn of some event that must take precedence over the conference, I may never even get as far as considering travel arrangements.

Bratman notes that intentions play a much stronger role in influencing action than other pro-attitudes, such as mere desires.

> My desire to play basketball this afternoon is merely a potential influ-encer of my conduct this afternoon. It must vie with my other relevant desires…before it is settled what I will do. In contrast, once I intend

to play basketball this afternoon, the matter is settled: I normally need not continue to weigh the pros and cons. When the afternoon arrives, I will normally just proceed to execute my intentions.

(Bratman, 1990, p. 22)

The second main property of intentions is that they *persist*. If I adopt an intention to become an academic, then I should persist with this intention and attempt to achieve it. For if I immediately drop my intentions without devoting any resources to achieving them, then I will not be acting rationally. Indeed, you might be inclined to say that I never really had intentions in the first place.

Of course, I should not persist with my intention for too long – if it becomes clear to me that I will never become an academic, then it is only rational to drop my intention to do so. Similarly, if the reason for having an intention goes away, then it would be rational for me to drop the intention. For example, if I adopted the intention to become an academic because I believed it would be an easy life, but then discover that this is not the case (e.g. I might be expected to actually teach!), then the justification for the intention is no longer present, and I should drop the intention.

If I initially fail to achieve an intention, then you would expect me to *try again* – you would not expect me to simply give up. For example, if my first application for a PhD program is rejected, then you might expect me to apply to alternative universities.

The third main property of intentions is that once I have adopted an intention, the very fact of having this intention will constrain my future practical reasoning. For example, while I hold some particular intention, I will not subsequently entertain options that are *inconsistent* with that intention. Intending to write a book, for example, would preclude the option of partying every night: the two are mutually exclusive. This is in fact a highly desirable property from the point of view of implementing rational agents, because in providing a 'filter of admissibility', intentions can be seen to constrain the space of possible intentions that an agent needs to consider.

Finally, intentions are closely related to beliefs about the future. For example, if I intend to become an academic, then I should believe that, assuming some certain background conditions are satisfied, I will indeed become an academic. For if I truly believe that I will never be an academic, it would be nonsensical of me to have an intention to become one. Thus if I intend to become an academic, I should at least believe that there is a good chance I will indeed become one. However, there is what appears at first sight to be a paradox here. While I might believe that I will indeed succeed in achieving my intention, if I am rational, then I must also recognize the possibility that I can *fail* to bring it about – that there is some circumstance under which my intention is not satisfied.

From this discussion, we can identify the following closely related situations.

- Having an intention to bring about φ, while believing that you will not bring about φ is called *intention-belief inconsistency*, and is not rational (see, for example, Bratman, 1987, pp. 37, 38).

- Having an intention to achieve φ without believing that φ will be the case is *intention-belief incompleteness*, and is an acceptable property of rational agents (see, for example, Bratman, 1987, p. 38).

The distinction between these two cases is known as the *asymmetry thesis* (Bratman, 1987, pp. 37–41).

Summarizing, we can see that intentions play the following important roles in practical reasoning.

Intentions drive means–ends reasoning. If I have formed an intention, then I will attempt to achieve the intention, which involves, among other things, deciding *how* to achieve it. Moreover, if one particular course of action fails to achieve an intention, then I will typically attempt others.

Intentions persist. I will not usually give up on my intentions without good reason – they will persist, typically until I believe I have successfully achieved them, I believe I cannot achieve them, or I believe the reason for the intention is no longer present.

Intentions constrain future deliberation. I will not entertain options that are inconsistent with my current intentions.

Intentions influence beliefs upon which future practical reasoning is based. If I adopt an intention, then I can plan for the future on the assumption that I will achieve the intention. For if I intend to achieve some state of affairs while simultaneously believing that I will not achieve it, then I am being irrational.

Notice from this discussion that intentions *interact* with an agent's beliefs and other mental states. For example, having an intention to φ implies that I do not believe φ is impossible, and moreover that I believe given the right circumstances, φ will be achieved. However, satisfactorily capturing the interaction between intention and belief turns out to be surprisingly hard – some discussion on this topic appears in Chapter 12.

Throughout the remainder of this chapter, I make one important assumption: that the agent maintains some explicit *representation* of its beliefs, desires, and intentions. However, I will not be concerned with *how* beliefs and the like are represented. One possibility is that they are represented *symbolically*, for example as logical statements *a là* Prolog facts (Clocksin and Mellish, 1981). However, the assumption that beliefs, desires, and intentions are symbolically represented is by no means necessary for the remainder of the book. I use B to denote a variable that holds the agent's current beliefs, and let *Bel* be the set of all such beliefs. Similarly, I use D as a variable for desires, and *Des* to denote the set of all desires.

Finally, the variable I represents the agent's intentions, and Int is the set of all possible intentions.

In what follows, deliberation will be modelled via two functions:

- an option generation function; and
- a filtering function.

The signature of the option generation function *options* is as follows:

$$options : \wp(Bel) \times \wp(Int) \rightarrow \wp(Des).$$

This function takes the agent's current beliefs and current intentions, and on the basis of these produces a set of possible options or desires.

In order to select between competing options, an agent uses a *filter* function. Intuitively, the filter function must simply select the 'best' option(s) for the agent to commit to. We represent the filter process through a function $filter$, with a signature as follows:

$$filter : \wp(Bel) \times \wp(Des) \times \wp(Int) \rightarrow \wp(Int).$$

An agent's belief update process is modelled through a *belief revision function*:

$$brf : \wp(Bel) \times Per \rightarrow \wp(Bel).$$

4.2 Means–Ends Reasoning

Means–ends reasoning is the process of deciding how to achieve an end (i.e. an intention that you have) using the available means (i.e. the actions that you can perform). Means–ends reasoning is perhaps better known in the AI community as *planning*.

Planning is essentially automatic programming. A planner is a system that takes as input representations of the following.

(1) A *goal*, *intention* or (in the terminology of Chapter 2) a *task*. This is something that the agent wants to achieve (in the case of achievement tasks – see Chapter 2), or a state of affairs that the agent wants to maintain or avoid (in the case of maintenance tasks – see Chapter 2).

(2) The current *state of the environment* – the agent's *beliefs*.

(3) The *actions* available to the agent.

As output, a planning algorithm generates a *plan* (see Figure 4.1). This is a course of action – a 'recipe'. If the planning algorithm does its job correctly, then if the agent executes this plan ('follows the recipe') from a state in which the world is as described in (2), then once the plan has been completely executed, the goal/intention/task described in (1) will be carried out.

The first real planner was the STRIPS system, developed by Fikes in the late 1960s/early 1970s (Fikes and Nilsson, 1971). The two basic components of STRIPS

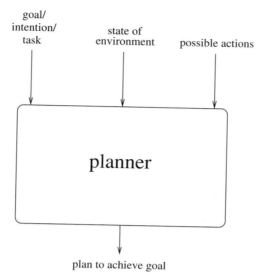

Figure 4.1   Planning.

were a model of the world as a set of formulae of first-order logic, and a set of *action schemata*, which describe the preconditions and effects of all the actions available to the planning agent. This latter component has perhaps proved to be STRIPS' most lasting legacy in the AI planning community: nearly all implemented planners employ the 'STRIPS formalism' for action, or some variant of it. The STRIPS planning algorithm was based on a principle of finding the 'difference' between the current state of the world and the goal state, and reducing this difference by applying an action. Unfortunately, this proved to be an inefficient process for formulating plans, as STRIPS tended to become 'lost' in low-level plan detail.

There is not scope in this book to give a detailed technical introduction to planning algorithms and technologies, and in fact it is probably not appropriate to do so. Nevertheless, it is at least worth giving a short overview of the main concepts.

The Blocks World

In time-honoured fashion, I will illustrate the techniques with reference to a *Blocks World*. The Blocks World contains three blocks (*A*, *B*, and *C*) of equal size, a robot arm capable of picking up and moving one block at a time, and a table top. The blocks may be placed on the table top, or one may be placed on top of the other. Figure 4.2 shows one possible configuration of the Blocks World.

Notice that in the description of planning algorithms I gave above, I stated that planning algorithms take as input *representations* of the goal, the current state of the environment, and the actions available. The first issue is exactly what form these representations take. The STRIPS system made use of representations based

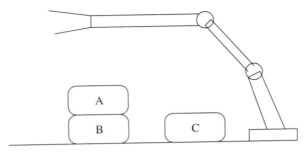

Figure 4.2   The Blocks World.

on first-order logic. I will use the predicates in Table 4.1 to represent the Blocks World.

A description of the Blocks World in Figure 4.2 is using these predicates as follows:

$$\{Clear(A), On(A, B), OnTable(B), OnTable(C), Clear(C)\}.$$

I am implicitly making use of the *closed world* assumption: if something is not explicitly stated to be true, then it is assumed false.

The next issue is how to represent goals. Again, we represent a goal as a set of formulae of first-order logic:

$$\{OnTable(A), OnTable(B), OnTable(C)\}.$$

So the goal is that all the blocks are on the table. To represent actions, we make use of the precondition/delete/add list notation – the STRIPS formalism. In this formalism, each action has

- a *name* – which may have arguments;
- a *precondition list* – a list of facts which must be true for the action to be executed;
- a *delete list* – a list of facts that are no longer true after the action is performed; and
- an *add list* – a list of facts made true by executing the action.

The *stack* action occurs when the robot arm places the object x it is holding on top of object y:

$$Stack(x, y)$$
$$\text{pre} \quad \{Clear(y), Holding(x)\}$$
$$\text{del} \quad \{Clear(y), Holding(x)\}$$
$$\text{add} \quad \{ArmEmpty, On(x, y)\}$$

The *unstack* action occurs when the robot arm picks an object x up from on top of another object y:

Table 4.1 Predicates for describing the Blocks World.

Predicate	Meaning
$On(x, y)$	object x on top of object y
$OnTable(x)$	object x is on the table
$Clear(x)$	nothing is on top of object x
$Holding(x)$	robot arm is holding x
$ArmEmpty$	robot arm empty (not holding anything)

$UnStack(x, y)$
pre $\{On(x, y), Clear(x), ArmEmpty\}$
del $\{On(x, y), ArmEmpty\}$
add $\{Holding(x), Clear(y)\}$

The *pickup* action occurs when the arm picks up an object x from the table:

$Pickup(x)$
pre $\{Clear(x), OnTable(x), ArmEmpty\}$
del $\{OnTable(x), ArmEmpty\}$
add $\{Holding(x)\}$

The *putdown* action occurs when the arm places the object x onto the table:

$PutDown(x)$
pre $\{Holding(x)\}$
del $\{Holding(x)\}$
add $\{ArmEmpty, OnTable(x)\}$

Let us now describe what is going on somewhat more formally. First, as we have throughout the book, we assume a fixed set of actions $Ac = \{\alpha_1, \ldots, \alpha_n\}$ that the agent can perform. A *descriptor* for an action $\alpha \in Ac$ is a triple

$$\langle P_\alpha, D_\alpha, A_\alpha \rangle,$$

where

- P_α is a set of formulae of first-order logic that characterize the *precondition* of action α;

- D_α is a set of formulae of first-order logic that characterize those facts made *false* by the performance of α (the *delete list*); and

- A_α is a set of formulae of first-order logic that characterize those facts made *true* by the performance of α (the *add list*).

For simplicity, we will assume that the precondition, delete, and add lists are constrained to only contain *ground atoms* – individual predicates, which do not contain logical connectives or variables.

A *planning problem* (over the set of actions *Ac*) is then determined by a triple

$$\langle \Delta, O, \gamma \rangle,$$

where

- Δ is the beliefs of the agent about the *initial* state of the world – these beliefs will be a set of formulae of first order (cf. the vacuum world in Chapter 2);
- $O = \{ \langle P_\alpha, D_\alpha, A_\alpha \rangle \mid \alpha \in Ac \}$ is an indexed set of operator descriptors, one for each available action α; and
- γ is a set of formulae of first-order logic, representing the *goal/task/intention* to be achieved.

A *plan* π is a sequence of actions

$$\pi = (\alpha_1, \ldots, \alpha_n),$$

where each α_i is a member of *Ac*.

With respect to a planning problem $\langle \Delta, O, \gamma \rangle$, a plan $\pi = (\alpha_1, \ldots, \alpha_n)$ determines a sequence of $n + 1$ *environment models*

$$\Delta_0, \Delta_1, \ldots, \Delta_n,$$

where

$$\Delta_0 = \Delta$$

and

$$\Delta_i = (\Delta_{i-1} \setminus D_{\alpha_i}) \cup A_{\alpha_i} \quad \text{for } 1 \leqslant i \leqslant n.$$

A (linear) plan $\pi = (\alpha_1, \ldots, \alpha_n)$ is said to be *acceptable* with respect to the problem $\langle \Delta, O, \gamma \rangle$ if, and only if, the precondition of every action is satisfied in the preceding environment model, i.e. if $\Delta_{i-1} \vDash P_{\alpha_i}$, for all $1 \leqslant i \leqslant n$. A plan $\pi = (\alpha_1, \ldots, \alpha_n)$ is *correct* with respect to $\langle \Delta, O, \gamma \rangle$ if and only if

(1) it is acceptable; and

(2) $\Delta_n \vDash \gamma$ (i.e. if the goal is achieved in the final environment state generated by the plan).

The problem to be solved by a planning system can then be stated as follows.

> Given a planning problem $\langle \Delta, O, \gamma \rangle$, find a correct plan for $\langle \Delta, O, \gamma \rangle$ or else announce that none exists).

(It is worth comparing this discussion with that on the synthesis of agents in Chapter 3 – similar comments apply with respect to the issues of soundness and completeness.)

We will use π (with decorations: $\pi', \pi_1, \ldots$) to denote plans, and let *Plan* be the set of all plans (over some set of actions *Ac*). We will make use of a number of auxiliary definitions for manipulating plans (some of these will not actually be required until later in this chapter):

- if π is a plan, then we write $pre(\pi)$ to denote the precondition of π, and $body(\pi)$ to denote the body of π;

- if π is a plan, then we write $empty(\pi)$ to mean that plan π is the empty sequence (thus $empty(\ldots)$ is a Boolean-valued function);

- $execute(\ldots)$ is a procedure that takes as input a single plan and executes it without stopping – executing a plan simply means executing each action in the plan body in turn;

- if π is a plan, then by $hd(\pi)$ we mean the plan made up of the first action in the plan body of π; for example, if the body of π is $\alpha_1, \ldots, \alpha_n$, then the body of $hd(\pi)$ contains only the action α_1;

- if π is a plan, then by $tail(\pi)$ we mean the plan made up of all but the first action in the plan body of π; for example, if the body of π is $\alpha_1, \alpha_2, \ldots, \alpha_n$, then the body of $tail(\pi)$ contains actions $\alpha_2, \ldots, \alpha_n$;

- if π is a plan, $I \subseteq Int$ is a set of intentions, and $B \subseteq Bel$ is a set of beliefs, then we write $sound(\pi, I, B)$ to mean that π is a correct plan for intentions I given beliefs B (Lifschitz, 1986).

An agent's means–ends reasoning capability is represented by a function

$$plan : \wp(Bel) \times \wp(Int) \times \wp(Ac) \rightarrow Plan,$$

which, on the basis of an agent's current beliefs and current intentions, determines a plan to achieve the intentions.

Notice that there is nothing in the definition of the $plan(\ldots)$ function which requires an agent to engage in *plan generation* – constructing a plan from scratch (Allen *et al.*, 1990). In many implemented practical reasoning agents, the $plan(\ldots)$ function is implemented by giving the agent a *plan library* (Georgeff and Lansky, 1987). A plan library is a pre-assembled collection of plans, which an agent designer gives to an agent. Finding a plan to achieve an intention then simply involves a single pass through the plan library to find a plan that, when executed, will have the intention as a postcondition, and will be sound given the agent's current beliefs. Preconditions and postconditions for plans are often represented as (lists of) atoms of first-order logic, and beliefs and intentions as ground atoms of first-order logic. Finding a plan to achieve an intention then reduces to finding a plan whose precondition unifies with the agent's beliefs, and whose postcondition unifies with the intention. At the end of this chapter, we will see how this idea works in the PRS system.

4.3 Implementing a Practical Reasoning Agent

We can now discuss the overall control structure of a practical reasoning agent. Figure 4.3 gives the pseudo-code for the control cycle of such an agent. The basic structure of the decision-making process is a loop, in which the agent continually

```
Algorithm: Practical Reasoning Agent Control Loop
1.
2.   B ← B₀;      /* B₀ are initial beliefs */
3.   I ← I₀;      /* I₀ are initial intentions */
4.   while true do
5.       get next percept ρ through see(...) function;
6.       B ← brf(B,ρ);
7.       D ← options(B,I);
8.       I ← filter(B,D,I);
9.       π ← plan(B,I,Ac);
10.      while not (empty(π) or succeeded(I,B) or impossible(I,B)) do
11.          α ← hd(π);
12.          execute(α);
13.          π ← tail(π);
14.          get next percept ρ through see(...) function;
15.          B ← brf(B,ρ);
16.          if reconsider(I,B) then
17.                  D ← options(B,I);
18.                  I ← filter(B,D,I);
19.          end-if
20.          if not sound(π,I,B) then
21.                  π ← plan(B,I,Ac);
22.          end-if
23.      end-while
24. end-while
```

Figure 4.3   A practical reasoning agent.

- observes the world, and updates beliefs;

- deliberates to decide what intention to achieve (deliberation being done by first determining the available options and then by filtering);

- uses means-ends reasoning to find a plan to achieve these intentions;

- executes the plan.

However, this basic control loop is complicated by a number of concerns. The first of these is that of *commitment* - and, in particular, how committed an agent is to both ends (the intention) and means (the plan to achieve the intention).

Commitment to ends and means

When an option successfully passes through the *filter* function and is hence chosen by the agent as an intention, we say that the agent has made a *commitment* to that option. Commitment implies *temporal persistence* - an intention, once adopted, should not immediately evaporate. A critical issue is just *how* committed an agent should be to its intentions. That is, how long should an intention persist? Under what circumstances should an intention vanish?

To motivate the discussion further, consider the following scenario.

> Some time in the not-so-distant future, you are having trouble with your new household robot. You say "Willie, bring me a beer." The robot replies "OK boss." Twenty minutes later, you screech "Willie, why didn't you bring me that beer?" It answers "Well, I intended to get you the beer, but I decided to do something else." Miffed, you send the wise guy back to the manufacturer, complaining about a lack of commitment. After retrofitting, Willie is returned, marked "Model C: The Committed Assistant." Again, you ask Willie to bring you a beer. Again, it accedes, replying "Sure thing." Then you ask: "What kind of beer did you buy?" It answers: "Genessee." You say "Never mind." One minute later, Willie trundles over with a Genessee in its gripper. This time, you angrily return Willie for overcommitment. After still more tinkering, the manufacturer sends Willie back, promising no more problems with its commitments. So, being a somewhat trusting customer, you accept the rascal back into your household, but as a test, you ask it to bring you your last beer. Willie again accedes, saying "Yes, Sir." (Its attitude problem seems to have been fixed.) The robot gets the beer and starts towards you. As it approaches, it lifts its arm, wheels around, deliberately smashes the bottle, and trundles off. Back at the plant, when interrogated by customer service as to why it had abandoned its commitments, the robot replies that according to its specifications, it kept its commitments as long as required – commitments must be dropped when fulfilled or impossible to achieve. By smashing the bottle, the commitment became unachievable.
>
> (Cohen and Levesque, 1990a, pp. 213, 214)

The mechanism an agent uses to determine when and how to drop intentions is known as a *commitment strategy*. The following three commitment strategies are commonly discussed in the literature of rational agents (Rao and Georgeff, 1991b).

Blind commitment. A blindly committed agent will continue to maintain an intention until it believes the intention has actually been achieved. Blind commitment is also sometimes referred to as *fanatical* commitment.

Single-minded commitment. A single-minded agent will continue to maintain an intention until it believes that either the intention has been achieved, or else that it is no longer possible to achieve the intention.

Open-minded commitment. An open-minded agent will maintain an intention as long as it is still believed possible.

Note that an agent has commitment both to *ends* (i.e. the state of affairs it wishes to bring about) and *means* (i.e. the mechanism via which the agent wishes to achieve the state of affairs).

With respect to commitment to means (i.e. plans), the solution adopted in Figure 4.3 is as follows. An agent will maintain a commitment to an intention until (i) it believes the intention has succeeded; (ii) it believes the intention is impossible, or (iii) there is nothing left to execute in the plan. This is single-minded commitment. I write $succeeded(I, B)$ to mean that given beliefs B, the intentions I can be regarded as having been satisfied. Similarly, we write $impossible(I, B)$ to mean that intentions I are impossible given beliefs B. The main loop, capturing this commitment to means, is in lines (10)–(23).

How about commitment to ends? When should an agent stop to *reconsider* its intentions? One possibility is to reconsider intentions at every opportunity – in particular, after executing every possible action. If option generation and filtering were computationally cheap processes, then this would be an acceptable strategy. Unfortunately, we know that deliberation is not cheap – it takes a considerable amount of time. While the agent is deliberating, the environment in which the agent is working is changing, possibly rendering its newly formed intentions irrelevant.

We are thus presented with a dilemma:

- an agent that does not stop to reconsider its intentions sufficiently often will continue attempting to achieve its intentions even after it is clear that they cannot be achieved, or that there is no longer any reason for achieving them;

- an agent that *constantly* reconsiders its attentions may spend insufficient time actually working to achieve them, and hence runs the risk of never actually achieving them.

There is clearly a trade-off to be struck between the degree of commitment and reconsideration at work here. To try to capture this trade-off, Figure 4.3 incorporates an explicit *meta-level control* component. The idea is to have a Boolean-valued function, $reconsider$, such that $reconsider(I, B)$ evaluates to 'true' just in case it is appropriate for the agent with beliefs B and intentions I to reconsider its intentions. Deciding whether to reconsider intentions thus falls to this function.

It is interesting to consider the circumstances under which this function can be said to behave *optimally*. Suppose that the agent's deliberation and plan generation functions are in some sense perfect: that deliberation always chooses the 'best' intentions (however that is defined for the application at hand), and planning always produces an appropriate plan. Further suppose that time expended always has a cost – the agent does not benefit by doing nothing. Then it is not difficult to see that the function $reconsider(\ldots)$ will be behaving optimally if, and only if, whenever it chooses to deliberate, the agent changes intentions (Wooldridge and Parsons, 1999). For if the agent chose to deliberate but did not change intentions, then the effort expended on deliberation was wasted. Similarly, if an agent

Table 4.2   Practical reasoning situations (cf. Bratman *et al.*, 1988, p. 353).

Situation number	Chose to deliberate?	Changed intentions?	Would have changed intentions?	$reconsider(...)$ optimal?
1.	No	—	No	Yes
2.	No	—	Yes	No
3.	Yes	No	—	No
4.	Yes	Yes	—	Yes

should have changed intentions, but failed to do so, then the effort expended on attempting to achieve its intentions was also wasted.

The possible interactions between deliberation and meta-level control (the function $reconsider(...)$) are summarized in Table 4.2.

- In situation (1), the agent did not choose to deliberate, and as a consequence, did not choose to change intentions. Moreover, if it *had* chosen to deliberate, it would not have changed intentions. In this situation, the $reconsider(...)$ function is behaving optimally.

- In situation (2), the agent did not choose to deliberate, but if it had done so, it *would* have changed intentions. In this situation, the $reconsider(...)$ function is not behaving optimally.

- In situation (3), the agent chose to deliberate, but did not change intentions. In this situation, the $reconsider(...)$ function is not behaving optimally.

- In situation (4), the agent chose to deliberate, and did change intentions. In this situation, the $reconsider(...)$ function is behaving optimally.

Notice that there is an important assumption implicit within this discussion: that the cost of executing the $reconsider(...)$ function is *much* less than the cost of the deliberation process itself. Otherwise, the $reconsider(...)$ function could simply use the deliberation process as an oracle, running it as a subroutine and choosing to deliberate just in case the deliberation process changed intentions.

The nature of the trade-off was examined by David Kinny and Michael Georgeff in a number of experiments carried out using a BDI agent system (Kinny and Georgeff, 1991). The aims of Kinny and Georgeff's investigation were to

(1) assess the feasibility of experimentally measuring agent effectiveness in a simulated environment (2) investigate how commitment to goals contributes to effective agent behaviour and (3) compare the properties of different strategies for reacting to change.

(Kinny and Georgeff, 1991, p. 82)

In Kinny and Georgeff's experiments, two different types of reconsideration strategy were used: *bold* agents, which never pause to reconsider their intentions before their current plan is fully executed; and *cautious* agents, which stop to reconsider after the execution of every action. These characteristics are defined by a *degree of boldness*, which specifies the maximum number of plan steps the agent executes before reconsidering its intentions. Dynamism in the environment is represented by the *rate of environment change*. Put simply, the rate of environment change is the ratio of the speed of the agent's control loop to the rate of change of the environment. If the rate of world change is 1, then the environment will change no more than once for each time the agent can execute its control loop. If the rate of world change is 2, then the environment can change twice for each pass through the agent's control loop, and so on. The performance of an agent is measured by the ratio of number of intentions that the agent managed to achieve to the number of intentions that the agent had at any time. Thus if effectiveness is 1, then the agent achieved all its intentions. If effectiveness is 0, then the agent failed to achieve any of its intentions. The key results of Kinny and Georgeff were as follows.

- If the rate of world change is low (i.e. the environment does not change quickly), then bold agents do well compared with cautious ones. This is because cautious ones waste time reconsidering their commitments while bold agents are busy working towards – and achieving – their intentions.

- If the rate of world change is high (i.e. the environment changes frequently), then cautious agents tend to outperform bold agents. This is because they are able to recognize when intentions are doomed, and also to take advantage of serendipitous situations and new opportunities when they arise.

The bottom line is that different environment types require different intention reconsideration and commitment strategies. In static environments, agents that are strongly committed to their intentions will perform well. But in dynamic environments, the ability to react to changes by modifying intentions becomes more important, and weakly committed agents will tend to outperform bold agents.

4.4   HOMER: an Agent That Plans

An interesting experiment in the design of intelligent agents was conducted by Vere and Bickmore (1990). They argued that the enabling technologies for intelligent agents were sufficiently developed to be able to construct a prototype autonomous agent, with linguistic ability, planning and acting capabilities, and so on. They developed such an agent, and christened it HOMER. This agent is a simulated robot submarine, which exists in a two-dimensional 'Seaworld', about which it has only partial knowledge. HOMER takes instructions from a user in a limited subset of English with about an 800 word vocabulary; instructions can contain moderately sophisticated temporal references. HOMER can plan how to achieve its instructions (which typically relate to collecting and moving items around the

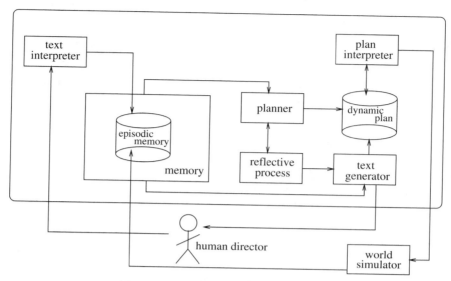

Figure 4.4 The HOMER architecture.

Seaworld), and can then execute its plans, modifying them as required during execution. The agent has a limited *episodic memory*, and using this, is able to answer questions about its past experiences. The architecture of HOMER is illustrated in Figure 4.4.

Here is an example of a dialogue with HOMER: the user begins by asking HOMER what he sees in front of him.

```
USER: What is in front of you?
HOMER: A log.
USER: Do you own the log.
HOMER: No, I don't.
```

The user then tells HOMER that he owns the log; this is new information, and so HOMER expresses surprise.

```
USER: The log belongs to you.
HOMER: Oh.
```

At this point, the user tells HOMER to move, so that he can no longer see the log, and moves the log while it is hidden from HOMER's sight. When he turns around, HOMER expects to see the log, and expresses surprise.

```
USER: Turn away from your log.
HOMER: OK, I am turning.
[LOG IS MOVED]
USER: Turn around.
HOMER: OK, I'm turning.
HOMER: I've lost the log!
```

In the following dialogue, the user gives HOMER a task to accomplish.

```
USER: Drop the package at the barge next Saturday at 9pm.
HOMER: OK.
```

HOMER then generates an appropriate plan for this task. When asked about his plans for Saturday, HOMER demonstrates that he has realized travelling to the barge will take some time.

```
USER: Are you going to the barge next Saturday?
HOMER: Yes.
USER: What time?
HOMER: 8.56pm.
```

4.5 The Procedural Reasoning System

The Procedural Reasoning System (PRS), originally developed at Stanford Research Institute by Michael Georgeff and Amy Lansky, was perhaps the first agent architecture to explicitly embody the belief–desire–intention paradigm, and proved to be the most durable agent architecture developed to date. It has been applied in several of the most significant multiagent applications so far built, including an air-traffic control system called OASIS that is currently undergoing field trials at Sydney airport, a simulation system for the Royal Australian Air Force called SWARMM, and a business process management system called SPOC (Single Point of Contact), that is currently being marketed by Agentis Solutions (Georgeff and Rao, 1996).

An illustration of the PRS architecture is given in Figure 4.5. The PRS is often referred to as a *belief-desire-intention* (BDI) architecture, because it contains explicitly represented data structures loosely corresponding to these mental states (Wooldridge, 2000b).

In the PRS, an agent does no planning from first principles. Instead, it is equipped with a library of pre-compiled plans. These plans are manually constructed, in advance, by the agent programmer. Plans in the PRS each have the following components:

- a *goal* – the postcondition of the plan;
- a *context* – the precondition of the plan; and
- a *body* – the 'recipe' part of the plan – the course of action to carry out.

The goal and context part of PRS plans are fairly conventional, but the body is slightly unusual. In the plans that we saw earlier in this chapter, the body of a plan was simply a sequence of actions. Executing the plan involves executing each action in turn. Such plans are possible in the PRS, but much richer kinds of plans are also possible. The first main difference is that as well has having individual

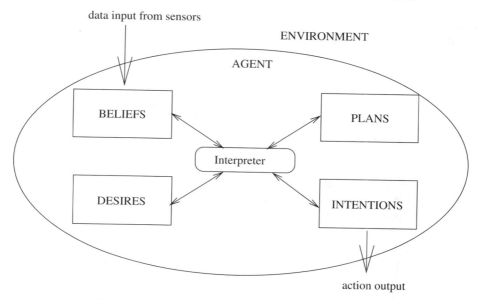

Figure 4.5   The Procedural Reasoning System (PRS).

primitive actions as the basic components of plans, it is possible to have *goals*. The idea is that when a plan includes a goal at a particular point, this means that this goal must then be achieved at this point before the remainder of the plan can be executed. It is also possible to have disjunctions of goals ('achieve φ or achieve ψ'), and loops ('keep achieving φ until ψ'), and so on.

At start-up time a PRS agent will have a collection of such plans, and some initial beliefs about the world. Beliefs in the PRS are represented as Prolog-like facts – essentially, as atoms of first-order logic, in exactly the same way that we saw in deductive agents in the preceding chapter. In addition, at start-up, the agent will typically have a top-level goal. This goal acts in a rather similar way to the 'main' method in Java or C.

When the agent starts up, the goal to be achieved is pushed onto a stack, called the *intention stack*. This stack contains all the goals that are pending achievement. The agent then searches through its plan library to see what plans have the goal on the top of the intention stack as their postcondition. Of these, only some will have their precondition satisfied, according to the agent's current beliefs. The set of plans that (i) achieve the goal, and (ii) have their precondition satisfied, become the possible *options* for the agent (cf. the *options* function described earlier in this chapter).

The process of selecting between different possible plans is, of course, deliberation, a process that we have already discussed above. There are several ways of deliberating between competing options in PRS-like architectures. In the original PRS deliberation is achieved by the use of *meta-level plans*. These are literally plans about plans. They are able to modify an agent's intention structures at run-time, in order to change the focus of the agent's practical reasoning. However, a simpler method is to use *utilities* for plans. These are numerical values; the agent simply chooses the plan that has the highest utility.

The chosen plan is then executed in its turn; this may involve pushing further goals onto the intention stack, which may then in turn involve finding more plans to achieve these goals, and so on. The process bottoms out with individual actions that may be directly computed (e.g. simple numerical calculations). If a particular plan to achieve a goal fails, then the agent is able to select another plan to achieve this goal from the set of all candidate plans.

To illustrate all this, Figure 4.6 shows a fragment of a Jam system (Huber, 1999). Jam is a second-generation descendant of the PRS, implemented in Java. The basic ideas are identical. The top level goal for this system, which is another Blocks World example, is to have achieved the goal blocks_stacked. The initial beliefs of the agent are spelled out in the FACTS section. Expressed in conventional logic notation, the first of these is $On(Block5, Block4)$, i.e. 'block 5 is on top of block 4'.

The system starts by pushing the goal blocks_stacked onto the intention stack. The agent must then find a candidate plan for this; these is just one plan that has this goal as a GOAL: the 'top level plan'. The context of this plan is empty, that is to say, true, and so this plan can be directly executed. Executing the body of the plan involves pushing the following goal onto the intention stack:

$$On(block3, table).$$

This is immediately achieved, as it is a FACT. The second sub-goal is then posted:

$$On(block2, block3)$$

To achieve this, the 'stack blocks that are clear' plan is used; the first sub-goals involve clearing both $block2$ and $block3$, which in turn will be done by two invocations of the 'clear a block' plan. When this is done, the move action is directly invoked to move $block2$ onto $block3$.

I leave the detailed behaviour as an exercise.

Notes and Further Reading

Some reflections on the origins of the BDI model, and on its relationship to other models of agency, may be found in Georgeff *et al.* (1999). Belief–desire–intention architectures originated in the work of the Rational Agency project at Stanford Research Institute in the mid-1980s. Key figures were Michael Bratman, Phil Cohen, Michael Georgeff, David Israel, Kurt Konolige, and Martha Pollack. The origins of the model lie in the theory of human practical reasoning developed by the philosopher Michael Bratman (Bratman, 1987), which focuses particularly on

```
GOALS:
  ACHIEVE blocks_stacked;
FACTS:
  FACT ON "Block5" "Block4";     FACT ON "Block4" "Block3";
  FACT ON "Block1" "Block2";     FACT ON "Block2" "Table";
  FACT ON "Block3" "Table";      FACT CLEAR "Block1";
  FACT CLEAR "Block5";           FACT CLEAR "Table";
Plan: {
  NAME: "Top-level plan"
  GOAL: ACHIEVE blocks_stacked;
  CONTEXT:
  BODY:      ACHIEVE ON "Block3" "Table";
             ACHIEVE ON "Block2" "Block3";
             ACHIEVE ON "Block1" "Block2";
}
Plan: {
  NAME: "Stack blocks that are already clear"
  GOAL: ACHIEVE ON $OBJ1 $OBJ2;
  CONTEXT:
  BODY:      ACHIEVE CLEAR $OBJ1;
             ACHIEVE CLEAR $OBJ2;
             PERFORM move $OBJ1 $OBJ2;
  UTILITY: 10;
  FAILURE: EXECUTE print "\n\nStack blocks failed!\n\n";
}
Plan: {
  NAME: "Clear a block"
  GOAL: ACHIEVE CLEAR $OBJ;
  CONTEXT: FACT ON $OBJ2 $OBJ;
  BODY:      ACHIEVE ON $OBJ2 "Table";
  EFFECTS: RETRACT ON $OBJ1 $OBJ;
  FAILURE: EXECUTE print "\n\nClearing block failed!\n\n";
}
```

Figure 4.6   The Blocks World in Jam.

the role of intentions in practical reasoning. The conceptual framework of the BDI model is described in Bratman *et al.* (1988), which also describes a specific BDI agent architecture called IRMA.

The best-known implementation of the BDI model is the PRS system, developed by Georgeff and colleagues (Georgeff and Lansky, 1987; Georgeff and Ingrand, 1989). The PRS has been re-implemented several times since the mid-1980s, for example in the Australian AI Institute's DMARS system (d'Inverno *et al.*, 1997), the University of Michigan's C++ implementation UM-PRS, and a Java version called

Jam! (Huber, 1999). Jack is a commercially available programming language, which extends the Java language with a number of BDI features (Busetta *et al.*, 2000).

The description of the BDI model given here draws upon Bratman *et al.* (1988) and Rao and Georgeff (1992), but is not strictly faithful to either. The most obvious difference is that I do not incorporate the notion of the 'filter override' mechanism described in Bratman *et al.* (1988), and I also assume that plans are linear sequences of actions (which is a fairly 'traditional' view of plans), rather than the hierarchically structured collections of goals used by PRS.

Plans are central to the BDI model of agency. An excellent discussion on the BDI model, focusing in particular on the role of plans in practical reasoning, is Martha Pollack's 1991 *Computers and Thought* award lecture, presented at the IJCAI-91 conference in Sydney, Australia, and published as 'The Uses of Plans' (Pollack, 1992). Another article, which focuses on the distinction between 'plans as recipes' and 'plans as mental states' is Pollack (1990). It is worth emphasizing that the BDI model is only one solution to the problem of building autonomous rational agents. Many other software architectures for agent systems have been described in the literature (Wooldridge and Jennings, 1995; Brooks, 1999). Other practical reasoning-style architectures include Fischer *et al.* (1996), Jung (1999), Móra *et al.* (1999) and Busetta *et al.* (2000).

The BDI model is also interesting because a great deal of effort has been devoted to formalizing it. In particular, Anand Rao and Michael Georgeff have developed a range of BDI logics, which they use to axiomatize properties of BDI-based practical reasoning agents (Rao and Georgeff, 1991a; Rao *et al.*, 1992; Rao and Georgeff, 1991b; Rao and Georgeff, 1992; Rao and Georgeff, 1993; Rao, 1996b). These models have been extended by others to deal with, for example, communication between agents (Haddadi, 1996).

Class reading: Bratman *et al.* (1988).   This is an interesting, insightful article, with not too much technical content. It introduces the IRMA architecture for practical reasoning agents, which has been very influential in the design of subsequent systems.

Exercises

(1) [Level 1.]

Imagine a mobile robot, capable of moving around an office environment. Ultimately, this robot must be controlled by very low-level instructions along the lines of 'motor on', and so on. How easy would it be to develop STRIPS operators to represent these properties? Try it.

(2) [Level 2.]

Recall the vacuum-world example discussed in the preceding chapter. Formulate the operations available to the agent using the STRIPS notation.

(3) [Level 2.]

Consider an agent that must move from one location to another, collecting items from one site and moving them. The agent is able to move by taxi, bus, bicycle, or car.

Formalize the operations available to the agent (move by taxi, move by car, etc.) using the STRIPS notation. (Hint: preconditions might be having money or energy.)

(4) [Level 3.]

Read Kinny and Georgeff (1991), and implement these experiments in the programming language of your choice. (This is not as difficult as its sounds: it should be possible in a couple of days at most.) Now carry out the experiments described in Kinny and Georgeff (1991) and see if you get the same results.

(5) [Level 3.]

Building on the previous question, investigate the following.

The effect that reducing perceptual capabilities on agent performance. The idea here is to reduce the amount of environment that the agent can see, until it can finally see only the grid square on which it is located. Can 'free' planning compensate for the inability to see very far?

The effect of non-deterministic actions. If actions are allowed to become non-deterministic (so that in attempting to move from one grid square to another, there is a certain probability that the agent will in fact move to an entirely different grid square), what effect does this have on the effectiveness of an agent?

5

Reactive and Hybrid Agents

The many problems with symbolic/logical approaches to building agents led some researchers to question, and ultimately reject, the assumptions upon which such approaches are based. These researchers have argued that minor changes to the symbolic approach, such as weakening the logical representation language, will not be sufficient to build agents that can operate in time-constrained environments: nothing less than a whole new approach is required. In the mid to late 1980s, these researchers began to investigate alternatives to the symbolic AI paradigm. It is difficult to neatly characterize these different approaches, since their advocates are united mainly by a rejection of symbolic AI, rather than by a common manifesto. However, certain themes do recur:

- the rejection of symbolic representations, and of decision making based on syntactic manipulation of such representations;

- the idea that intelligent, rational behaviour is seen as innately linked to the *environment* an agent occupies – intelligent behaviour is not disembodied, but is a product of the *interaction* the agent maintains with its environment;

- the idea that intelligent behaviour *emerges* from the interaction of various simpler behaviours.

Alternative approaches to agency are sometime referred to as *behavioural* (since a common theme is that of developing and combining individual behaviours), *situated* (since a common theme is that of agents actually situated in some environment, rather than being disembodied from it), and finally – the term used in this chapter – *reactive* (because such systems are often perceived as simply reacting to an environment, without reasoning about it).

5.1   Brooks and the Subsumption Architecture

This section presents a survey of the *subsumption architecture*, which is arguably the best-known reactive agent architecture. It was developed by Rodney Brooks – one of the most vocal and influential critics of the symbolic approach to agency to have emerged in recent years. Brooks has propounded three key theses that have guided his work as follows (Brooks, 1991b; Brooks, 1991a).

(1) Intelligent behaviour can be generated *without* explicit representations of the kind that symbolic AI proposes.

(2) Intelligent behaviour can be generated *without* explicit abstract reasoning of the kind that symbolic AI proposes.

(3) Intelligence is an *emergent* property of certain complex systems.

Brooks also identifies two key ideas that have informed his research.

(1) Situatedness and embodiment. 'Real' intelligence is situated in the world, not in disembodied systems such as theorem provers or expert systems.

(2) Intelligence and emergence. 'Intelligent' behaviour arises as a result of an agent's interaction with its environment. Also, intelligence is 'in the eye of the beholder' – it is not an innate, isolated property.

These ideas were made concrete in the subsumption architecture. There are two defining characteristics of the subsumption architecture. The first is that an agent's decision-making is realized through a set of *task-accomplishing behaviours*; each behaviour may be thought of as an individual *action* function, as we defined above, which continually takes perceptual input and maps it to an action to perform. Each of these behaviour modules is intended to achieve some particular task. In Brooks's implementation, the behaviour modules are finite-state machines. An important point to note is that these task-accomplishing modules are assumed to include *no* complex symbolic representations, and are assumed to do *no* symbolic reasoning at all. In many implementations, these behaviours are implemented as rules of the form

$$\text{situation} \longrightarrow \text{action},$$

which simply map perceptual input directly to actions.

The second defining characteristic of the subsumption architecture is that many behaviours can 'fire' simultaneously. There must obviously be a mechanism to choose between the different actions selected by these multiple actions. Brooks proposed arranging the modules into a *subsumption hierarchy*, with the

```
Function: Action Selection in the Subsumption Architecture
1.  function action(p : P) : A
2.  var fired : ℘(R)
3.  var selected : A
4.  begin
5.      fired ← {(c,a) | (c,a) ∈ R and p ∈ c}
6.      for each (c,a) ∈ fired do
7.          if ¬(∃(c′,a′) ∈ fired such that (c′,a′) ≺ (c,a)) then
8.              return a
9.          end-if
10.     end-for
11.     return null
12. end function action
```

Figure 5.1   Action Selection in the subsumption architecture.

behaviours arranged into *layers*. Lower layers in the hierarchy are able to *inhibit* higher layers: the lower a layer is, the higher is its priority. The idea is that higher layers represent more abstract behaviours. For example, one might desire a behaviour in a mobile robot for the behaviour 'avoid obstacles'. It makes sense to give obstacle avoidance a high priority – hence this behaviour will typically be encoded in a *low-level* layer, which has *high* priority. To illustrate the subsumption architecture in more detail, we will now present a simple formal model of it, and illustrate how it works by means of a short example. We then discuss its relative advantages and shortcomings, and point at other similar reactive architectures.

The *see* function, which represents the agent's perceptual ability, is assumed to remain unchanged. However, in implemented subsumption architecture systems, there is assumed to be quite tight coupling between perception and action – raw sensor input is not processed or transformed much, and there is certainly no attempt to transform images to symbolic representations.

The decision function *action* is realized through a set of behaviours, together with an *inhibition* relation holding between these behaviours. A behaviour is a pair (c, a), where $c \subseteq P$ is a set of percepts called the *condition*, and $a \in A$ is an action. A behaviour (c, a) will *fire* when the environment is in state $s \in S$ if and only if $see(s) \in c$. Let $Beh = \{(c, a) \mid c \subseteq P \text{ and } a \in A\}$ be the set of all such rules.

Associated with an agent's set of behaviour rules $R \subseteq Beh$ is a binary *inhibition relation* on the set of behaviours: $\prec \subseteq R \times R$. This relation is assumed to be a strict total ordering on R (i.e. it is transitive, irreflexive, and antisymmetric). We write $b_1 \prec b_2$ if $(b_1, b_2) \in \prec$, and read this as 'b_1 inhibits b_2', that is, b_1 is lower in the hierarchy than b_2, and will hence get priority over b_2. The action function is then as shown in Figure 5.1.

Thus action selection begins by first computing the set *fired* of all behaviours that fire (5). Then, each behaviour (c, a) that fires is checked, to determine whether there is some other higher priority behaviour that fires. If not, then the action part of the behaviour, a, is returned as the selected action (8). If no behaviour fires, then the distinguished action *null* will be returned, indicating that no action has been chosen.

Given that one of our main concerns with logic-based decision making was its theoretical complexity, it is worth pausing to examine how well our simple behaviour-based system performs. The overall time complexity of the subsumption action function is no worse than $O(n^2)$, where n is the larger of the number of behaviours or number of percepts. Thus, even with the naive algorithm above, decision making is tractable. In practice, we can do *much* better than this: the decision-making logic can be encoded into hardware, giving *constant* decision time. For modern hardware, this means that an agent can be guaranteed to select an action within microseconds. Perhaps more than anything else, this computational simplicity is the strength of the subsumption architecture.

Steels's Mars explorer experiments

We will see how subsumption architecture agents were built for the following scenario (this example is adapted from Steels (1990)).

> The objective is to explore a distant planet, more concretely, to collect samples of a particular type of precious rock. The location of the rock samples is not known in advance, but they are typically clustered in certain spots. A number of autonomous vehicles are available that can drive around the planet collecting samples and later reenter a mother ship spacecraft to go back to Earth. There is no detailed map of the planet available, although it is known that the terrain is full of obstacles – hills, valleys, etc. – which prevent the vehicles from exchanging any communication.

The problem we are faced with is that of building an agent control architecture for each vehicle, so that they will cooperate to collect rock samples from the planet surface as efficiently as possible. Luc Steels argues that logic-based agents, of the type we described above, are 'entirely unrealistic' for this problem (Steels, 1990). Instead, he proposes a solution using the subsumption architecture.

The solution makes use of two mechanisms introduced by Steels. The first is a *gradient field*. In order that agents can know in which direction the mother ship lies, the mother ship generates a radio signal. Now this signal will obviously weaken as distance from the source increases – to find the direction of the mother ship, an agent need therefore only travel 'up the gradient' of signal strength. The signal need not carry any information – it need only exist.

The second mechanism enables agents to communicate with one another. The characteristics of the terrain prevent direct communication (such as message passing), so Steels adopted an *indirect* communication method. The idea is that agents will carry 'radioactive crumbs', which can be dropped, picked up, and detected by passing robots. Thus if an agent drops some of these crumbs in a particular location, then later another agent happening upon this location will be able to detect them. This simple mechanism enables a quite sophisticated form of cooperation.

The behaviour of an individual agent is then built up from a number of behaviours, as we indicated above. First, we will see how agents can be programmed to *individually* collect samples. We will then see how agents can be programmed to generate a *cooperative* solution.

For individual (non-cooperative) agents, the lowest-level behaviour (and hence the behaviour with the highest 'priority') is obstacle avoidance. This behaviour can be represented in the rule:

$$\textit{if} \text{ detect an obstacle } \textit{then} \text{ change direction.} \tag{5.1}$$

The second behaviour ensures that any samples carried by agents are dropped back at the mother ship:

$$\textit{if} \text{ carrying samples } \textit{and} \text{ at the base } \textit{then} \text{ drop samples;} \tag{5.2}$$
$$\textit{if} \text{ carrying samples and } \textit{not} \text{ at the base } \textit{then} \text{ travel up gradient.} \tag{5.3}$$

Behaviour (5.3) ensures that agents carrying samples will return to the mother ship (by heading towards the origin of the gradient field). The next behaviour ensures that agents will collect samples they find:

$$\textit{if} \text{ detect a sample } \textit{then} \text{ pick sample up.} \tag{5.4}$$

The final behaviour ensures that an agent with 'nothing better to do' will explore randomly:

$$\textit{if} \text{ true } \textit{then} \text{ move randomly.} \tag{5.5}$$

The precondition of this rule is thus assumed to always fire. These behaviours are arranged into the following hierarchy:

$$(5.1) \prec (5.2) \prec (5.3) \prec (5.4) \prec (5.5).$$

The subsumption hierarchy for this example ensures that, for example, an agent will *always* turn if any obstacles are detected; if the agent is at the mother ship and is carrying samples, then it will *always* drop them if it is not in any immediate danger of crashing, and so on. The 'top level' behaviour – a random walk – will only ever be carried out if the agent has nothing more urgent to do. It is not difficult to see how this simple set of behaviours will solve the problem: agents will search for samples (ultimately by searching randomly), and when they find them, will return them to the mother ship.

If the samples are distributed across the terrain entirely at random, then equipping a large number of robots with these very simple behaviours will work extremely well. But we know from the problem specification, above, that this is not the case: the samples tend to be located in clusters. In this case, it makes sense to have agents *cooperate* with one another in order to find the samples.

Thus when one agent finds a large sample, it would be helpful for it to communicate this to the other agents, so they can help it collect the rocks. Unfortunately, we also know from the problem specification that *direct* communication is impossible. Steels developed a simple solution to this problem, partly inspired by the foraging behaviour of ants. The idea revolves around an agent creating a 'trail' of radioactive crumbs whenever it finds a rock sample. The trail will be created when the agent returns the rock samples to the mother ship. If at some later point, another agent comes across this trail, then it need only follow it down the gradient field to locate the source of the rock samples. Some small refinements improve the efficiency of this ingenious scheme still further. First, as an agent follows a trail to the rock sample source, it picks up some of the crumbs it finds, hence making the trail fainter. Secondly, the trail is *only* laid by agents returning to the mother ship. Hence if an agent follows the trail out to the source of the nominal rock sample only to find that it contains no samples, it will reduce the trail on the way out, and will not return with samples to reinforce it. After a few agents have followed the trail to find no sample at the end of it, the trail will in fact have been removed.

The modified behaviours for this example are as follows. Obstacle avoidance (5.1) remains unchanged. However, the two rules determining what to do if carrying a sample are modified as follows:

$$\textit{if} \text{ carrying samples } \textit{and} \text{ at the base } \textit{then} \text{ drop samples;} \qquad (5.6)$$

$$\begin{aligned}\textit{if} \text{ carrying samples and } \textit{not} \text{ at the base} \\ \textit{then} \text{ drop 2 crumbs } \textit{and} \text{ travel up gradient.}\end{aligned} \qquad (5.7)$$

The behaviour (5.7) requires an agent to drop crumbs when returning to base with a sample, thus either reinforcing or creating a trail. The 'pick up sample' behaviour (5.4) remains unchanged. However, an additional behaviour is required for dealing with crumbs:

$$\textit{if} \text{ sense crumbs } \textit{then} \text{ pick up 1 crumb } \textit{and} \text{ travel down gradient.} \qquad (5.8)$$

Finally, the random movement behaviour (5.5) remains unchanged. These behaviour are then arranged into the following subsumption hierarchy:

$$(5.1) \prec (5.6) \prec (5.7) \prec (5.4) \prec (5.8) \prec (5.5).$$

Steels shows how this simple adjustment achieves near-optimal performance in many situations. Moreover, the solution is *cheap* (the computing power required by each agent is minimal) and *robust* (the loss of a single agent will not affect the overall system significantly).

Agre and Chapman – PENGI

At about the same time as Brooks was describing his first results with the subsumption architecture, Chapman was completing his Master's thesis, in which he reported the theoretical difficulties with planning described above, and was coming to similar conclusions about the inadequacies of the symbolic AI model himself. Together with his co-worker Agre, he began to explore alternatives to the AI planning paradigm (Chapman and Agre, 1986).

Agre observed that most everyday activity is 'routine' in the sense that it requires little – if any – new abstract reasoning. Most tasks, once learned, can be accomplished in a routine way, with little variation. Agre proposed that an efficient agent architecture could be based on the idea of 'running arguments'. Crudely, the idea is that as most decisions are routine, they can be encoded into a low-level structure (such as a digital circuit), which only needs periodic updating, perhaps to handle new kinds of problems. His approach was illustrated with the celebrated PENGI system (Agre and Chapman, 1987). PENGI is a simulated computer game, with the central character controlled using a scheme such as that outlined above.

Rosenschein and Kaelbling – situated automata

Another sophisticated approach is that of Rosenschein and Kaelbling (see Rosenschein, 1985; Rosenschein and Kaelbling, 1986; Kaelbling and Rosenschein, 1990; Kaelbling, 1991). They observed that just because an agent is conceptualized in logical terms, it need not be implemented as a theorem prover. In their *situated automata* paradigm, an agent is specified in declarative terms. This specification is then compiled down to a digital machine, which satisfies the declarative specification. This digital machine can operate in a provably time-bounded fashion; it does not do any symbol manipulation, and in fact no symbolic expressions are represented in the machine at all. The logic used to specify an agent is essentially a logic of knowledge:

> [An agent] x is said to carry the information that p in world state s, written $s \models K(x,p)$, if for all world states in which x has the same value as it does in s, the proposition p is true.
>
> (Kaelbling and Rosenschein, 1990, p. 36)

An agent is specified in terms of two components: perception and action. Two programs are then used to synthesize agents: RULER is used to specify the perception component of an agent; GAPPS is used to specify the action component.

RULER takes as its input three components as follows.

> [A] specification of the semantics of the [agent's] inputs ('whenever bit 1 is on, it is raining'); a set of static facts ('whenever it is raining, the ground is wet'); and a specification of the state transitions of the world ('if the ground is wet, it stays wet until the sun comes out'). The programmer then specifies the desired semantics for the output ('if this bit is on, the ground is wet'), and the compiler...[synthesizes] a circuit

whose output will have the correct semantics. ... All that declarative 'knowledge' has been reduced to a very simple circuit.

(Kaelbling, 1991, p. 86)

The GAPPS program takes as its input a set of *goal reduction rules* (essentially rules that encode information about how goals can be achieved) and a top level goal, and generates a program that can be translated into a digital circuit in order to realize the goal. Once again, the generated circuit does not represent or manipulate symbolic expressions; all symbolic manipulation is done at compile time.

The situated automata paradigm has attracted much interest, as it appears to combine the best elements of both reactive and symbolic declarative systems. However, at the time of writing, the theoretical limitations of the approach are not well understood; there are similarities with the automatic synthesis of programs from temporal logic specifications, a complex area of much ongoing work in mainstream computer science (see the comments in Emerson (1990)).

Maes – agent network architecture

Pattie Maes has developed an agent architecture in which an agent is defined as a set of *competence modules* (Maes, 1989, 1990b, 1991). These modules loosely resemble the behaviours of Brooks's subsumption architecture (above). Each module is specified by the designer in terms of preconditions and postconditions (rather like STRIPS operators), and an *activation level*, which gives a real-valued indication of the *relevance* of the module in a particular situation. The higher the activation level of a module, the more likely it is that this module will influence the behaviour of the agent. Once specified, a set of competence modules is compiled into a *spreading activation network*, in which the modules are linked to one another in ways defined by their preconditions and postconditions. For example, if module a has postcondition φ, and module b has precondition φ, then a and b are connected by a *successor* link. Other types of link include predecessor links and conflicter links. When an agent is executing, various modules may become more active in given situations, and may be executed. The result of execution may be a command to an effector unit, or perhaps the increase in activation level of a successor module.

There are obvious similarities between the agent network architecture and neural network architectures. Perhaps the key difference is that it is difficult to say what the meaning of a node in a neural net is; it only has a meaning in the context of the net itself. Since competence modules are defined in declarative terms, however, it is very much easier to say what their meaning is.

5.2   The Limitations of Reactive Agents

There are obvious advantages to reactive approaches such as Brooks's subsumption architecture: simplicity, economy, computational tractability, robustness against failure, and elegance all make such architectures appealing. But there are some fundamental, unsolved problems, not just with the subsumption architecture, but with other purely reactive architectures.

- If agents do not employ models of their environment, then they must have sufficient information available in their *local* environment to determine an acceptable action.

- Since purely reactive agents make decisions based on *local* information (i.e. information about the agents *current* state), it is difficult to see how such decision making could take into account *non-local* information – it must inherently take a 'short-term' view.

- It is difficult to see how purely reactive agents can be designed that *learn* from experience, and improve their performance over time.

- One major selling point of purely reactive systems is that overall behaviour *emerges* from the interaction of the component behaviours when the agent is placed in its environment. But the very term 'emerges' suggests that the relationship between individual behaviours, environment, and overall behaviour is not understandable. This necessarily makes it very hard to *engineer* agents to fulfil specific tasks. Ultimately, there is no principled *methodology* for building such agents: one must use a laborious process of experimentation, trial, and error to engineer an agent.

- While effective agents can be generated with small numbers of behaviours (typically less than ten layers), it is *much* harder to build agents that contain many layers. The dynamics of the interactions between the different behaviours become too complex to understand.

Various solutions to these problems have been proposed. One of the most popular of these is the idea of *evolving* agents to perform certain tasks. This area of work has largely broken away from the mainstream AI tradition in which work on, for example, logic-based agents is carried out, and is documented primarily in the *artificial life* (alife) literature.

5.3 Hybrid Agents

Given the requirement that an agent be capable of reactive and proactive behaviour, an obvious decomposition involves creating separate subsystems to deal with these different types of behaviours. This idea leads naturally to a class of architectures in which the various subsystems are arranged into a hierarchy of interacting *layers*. In this section, we will consider some general aspects of layered architectures, and then go on to consider two examples of such architectures: InteRRaP and TouringMachines.

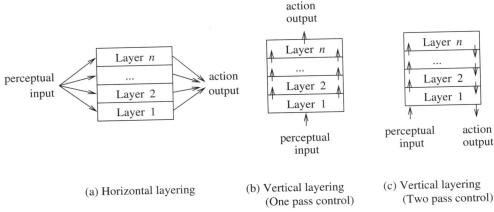

(a) Horizontal layering   (b) Vertical layering   (c) Vertical layering
                              (One pass control)   (Two pass control)

Figure 5.2 Information and control flows in three types of layered agent architecture. (Source: Müller *et al.* (1995, p. 263).)

Typically, there will be at least two layers, to deal with reactive and proactive behaviours, respectively. In principle, there is no reason why there should not be many more layers. It is useful to characterize such architectures in terms of the information and control flows within the layers. Broadly speaking, we can identify two types of control flow within layered architectures as follows (see Figure 5.2).

Horizontal layering. In horizontally layered architectures (Figure 5.2(a)), the software layers are each directly connected to the sensory input and action output. In effect, each layer itself acts like an agent, producing suggestions as to what action to perform.

Vertical layering. In vertically layered architectures (see parts (b) and (c) of Figure 5.2), sensory input and action output are each dealt with by at most one layer.

The great advantage of horizontally layered architectures is their conceptual simplicity: if we need an agent to exhibit n different types of behaviour, then we implement n different layers. However, because the layers are each in effect competing with one another to generate action suggestions, there is a danger that the *overall* behaviour of the agent will not be coherent. In order to ensure that horizontally layered architectures *are* consistent, they generally include a *mediator* function, which makes decisions about which layer has 'control' of the agent at any given time. The need for such central control is problematic: it means that the designer must potentially consider all possible interactions between layers. If there are n layers in the architecture, and each layer is capable of suggesting m possible actions, then this means there are m^n such interactions to be considered. This is clearly difficult from a design point of view in any but the most simple system. The introduction of a central control system also introduces a *bottleneck* into the agent's decision making.

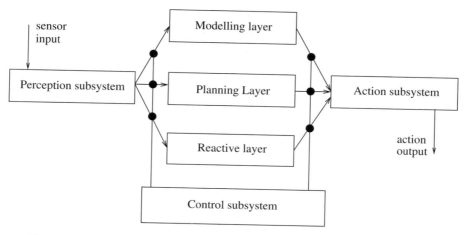

Figure 5.3 TouringMachines: a horizontally layered agent architecture.

These problems are partly alleviated in a vertically layered architecture. We can subdivide vertically layered architectures into *one-pass* architectures (Figure 5.2(b)) and *two-pass* architectures (Figure 5.2(c)). In one-pass architectures, control flows sequentially through each layer, until the final layer generates action output. In two-pass architectures, information flows up the architecture (the first pass) and control then flows back down. There are some interesting similarities between the idea of two-pass vertically layered architectures and the way that organizations work, with information flowing up to the highest levels of the organization, and commands then flowing down. In both one-pass and two-pass vertically layered architectures, the complexity of interactions between layers is reduced: since there are $n - 1$ interfaces between n layers, then if each layer is capable of suggesting m actions, there are at most $m^2(n - 1)$ interactions to be considered between layers. This is clearly much simpler than the horizontally layered case. However, this simplicity comes at the cost of some flexibility: in order for a vertically layered architecture to make a decision, control must pass between *each* different layer. This is not fault tolerant: failures in any one layer are likely to have serious consequences for agent performance.

In the remainder of this section, we will consider two examples of layered architectures: Innes Ferguson's TouringMachines, and Jörg Müller's InteRRaP. The former is an example of a horizontally layered architecture; the latter is a (two-pass) vertically layered architecture.

5.3.1 TouringMachines

The TouringMachines architecture is illustrated in Figure 5.3. As this figure shows, TouringMachines consists of three *activity producing layers*. That is, each layer continually produces 'suggestions' for what actions the agent should perform.

The *reactive layer* provides a more-or-less immediate response to changes that occur in the environment. It is implemented as a set of situation–action rules, like the behaviours in Brooks's subsumption architecture (see Chapter 5). These rules map sensor input directly to effector output. The original demonstration scenario for TouringMachines was that of autonomous vehicles driving between locations through streets populated by other similar agents. In this scenario, reactive rules typically deal with functions like obstacle avoidance. For example, here is an example of a reactive rule for avoiding the kerb (from (Ferguson, 1992a, p. 59)):

```
rule-1: kerb-avoidance
    if
        is-in-front(Kerb, Observer) and
        speed(Observer) > 0 and
        separation(Kerb, Observer) < KerbThreshHold
    then
        change-orientation(KerbAvoidanceAngle)
```

Here change-orientation(...) is the action suggested if the rule fires. The rules can only make references to the agent's current state – they cannot do any explicit reasoning about the world, and on the right-hand side of rules are *actions*, not predicates. Thus if this rule fired, it would not result in any central environment model being updated, but would just result in an action being suggested by the reactive layer.

The TouringMachines *planning layer* achieves the agent's proactive behaviour. Specifically, the planning layer is responsible for the 'day-to-day' running of the agent – under normal circumstances, the planning layer will be responsible for deciding what the agent does. However, the planning layer does not do 'first-principles' planning. That is, it does not attempt to generate plans from scratch. Rather, the planning layer employs a *library* of plan 'skeletons' called *schemas*. These skeletons are in essence hierarchically structured plans, which the Touring-Machines planning layer elaborates at run time in order to decide what to do (cf. the PRS architecture discussed in Chapter 4). So, in order to achieve a goal, the planning layer attempts to find a schema in its library which matches that goal. This schema will contain sub-goals, which the planning layer elaborates by attempting to find other schemas in its plan library that match these sub-goals.

The *modelling* layer represents the various entities in the world (including the agent itself, as well as other agents). The modelling layer thus predicts conflicts between agents, and generates new goals to be achieved in order to resolve these conflicts. These new goals are then posted down to the planning layer, which makes use of its plan library in order to determine how to satisfy them.

The three control layers are embedded within a *control subsystem*, which is effectively responsible for deciding which of the layers should have control over the agent. This control subsystem is implemented as a set of *control rules*. Control

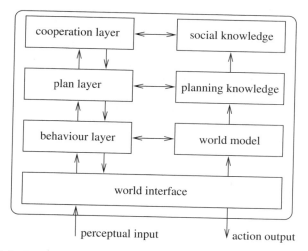

Figure 5.4   InteRRaP – a vertically layered two-pass agent architecture.

rules can either *suppress* sensor information between the control rules and the control layers, or else *censor* action outputs from the control layers. Here is an example censor rule (Ferguson, 1995, p. 207):

```
censor-rule-1:
    if
        entity(obstacle-6) in perception-buffer
    then
        remove-sensory-record(layer-R, entity(obstacle-6))
```

This rule prevents the reactive layer from ever knowing about whether `obstacle-6` has been perceived. The intuition is that although the reactive layer will in general be the most appropriate layer for dealing with obstacle avoidance, there are certain obstacles for which other layers are more appropriate. This rule ensures that the reactive layer never comes to know about these obstacles.

5.3.2   InteRRaP

InteRRaP is an example of a vertically layered two-pass agent architecture – see Figure 5.4. As Figure 5.4 shows, InteRRaP contains three control layers, as in TouringMachines. Moreover, the purpose of each InteRRaP layer appears to be rather similar to the purpose of each corresponding TouringMachines layer. Thus the lowest (*behaviour-based*) layer deals with reactive behaviour; the middle (*local planning*) layer deals with everyday planning to achieve the agent's goals, and the uppermost (*cooperative planning*) layer deals with social interactions. Each layer has associated with it a *knowledge base*, i.e. a representation of the world appropriate for that layer. These different knowledge bases represent the agent and its environment at different levels of abstraction. Thus the highest level knowledge base represents the plans and actions of other agents in the environment; the middle-level knowledge base represents the plans and actions of the agent itself; and the lowest level knowledge base represents 'raw' information about the environment. The explicit introduction of these knowledge bases distinguishes TouringMachines from InteRRaP.

The way the different layers in InteRRaP conspire to produce behaviour is also quite different from TouringMachines. The main difference is in the way the layers interact with the environment. In TouringMachines, each layer was directly coupled to perceptual input and action output. This necessitated the introduction of a supervisory control framework, to deal with conflicts or problems between layers. In InteRRaP, layers interact with *each other* to achieve the same end. The two main types of interaction between layers are *bottom-up activation* and *top-down execution*. Bottom-up activation occurs when a lower layer passes control to a higher layer because it is not *competent* to deal with the current situation. Top-down execution occurs when a higher layer makes use of the facilities provided by a lower layer to achieve one of its goals. The basic flow of control in InteRRaP begins when perceptual input arrives at the lowest layer in the architecture. If the reactive layer can deal with this input, then it will do so; otherwise, bottom-up activation will occur, and control will be passed to the local planning layer. If the local planning layer can handle the situation, then it will do so, typically by making use of top-down execution. Otherwise, it will use bottom-up activation to pass control to the highest layer. In this way, control in InteRRaP will flow from the lowest layer to higher layers of the architecture, and then back down again.

The internals of each layer are not important for the purposes of this chapter. However, it is worth noting that each layer implements two general functions. The first of these is a *situation recognition and goal activation* function. It maps a knowledge base (one of the three layers) and current goals to a new set of goals. The second function is responsible for *planning and scheduling* – it is responsible for selecting which plans to execute, based on the current plans, goals, and knowledge base of that layer.

Layered architectures are currently the most popular general class of agent architecture available. Layering represents a natural decomposition of functionality: it is easy to see how reactive, proactive, social behaviour can be generated by the reactive, proactive, and social layers in an architecture. The main problem with layered architectures is that while they are arguably a *pragmatic* solution, they lack the conceptual and semantic clarity of unlayered approaches. In particular, while logic-based approaches have a clear logical semantics, it is difficult to see how such a semantics could be devised for a layered architecture. Another issue is that of interactions between layers. If each layer is an independent activity-producing process (as in TouringMachines), then it is necessary to consider all possible ways that the layers can interact with one another. This problem is partly alleviated in two-pass vertically layered architecture such as InteRRaP.

Notes and Further Reading

The introductory discussion of layered architectures given here draws upon Müller *et al.* (1995, pp. 262–264). The best reference to TouringMachines is Ferguson (1992a); more accessible references include Ferguson (1992b, 1995). The definitive reference to InteRRaP is Müller (1997), although Fischer *et al.* (1996) is also a useful reference. Other examples of layered architectures include the subsumption architecture (Brooks, 1986) (see Chapter 5), and the 3T architecture (Bonasso *et al.*, 1996).

Brooks's original paper on the subsumption architecture – the one that started all the fuss – was published as Brooks (1986). The description and discussion here is partly based on Ferber (1996). This original paper seems to be somewhat less radical than many of his later ones, which include Brooks (1990, 1991b). The version of the subsumption architecture used in this chapter is actually a simplification of that presented by Brooks. The subsumption architecture is probably the best-known reactive architecture around – but there are many others. The collection of papers edited by Maes (1990a) contains papers that describe many of these, as does the collection by Agre and Rosenschein (1996). Other approaches include:

- Nilsson's *teleo reactive programs* (Nilsson, 1992);
- Schoppers' *universal plans* – which are essentially decision trees that can be used to efficiently determine an appropriate action in any situation (Schoppers, 1987);
- Firby's *reactive action packages* (Firby, 1987).

Kaelbling (1986) gives a good discussion of the issues associated with developing resource-bounded rational agents, and proposes an agent architecture somewhat similar to that developed by Brooks.

Ginsberg (1989) gives a critique of reactive agent architectures based on cached plans; Etzioni (1993) gives a critique of the claim by Brooks that intelligent agents must be situated 'in the real world'. He points out that *software environments* (such as computer operating systems and computer networks) can provide a challenging environment in which agents might work.

Class reading: Brooks (1986).   A provocative, fascinating article, packed with ideas. It is interesting to compare this with some of Brooks's later – arguably more controversial – articles.

Exercises

(1) [Level 2.]

Develop a solution to the vacuum-world example described in Chapter 3 using Brooks's subsumption architecture. How does it compare with the logic-based example?

(2) [Level 2.]

Try developing a solution to the Mars explorer example using the logic-based approach described in Chapter 3. How does it compare with the reactive solution?

(3) [Level 3.]

In the programming language of your choice, implement the Mars explorer example using the subsumption architecture. (To do this, you may find it useful to implement a simple subsumption architecture 'shell' for programming different behaviours.) Investigate the performance of the two approaches described, and see if you can do better.

(4) [Level 3.]

Using the simulator implemented for the preceding question, see what happens as you increase the number of agents. Eventually, you should see that overcrowding leads to a sub-optimal solution – agents spend too much time getting out of each other's way to get any work done. Try to get around this problem by allowing agents to pass samples to each other, thus implementing *chains*. (See the description in Ferber (1996, p. 305).)

6

Multiagent Interactions

So far in this book, we have been focusing on the problem of how to build an individual agent. Except in passing, we have not examined the issues associated in putting these agents together. But there is a popular slogan in the multiagent systems community:

> There's no such thing as a single agent system.

The point of the slogan is that interacting systems, which used to be regarded as rare and unusual beasts, are in fact the norm in the everyday computing world. All but the most trivial of systems contains a number of sub-systems that must interact with one another in order to successfully carry out their tasks. In this chapter, I will start to change the emphasis of the book, from the problem of 'how to build an agent', to 'how to build an agent society'. I begin by defining what we mean by a multiagent system.

Figure 6.1 (from Jennings (2000)) illustrates the typical structure of a multiagent system. The system contains a number of agents, which interact with one another through communication. The agents are able to act in an environment; different agents have different 'spheres of influence', in the sense that they will have control over – or at least be able to influence – different parts of the environment. These spheres of influence may coincide in some cases. The fact that these spheres of influence may coincide may give rise to dependency relationships between the agents. For example, two robotic agents may both be able to move through a door – but they may not be able to do so simultaneously. Finally, agents will also typically be linked by other relationships. Examples might be 'power' relationships, where one agent is the 'boss' of another.

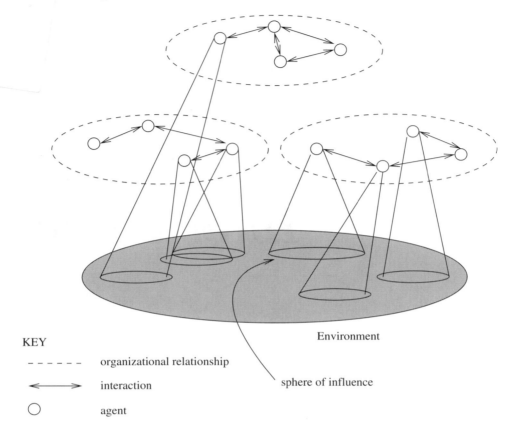

KEY

– – – – – – organizational relationship

←——→ interaction   sphere of influence

○ agent

Figure 6.1 Typical structure of a multiagent system.

The most important lesson of this chapter – and perhaps one of the most important lessons of multiagent systems generally – is that when faced with what appears to be a multiagent domain, it is critically important to understand the *type* of interaction that takes place between the agents. To see what I mean by this, let us start with some notation.

6.1 Utilities and Preferences

First, let us simplify things by assuming that we have just two agents; things tend to be much more complicated when we have more than two. Call these agents i and j, respectively. Each of the agents is assumed to be *self-interested*. That is, each agent has its own preferences and desires about how the world should be. For the moment, we will not be concerned with where these preferences come from; just assume that they are the preferences of the agent's user or owner. Next, we will assume that there is a set $\Omega = \{\omega_1, \omega_2, \dots\}$ of 'outcomes' or 'states' that the agents have preferences over. To make this concrete, just think of these as outcomes of a game that the two agents are playing.

We formally capture the preferences that the two agents have by means of *utility functions*, one for each agent, which assign to every outcome a real number, indicating how 'good' the outcome is for that agent. The larger the number the better from the point of view of the agent with the utility function. Thus agent i's preferences will be captured by a function

$$u_i : \Omega \rightarrow \mathbb{R}$$

and agent j's preferences will be captured by a function

$$u_j : \Omega \rightarrow \mathbb{R}.$$

(Compare with the discussion in Chapter 2 on tasks for agents.) It is not difficult to see that these utility function lead to a *preference ordering* over outcomes. For example, if ω and ω' are both possible outcomes in Ω, and $u_i(\omega) \geqslant u_i(\omega')$, then outcome ω is *preferred* by agent i at least as much as ω'. We can introduce a bit more notation to capture this preference ordering. We write

$$\omega \succeq_i \omega'$$

as an abbreviation for

$$u_i(\omega) \geqslant u_i(\omega').$$

Similarly, if $u_i(\omega) > u_i(\omega')$, then outcome ω is *strictly preferred* by agent i over ω'. We write

$$\omega \succ_i \omega'$$

as an abbreviation for

$$u_i(\omega) > u_i(\omega').$$

In other words,

$\omega \succ_i \omega'$ if and only if $u_i(\omega) \geqslant u_i(\omega')$ and not $u_i(\omega) = u_i(\omega')$.

We can see that the relation $\succeq_i$ really is an ordering, over Ω, in that it has the following properties.

Reflexivity: for all $\omega \in \Omega$, we have that $\omega \succeq_i \omega$.

Transitivity: if $\omega \succeq_i \omega'$, and $\omega' \succeq_i \omega''$, then $\omega \succeq_i \omega''$.

Comparability: for all $\omega \in \Omega$ and $\omega' \in \Omega$ we have that either $\omega \succeq_i \omega'$ or $\omega' \succeq_i \omega$.

The strict preference relation will satisfy the second and third of these properties, but will clearly not be reflexive.

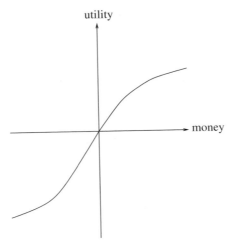

Figure 6.2   The relationship between money and utility.

What is utility?

Undoubtedly the simplest way to think about utilities is as money; the more money, the better. But resist the temptation to think that this is all that utilities are. Utility functions are *just a way of representing an agent's preferences.* They *do not* simply equate to money.

To see what I mean by this, suppose (and this really *is* a supposition) that I have US$500 million in the bank, while you are absolutely penniless. A rich benefactor appears, with one million dollars, which he generously wishes to donate to one of us. If the benefactor gives the money to me, what will the increase in the utility of my situation be? Well, I have more money, so there will clearly be *some* increase in the utility of my situation. But there will not be much: after all, there is not much that you can do with US$501 million that you cannot do with US$500 million. In contrast, if the benefactor gave the money to you, the increase in your utility would be *enormous*; you go from having no money at all to being a millionaire. That is a *big* difference.

This works the other way as well. Suppose I am in *debt* to the tune of US$500 million; well, there is frankly not that much difference in utility between owing US$500 million and owing US$499 million; they are both pretty bad. In contrast, there is a very big difference between being US$1 million in debt and not being in debt at all. A graph of the relationship between utility and money is shown in Figure 6.2.

6.2   Multiagent Encounters

Now that we have our model of agent's preferences, we need to introduce a model of the environment in which these agents will act. The idea is that our two agents will simultaneously choose an action to perform in the environment, and as a result of the actions they select, an outcome in Ω will result. The *actual* outcome that will result will depend on the particular *combination* of actions performed. Thus *both* agents can influence the outcome. We will also assume that the agents have no choice about whether to perform an action – they have to simply go ahead and perform one. Further, it is assumed that they cannot see the action performed by the other agent.

To make the analysis a bit easier, we will assume that each agent has just two possible actions that it can perform. We will call these two actions 'C', for 'cooperate', and 'D', for 'defect'. (The rationale for this terminology will become clear below.) Let $Ac = \{C, D\}$ be the set of these actions. The way the *environment* behaves is then determined by a function

$$\tau : \underbrace{Ac}_{\text{agent } i\text{'s action}} \times \underbrace{Ac}_{\text{agent } j\text{'s action}} \to \Omega.$$

(This is essentially a state transformer function, as discussed in Chapter 2.) In other words, on the basis of the action (either C or D) selected by agent i, and the action (also either C or D) chosen by agent j an outcome will result.

Here is an example of an environment function:

$$\tau(D,D) = \omega_1, \quad \tau(D,C) = \omega_2, \quad \tau(C,D) = \omega_3, \quad \tau(C,C) = \omega_4. \tag{6.1}$$

This environment maps each combination of actions to a *different* outcome. This environment is thus sensitive to the actions that each agent performs. At the other extreme, we can consider an environment that maps each combination of actions to the *same* outcome.

$$\tau(D,D) = \omega_1, \quad \tau(D,C) = \omega_1, \quad \tau(C,D) = \omega_1, \quad \tau(C,C) = \omega_1. \tag{6.2}$$

In this environment, it does not matter what the agents do: the outcome will be the same. Neither agent has any influence in such a scenario. We can also consider an environment that is only sensitive to the actions performed by one of the agents.

$$\tau(D,D) = \omega_1, \quad \tau(D,C) = \omega_2, \quad \tau(C,D) = \omega_1, \quad \tau(C,C) = \omega_2. \tag{6.3}$$

In this environment, it does not matter what agent i does: the outcome depends solely on the action performed by j. If j chooses to defect, then outcome ω_1 will result; if j chooses to cooperate, then outcome ω_2 will result.

The interesting story begins when we put an environment together with the preferences that agents have. To see what I mean by this, suppose we have the most general case, characterized by (6.1), where both agents are able to exert some influence over the environment. Now let us suppose that the agents have utility functions defined as follows:

$$\begin{aligned} u_i(\omega_1) = 1, \quad & u_i(\omega_2) = 1, \quad && u_i(\omega_3) = 4, \quad && u_i(\omega_4) = 4, \\ u_j(\omega_1) = 1, \quad & u_j(\omega_2) = 4, \quad && u_j(\omega_3) = 1, \quad && u_j(\omega_4) = 4. \end{aligned} \tag{6.4}$$

Since we know that every different combination of choices by the agents are mapped to a different outcome, we can abuse notation somewhat by writing the following:

$$u_i(D,D) = 1, \quad u_i(D,C) = 1, \quad u_i(C,D) = 4, \quad u_i(C,C) = 4, \\ u_j(D,D) = 1, \quad u_j(D,C) = 4, \quad u_j(C,D) = 1, \quad u_j(C,C) = 4. \tag{6.5}$$

We can then characterize agent i's preferences over the possible outcomes in the following way:

$$C,C \succeq_i C,D \succ_i D,C \succeq_i D,D.$$

Now, consider the following question.

> If you were agent i in this scenario, what would you choose to do – cooperate or defect?

In this case (I hope), the answer is pretty unambiguous. Agent i prefers *all* the outcomes in which it cooperates over *all* the outcomes in which it defects. Agent i's choice is thus clear: it should cooperate. It does not matter what agent j chooses to do.

In just the same way, agent j prefers all the outcomes in which *it* cooperates over all the outcomes in which it defects. Notice that in this scenario, neither agent has to expend any effort worrying about what the other agent will do: the action it should perform does not depend in any way on what the other does.

If both agents in this scenario act rationally, that is, they both choose to perform the action that will lead to their preferred outcomes, then the 'joint' action selected will be C, C: both agents will cooperate.

Now suppose that, for the same environment, the agents' utility functions were as follows:

$$u_i(D,D) = 4, \quad u_i(D,C) = 4, \quad u_i(C,D) = 1, \quad u_i(C,C) = 1, \\ u_j(D,D) = 4, \quad u_j(D,C) = 1, \quad u_j(C,D) = 4, \quad u_j(C,C) = 1. \tag{6.6}$$

Agent i's preferences over the possible outcomes are thus as follows:

$$D,D \succeq_i D,C \succ_i C,D \succeq_i C,C.$$

In this scenario, agent i can do no better than to defect. The agent prefers *all* the outcomes in which it defects over *all* the outcomes in which it cooperates. Similarly, agent j can do no better than defect: it also prefers all the outcomes in which it defects over all the outcomes in which it cooperates. Once again, the agents do not need to engage in *strategic* thinking (worrying about what the other agent will do): the best action to perform is entirely independent of the other agent's choice. I emphasize that in most multiagent scenarios, the choice an agent should make is not so clear cut; indeed, most are much more difficult.

We can neatly summarize the previous interaction scenario by making use of a standard game-theoretic notation known as a *payoff matrix*:

	i defects	*i* cooperates
j defects	4 4	1 4
j cooperates	4 1	1 1

The way to read such a payoff matrix is as follows. Each of the four cells in the matrix corresponds to one of the four possible outcomes. For example, the top-right cell corresponds to the outcome in which *i* cooperates and *j* defects; the bottom-left cell corresponds to the outcome in which *i* defects and *j* cooperates. The payoffs received by the two agents are written in the cell. The value in the top right of each cell is the payoff received by player *i* (the *column player*), while the value in the bottom left of each cell is the payoff received by agent *j* (the *row player*). As payoff matrices are standard in the literature, and are a much more succinct notation than the alternatives, we will use them as standard in the remainder of this chapter.

Before proceeding to consider any specific examples of multiagent encounter, let us introduce some of the theory that underpins the kind of analysis we have informally discussed above.

6.3 Dominant Strategies and Nash Equilibria

Given a particular multiagent encounter involving two agents *i* and *j*, there is one critically important question that both agents want answered: *what should I do?* We have already seen some multiagent encounters, and informally argued what the best possible outcome should be. In this section, we will define some of the concepts that are used in answering this question.

The first concept we will introduce is that of *dominance*. To understand what is meant by dominance, suppose we have two subsets of Ω, which we refer to as Ω_1 and Ω_2, respectively. We will say that Ω_1 *dominates* Ω_2 for agent *i* if *every* outcome in Ω_1 is preferred by *i* over *every* outcome in Ω_2. For example, suppose that

- $\Omega = \{\omega_1, \omega_2, \omega_3, \omega_4\}$;

- $\omega_1 \succ_i \omega_2 \succ_i \omega_3 \succ_i \omega_4$;

- $\Omega_1 = \{\omega_1, \omega_2\}$; and

- $\Omega_2 = \{\omega_3, \omega_4\}$.

Then Ω_1 strongly dominates Ω_2 since $\omega_1 \succ_i \omega_3$, $\omega_1 \succ_i \omega_4$, $\omega_2 \succ_i \omega_3$, and $\omega_2 \succ_i \omega_4$. However, Ω_2 does not strongly dominate Ω_1, since (for example), it is not the case that $\omega_3 \succ_i \omega_1$.

Formally, a set of outcomes Ω_1 strongly dominates set Ω_2 if the following condition is true:

$$\forall \omega_1 \in \Omega_1, \quad \forall \omega_2 \in \Omega_2, \quad \text{we have } \omega_1 \succ_i \omega_2.$$

Now, in order to bring ourselves in line with the game-theory literature, we will start referring to actions (members of the set Ac) as *strategies*. Given any particular strategy s for an agent i in a multiagent interaction scenario, there will be a number of possible outcomes. Let us denote by s^* the outcomes that may arise by i playing strategy s. For example, referring to the example environment in Equation (6.1), from agent i's point of view we have $C^* = \{\omega_3, \omega_4\}$, while $D^* = \{\omega_1, \omega_2\}$.

Now, we will say a *strategy* s_1 dominates a strategy s_2 if the set of outcomes possible by playing s_1 dominates the set possible by playing s_2, that is, if s_1^* dominates s_2^*. Again, referring back to the example of (6.5), it should be clear that, for agent i, cooperate strongly dominates defect. Indeed, as there are only two strategies available, the cooperate strategy is *dominant*: it is not dominated by any other strategy. The presence of a dominant strategy makes the decision about what to do extremely easy: the agent guarantees its best outcome by performing the dominant strategy. In following a dominant strategy, an agent guarantees itself the best possible payoff.

Another way of looking at dominance is that if a strategy s is dominated by another strategy s', then a rational agent will not follow s (because it can guarantee to do better with s'). When considering what to do, this allows us to *delete* dominated strategies from our consideration, simplifying the analysis considerably. The idea is to iteratively consider each strategy s in turn, and if there is another remaining strategy that strongly dominates it, then delete strategy s from consideration. If we end up with a single strategy remaining, then this will be the dominant strategy, and is clearly the rational choice. Unfortunately, for many interaction scenarios, there will not be a strongly dominant strategy; after deleting strongly dominated strategies, we may find more than one strategy remaining. What to do then? Well, we can start to delete *weakly* dominated strategies. A strategy s_1 is said to weakly dominate strategy s_2 if every outcome s_1^* is preferred at least as much as every outcome s_2^*. The problem is that if a strategy is only weakly dominated, then it is not necessarily irrational to use it; in deleting weakly dominated strategies, we may therefore 'throw away' a strategy that would in fact have been useful to use. We will not take this discussion further; see the *Notes and Further Reading* section at the end of this chapter for pointers to the literature.

The next notion we shall discuss is one of the most important concepts in the game-theory literature, and in turn is one of the most important concepts in analysing multiagent systems. The notion is that of *equilibrium*, and, more specifically, *Nash equilibrium*. The intuition behind equilibrium is perhaps best explained by example. Every time you drive a car, you need to decide which side of the road to drive on. The choice is not a very hard one: if you are in the UK, for example, you will probably choose to drive on the left; if you are in the US or continental Europe, you will drive on the right. The reason the choice is not hard is that it is a Nash equilibrium strategy. Assuming everyone else is driving on the left, you can do no better than drive on the left also. From everyone else's point of view, assuming you are driving on the left then everyone else can do no better than drive on the left also.

In general, we will say that two strategies s_1 and s_2 are in Nash equilibrium if:

(1) under the assumption that agent i plays s_1, agent j can do no better than play s_2; and

(2) under the assumption that agent j plays s_2, agent i can do no better than play s_1.

The *mutual* form of an equilibrium is important because it 'locks the agents in' to a pair of strategies. *Neither agent has any incentive to deviate from a Nash equilibrium.* To see why, suppose s_1, s_2 are a pair of strategies in Nash equilibrium for agents i and j, respectively, and that agent i chooses to play some other strategy, s_3 say. Then by definition, i will do no better, and may possibly do worse than it would have done by playing s_1.

The presence of a Nash equilibrium pair of strategies in a game might appear to be the definitive answer to the question of what to do in any given scenario. Unfortunately, there are two important results in the game-theory literature which serve to make life difficult:

(1) *not every interaction scenario has a Nash equilibrium*; and

(2) *some interaction scenarios have more than one Nash equilibrium.*

Despite these negative results, Nash equilibrium is an extremely important concept, and plays an important role in the analysis of multiagent systems.

6.4 Competitive and Zero-Sum Interactions

Suppose we have some scenario in which an outcome $\omega \in \Omega$ is preferred by agent i over an outcome ω' if, and only if, ω' is preferred over ω by agent j. Formally,

$$\omega \succ_i \omega' \text{ if and only if } \omega' \succ_j \omega.$$

The preferences of the players are thus diametrically opposed to one another: one agent can only improve its lot (i.e. get a more preferred outcome) at the expense of the other. An interaction scenario that satisfies this property is said to be *strictly competitive*, for hopefully obvious reasons.

Zero-sum encounters are those in which, for any particular outcome, the utilities of the two agents sum to zero. Formally, a scenario is said to be zero sum if the following condition is satisfied:

$$u_i(\omega) + u_j(\omega) = 0 \quad \text{for all } \omega \in \Omega.$$

It should be easy to see that any zero-sum scenario is strictly competitive. Zero-sum encounters are important because they are the most 'vicious' types of encounter conceivable, allowing for no possibility of cooperative behaviour. If you allow your opponent positive utility, then this means that you get *negative* utility – intuitively, you are worse off than you were before the interaction.

Games such as chess and chequers are the most obvious examples of strictly competitive interactions. Indeed, any game in which the possible outcomes are win or lose will be strictly competitive. Outside these rather abstract settings, however, it is hard to think of real-world examples of zero-sum encounters. War might be cited as a zero-sum interaction between nations, but even in the most extreme wars, there will usually be at least *some* common interest between the participants (e.g. in ensuring that the planet survives). Perhaps games like chess – which are a highly stylized form of interaction – are the only real-world examples of zero-sum encounters.

For these reasons, some social scientists are sceptical about whether zero-sum games exist in real-world scenarios (Zagare, 1984, p. 22). Interestingly, however, people interacting in many scenarios have a tendency to treat them *as if they were zero sum*. Below, we will see that in some scenarios – where there is the possibility of mutually beneficial cooperation – this type of behaviour can be damaging.

Enough abstract theory! Let us now apply this theory to some actual multiagent scenarios. First, let us consider what is perhaps the best-known scenario: the *prisoner's dilemma*.

6.5 The Prisoner's Dilemma

Consider the following scenario.

> Two men are collectively charged with a crime and held in separate cells. They have no way of communicating with each other or making any kind of agreement. The two men are told that:
>
> (1) if one of them confesses to the crime and the other does not, the confessor will be freed, and the other will be jailed for three years; and
>
> (2) if both confess to the crime, then each will be jailed for two years.
>
> Both prisoners know that if neither confesses, then they will each be jailed for one year.

We refer to confessing as defection, and not confessing as cooperating. Before reading any further, stop and think about this scenario: if you were one of the prisoners, what would you do? (Write down your answer somewhere, together with your reasoning; after you have read the discussion below, return and see how you fared.)

There are four possible outcomes to the prisoner's dilemma, depending on whether the agents cooperate or defect, and so the environment is of type (6.1). Abstracting from the scenario above, we can write down the utility functions for each agent in the following payoff matrix:

	i defects	i cooperates
j defects	2 2	0 5
j cooperates	5 0	3 3

Note that the numbers in the payoff matrix do not refer to years in prison. They capture how good an outcome is for the agents – the shorter jail term, the better. In other words, the utilities are

$$u_i(D,D) = 2, \quad u_i(D,C) = 5, \quad u_i(C,D) = 0, \quad u_i(C,C) = 3,$$
$$u_j(D,D) = 2, \quad u_j(D,C) = 0, \quad u_j(C,D) = 5, \quad u_j(C,C) = 3,$$

and the preferences are

$$D,C \succ_i C,C \succ_i D,D \succ_i C,D,$$
$$C,D \succ_j C,C \succ_j D,D \succ_j D,C.$$

What should a prisoner do? The answer is not as clear cut as the previous examples we looked at. It is not the case a prisoner prefers all the outcomes in which it cooperates over all the outcomes in which it defects. Similarly, it is not the case that a prisoner prefers all the outcomes in which it defects over all the outcomes in which it cooperates.

The 'standard' approach to this problem is to put yourself in the place of a prisoner, i say, and reason as follows.

- Suppose I cooperate. Then if j cooperates, we will both get a payoff of 3. But if j defects, then I will get a payoff of 0. So the best payoff I can be *guaranteed* to get if I cooperate is 0.

- Suppose I defect. Then if j cooperates, then I get a payoff of 5, whereas if j defects, then I will get a payoff of 2. So the best payoff I can be guaranteed to get if I defect is 2.

- So, if I cooperate, the worst case is I will get a payoff of 0, whereas if I defect, the worst case is that I will get 2.

- I would prefer a guaranteed payoff of 2 to a guaranteed payoff of 0, so I should defect.

Since the scenario is symmetric (i.e. both agents reason the same way), then the outcome that will emerge – if both agents reason 'rationally' – is that *both agents will defect*, giving them each a payoff off 2.

Notice that neither strategy strongly dominates in this scenario, so our first route to finding a choice of strategy is not going to work. Turning to Nash equilibria, there is a single Nash equilibrium of D, D. Thus under the assumption that i will play D, j can do no better than play D, and under the assumption that j will play D, i can also do no better than play D.

Is this the best they can do? *Naive intuition says not.* Surely if they both *cooperated*, then they could do better – they would receive a payoff of 3. But if you assume the other agent will cooperate, then the rational thing to do – the thing that maximizes your utility – is to defect. The conclusion seems inescapable: the rational thing to do in the prisoner's dilemma is defect, even though this appears to 'waste' some utility. (The fact that our naive intuition tells us that utility appears to be wasted here, and that the agents could do better by cooperating, even though the rational thing to do is to defect, is why this is referred to as a dilemma.)

The prisoner's dilemma may seem an abstract problem, but it turns out to be very common indeed. In the real world, the prisoner's dilemma appears in situations ranging from nuclear weapons treaty compliance to negotiating with one's children. Consider the problem of nuclear weapons treaty compliance. Two countries i and j have signed a treaty to dispose of their nuclear weapons. Each country can then either cooperate (i.e. get rid of their weapons), or defect (i.e. keep their weapons). But if you get rid of your weapons, you run the risk that the other side keeps theirs, making them very well off while you suffer what is called the 'sucker's payoff'. In contrast, if you keep yours, then the possible outcomes are that you will have nuclear weapons while the other country does not (a very good outcome for you), or else at worst that you both retain your weapons. This may not be the best possible outcome, but is certainly better than you giving up your weapons while your opponent kept theirs, which is what you risk if your give up your weapons.

Many people find the conclusion of this analysis – that the rational thing to do in the prisoner's dilemma is defect – deeply upsetting. For the result *seems* to imply that cooperation can only arise as a result of *irrational* behaviour, and that cooperative behaviour can be exploited by those who behave rationally. The apparent conclusion is that nature really is 'red in tooth and claw'. Particularly for those who are inclined to a liberal view of the world, this is unsettling and perhaps even distasteful. As civilized beings, we tend to pride ourselves on somehow 'rising above' the other animals in the world, and believe that we are capable of nobler behaviour: to argue in favour of such an analysis is therefore somehow immoral, and even demeaning to the entire human race.

Naturally enough, there have been several attempts to respond to this analysis of the prisoner's dilemma, in order to 'recover' cooperation (Binmore, 1992, pp. 355–382).

We are not all Machiavelli!

The first approach is to argue that we are not all such 'hard-boiled' individuals as the prisoner's dilemma (and more generally, this kind of game-theoretic analysis) implies. We are *not* seeking to constantly maximize our own welfare, possibly at the expense of others. Proponents of this kind of argument typically point to real-world examples of *altruism* and spontaneous, mutually beneficial cooperative behaviour in order to justify their claim.

There is some strength to this argument: we do not (or at least, most of us do not) constantly deliberate about how to maximize our welfare without any consideration for the welfare of our peers. Similarly, in many scenarios, we would be happy to trust our peers to recognize the value of a cooperative outcome without even mentioning it to them, being no more than mildly annoyed if we get the 'sucker's payoff'.

There are several counter responses to this. First, it is pointed out that many real-world examples of spontaneous cooperative behaviour are not really the prisoner's dilemma. Frequently, there is some built-in mechanism that makes it in the interests of participants to cooperate. For example, consider the problem of giving up your seat on the bus. We will frequently give up our seat on the bus to an older person, mother with children, etc., apparently at some discomfort (i.e. loss of utility) to ourselves. But it could be argued that in such scenarios, society has ways of punishing non-cooperative behaviour: suffering the hard and unforgiving stares of fellow passengers when we do not give up our seat, or worse, being accused in public of being uncouth!

Second, it is argued that many 'counter-examples' of cooperative behaviour arising do not stand up to inspection. For example, consider a public transport system, which relies on everyone cooperating and honestly paying their fare every time they travel, even though whether they have paid is not verified. The fact that such a system works would appear to be evidence that relying on spontaneous cooperation can work. But the fact that such a system works does not mean that it is not exploited. It will be, and if there is no means of checking whether or not someone has paid their fare and punishing non-compliance, then all other things being equal, those individuals that do exploit the system (defect) will be better off than those that pay honestly (cooperate). Unpalatable, perhaps, but true nevertheless.

The other prisoner is my twin!

A second line of attack is to argue that two prisoner's will 'think alike', and recognize that cooperation is the best outcome. For example, suppose the two prisoners are twins, unseparated since birth; then, it is argued, if their thought processes are sufficiently aligned, they will both recognize the benefits of cooperation, and behave accordingly. The answer to this is that it implies there are not actually two prisoners playing the game. If I can make my twin select a course of action simply by 'thinking it', then we are not playing the prisoner's dilemma at all.

This 'fallacy of the twins' argument often takes the form 'what if everyone were to behave like that' (Binmore, 1992, p. 311). The answer (as Yossarian pointed out in Joseph Heller's *Catch 22*) is that if everyone else behaved like that, you would be a damn fool to behave any other way.

People are not rational!

Some would argue – and game theorist Ken Binmore certainly did at the UKMAS workshop in December 1998 – that we might indeed be happy to risk cooperation as opposed to defection when faced with situations where the sucker's payoff really does not matter very much. For example, paying a bus fare that amounts to a few pennies does not really hurt us much, even if everybody else is defecting and hence exploiting the system. But, it is argued, when we are faced with situations where the sucker's payoff really *hurts* us – life or death situations and the like – we will choose the 'rational' course of action that maximizes our welfare, and defect.

The shadow of the future

Lest the discussion has so far proved too depressing, it should be emphasized that there are quite natural variants of the prisoner's dilemma in which cooperation *is* the rational thing to do. One idea is to *play the game more than once*. In the *iterated prisoner's dilemma*, the 'game' of the prisoner's dilemma is played a number of times. Each play is referred to as a 'round'. Critically, it is assumed that each agent can see what the opponent did on the previous round: player i can see whether j defected or not, and j can see whether i defected or not.

Now, for the sake of argument, assume that the agents will continue to play the game *forever*: every round will be followed by another round. Now, under these assumptions, what is the rational thing to do? If you know that you will be meeting the same opponent in future rounds, the incentive to defect appears to be considerably diminished, for two reasons.

- If you defect now, your opponent can *punish* you by also defecting. Punishment is not possible in the one-shot prisoner's dilemma.

- If you 'test the water' by cooperating initially, and receive the sucker's payoff on the first round, then because you are playing the game indefinitely, this loss of utility (one util) can be 'amortized' over the future rounds. When taken into the context of an infinite (or at least very long) run, then the loss of a single unit of utility will represent a small percentage of the overall utility gained.

So, if you play the prisoner's dilemma game indefinitely, then cooperation is a rational outcome (Binmore, 1992, p. 358). The 'shadow of the future' encourages us to cooperate in the infinitely repeated prisoner's dilemma game.

This seems to be very good news indeed, as truly one-shot games are comparatively scarce in real life. When we interact with someone, then there is often a good chance that we will interact with them in the future, and rational cooperation begins to look possible. However, there is a catch.

Suppose you agree to play the iterated prisoner's dilemma a *fixed* number of times (say 100). You need to decide (presumably in advance) what your strategy for playing the game will be. Consider the last round (i.e. the 100th game). Now, on this round, you know – as does your opponent – that you will not be interacting again. In other words, the last round is in effect a one-shot prisoner's dilemma game. As we know from the analysis above, the rational thing to do in a one-shot prisoner's dilemma game is defect. Your opponent, as a rational agent, will presumably reason likewise, and will also defect. On the 100th round, therefore, you will both defect. But this means that the last 'real' round, is 99. But similar reasoning leads us to the conclusion that this round will also be treated in effect like a one-shot prisoner's dilemma, and so on. Continuing this *backwards induction* leads inevitably to the conclusion that, in the iterated prisoner's dilemma with a fixed, predetermined, commonly known number of rounds, defection is the dominant strategy, as in the one-shot version (Binmore, 1992, p. 354).

Whereas it seemed to be very good news that rational cooperation is possible in the iterated prisoner's dilemma with an infinite number of rounds, it seems to be very bad news that this possibility appears to evaporate if we restrict ourselves to repeating the game a predetermined, fixed number of times. Returning to the real-world, we know that in reality, we will only interact with our opponents a finite number of times (after all, one day the world will end). We appear to be back where we started.

The story is actually better than it might at first appear, for several reasons. The first is that *actually* playing the game an infinite number of times is not necessary. As long as the 'shadow of the future' looms sufficiently large, then it can encourage cooperation. So, rational cooperation can become possible if both players know, with sufficient probability, that they will meet and play the game again in the future.

The second reason is that, even though a cooperative agent can suffer when playing against a defecting opponent, it can do well overall provided it gets sufficient opportunity to interact with other cooperative agents. To understand how this idea works, we will now turn to one of the best-known pieces of multiagent systems research: Axelrod's prisoner's dilemma tournament.

Axelrod's tournament

Robert Axelrod was (indeed, is) a political scientist interested in how cooperation can arise in societies of self-interested agents. In 1980, he organized a public tournament in which political scientists, psychologists, economists, and game theoreticians were invited to submit a computer program to play the iterated prisoner's dilemma. Each computer program had available to it the previous choices made by its opponent, and simply selected either C or D on the basis of these. Each computer program was played against each other for five games, each game consisting of two hundred rounds. The 'winner' of the tournament was the program that did best *overall*, i.e. best when considered against the whole range of programs. The computer programs ranged from 152 lines of program code to just five lines. Here are some examples of the kinds of strategy that were submitted.

ALL-D. This is the 'hawk' strategy, which encodes what a game-theoretic analysis tells us is the 'rational' strategy in the finitely iterated prisoner's dilemma: always defect, no matter what your opponent has done.

RANDOM. This strategy is a control: it ignores what its opponent has done on previous rounds, and selects either C or D at random, with equal probability of either outcome.

TIT-FOR-TAT. This strategy is as follows:

(1) on the first round, cooperate;

(2) on round $t > 1$, do what your opponent did on round $t - 1$.

TIT-FOR-TAT was actually the simplest strategy entered, requiring only five lines of Fortran code.

TESTER. This strategy was intended to exploit computer programs that did not punish defection: as its name suggests, on the first round it tested its opponent by defecting. If the opponent ever retaliated with defection, then it subsequently played TIT-FOR-TAT. If the opponent did not defect, then it played a repeated sequence of cooperating for two rounds, then defecting.

JOSS. Like TESTER, the JOSS strategy was intended to exploit 'weak' opponents. It is essentially TIT-FOR-TAT, but 10% of the time, instead of cooperating, it will defect.

Before proceeding, consider the following two questions.

(1) On the basis of what you know so far, and, in particular, what you know of the game-theoretic results relating to the finitely iterated prisoner's dilemma, which strategy do you think would do best overall?

(2) If you were entering the competition, which strategy would you enter?

After the tournament was played, the result was that the overall winner was TIT-FOR-TAT: the simplest strategy entered. At first sight, this result seems extraordinary. It appears to be empirical proof that the game-theoretic analysis of the iterated prisoner's dilemma is wrong: cooperation *is* the rational thing to do, after all! But the result, while significant, is more subtle (and possibly less encouraging) than this. TIT-FOR-TAT won because the overall score was computed by taking into account *all* the strategies that it played against. The result when TIT-FOR-TAT was played against ALL-D was exactly as might be expected: ALL-D came out on top. Many people have misinterpreted these results as meaning that TIT-FOR-TAT is the optimal strategy in the iterated prisoner's dilemma. *You should be careful not to interpret Axelrod's results in this way.* TIT-FOR-TAT was able to succeed because it had the opportunity to play against other programs that were also inclined to cooperate. Provided the environment in which TIT-FOR-TAT plays contains sufficient opportunity to interact with other 'like-minded' strategies, TIT-FOR-TAT can prosper. The TIT-FOR-TAT strategy will not prosper if it is forced to interact with strategies that tend to defect.

Axelrod attempted to characterize the reasons for the success of TIT-FOR-TAT, and came up with the following four rules for success in the iterated prisoner's dilemma.

(1) Do not be envious. In the prisoner's dilemma, it is not necessary for you to 'beat' your opponent in order for you to do well.

(2) Do not be the first to defect. Axelrod refers to a program as 'nice' if it starts by cooperating. He found that whether or not a rule was nice was the single best predictor of success in his tournaments. There is clearly a risk in starting with cooperation. But the loss of utility associated with receiving the sucker's payoff on the first round will be comparatively small compared with possible benefits of mutual cooperation with another nice strategy.

(3) Reciprocate cooperation and defection. As Axelrod puts it, 'TIT-FOR-TAT represents a balance between punishing and being forgiving' (Axelrod, 1984, p. 119): the combination of punishing defection and rewarding cooperation seems to encourage cooperation. Although TIT-FOR-TAT can be exploited on the first round, it retaliates relentlessly for such non-cooperative behaviour. Moreover, TIT-FOR-TAT punishes with *exactly* the same degree of violence that it was the recipient of: in other words, it never 'overreacts' to defection. In addition, because TIT-FOR-TAT is *forgiving* (it rewards cooperation), it is possible for cooperation to become established even following a poor start.

(4) Do not be too clever. As noted above, TIT-FOR-TAT was the simplest program entered into Axelrod's competition. Either surprisingly or not, depending on your point of view, it fared significantly better than other programs that attempted to make use of comparatively advanced programming techniques in order to decide what to do. Axelrod suggests three reasons for this:

  (a) the most complex entries attempted to develop a model of the behaviour of the other agent while ignoring the fact that this agent was in turn watching the original agent – they lacked a model of the reciprocal learning that actually takes place;

(b) most complex entries over generalized when seeing their opponent defect, and did not allow for the fact that cooperation was still possible in the future – they were not *forgiving*;

(c) many complex entries exhibited behaviour that was too complex to be understood – to their opponent, they may as well have been acting randomly.

From the amount of space we have devoted to discussing it, you might assume that the prisoner's dilemma was the *only* type of multiagent interaction there is. This is not the case.

6.6 Other Symmetric 2 × 2 Interactions

Recall the ordering of agent i's preferences in the prisoner's dilemma:

$$D, C \succ_i C, C \succ_i D, D \succ_i C, D.$$

This is just one of the possible orderings of outcomes that agents may have. If we restrict our attention to interactions in which there are two agents, each agent has two possible actions (C or D), and the scenario is *symmetric*, then there are 4! = 24 possible orderings of preferences, which for completeness I have summarized in Table 6.1. (In the game-theory literature, these are referred to as symmetric 2 × 2 games.)

In many of these scenarios, what an agent should do is clear-cut. For example, agent i should clearly cooperate in scenarios (1) and (2), as both of the outcomes in which i cooperates are preferred over both of the outcomes in which i defects. Similarly, in scenarios (23) and (24), agent i should clearly defect, as both outcomes in which it defects are preferred over both outcomes in which it cooperates. Scenario (14) is the prisoner's dilemma, which we have already discussed at length, which leaves us with two other interesting cases to examine: the *stag hunt* and the *game of chicken*.

The stag hunt

The stag hunt is another example of a social dilemma. The name stag hunt arises from a scenario put forward by the Swiss philosopher Jean-Jacques Rousseau in his 1775 *Discourse on Inequality*. However, to explain the dilemma, I will use a scenario that will perhaps be more relevant to readers at the beginning of the 21st century (Poundstone, 1992, pp. 218, 219).

> You and a friend decide it would be a great joke to show up on the last day of school with some ridiculous haircut. Egged on by your clique, you both *swear* you'll get the haircut.

Table 6.1 The possible preferences that agent i can have in symmetric interaction scenarios where there are two agents, each of which has two available actions, C (cooperate) and D (defect); recall that X, Y means the outcome in which agent i plays X and agent j plays Y.

Scenario	Preferences over outcomes	Comment
1.	$C,C \succ_i C,D \succ_i D,C \succ_i D,D$	cooperation dominates
2.	$C,C \succ_i C,D \succ_i D,D \succ_i D,C$	cooperation dominates
3.	$C,C \succ_i D,C \succ_i C,D \succ_i D,D$	
4.	$C,C \succ_i D,C \succ_i D,D \succ_i C,D$	stag hunt
5.	$C,C \succ_i D,D \succ_i C,D \succ_i D,C$	
6.	$C,C \succ_i D,D \succ_i D,C \succ_i C,D$	
7.	$C,D \succ_i C,C \succ_i D,C \succ_i D,D$	
8.	$C,D \succ_i C,C \succ_i D,D \succ_i D,C$	
9.	$C,D \succ_i D,C \succ_i C,C \succ_i D,D$	
10.	$C,D \succ_i D,C \succ_i D,D \succ_i C,C$	
11.	$C,D \succ_i D,D \succ_i C,C \succ_i D,C$	
12.	$C,D \succ_i D,D \succ_i D,C \succ_i C,C$	
13.	$D,C \succ_i C,C \succ_i C,D \succ_i D,D$	game of chicken
14.	$D,C \succ_i C,C \succ_i D,D \succ_i C,D$	prisoner's dilemma
15.	$D,C \succ_i C,D \succ_i C,C \succ_i D,D$	
16.	$D,C \succ_i C,D \succ_i D,D \succ_i C,C$	
17.	$D,C \succ_i D,D \succ_i C,C \succ_i C,D$	
18.	$D,C \succ_i D,D \succ_i C,D \succ_i C,C$	
19.	$D,D \succ_i C,C \succ_i C,D \succ_i D,C$	
20.	$D,D \succ_i C,C \succ_i D,C \succ_i C,D$	
21.	$D,D \succ_i C,D \succ_i C,C \succ_i D,C$	
22.	$D,D \succ_i C,D \succ_i D,C \succ_i C,C$	
23.	$D,D \succ_i D,C \succ_i C,C \succ_i C,D$	defection dominates
24.	$D,D \succ_i D,C \succ_i C,D \succ_i C,C$	defection dominates

A night of indecision follows. As you anticipate your parents' and teachers' reactions...you start wondering if your friend is really going to go through with the plan.

Not that you do not want the plan to succeed: the best possible outcome would be for both of you to get the haircut.

The trouble is, it would be awful to be the *only* one to show up with the haircut. That would be the worst possible outcome.

You're not above enjoying your friend's embarrassment. If you *didn't* get the haircut, but the friend did, and looked like a real jerk, that would be almost as good as if you both got the haircut.

This scenario is obviously very close to the prisoner's dilemma: the difference is that in this scenario, mutual cooperation is the most preferred outcome, rather than you defecting while your opponent cooperates. Expressing the game in a payoff matrix (picking rather arbitrary payoffs to give the preferences):

	i defects	*i* cooperates
j defects	1 1	0 2
j cooperates	2 0	3 3

It should be clear that there are *two* Nash equilibria in this game: mutual defection, or mutual cooperation. If you trust your opponent, and believe that he will cooperate, then you can do no better than cooperate, and vice versa, your opponent can also do no better than cooperate. Conversely, if you believe your opponent will defect, then you can do no better than defect yourself, and vice versa.

Poundstone suggests that 'mutiny' scenarios are examples of the stag hunt: 'We'd all be better off if we got rid of Captain Bligh, but we'll be hung as mutineers if not enough of us go along' (Poundstone, 1992, p. 220).

The game of chicken

The game of chicken (row 13 in Table 6.1) is characterized by agent *i* having the following preferences:

$$D, C \succ_i C, C \succ_i C, D \succ_i D, D.$$

As with the stag hunt, this game is also closely related to the prisoner's dilemma. The difference here is that mutual defection is agent *i*'s most feared outcome, rather than *i* cooperating while *j* defects. The game of chicken gets its name from a rather silly, macho 'game' that was supposedly popular amongst juvenile delinquents in 1950s America; the game was immortalized by James Dean in the film *Rebel Without a Cause*. The purpose of the game is to establish who is bravest out of two young thugs. The game is played by both players driving their cars at high speed towards a cliff. The idea is that the least brave of the two (the 'chicken') will be the first to drop out of the game by steering away from the cliff. The winner is the one who lasts longest in the car. Of course, if *neither* player steers away, then both cars fly off the cliff, taking their foolish passengers to a fiery death on the rocks that undoubtedly lie below.

So, how should agent *i* play this game? It depends on how brave (or foolish) *i* believes *j* is. If *i* believes that *j* is braver than *i*, then *i* would do best to steer away from the cliff (i.e. cooperate), since it is unlikely that *j* will steer away from the cliff. However, if *i* believes that *j* is *less* brave than *i*, then *i* should stay in the car; because *j* is less brave, he will steer away first, allowing *i* to win. The difficulty arises when both agents mistakenly believe that the other is less brave; in this case, both agents will stay in their car (i.e. defect), and the worst outcome arises.

Expressed as a payoff matrix, the game of chicken is as follows:

	i defects	i cooperates
j defects	0 0	1 3
j cooperates	3 1	2 2

It should be clear that the game of chicken has two Nash equilibria, corresponding to the above-right and below-left cells. Thus if you believe that your opponent is going to drive straight (i.e. defect), then you can do no better than to steer away from the cliff, and vice versa. Similarly, if you believe your opponent is going to steer away, then you can do no better than to drive straight.

6.7 Dependence Relations in Multiagent Systems

Before leaving the issue of interactions, I will briefly discuss another approach to understanding how the properties of a multiagent system can be understood. This approach, due to Sichman and colleagues, attempts to understand the *dependencies* between agents (Sichman *et al.*, 1994; Sichman and Demazeau, 1995). The basic idea is that a dependence relation exists between two agents if one of the agents requires the other in order to achieve one of its goals. There are a number of possible dependency relations.

Independence. There is no dependency between the agents.

Unilateral. One agent depends on the other, but not vice versa.

Mutual. Both agents depend on each other with respect to the same goal.

Reciprocal dependence. The first agent depends on the other for some goal, while the second also depends on the first for some goal (the two goals are not necessarily the same). Note that mutual dependence implies reciprocal dependence.

These relationships may be qualified by whether or not they are *locally believed* or *mutually believed*. There is a locally believed dependence if one agent believes the dependence exists, but does not believe that the other agent believes it exists. A mutually believed dependence exists when the agent believes the dependence exists, and also believes that the other agent is aware of it. Sichman and colleagues implemented a *social reasoning system* called DepNet (Sichman *et al.*, 1994). Given a description of a multiagent system, DepNet was capable of computing the relationships that existed between agents in the system.

Notes and Further Reading

Ken Binmore, in his lucid and entertaining introduction to game theory, *Fun and Games*, discusses the philosophical implications of the prisoner's dilemma at length (Binmore, 1992, p. 310–316). This text is recommended as a readable – albeit mathematically demanding – introduction to game theory, which provides extensive pointers into the literature.

There are many other interesting aspects of Axelrod's tournaments that I can only briefly mention due to space restrictions. The first is that of *noise*. I mentioned above that the iterated prisoner's dilemma is predicated on the assumption that the participating agents can see the move made by their opponent: they can see, in other words, whether their opponent defects or cooperates. But suppose the game allows for a certain probability that on any given round, an agent will *misinterpret* the actions of its opponent, and perceive cooperation to be defection and vice versa. Suppose two agents are playing the iterated prisoner's dilemma against one another, and both are playing TIT-FOR-TAT. Then both agents will start by cooperating, and in the absence of noise, will continue to enjoy the fruits of mutual cooperation. But if noise causes one of them to misinterpret defection as cooperation, then this agent will retaliate to the perceived defection with defection. The other agent will retaliate in turn, and both agents will defect, then retaliate, and so on, losing significant utility as a consequence. Interestingly, cooperation can be restored if further noise causes one of the agents to misinterpret defection as cooperation – this will then cause the agents to begin cooperating again! Axelrod (1984) is recommended as a point of departure for further reading; Mor and Rosenschein (1995) provides pointers into recent prisoner's dilemma literature; a collection of Axelrod's more recent essays was published as Axelrod (1997). A non-mathematical introduction to game theory, with an emphasis on the applications of game theory in the social sciences, is Zagare (1984).

Exercises

(1) **[Level 1.]**

Consider the following sets of outcomes and preferences:

- $\Omega = \{w_1, w_2, w_3, w_4, w_5, w_6\}$;
- $w_6 \succ_i w_2 \succ_i w_3 \succ_i w_1 \succ_i w_5 \succ_i w_4$;
- $\Omega_1 = \{w_1, w_3\}$;
- $\Omega_2 = \{w_3, w_4\}$;
- $\Omega_3 = \{w_3\}$; and
- $\Omega_4 = \{w_2, w_6\}$.

Which of these sets (if any) dominates the others? Where neither set dominates the other, indicate this.

(2) **[Level 2.]**

Consider the following interaction scenarios:

	i defects	i cooperates
j defects	3 3	4 2
j cooperates	1 1	2 4

	i defects	i cooperates
j defects	−1 −1	2 1
j cooperates	1 2	−1 −1

	i defects	i cooperates
j defects	3 3	4 2
j cooperates	1 1	2 4

Now, for each of these scenarios,

- begin by informally analysing the scenario to determine what the two agents should do;
- classify the preferences that agents have with respect to outcomes;
- determine which strategies are strongly or weakly dominated;
- use the idea of deleting strongly dominated strategies to simplify the scenario where appropriate;
- identify any Nash equilibria.

(3) **[Class discussion.]**

This is best done as a class exercise, in groups of three: play the prisoner's dilemma. Use one of the three as 'umpire', to keep track of progress and scores, and to stop any outbreaks of violence. First try playing the one-shot game a few times, and then try the iterated version, first for an agreed, predetermined number of times, and then allowing the umpire to choose how many times to iterate without telling the players.

- Which strategies do best in the one-shot and iterated prisoner's dilemma?

- Try playing people against strategies such as TIT-FOR-TAT, and ALL-D.

- Try getting people to define their strategy precisely in advance (by writing it down), and then see if you can determine their strategy while playing the game; distribute their strategy, and see if it can be exploited.

(4) **[Level 2.]**

For each of the scenarios in Table 6.1 that was not discussed in the text,

- draw up a payoff matrix that characterizes the scenario (remembering that these are *symmetric* interaction scenarios);

- attempt to determine what an agent should do;

- identify, if possible, a real-world interaction situation that corresponds to the abstract scenario.

7

Reaching Agreements

An obvious problem, related to the issue of cooperation, is that of *reaching agreements* in a society of self-interested agents. In the multiagent world that we all inhabit every day, we are regularly required to interact with other individuals with whom we may well not share common goals. In the most extreme scenario, as discussed in the preceding chapter, we may find ourselves in a zero-sum encounter. In such an encounter, the only way we can profit is at the expense of our opponents. In general, however, most scenarios in which we find ourselves are not so extreme – in most realistic scenarios, there is some potential for agents to reach *mutually beneficial agreement* on matters of common interest. The ability to reach agreements (without a third party dictating terms!) is a fundamental capability of intelligent autonomous agents – without this capability, we would surely find it impossible to function in society. The capabilities of *negotiation* and *argumentation* are central to the ability of an agent to reach agreement.

Negotiation scenarios do not occur in a vacuum: they will be governed by a particular *mechanism*, or *protocol*. The protocol defines the 'rules of encounter' between agents (Rosenschein and Zlotkin, 1994). It is possible to design protocols so that any particular negotiation history has certain desirable properties – this is *mechanism design*, and is discussed in more detail below.

A second issue is, given a particular protocol, how can a particular *strategy* be designed that individual agents can use while negotiating – an agent will aim to use a strategy that maximizes its own individual welfare. A key issue here is that, since we are interested in actually *building* agents that will be capable of negotiating on our behalf, it is not enough simply to have agents that get the best outcome *in theory* – they must be able to obtain the best outcome *in practice*.

In the remainder of this chapter, I will discuss the process of reaching agreements through negotiation and argumentation. I will start by considering the issue of mechanism design – broadly, what properties we might want a negotiation or argumentation protocol to have – and then go on to discuss auctions, negotiation protocols and strategies, and finally argumentation.

7.1   Mechanism Design

As noted above, *mechanism design* is the design of protocols for governing multiagent interactions, such that these protocols have certain desirable properties. When we design 'conventional' communication protocols, we typically aim to design them so that (for example) they are provably free of deadlocks, livelocks, and so on (Holzmann, 1991). In multiagent systems, we are still concerned with such issues of course, but for negotiation protocols, the properties we would like to prove are slightly different. Possible properties include, for example (Sandholm, 1999, p. 204), the following.

Guaranteed success. A protocol guarantees success if it ensures that, eventually, agreement is certain to be reached.

Maximizing social welfare. Intuitively, a protocol maximizes social welfare if it ensures that any outcome maximizes the sum of the utilities of negotiation participants. If the utility of an outcome for an agent was simply defined in terms of the amount of money that agent received in the outcome, then a protocol that maximized social welfare would maximize the *total* amount of money 'paid out'.

Pareto efficiency. A negotiation outcome is said to be pareto efficient if there is no other outcome that will make at least one agent better off without making at least one other agent worse off. Intuitively, if a negotiation outcome is not pareto efficient, then there is another outcome that will make at least one agent happier while keeping everyone else at least as happy.

Individual rationality. A protocol is said to be individually rational if following the protocol – 'playing by the rules' – is in the best interests of negotiation participants. Individually rational protocols are essential because without them, there is no incentive for agents to engage in negotiations.

Stability. A protocol is *stable* if it provides all agents with an incentive to behave in a particular way. The best-known kind of stability is *Nash equilibrium*, as discussed in the preceding chapter.

Simplicity. A 'simple' protocol is one that makes the appropriate strategy for a negotiation participant 'obvious'. That is, a protocol is simple if using it, a participant can easily (tractably) determine the optimal strategy.

Distribution. A protocol should ideally be designed to ensure that there is no 'single point of failure' (such as a single arbitrator) and, ideally, so as to minimize communication between agents.

The fact that even quite simple negotiation protocols can be proven to have such desirable properties accounts in no small part for the success of game-theoretic techniques for negotiation (Kraus, 1997).

7.2 Auctions

Auctions used to be comparatively rare in everyday life; every now and then, one would hear of astronomical sums paid at auction for a painting by Monet or Van Gogh, but other than this, they did not enter the lives of the majority. The Internet and Web fundamentally changed this. The Web made it possible for auctions with a large, international audience to be carried out at very low cost. This in turn made it possible for goods to be put up for auction which hitherto would have been too uneconomical. Large businesses have sprung up around the idea of online auctions, with eBay being perhaps the best-known example (EBAY, 2001).

One of the reasons why online auctions have become so popular is that auctions are extremely simple interaction scenarios. This means that it is easy to automate auctions; this makes them a good first choice for consideration as a way for agents to reach agreements. Despite their simplicity, auctions present both a rich collection of problems for researchers, and a powerful tool that automated agents can use for allocating goods, tasks, and resources.

Abstractly, an auction takes place between an agent known as the *auctioneer* and a collection of agents known as the *bidders*. The goal of the auction is for the auctioneer to allocate the *good* to one of the bidders. In most settings – and certainly most traditional auction settings – the auctioneer desires to maximize the price at which the good is allocated, while bidders desire to minimize price. The auctioneer will attempt to achieve his desire through the design of an appropriate auction mechanism – the rules of encounter – while bidders attempt to achieve their desires by using a strategy that will conform to the rules of encounter, but that will also deliver an optimal result.

There are several factors that can affect both the protocol and the strategy that agents use. The most important of these is whether the good for auction has a *private* or a *public/common* value. Consider an auction for a one dollar bill. How much is this dollar bill worth to you? Assuming it is a 'typical' dollar bill, then it should be worth exactly $1; if you paid $2 for it, you would be $1 worse off than you were. The same goes for anyone else involved in this auction. A typical dollar bill thus has a *common value*: it is worth exactly the same to all bidders in the auction. However, suppose you were a big fan of the Beatles, and the dollar bill happened to be the last dollar bill that John Lennon spent. Then it may well be that, for sentimental reasons, this dollar bill was worth considerably more to you – you might be willing to pay $100 for it. To a fan of the Rolling Stones, with no interest in or liking for the Beatles, however, the bill might not have the same value. Someone with no interest in the Beatles whatsoever might value the one dollar bill at exactly $1. In this case, the good for auction – the dollar bill – is said to have a *private value*: each agent values it differently.

A third type of valuation is *correlated value*: in such a setting, an agent's valuation of the good depends partly on private factors, and partly on other agent's valuation of it. An example might be where an agent was bidding for a painting that it liked, but wanted to keep open the option of later selling the painting. In this case, the amount you would be willing to pay would depend partly on how much you liked it, but also partly on how much you believed other agents might be willing to pay for it if you put it up for auction later.

Let us turn now to consider some of the dimensions along which auction protocols may vary. The first is that of *winner determination*: who gets the good that the bidders are bidding for. In the auctions with which we are most familiar, the answer to this question is probably self-evident: the agent that bids the most is allocated the good. Such protocols are known as *first-price* auctions. This is not the only possibility, however. A second possibility is to allocate the good to the agent that bid the highest, but this agent pays only the amount of the *second highest* bid. Such auctions are known as *second-price* auctions.

At first sight, it may seem bizarre that there are any settings in which a second-price auction is desirable, as this implies that the auctioneer does not get as much for the good as it could do. However, we shall see below that there are indeed some settings in which a second-price auction is desirable.

The second dimension along which auction protocols can vary is whether or not the bids made by the agents are known to each other. If every agent can see what every other agent is bidding (the terminology is that the bids are *common knowledge*), then the auction is said to be *open cry*. If the agents are not able to determine the bids made by other agents, then the auction is said to be a *sealed-bid* auction.

A third dimension is the mechanism by which bidding proceeds. The simplest possibility is to have a single round of bidding, after which the auctioneer allocates the good to the winner. Such auctions are known as *one shot*. The second possibility is that the price starts low (often at a *reservation price*) and successive bids are for increasingly large amounts. Such auctions are known as *ascending*. The alternative – *descending* – is for the auctioneer to start off with a high value, and to decrease the price in successive rounds.

English auctions

English auctions are the most commonly known type of auction, made famous by such auction houses as Sothebys. English auction are *first-price, open cry, ascending* auctions:

- the auctioneer starts off by suggesting a *reservation price* for the good (which may be 0) – if no agent is willing to bid more than the reservation price, then the good is allocated to the auctioneer for this amount;

- bids are then invited from agents, who must bid more than the current highest bid – all agents can see the bids being made, and are able to participate in the bidding process if they so desire;

- when no agent is willing to raise the bid, then the good is allocated to the agent that has made the current highest bid, and the price they pay for the good is the amount of this bid.

What strategy should an agent use to bid in English auctions? It turns out that the dominant strategy is for an agent to successively bid a small amount more than the current highest bid until the bid price reaches their current valuation, and then to withdraw.

Simple though English auctions are, it turns out that they have some interesting properties. One interesting feature of English auctions arises when there is uncertainty about the true value of the good being auctioned. For example, suppose an auctioneer is selling some land to agents that want to exploit it for its mineral resources, and that there is limited geological information available about this land. None of the agents thus knows exactly what the land is worth. Suppose now that the agents engage in an English auction to obtain the land, each using the dominant strategy described above. When the auction is over, should the winner feel happy that they have obtained the land for less than or equal to their private valuation? Or should they feel worried *because no other agent valued the land so highly*? This situation, where the winner is the one who overvalues the good on offer, is known as the *winner's curse*. Its occurrence is not limited to English auctions, but occurs most frequently in these.

Dutch auctions

Dutch auctions are examples of *open-cry descending* auctions:

- the auctioneer starts out offering the good at some artificially high value (above the expected value of any bidder's valuation of it);

- the auctioneer then continually lowers the offer price of the good by some small value, until some agent makes a bid for the good which is equal to the current offer price;

- the good is then allocated to the agent that made the offer.

Notice that Dutch auctions are also susceptible to the winner's curse. There is no dominant strategy for Dutch auctions in general.

First-price sealed-bid auctions

First-price sealed-bid auctions are examples of one-shot auctions, and are perhaps the simplest of all the auction types we will consider. In such an auction, there is a single round, in which bidders submit to the auctioneer a bid for the good; there are no subsequent rounds, and the good is awarded to the agent that made the highest bid. The winner pays the price of the highest bid. There are hence no opportunities for agents to offer larger amounts for the good.

How should an agent act in first-price sealed-bid auctions? Suppose every agent bids their true valuation; the good is then awarded to the agent that bid the highest amount. But consider the amount bid by the second highest bidder. The winner could have offered just a tiny fraction more than the second highest price, and still been awarded the good. Hence most of the difference between the highest and second highest price is, in effect, money wasted as far as the winner is concerned. The best strategy for an agent is therefore to bid less than its true valuation. How *much* less will of course depend on what the other agents bid – there is no general solution.

Vickrey auctions

The next type of auction is the most unusual and perhaps most counterintuitive of all the auction types we shall consider. Vickrey auctions are *second-price sealed-bid* auctions. This means that there is a single negotiation round, during which each bidder submits a single bid; bidders do not get to see the bids made by other agents. The good is awarded to the agent that made the highest bid; however the price this agent pays is not the price of the highest bid, but the price of the *second highest* bid. Thus if the highest bid was made by agent i, who bid $9, and the second highest bid was by agent j, who bid $8, then agent i would win the auction and be allocated the good, *but agent i would only pay $8.*

Why would one even consider using Vickrey auctions? The answer is that Vickrey auctions make truth telling the dominant strategy: *a bidder's dominant strategy in a private value Vickrey auction is to bid his true valuation.* Consider why this is.

- Suppose that you bid *more* than your true valuation. In this case, you may be awarded the good, but you run the risk of being awarded the good but at more than the amount of your private valuation. If you win in such a circumstance, then you make a loss (since you paid more than you believed the good was worth).

- Suppose you bid *less* than your true valuation. In this case, note that you stand less chance of winning than if you had bid your true valuation. But, even if you do win, the amount you pay will not have been affected by the fact that you bid less than your true valuation, because you will pay the price of the second highest bid.

Thus the best thing to do in a Vickrey auction is to bid truthfully: to bid to your private valuation – no more and no less.

Because they make truth telling the dominant strategy, Vickrey auctions have received a lot of attention in the multiagent systems literature (see Sandholm (1999, p. 213) for references). However, they are not widely used in human auctions. There are several reasons for this, but perhaps the most important is that humans frequently find the Vickrey mechanism hard to understand, because at first sight it seems so counterintuitive. In terms of the desirable attributes that we discussed above, it is not *simple* for humans to understand.

Note that Vickrey auctions make it possible for *antisocial* behaviour. Suppose you want some good and your private valuation is $90, but you know that some other agent wants it and values it at $100. As truth telling is the dominant strategy, you can do no better than bid $90; your opponent bids $100, is awarded the good, but pays only $90. Well, maybe you are not too happy about this: maybe you would like to 'punish' your successful opponent. How can you do this? Suppose you bid $99 instead of $90. Then you still lose the good to your opponent – *but he pays $9 more than he would do if you had bid truthfully*. To make this work, of course, you have to be very confident about what your opponent will bid – you do not want to bid $99 only to discover that your opponent bid $95, and you were left with a good that cost $5 more than your private valuation. This kind of behaviour occurs in commercial situations, where one company may not be able to compete directly with another company, but uses their position to try to force the opposition into bankruptcy.

Expected revenue

There are several issues that should be mentioned relating to the types of auctions discussed above. The first is that of *expected revenue*. If you are an auctioneer, then as mentioned above, your overriding consideration will in all likelihood be to maximize your revenue: you want an auction protocol that will get you the highest possible price for the good on offer. You may well not be concerned with whether or not agents tell the truth, or whether they are afflicted by the winner's curse. It may seem that some protocols – Vickrey's mechanism in particular – do not encourage this. So, which should the auctioneer choose?

For private value auctions, the answer depends partly on the attitude to risk of both auctioneers and bidders (Sandholm, 1999, p. 214).

- For *risk-neutral bidders*, the expected revenue to the auctioneer is provably identical in all four types of auctions discussed above (under certain simple assumptions). That is, the auctioneer can expect on average to get the same revenue for the good using all of these types of auction.

- For *risk-averse bidders* (i.e. bidders that would prefer to get the good even if they paid slightly more for it than their private valuation), Dutch and first-price sealed-bid protocols lead to higher expected revenue for the auctioneer. This is because in these protocols, a risk-averse agent can 'insure' himself by bidding slightly more for the good than would be offered by a risk-neutral bidder.

- *Risk-averse auctioneers*, however, do better with Vickrey or English auctions.

Note that these results should be treated very carefully. For example, the first result, relating to the revenue equivalence of auctions given risk-neutral bidders, depends critically on the fact that bidders really do have private valuations. In choosing an appropriate protocol, it is therefore critical to ensure that the properties of the auction scenario – and the bidders – are understood correctly.

Lies and collusion

An interesting question is the extent to which the protocols we have discussed above are susceptible to lying and collusion by both bidders and auctioneer. Ideally, as an auctioneer, we would like a protocol that was immune to collusion by bidders, i.e. that made it against a bidder's best interests to engage in collusion with other bidders. Similarly, as a potential bidder in an auction, we would like a protocol that made honesty on the part of the auctioneer the dominant strategy.

None of the four auction types discussed above is immune to collusion. For any of them, the 'grand coalition' of all agents involved in bidding for the good can agree beforehand to collude to put forward artificially low bids for the good on offer. When the good is obtained, the bidders can then obtain its true value (higher than the artificially low price paid for it), and split the profits amongst themselves. The most obvious way of preventing collusion is to modify the protocol so that bidders cannot identify each other. Of course, this is not popular with bidders in open-cry auctions, because bidders will want to be sure that the information they receive about the bids placed by other agents is accurate.

With respect to the honesty or otherwise of the auctioneer, the main opportunity for lying occurs in Vickrey auctions. The auctioneer can lie to the winner about the price of the second highest bid, by overstating it and thus forcing the winner to pay more than they should. One way around this is to 'sign' bids in some way (e.g. through the use of a digital signature), so that the winner can independently verify the value of the second highest bid. Another alternative is to use a trusted third party to handle bids. In open-cry auction settings, there is no possibility for lying by the auctioneer, because all agents can see all other bids; first-price sealed-bid auctions are not susceptible because the winner will know how much they offered.

Another possible opportunity for lying by the auctioneer is to place bogus bidders, known as *shills*, in an attempt to artificially inflate the current bidding price. Shills are only a potential problem in English auctions.

Counterspeculation

Before we leave auctions, there is at least one other issue worth mention *counterspeculation*. This is the process of a bidder engaging in an activ to obtain information either about the true value of the good on offe the valuations of other bidders. Clearly, if counterspeculation was free (i.e. it did not cost anything in terms of time or money) and accurate (i.e. counterspeculation would accurately reduce an agent's uncertainty either about the true value of the good or the value placed on it by other bidders), then every agent would engage in it at every opportunity. However, in most settings, counterspeculation is not free: it may have a time cost and a monetary cost. The time cost will matter in auction settings (e.g. English or Dutch) that depend heavily on the time at which a bid is made. Similarly, investing money in counterspeculation will only be worth it if, as a result, the bidder can expect to be no worse off than if it did not counterspeculate. In deciding whether to speculate, there is clearly a tradeoff to be made, balancing the potential gains of counterspeculation against the costs (money and time) that it will entail. (It is worth mentioning that counterspeculation can be thought of as a kind of meta-level reasoning, and the nature of these tradeoffs is thus very similar to that of the tradeoffs discussed in practical reasoning agents as discussed in earlier chapters.)

7.3 Negotiation

Auctions are a very useful techniques for allocating goods to agents. However, they are too simple for many settings: they are *only* concerned with the allocation of goods. For more general settings, where agents must reach agreements on matters of mutual interest, richer techniques for reaching agreements are required. *Negotiation* is the generic name given to such techniques. In this section, we will consider some negotiation techniques that have been proposed for use by artificial agents – we will focus on the work of Rosenschein and Zlotkin (1994). One of the most important contributions of their work was to introduce a distinction between different types of negotiation domain: in particular, they distinguished between *task-oriented domains* and *worth-oriented domains*.

Before we start to discuss this work, however, it is worth saying a few words about negotiation techniques in general. In general, any negotiation setting will have four different components.

- A negotiation set, which represents the space of possible proposals that agents can make.
- A protocol, which defines the legal proposals that agents can make, as a function of prior negotiation history.
- A collection of strategies, one for each agent, which determine what proposals the agents will make. Usually, the strategy that an agent plays is *private*:

the fact that an agent is using a particular strategy is not generally visible to other negotiation participants (although most negotiation settings are 'open cry', in the sense that the actual proposals that are made *are* seen by all participants).

· A rule that determines when a deal has been struck, and what this agreement deal is.

Negotiation usually proceeds in a series of rounds, with every agent making a proposal at every round. The proposals that agents make are defined by their strategy, must be drawn from the negotiation set, and must be legal, as defined by the protocol. If agreement is reached, as defined by the agreement rule, then negotiation terminates with the agreement deal.

These four parameters lead to an extremely rich and complex environment for analysis.

The first attribute that may complicate negotiation is where *multiple issues* are involved. An example of a single-issue negotiation scenario might be where two agents were negotiating only the price of a particular good for sale. In such a scenario, the preferences of the agents are symmetric, in that a deal which is more preferred from one agent's point of view is guaranteed to be less preferred from the other's point of view, and vice versa. Such symmetric scenarios are simple to analyse because it is always obvious what represents a concession: in order for the seller to concede, he must lower the price of his proposal, while for the buyer to concede, he must raise the price of his proposal. In *multiple-issue* negotiation scenarios, agents negotiate over not just the value of a single attribute, but over the values of multiple attributes, which may be interrelated. For example, when buying a car, price is not the only issue to be negotiated (although it may be the dominant one). In addition, the buyer might be interested in the length of the guarantee, the terms of after-sales service, the extras that might be included such as air conditioning, stereos, and so on. In multiple-issue negotiations, it is usually much less obvious what represents a true concession: it is not simply the case that all attribute values must be either increased or decreased. (Salesmen in general, and car salesmen in particular, often exploit this fact during negotiation by making 'concessions' that are in fact no such thing.)

Multiple attributes also lead to an exponential growth in the space of possible deals. Let us take an example of a domain in which agents are negotiating over the value of n Boolean variables, $v_1, \ldots, v_n$. A deal in such a setting consists of an assignment of either true or false to each variable v_i. Obviously, there are 2^n possible deals in such a domain. This means that, in attempting to decide what proposal to make next, it will be entirely unfeasible for an agent to explicitly consider every possible deal in domains of moderate size. Most negotiation domains are, of course, much more complex than this. For example, agents may need to negotiate about the value of attributes where these attributes can have m possible values, leading to a set of m^n possible deals. Worse, the objects of negotiation may be individually very complex indeed. In real-world negotiation settings – such as labour disputes or (to pick a rather extreme example) the kind of negotiation that, at the time of writing, was still going on with respect to the political future of Northern Ireland, there are not only many attributes, but the value of these attributes may be laws, procedures, and the like.

The negotiation participants may even have difficulty reaching agreement on what the attributes under negotiation actually are – a rather depressing real-world example, again from Northern Ireland, is whether or not the decommissioning of paramilitary weapons should be up for negotiation. At times, it seems that the different sides in this long-standing dispute have simultaneously had different beliefs about whether decommissioning was up for negotiation or not.

Another source of complexity in negotiation is the number of agents involved in the process, and the way in which these agents interact. There are three obvious possibilities.

One-to-one negotiation. In which one agent negotiates with just one other agent. A particularly simple case of one-to-one negotiation is that where the agents involved have symmetric preferences with respect to the possible deals. An example from everyday life would be the type of negotiation we get involved in when discussing terms with a car salesman. We will see examples of such symmetric negotiation scenarios later.

Many-to-one negotiation. In this setting, a single agent negotiates with a number of other agents. Auctions, as discussed above, are one example of many-to-one negotiation. For the purposes of analysis, many-to-one negotiations can often be treated as a number of concurrent one-to-one negotiations.

Many-to-many negotiation. In this setting, many agents negotiate with many other agents simultaneously. In the worst case, where there are n agents involved in negotiation in total, this means there can be up to $n(n-1)/2$ negotiation threads. Clearly, from an analysis point of view, this makes such negotiations hard to handle.

For these reasons, most attempts to automate the negotiation process have focused on rather simple settings. Single-issue, symmetric, one-to-one negotiation is the most commonly analysed, and it is on such settings that I will mainly focus.

7.3.1 Task-oriented domains

The first type of negotiation domains we shall consider in detail are the *task-oriented domains* of Rosenschein and Zlotkin (1994, pp. 29–52). Consider the following example.

magine that you have three children, each of whom needs to be deliv-
red to a different school each morning. Your neighbour has four children, and also needs to take them to school. Delivery of each child
can be modelled as an indivisible task. You and your neighbour can
discuss the situation, and come to an agreement that it is better for
both of you (for example, by carrying the other's child to a shared destination, saving him the trip). There is no concern about being able to
achieve your task by yourself. The worst that can happen is that you
and your neighbour will not come to an agreement about setting up
a car pool, in which case you are no worse off than if you were alone.
You can only benefit (or do no worse) from your neighbour's tasks.

Assume, though, that one of my children and one of my neighbours'
children both go to the same school (that is, the cost of carrying out
these two deliveries, or two tasks, is the same as the cost of carrying
out one of them). It obviously makes sense for both children to be
taken together, and only my neighbour or I will need to make the trip
to carry out both tasks.

What kinds of agreement might we reach? We might decide that I will
take the children on even days each month, and my neighbour will
take them on odd days; perhaps, if there are other children involved,
we might have my neighbour always take those two specific children,
while I am responsible for the rest of the children.

(Rosenschein and Zlotkin, 1994, p. 29)

To formalize this kind of situation, Rosenschein and Zlotkin defined the notion
of a *task-oriented domain* (TOD). A task-oriented domain is a triple

$$\langle T, Ag, c \rangle,$$

where

- T is the (finite) set of all possible tasks;
- $Ag = \{1, \ldots, n\}$ is the (finite) set of negotiation participant agents;
- $c : \wp(T) \to \mathbb{R}^+$ is a function which defines the *cost* of executing each subset
  of tasks: the cost of executing any set of tasks is a positive real number.

The cost function must satisfy two constraints. First, it must be *monotonic*. Intuitively, this means that adding tasks never decreases the cost. Formally, this constraint is defined as follows:

If $T_1, T_2 \subseteq T$ are sets of tasks such that $T_1 \subseteq T_2$, then $c(T_1) \leqslant c(T_2)$.

The second constraint is that the cost of doing nothing is zero, i.e. $c(\varnothing) = 0$.

An *encounter* within a task-oriented domain $\langle T, Ag, c \rangle$ occurs when the agents
Ag are assigned tasks to perform from the set T. Intuitively, when an encounter

occurs, there is potential for the agents to reach a deal by reallocating the tasks amongst themselves; as we saw in the informal car pool example above, by reallocating the tasks, the agents can potentially do better than if they simply performed their tasks themselves. Formally, an encounter in a TOD $\langle T, Ag, c \rangle$ is a collection of tasks

$$\langle T_1, \ldots, T_n \rangle,$$

where, for all i, we have that $i \in Ag$ and $T_i \subseteq T$. Notice that a TOD together with an encounter in this TOD is a type of *task environment*, of the kind we saw in Chapter 2. It defines both the characteristics of the environment in which the agent must operate, together with a task (or rather, set of tasks), which the agent must carry out in the environment.

Hereafter, we will restrict our attention to one-to-one negotiation scenarios, as discussed above: we will assume the two agents in question are $\{1, 2\}$. Now, given an encounter $\langle T_1, T_2 \rangle$, a *deal* will be very similar to an encounter: it will be an allocation of the tasks $T_1 \cup T_2$ to the agents 1 and 2. Formally, a pure deal is a pair $\langle D_1, D_2 \rangle$ where $D_1 \cup D_2 = T_1 \cup T_2$. The semantics of a deal $\langle D_1, D_2 \rangle$ is that agent 1 is committed to performing tasks D_1 and agent 2 is committed to performing tasks D_2.

The *cost* to agent i of a deal $\delta = \langle D_1, D_2 \rangle$ is defined to be $c(D_i)$, and will be denoted $cost_i(\delta)$. The *utility* of a deal δ to an agent i is the difference between the cost of agent i doing the tasks T_i that it was originally assigned in the encounter, and the cost $cost_i(\delta)$ of the tasks it is assigned in δ:

$$utility_i(\delta) = c(T_i) - cost_i(\delta).$$

Thus the utility of a deal represents how much the agent has to gain from the deal; if the utility is negative, then the agent is *worse off* than if it simply performed the tasks it was originally allocated in the encounter.

What happens if the agents *fail* to reach agreement? In this case, they must perform the tasks $\langle T_1, T_2 \rangle$ that they were originally allocated. This is the intuition behind the terminology that the *conflict deal*, denoted Θ, is the deal $\langle T_1, T_2 \rangle$ consisting of the tasks originally allocated.

The notion of *dominance*, as discussed in the preceding chapter, can be easily extended to deals. A deal δ_1 is said to dominate deal δ_2 (written $\delta_1 \succ \delta_2$) if and only if the following hold.

(1) Deal δ_1 is at least as good for every agent as δ_2:

$$\forall i \in \{1, 2\}, utility_i(\delta_1) \geqslant utility_i(\delta_2).$$

(2) Deal δ_1 is better for some agent than δ_2:

$$\exists i \in \{1, 2\}, utility_i(\delta_1) > utility_i(\delta_2).$$

If deal δ_1 dominates another deal δ_2, then it should be clear to all participants that δ_1 is better than δ_2. That is, all 'reasonable' participants would prefer δ_1 to

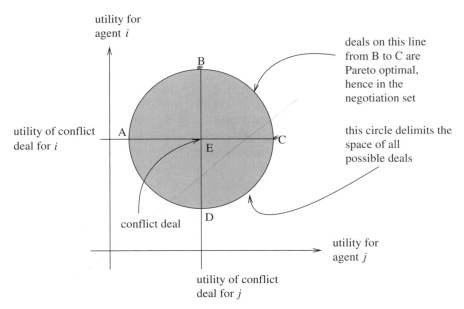

Figure 7.1   The negotiation set.

δ_2. Deal δ_1 is said to weakly dominate δ_2 (written $\delta_1 \succeq \delta_2$) if at least the first condition holds.

A deal that is not dominated by any other deal is said to be *pareto optimal*. Formally, a deal δ is pareto optimal if there is no deal δ' such that $\delta' \succ \delta$. If a deal is pareto optimal, then there is no alternative deal that will improve the lot of one agent except at some cost to another agent (who presumably would not be happy about it!). If a deal is not pareto optimal, however, then the agents could improve the lot of at least one agent, without making anyone else worse off.

A deal δ is said to be *individual rational* if it weakly dominates the conflict deal. If a deal is *not* individual rational, then at least one agent can do better by simply performing the tasks it was originally allocated – hence it will prefer the conflict deal. Formally, deal δ is individual rational if and only if $\delta \succeq \Theta$.

We are now in a position to define the space of possible proposals that agents can make. The *negotiation set* consists of the set of deals that are (i) individual rational, and (ii) pareto optimal. The intuition behind the first constraint is that there is no purpose in proposing a deal that is less preferable to some agent than the conflict deal (as this agent would prefer conflict); the intuition behind the second condition is that there is no point in making a proposal if an alternative proposal could make some agent better off at nobody's expense.

The intuition behind the negotiation set is illustrated in Figure 7.1. In this graph, the space of all conceivable deals is plotted as points on a graph, with the utility to i on the y-axis, and utility to j on the x-axis. The shaded space enclosed by points

A, B, C, and D contains the space of all possible deals. (For convenience, I have illustrated this space as a circle, although of course it need not be.) The conflict deal is marked at point E. It follows that all deals to the left of the line B–D will not be individual rational for agent j (because j could do better with the conflict deal). For the same reason, all deals below line A–C will not be individual rational for agent i. This means that the negotiation set contains deals in the shaded area B–C–E. However, not all deals in this space will be pareto optimal. In fact, the only pareto optimal deals that are also individual rational for both agents will lie on the line B–C. Thus the deals that lie on this line are those in the negotiation set. Typically, agent i will start negotiation by proposing the deal at point B, and agent j will start by proposing the deal at point C.

The monotonic concession protocol

The protocol we will introduce for this scenario is known as the *monotonic concession protocol* (Rosenschein and Zlotkin, 1994, pp. 40, 41). The rules of this protocol are as follows.

- Negotiation proceeds in a series of rounds.

- On the first round, both agents simultaneously propose a deal from the negotiation set.

- An agreement is reached if the two agents propose deals δ_1 and δ_2, respectively, such that either (i) $utility_1(\delta_2) \geqslant utility_1(\delta_1)$ or (ii) $utility_2(\delta_1) \geqslant utility_2(\delta_2)$, i.e. if one of the agents finds that the deal proposed by the other is at least as good or better than the proposal it made.

  If agreement is reached, then the rule for determining the agreement deal is as follows. If both agents' offers match or exceed those of the other agent, then one of the proposals is selected at random. If only one proposal exceeds or matches the other's proposal, then this is the agreement deal.

- If no agreement is reached, then negotiation proceeds to another round of simultaneous proposals. In round $u + 1$, no agent is allowed to make a proposal that is less preferred by the other agent than the deal it proposed at time u.

- If neither agent makes a concession in some round $u > 0$, then negotiation terminates, with the conflict deal.

It should be clear that this protocol is effectively *verifiable*: it is easy for both parties to see that the rules of the protocol are being adhered to.

Using the monotonic concession protocol, negotiation is guaranteed to end (with or without agreement) after a finite number of rounds. Since the set of possible deals is finite, the agents cannot negotiate indefinitely: either the agents will reach agreement, or a round will occur in which neither agent concedes. However, the protocol does not guarantee that agreement will be reached *quickly*. Since the number of possible deals is $O(2^{|T|})$, it is conceivable that negotiation will continue for a number of rounds exponential in the number of tasks to be allocated.

The Zeuthen strategy

So far, we have said nothing about how negotiation participants might or should behave when using the monotonic concession protocol. On examining the protocol, it seems there are three key questions to be answered as follows.

- What should an agent's first proposal be?
- On any given round, *who should concede*?
- If an agent concedes, then *how much* should it concede?

The first question is straightforward enough to answer: an agent's first proposal should be its most preferred deal.

With respect to the second question, the idea of the Zeuthen strategy is to measure an agent's *willingness to risk conflict*. Intuitively, an agent will be more willing to risk conflict if the difference in utility between its current proposal and the conflict deal is low.

In contrast, if the difference between the agent's current proposal and the conflict deal is high, then the agent has more to lose from conflict and is therefore less willing to risk conflict – and thus should be more willing to concede.

Agent i's willingness to risk conflict at round t, denoted $risk_i^t$, is measured in the following way (Rosenschein and Zlotkin, 1994, p. 43):

$$risk_i^t = \frac{\text{utility } i \text{ loses by conceding and accepting } j\text{'s offer}}{\text{utility } i \text{ loses by not conceding and causing conflict}}.$$

The numerator on the right-hand side of this equation is defined to be the difference between the utility to i of its current proposal, and the utility to i of j's current proposal; the denominator is defined to be the utility of agent i's current proposal. Until an agreement is reached, the value of $risk_i^t$ will be a value between 0 and 1. Higher values of $risk_i^t$ (nearer to 1) indicate that i has less to lose from conflict, and so is more willing to risk conflict. Conversely, lower values of $risk_i^t$ (nearer to 0) indicate that i has more to lose from conflict, and so is less willing to risk conflict.

Formally, we have

$$risk_i^t = \begin{cases} 1 & \text{if } utility_i(\delta_i^t) = 0, \\ \dfrac{utility_i(\delta_i^t) - utility_i(\delta_j^t)}{utility_i(\delta_i^t)} & \text{otherwise.} \end{cases}$$

The idea of assigning risk the value 1 if $utility_i(\delta_i^t) = 0$ is that in this case, the utility to i of its current proposal is the same as from the conflict deal; in this case, i is completely willing to risk conflict by not conceding.

So, the Zeuthen strategy proposes that the agent to concede on round t of negotiation should be the one with the smaller value of risk.

The next question to answer is *how much should be conceded*? The simple answer to this question is *just enough*. If an agent does not concede enough, then on the next round, the balance of risk will indicate that it still has most to lose from conflict, and so should concede again. This is clearly inefficient. On the other hand, if an agent concedes too much, then it 'wastes' some of its utility. Thus an agent should make the *smallest* concession necessary to change the balance of risk – so that on the next round, the other agent will concede.

There is one final refinement that must be made to the strategy. Suppose that, on the final round of negotiation, both agents have *equal* risk. Hence, according to the strategy, both should concede. But, knowing this, one agent can 'defect' (cf. discussions in the preceding chapter) by not conceding, and so benefit from the other. If both agents behave in this way, then conflict will arise, and no deal will be struck. We extend the strategy by an agent 'flipping a coin' to decide who should concede if ever an equal risk situation is reached on the last negotiation step.

Now, given the protocol and the associated strategy, to what extent does it satisfy the desirable criteria for mechanisms discussed at the opening of this chapter? While the protocol does not guarantee success, it does guarantee termination; it does not guarantee to maximize social welfare, but it does guarantee that if agreement is reached, then this agreement will be pareto optimal; it is individual rational (if agreement is reached, then this agreement will be better for both agents than the default, conflict deal); and clearly there is no single point of failure – it does not require a central arbiter to monitor negotiation. With respect to simplicity and stability, a few more words are necessary. As we noted above, the space of possible deals may be exponential in the number of tasks allocated. For example, in order to execute his strategy, an agent may need to carry out $O(2^{|T|})$ computations of the cost function (Rosenschein and Zlotkin, 1994, p. 49). This is clearly not going to be feasible in practice for any realistic number of tasks.

With respect to stability, we here note that the Zeuthen strategy (with the equal risk rule) is in Nash equilibrium, as discussed in the previous chapter. Thus, under the assumption that one agent is using the strategy the other can do no better than use it himself.

> This is of particular interest to the designer of automated agents. It does away with any need for secrecy on the part of the programmer. An agent's strategy can be publicly known, and no other agent designer can exploit the information by choosing a different strategy. In fact, it is desirable that the strategy be known, to avoid inadvertent conflicts.
>
> (Rosenschein and Zlotkin, 1994, p. 46)

An interesting issue arises when one considers that agents need not necessarily be truthful when declaring their tasks in an encounter. By so doing, they can subvert the negotiation process. There are two obvious ways in which an agent can be deceitful in such domains as follows.

Phantom and decoy tasks. Perhaps the most obvious way in which an agent can deceive for personal advantage in task-oriented domains is by pretending to have been allocated a task that it has not been allocated. These are called *phantom* tasks. Returning to the car pool example, above, one might pretend that some additional task was necessary by saying that one had to collect a relative from a train station, or visit the doctor at the time when the children needed to be delivered to school. In this way, the apparent structure of the encounter is changed, so that outcome is in favour of the deceitful agent. The obvious response to this is to ensure that the tasks an agent has been assigned to carry out are *verifiable* by all negotiation participants. In some circumstances, it is possible for an agent to produce an artificial task when asked for it. Detection of such *decoy* tasks is essentially impossible, making it hard to be sure that deception will not occur in such domains. Whether or not introducing artificial tasks is beneficial to an agent will depend on the particular TOD in question.

Hidden tasks. Perhaps counterintuitively, it is possible for an agent to benefit from deception by *hiding* tasks that it has to perform. Again with respect to the car pool example, agent 1 might have two children to take to schools that are close to one another. It takes one hour for the agent to visit both schools, but only 45 minutes to visit just one. If the neighbour, agent 2, has to take a child to one of these schools, then by hiding his task of going to one of these schools, agent 1 can perhaps get agent 2 to take his child, thus improving his overall utility slightly.

Before we leave task-oriented domains, there are some final comments worth making. First, the attractiveness of the monotonic concession protocol and Zeuthen strategy is obvious. They closely mirror the way in which human negotiation seems to work – the assessment of risk in particular is appealing. The Nash equilibrium status of the (extended) Zeuthen strategy is also attractive. However, the computational complexity of the approach is a drawback. Moreover, extensions to $n > 2$ agent negotiation scenarios are not obvious – for the reasons discussed earlier, the technique works best with symmetric preferences. Nevertheless, variations of the monotonic concession protocol are in wide-scale use, and the simplicity of the protocol means that many variations on it have been developed.

7.3.2 Worth-oriented domains

We saw in earlier chapters that there are different ways of defining the task that an agent has to achieve. In task-oriented domains, the task(s) are explicitly defined in the encounter: each agent is given a set of tasks to accomplish, associated with which there is a cost. An agent attempts to minimize the overall cost of accomplishing these tasks. Intuitively, this corresponds to the idea of telling an agent what to do by explicitly giving to it a collection of programs that it should execute. In this section, we will discuss a more general kind of domain, in which the goals of an agent are specified by defining a *worth* function for the possible states of the environment. The goal of the agent is thus implicitly to bring about the state of the environment with the greatest value. How does an agent bring about a goal? We will assume that the collection of agents have available to them a set of *joint plans*. The plans are joint because executing one can require several different agents. These plans transform one state of the environment to another. Reaching agreement involves the agents negotiating not over a distribution of tasks to agents, as in task-oriented domains, but over the collection of joint plans. It is in an agent's interest to reach agreement on the plan that brings about the environment state with the greatest worth.

Formally, a worth-oriented domain (WOD) is a tuple (Rosenschein and Zlotkin, 1994, p. 55)

$$\langle E, Ag, J, c \rangle,$$

where

- E is the set of possible environment states;
- $Ag = \{1, \ldots, n\}$ is the set of possible agents;
- J is the set of possible joint plans; and
- $c : J \times Ag \rightarrow \mathbb{R}$ is a cost function, which assigns to every plan $j \in J$ and every agent $i \in Ag$ a real number which represents the cost $c(j, i)$ to i of executing the plan j.

An *encounter* in a WOD $\langle E, Ag, J, c \rangle$ is a tuple

$$\langle e, W \rangle,$$

where

- $e \in E$ is the *initial* state of the environment; and
- $W : E \times Ag \rightarrow \mathbb{R}$ is a *worth* function, which assigns to each environment state $e \in E$ and each agent $i \in Ag$ a real number $W(e, i)$ which represents the value, or worth, to agent i of state e.

I write plans using the notation $j : e_1 \leadsto e_2$; the intuitive reading of this is that the (joint) plan j can be executed in state e_1, and when executed in this state, will lead to state e_2.

Suppose for the sake of argument that agent i operates alone in an environment that is in initial state e_0. What should this agent do? In this case, it does not need to negotiate – it should simply pick the plan j_{opt}^i such that j_{opt}^i can be executed in state e_0 and, when executed, will bring about a state that maximizes the worth for agent i. Formally, j_{opt}^i will satisfy the following equation (Rosenschein and Zlotkin, 1994, p. 156):

$$j_{opt}^i = \arg \max_{j:e_0 \rightsquigarrow e \in J} W(i, e) - C(j, i).$$

Operating alone, the utility that i obtains by executing the plan j_{opt}^i represents the best it can do. Turning to multiagent encounters, it may at first seem that an agent can do no better than executing j_{opt}, but of course this is not true. An agent can *benefit* from the presence of other agents, by being able to execute joint plans – and hence bring about world states – that it would be unable to execute alone. If there is no joint plan that improves on j_{opt}^i for agent i, and there is no *interaction* between different plans, then negotiation is not individual rational: i may as well work on its own, and execute j_{opt}^i. How might plans interact? Suppose my individual optimal plan for tomorrow involves using the family car to drive to the golf course; my wife's individual optimal plan involves using the car to go elsewhere. In this case, our individual plans interact with one another because there is no way they can both be successfully executed. If plans interfere with one another, then agents have no choice but to negotiate.

It may be fruitful to consider in more detail exactly what agents are negotiating over in WODs. Unlike TODs, agents negotiating over WODs are not negotiating over a single issue: they are negotiating over both the *state* that they wish to bring about (which will have a different value for different agents), and over the *means* by which they will reach this state.

7.4 Argumentation

The game-theoretic approaches to reaching agreement that we have seen so far in this chapter have a number of advantages, perhaps the most important of which are that we can prove some desirable properties of the negotiation protocols we have considered. However, there are several disadvantages to such styles of negotiation (Jennings *et al.*, 2001) as follows.

Positions cannot be justified. When humans negotiate, they *justify* their negotiation stances. For example, if you attempt to sell a car to me, you may justify the price with respect to a list of some of the features that the car has – for example, a particularly powerful engine. In turn, I may justify my proposal for a lower price by pointing out that I intend to use the car for short inner-city journeys, rendering a powerful engine less useful. More generally, negotiating using a particular game-theoretic technique may make it very hard to understand *how* an agreement was reached. This issue is particularly important if we intend to delegate tasks such as buying and selling goods to agents. To see why, suppose you delegate the task of buying a car to your agent: after some time, the agent returns, having purchased a car using your credit card. Reasonably enough, you want to know how agreement was reached: Why did the agent pay *this much* for *this car*? But if the agent cannot explain how the agreement was reached in terms that you can easily understand and relate to, then you may find the agreement rather hard to accept. Notice that simply pointing to a sequence of complex equations *will not* count as an explanation for most people; nor will the claim that 'the agreement was the best for you'. If agents are to act on our behalf in such scenarios, then we will need to be able to trust and relate to the decisions they make.

Positions cannot be changed. Game theory tends to assume that an agent's utility function is fixed and immutable: it does not change as we negotiate. It could be argued that from the point of view of an objective, external, omniscient observer, this is in one sense true. However, from our *subjective, personal* point of view, our preferences certainly *do* change when we negotiate. Returning to the car-buying example, when I set out to buy a car, I may initially decide that I want a car with an electric sun roof. However, if I subsequently read that electric sun roofs are unreliable and tend to leak, then this might well change my preferences.

These limitations of game-theoretic negotiation have led to the emergence of *argumentation-based negotiation* (Sycara, 1989b; Parsons *et al.*, 1998). Put crudely, argumentation in a multiagent context is a process by which one agent attempts to convince another of the truth (or falsity) of some state of affairs. The process involves agents putting forward arguments for and against propositions, together with justifications for the acceptability of these arguments.

The philosopher Michael Gilbert suggests that if we consider argumentation as it occurs between humans, we can identify at least four different modes of argument (Gilbert, 1994) as follows.

(1) Logical mode. The logical mode of argumentation resembles mathematical proof. It tends to be deductive in nature ('if you accept that A and that A implies B, then you must accept that B'). The logical mode is perhaps the paradigm example of argumentation. It is the kind of argument that we generally expect (or at least hope) to see in courts of law and scientific papers.

(2) Emotional mode. The emotional mode of argumentation occurs when appeals are made to feelings, attitudes, and the like. An example is the 'how would you feel if it happened to you' type of argument.

(3) Visceral mode. The visceral mode of argumentation is the physical, social aspect of human argument. It occurs, for example, when one argumentation participant stamps their feet to indicate the strength of their feeling.

(4) Kisceral mode. Finally, the kisceral mode of argumentation involves appeals to the intuitive, mystical, or religious.

Of course, depending on the circumstances, we might not be inclined to accept some of these modes of argument. In a court of law in most western societies, for example, the emotional and kisceral modes of argumentation are not permitted. Of course, this does not stop lawyers trying to use them: one of the roles of a judge is to rule such arguments unacceptable when they occur. Other societies, in contrast, explicitly allow for appeals to be made to religious beliefs in legal settings. Similarly, while we might not expect to see arguments based on emotion accepted in a court of law, we might be happy to permit them when arguing with our children or spouse.

Logic-based argumentation

The logical mode of argumentation might be regarded as the 'purest' or 'most rational' kind of argument. In this subsection, I introduce a system of argumentation based upon that proposed by Fox and colleagues (Fox *et al.*, 1992; Krause *et al.*, 1995). This system works by constructing a series of logical steps (arguments) for and against propositions of interest. Because this closely mirrors the way that human dialectic argumentation (Jowett, 1875) proceeds, this system forms a promising basis for building a framework for dialectic argumentation by which agents can negotiate (Parsons and Jennings, 1996).

In classical logic, an argument is a sequence of inferences leading to a conclusion: we write $\Delta \vdash \varphi$ to mean that there is a sequence of inferences from premises Δ that will allow us to establish proposition φ. Consider the simple database Δ_1 which expresses some very familiar information in a Prolog-like notation in which variables are capitalized and ground terms and predicate names start with small letters:

$$human(Socrates). \qquad \Delta_1$$
$$human(X) \Rightarrow mortal(X).$$

The argument $\Delta_1 \vdash mortal(Socrates)$ may be correctly made from this database because $mortal(Socrates)$ follows from Δ_1 given the usual logical axioms and rules of inference of classical logic. Thus a correct argument simply yields a conclusion which in this case could be paraphrased '$mortal(Socrates)$ is true in the context of $human(Socrates)$ and $human(X) \Rightarrow mortal(X)$'. In the system of argumentation we adopt here, this traditional form of reasoning is extended by explicitly recording those propositions that are used in the derivation. This makes it possible to assess the strength of a given argument by examining the propositions on which it is based.

The basic form of arguments is as follows:

$$Database \vdash (Sentence, Grounds),$$

where

- *Database* is a (possibly inconsistent) set of logical formulae;
- *Sentence* is a logical formula known as the *conclusion*; and

- *Grounds* is a set of logical formulae such that

(1) *Grounds* ⊆ *Database*; and

(2) *Sentence* can be proved from *Grounds*.

The intuition is that *Database* is a set of formulae that is 'agreed' between the agents participating in the argumentation process. This database provides some common ground between the agents. Given this common ground, an agent makes the argument (*Sentence, Grounds*) in support of the claim that *Sentence* is true; the justification for this claim is provided by *Grounds*, which is a set of formulae such that *Sentence* can be proved from it.

Formally, if Δ is a database, then an argument over Δ is a pair (φ, Γ), where φ is a formula known as the conclusion, and $\Gamma \subseteq \Delta$ is a subset of Δ known as the *grounds*, or *support*, such that $\Gamma \vdash \varphi$. We denote the set of all such arguments over database Δ by $\mathcal{A}(\Delta)$, and use $Arg, Arg', Arg_1, \ldots$ to stand for members of $\mathcal{A}(\Delta)$.

Typically an agent will be able to build several arguments for a given proposition, some of which will be in favour of the proposition, and some of which will be against the proposition (in which case they are for its negation). In order to establish whether or not the set of arguments as a whole are in favour of the proposition, it is desirable to provide some means of *flattening* the set of arguments into some measure of how favoured the proposition is. One way of doing this is to attach a numerical or symbolic weight to arguments and then have a flattening function that combines these in a suitable way. However, it is also possible to use the structure of the arguments themselves to determine how good they are.

We can identify two important classes of arguments as follows.

Non-trivial argument. An argument (φ, Γ) is non-trivial if Γ is consistent.

Tautological argument. An argument (φ, Γ) is tautological if $\Gamma = \emptyset$.

The important idea of defeat between arguments is as follows.

Defeat. Let (φ_1, Γ_1) and (φ_2, Γ_2) be arguments from some database Δ. The argument (φ_2, Γ_2) can be defeated in one of two ways. Firstly, (φ_1, Γ_1) *rebuts* (φ_2, Γ_2) if φ_1 attacks φ_2. Secondly, (φ_1, Γ_1) *undercuts* (φ_2, Γ_2) if φ_1 attacks ψ for some $\psi \in \Gamma_2$.

In which attack is defined as follows.

Attack. For any two propositions φ and ψ, we say that φ attacks ψ if and only if $\varphi \equiv \neg\psi$.

Consider the following set of formulae, which extend the example of Δ_1 with information in common currency at the time of Plato:

$$human(Heracles)$$
$$father(Heracles, Zeus)$$
$$father(Apollo, Zeus)$$
$$divine(X) \Rightarrow \neg mortal(X)$$
$$father(X, Zeus) \Rightarrow divine(X)$$
$$\neg(father(X, Zeus) \Rightarrow divine(X)).$$

From this we can build the obvious argument, Arg_1 about $Heracles$,

$$(mortal(Heracles),$$
$$\{human(Heracles), human(X) \Rightarrow mortal(X)\}),$$

as well as a rebutting argument Arg_2,

$$(\neg mortal(Heracles),$$
$$\{father(Heracles, Zeus), father(X, Zeus) \Rightarrow divine(X),$$
$$divine(X) \Rightarrow \neg mortal(X)\}).$$

The second of these is undercut by Arg_3:

$$(\neg(father(X, Zeus) \Rightarrow divine(X)),$$
$$\{\neg(father(X, Zeus) \Rightarrow divine(X))\}).$$

The next step is to define an ordering over argument types, which approximately corresponds to increasing acceptability. The idea is that, when engaged in argumentation, we intuitively recognize that some types of argument are more 'powerful' than others. For example, given database $\Delta = \{p \Rightarrow q, p\}$, the arguments $Arg_1 = (p \vee \neg p, \varnothing)$ and $Arg_2 = (q, \{p \Rightarrow q, p\})$ are both acceptable members of $\mathcal{A}(\Delta)$. However, it is generally accepted that Arg_1 – a tautological argument – is stronger than Arg_2, for the simple reason that it is not possible to construct a scenario in which the conclusion of Arg_1 is false. Any agent that accepted classical propositional logic would have to accept Arg_1 (but an agent that only accepted intuitionistic propositional logic would not). In contrast, the argument for the conclusion of Arg_2 depends on two other propositions, both of which could be questioned.

In fact, we can identify five classes of argument type, which we refer to as A_1 to A_5, respectively. In order of increasing acceptability, these are as follows.

A_1 The class of all arguments that may be made from Δ.

A_2 The class of all non-trivial arguments that may be made from Δ.

A_3 The class of all arguments that may be made from Δ for which there are no rebutting arguments.

A_4 The class of all arguments that may be made from Δ for which there are no undercutting arguments.

A_5 The class of all tautological arguments that may be made from Δ.

There is an order, $\preceq$, over the acceptability classes:

$$A_1(\Delta) \preceq A_2(\Delta) \preceq A_3(\Delta) \preceq A_4(\Delta) \preceq A_5(\Delta),$$

meaning that arguments in higher numbered classes are *more acceptable* than arguments in lower numbered classes. The intuition is that there is less reason for thinking that there is something wrong with them – because, for instance, there is no argument which rebuts them. The idea that an undercut attack is less damaging than a rebutting attack is based on the notion that an undercut allows for another, undefeated, supporting argument for the same conclusion. This is common in the argumentation literature (see, for example, Krause *et al.*, 1995).

In the previous example, the argument

$$(divine(Heracles) \lor \neg divine(Heracles), \varnothing)$$

is in A_5, while Arg_1 and Arg_2 are mutually rebutting and thus in A_2, whereas Arg_4,

$$(\neg mortal(apollo),$$
$$\{father(apollo, Zeus), father(X, Zeus) \Rightarrow divine(X),$$
$$divine(X) \Rightarrow \neg mortal(X)\}),$$

is in A_4. This logic-based model of argumentation has been used in argumentation-based negotiation systems (Parsons and Jennings, 1996; Parsons *et al.*, 1998). The basic idea is as follows. You are attempting to negotiate with a peer over who will carry out a particular task. Then the idea is to argue for the other agent intending to carry this out, i.e. you attempt to convince the other agent of the acceptability of the argument that it should intend to carry out the task for you.

Dialogues and dialogue systems for argumentation

Many authors are concerned with agents that argue with themselves, either to resolve inconsistencies or else to determine which set of assumptions to adopt. In contrast, we are interested in agents that are involved in a *dialogue* with other agents. As we noted above, an agent engages in such a dialogue in order to convince another agent of some state of affairs. In this section, we define the notion of dialogue, and investigate the concept of *winning* an argument. Call the two agents involved in argumentation 0 and 1.

Intuitively, a dialogue is a series of arguments, with the first made by agent 0, the second by agent 1, the third by agent 0, and so on. Agent 0 engages in the dialogue in order to convince agent 1 of the conclusion of the first argument made. Agent 1 attempts to defeat this argument, by either undercutting or rebutting it. Agent 0 must respond to the counter argument if it can, by presenting an argument that defeats it, and so on. (For a concrete example of how this kind of argumentation can be used to solve negotiation problems, see Parsons *et al.* (1998) and Amgoud (1999).)

Each step of a dialogue is referred to as a *move*. A move is simply a pair $\langle Player, Arg \rangle$, where $Player \in \{0, 1\}$ is the agent making the argument, and $Arg \in \mathcal{A}(\Delta)$ is the argument being made. I use m (with decorations: $m, m', \dots$ and so on) to stand for moves.

Formally, a non-empty, finite sequence of moves

$$(m_0, m_1, \dots, m_k)$$

is a *dialogue history* if it satisfies the following conditions.

(1) $Player_0 = 0$

   (the first move is made by agent 0).

(2) $Player_u = 0$ if and only if u is even, $Player_u = 1$ if and only if u is odd

   (the agents take it in turns to make proposals).

(3) If $Player_u = Player_v$ and $u \neq v$ then $Arg_u \neq Arg_v$

   (agents are not allowed to make the same argument twice).

(4) Arg_u defeats Arg_{u-1}.

Consider the following dialogue in which agent 0 starts by making Arg_1 for r:

$$m_0 = (r, \{p, p \Rightarrow q, q \Rightarrow r\}).$$

Agent 1 undercuts this with an attack on the connection between p and q,

$$m_1 = (\neg(p \Rightarrow q), \{t, t \Rightarrow \neg(p \Rightarrow q)\}),$$

and agent 0 counters with an attack on the premise t using Arg_3,

$$m_2 = (\neg t, \{s, s \Rightarrow \neg t\}).$$

A dialogue has *ended* if there are no further moves possible. The *winner* of a dialogue that has ended is the last agent to move. If agent 0 was the last agent to move, then this means that agent 1 had no argument available to defeat 0's last argument. If agent 1 was the last agent to move, then agent 0 had no argument available to defeat 1's last argument. Viewed in this way, argument dialogues can be seen as a game played between proposers and opponents of arguments.

Types of dialogue

Walton and Krabbe (1995, p. 66) suggest a typology of six different modes of dialogues, which are summarized in Table 7.1. The first (type I) involves the 'canonical' form of argumentation, where one agent attempts to convince another of the

Table 7.1   Walton and Krabbe's dialogue types.

Type	Initial situation	Main goal	Participants aim
I. Persuasion	conflict of opinions	resolve the issue	persuade the other
II. Negotiation	conflict of interests	make a deal	get the best for oneself
III. Inquiry	general ignorance	growth of knowledge	find a 'proof'
IV. Deliberation	need for action	reach a decision	influence outcome
V. Information seeking	personal ignorance	spread knowledge	gain or pass on personal knowledge
VI. Eristics	conflict/ antagonism	reaching an accommodation	strike the other party
VII. Mixed	various	various	various

truth of something. Initially, agents involved in persuasion dialogues will have conflicting opinions about some state of affairs. To use a classic, if somewhat slightly morbid example, you may believe the murderer is Alice, while I believe the murderer is Bob. We engage in a persuasion dialogue in an attempt to convince one another of the truth of our positions.

In a persuasion dialogue, the elements at stake are primarily beliefs. In contrast, a negotiation (type II) dialogue directly involves utility. It may involve (as in Rosenschein and Zlotkin's TODs, discussed earlier in the chapter) attempting to reach agreement on a division of labour between us.

An inquiry (type III) dialogue is one that is related to a matter of common interest, where the object of the inquiry is a belief. A public inquest into some event (such as a train crash) is perhaps the best-known example of an inquiry. It takes place when a group of people have some mutual interest in determining something. Notice that the aim of an inquiry is simply to determine facts – what to believe. If the aim of a dialogue is for a group to decide upon a course of action, then the dialogue is a deliberation dialogue. An information-seeking (type V) dialogue is also related to an inquiry, but occurs when an agent attempts to find out something for itself. An eristic (type VI) dialogue occurs when agents have a conflict that they air in public. The aim of such a dialogue may be to reach an accommodation, but need not be. Finally, type VII or mixed dialogues occur when a number of different dialogue types are combined. Most committee meetings are of this kind: different parts of the meeting involve negotiation, deliberation, inquiry, and, frequently, eristic dialogues. Figure 7.2 shows how the type of a dialogue may be determined (Walton and Krabbe, 1995, p. 81).

Abstract argumentation

There is another, more abstract way of looking at arguments than the view we have adopted so far. In this view, we are not concerned with the internal structure of

Figure 7.2   Determining the type of a dialogue.

individual arguments, but rather with the *overall structure* of the argument. We can model such an *abstract argument system* $\mathcal{A}$ as a pair (Dung, 1995):

$$\mathcal{A} = \langle X, \rightarrow \rangle,$$

where

- X is a set of arguments (we are not concerned with exactly *what* members of X are); and
- $\rightarrow \subseteq X \times X$ is a binary relation on the set of arguments, representing the notion of *attack*.

I write $x \rightarrow y$ as a shorthand for $\langle x, y \rangle \in \rightarrow$. The expression $x \rightarrow y$ may be read as

- 'argument x attacks argument y';
- 'x is a counter-example of y'; or
- 'x is an attacker of y'.

Notice that, for the purposes of abstract argument systems, we are not concerned with the contents of the set X, nor are we concerned with 'where the attack relation comes from'. Instead, we simply look at the overall structure of the argument.

Given an abstract argument system, the obvious question is when an argument in it is considered 'safe' or 'acceptable'. Similarly important is the notion of a set of arguments being a 'defendable position', where such a position intuitively represents a set of arguments that are mutually defensive, and cannot be attacked. Such a set of arguments is referred to as being *admissible*.

There are different ways of framing this notion, and I will present just one of them (from Vreeswijk and Prakken, 2000, p. 242). Given an abstract argument system $\mathcal{A} = \langle X, \rightarrow \rangle$, we have the following.

- An argument $x \in X$ is attacked by a set of arguments $Y \subseteq X$ if at least one member of Y attacks x (i.e. if $y \rightarrow x$ for some $y \in X$).

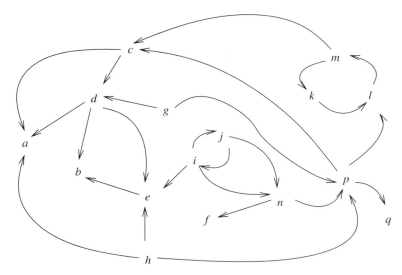

Figure 7.3   An abstract argument system.

- An argument $x \in X$ is *acceptable* (or 'in') with respect to a set of arguments $Y \subseteq X$ if every attacker of x in Y is also attacked.

- A set of arguments Y is *conflict free* if no argument in Y attacks some other argument in Y. A conflict-free set of arguments may be thought of as being in some sense consistent.

- A conflict-free set of arguments Y is *admissible* if each argument in Y is acceptable with respect to Y.

Figure 7.3 (from Vreeswijk and Prakken, 2000, pp. 241, 242) illustrates an abstract argument system. With respect to this example,

- argument h has no attackers, and so is clearly acceptable ('in');

- since h is in, and h attacks a, then a is not an acceptable argument – it is 'out';

- similarly, since h is in, and h attacks p, then p is out; and

- since p is out, and this is the only attacker of q, then q is in.

What of i and j, which attack each other? Well, at least *one* of them must be in, and since they both attack n, then this implies that at least one argument attacks n. Hence n has one undefeated attacker, and so n is out.

Implemented argumentation agents

Several agent systems have been developed which make use of argumentation-based negotiation. Probably the first of these was Sycara's PERSUADER system

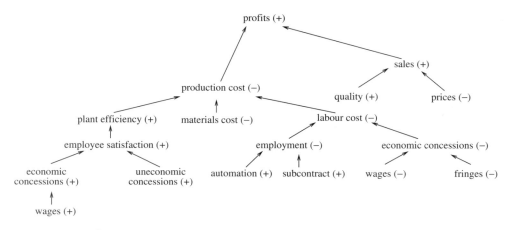

Figure 7.4   Argument structure in the PERSUADER system.

(Sycara, 1989a,b, 1990). PERSUADER operated in the domain of labour negotiation, and involved three agents (a labour union, a company, and a mediator). It modelled the iterative exchange of proposals and counter-proposals in order for the parties to reach agreement. The negotiation involved multiple issues (such as wages, pensions, seniority, and subcontracting).

Argumentation in PERSUADER makes use of a model of each agent's beliefs. An agent's beliefs in PERSUADER capture an agent's goals and the interrelationships among them. An example of an agent's beliefs (from Sycara, 1989b, p. 130) is given in Figure 7.4. This captures the beliefs of a company, the top-level goal of which is to maximize profit. So, for example, a decrease (−) in production costs will lead to an increase (+) in profit; an increase in quality or a decrease in prices will lead to an increase in sales, and so on. Sycara (1989b) gives an example of the following argument, addressed to a labour union that has refused to a proposed wage increase:

> If the company is forced to grant higher wage increases, then it will decrease employment.

To generate this argument, the system determines which goals (illustrated in Figure 7.4) are violated by the union's refusal, and then looks for compensating actions. In this case, a compensating action might be to reduce employment, either by subcontracting or increasing automation. Such a compensating action can violate a goal that the union rates more highly than higher wages. Figure 7.5 illustrates a run of PERSUADER (from Sycara, 1989b, p. 131), showing how the system generates the argument from the belief structure in Figure 7.4.

In general, PERSUADER can generate more than one possible argument for a particular position. These arguments are presented in order of 'severity', with the weakest type of argument first. The order of argument types (weakest first) is as follows (Sycara, 1989b, p. 131):

```
Importance of wage-goal1 is 6 for union1
Searching company1 goal-graph...
Increase in wage-goal1 by company1 will result in
    increase in economic-concessions, labour-cost1, production-cost1
Increase in wage-goal1 by company 1 will result in
    decrease in profits1
To compensate, company1 can decrease fringe-benefits1,
    decrease employment1, increase plant-efficiency1,
    increase sales1
Only decrease fringe-benefits1, decreases employment1
    violate goals of union1
Importance of fringe-benefits1 is 4 for union1
Importance of employment1 is 8 for union1
Since importance of employment1 > importance of wage-goal1
One possible argument found
```

Figure 7.5   PERSUADER generates an argument.

(1) appeal to universal principle;

(2) appeal to a theme;

(3) appeal to authority;

(4) appeal to 'status quo';

(5) appeal to 'minor standards';

(6) appeal to 'prevailing practice';

(7) appeal to precedents as counter-examples;

(8) threaten.

The idea is closely related to the way in which humans use arguments of different 'strength' in argumentation (Gilkinson *et al.*, 1954).

Notes and Further Reading

Despite their obvious advantages, there are a number of problems associated with the use of game theory when applied to negotiation problems.

- Game theory assumes that it is possible to characterize an agent's preferences with respect to possible outcomes. *Humans*, however, find it extremely hard to consistently define their preferences over outcomes – in general, human preferences cannot be characterized even by a simple ordering over outcomes, let alone by numeric utilities (Russell and Norvig, 1995, pp. 75–480). In scenarios where preferences are obvious (such as the case of a person buying a particular CD and attempting to minimize costs), game-theoretic techniques may work well. With more complex (multi-issue) preferences, it is much harder to use them.

- Most game-theoretic negotiation techniques tend to assume the availability of unlimited computational resources to find an optimal solution – they have the characteristics of NP-hard problems. (A well-known example is the problem of winner determination in combinatorial auctions.) In such cases, *approximations* of game-theoretic solutions may be more appropriate.

In writing this chapter, I drew heavily upon Tuomas Sandholm's very useful survey of distributed rational decision making (Sandholm, 1999). Tuomas presents many of the results and discussions in this chapter in a much more formal and rigorous way than I have attempted to do, and provides extensive references and pointers to further reading: his article is recommended for further reading. The negotiation text also drew heavily upon Rosenschein and Zlotkin's influential 1994 book *Rules of Encounter* (Rosenschein and Zlotkin, 1994). This book is essential reading if you wish to gain a more detailed understanding of game-theoretic negotiation techniques. Sarit Kraus presents a short survey of the negotiation literature in Kraus (1997), and an extensive advanced introduction to strategic negotiation in Kraus (2001). Another useful short survey of work on negotiation as applied to electronic commerce is Jennings *et al.* (2001).

Argumentation was originally studied by philosophers and logicians in an attempt to understand the 'informal logic' that humans use to interact with one another (van Eemeren *et al.*, 1996; Walton and Krabbe, 1995). More recently, argumentation has been found to have a number of applications in AI, particularly in decision making (Fox *et al.*, 1992; Krause *et al.*, 1995), the semantics of logic programming (Dung, 1995; Dimpoulos *et al.*, 1999), and defeasible reasoning (Loui, 1987; Pollock, 1992; Pollock, 1994). An excellent survey of work on argumentation was published as Prakken and Vreeswijk (2001), although this does not deal with the subject from the standpoint of multiagent systems. Building largely on the work of Sycara's PERSUADER system, several other agents capable of argumentation have been implemented. An attempt to formalize some of the ideas in PERSUADER using logic and then to implement this formal version was Kraus *et al.* (1998). A number of authors have proposed the use of variations of Walton and Krabbe's dialogue types for multiagent systems (Reed, 1998; Amgoud, 1999; Amgoud *et al.*, 2000).

Class reading: Kraus (1997).   This article provides an overview of negotiation techniques for multiagent systems. It provides a number of pointers into the research literature, and will be particularly useful for mathematically oriented students.

Exercises

(1) **[Class discussion.]**

Pick real-world examples of negotiation with which you are familiar (buying a second-hand car or house, for example). For these, identify what represents a 'deal'. Is the deal single attribute or multiple attribute? Is it a task-oriented domain or a worth-oriented domain? Or neither? Is it two agent or n agent? What represents a concession in such a domain? Is a particular protocol used when negotiating? What are the rules?

(2) **[Level 1.]**

Why are shills not a potential problem in Dutch, Vickrey, and first-price sealed-bid auctions?

(3) **[Level 2.]**

With respect to the argument system in Figure 7.3, state with justification the status of the arguments were not discussed in the text (i.e. a–q).

8

Communication

Communication has long been recognized as a topic of central importance in computer science, and many formalisms have been developed for representing the properties of communicating concurrent systems (Hoare, 1978; Milner, 1989). Such formalisms have tended to focus on a number of key issues that arise when dealing with systems that can interact with one another.

Perhaps the characteristic problem in communicating concurrent systems research is that of *synchronizing* multiple processes, which was widely studied throughout the 1970s and 1980s (Ben-Ari, 1990). Essentially, two processes (cf. agents) need to be synchronized if there is a possibility that they can interfere with one another in a destructive way. The classic example of such interference is the 'lost update' scenario. In this scenario, we have two processes, p_1 and p_2, both of which have access to some shared variable v. Process p_1 begins to update the value of v, by first reading it, then modifying it (perhaps by simply incrementing the value that it obtained), and finally saving this updated value in v. But between p_1 reading and again saving the value of v, process p_2 updates v, by saving some value in it. When p_1 saves its modified value of v, the update performed by p_2 is thus lost, which is almost certainly not what was intended. The lost update problem is a very real issue in the design of programs that communicate through shared data structures.

So, if we do not treat communication in such a 'low-level' way, then how *is* communication treated by the agent community? In order to understand the answer, it is helpful to first consider the way that communication is treated in the object-oriented programming community, that is, communication as method invocation. Suppose we have a Java system containing two objects, o_1 and o_2, and that o_1 has a publicly available method m_1. Object o_2 can communicate with o_1 by invoking method m_1. In Java, this would mean o_2 executing an instruction that looks something like `o1.m1(arg)`, where `arg` is the argument that o_2 wants to communicate to o_1. But consider: which object makes the decision about the execution of method m_1? Is it object o_1 or object o_2? In this scenario, object o_1 has *no control* over the execution of m_1: the decision about whether to execute m_1 lies entirely with o_2.

Now consider a similar scenario, but in an agent-oriented setting. We have two agents i and j, where i has the capability to perform action α, which corresponds loosely to a method. But there is no concept in the agent-oriented world of agent j 'invoking a method' on i. This is because i is an *autonomous agent*: it has control over both its state and its behaviour. It cannot be taken for granted that agent i will execute action α just because another agent j wants it to. Performing the action α may not be in the best interests of agent i. The locus of control with respect to the decision about whether to execute an action is thus very different in agent and object systems.

In general, agents can neither force other agents to perform some action, nor write data onto the internal state of other agents. This does not mean they cannot communicate, however. What they *can* do is perform actions – communicative actions – in an attempt to *influence* other agents appropriately. For example, suppose I say to you 'It is raining in London', in a sincere way. Under normal circumstances, such a communication action is an attempt by me to modify your beliefs. Of course, simply uttering the sentence 'It is raining in London' is not usually enough to bring about this state of affairs, for all the reasons that were discussed above. You have control over your own beliefs (desires, intentions). You may believe that I am notoriously unreliable on the subject of the weather, or even that I am a pathological liar. But in performing the communication action of uttering 'It is raining in London', I am attempting to change your internal state. Furthermore, since this utterance is an action that I perform, I am performing it for some purpose – presumably because I intend that you believe it is raining.

8.1 Speech Acts

Speech act theory treats communication as action. It is predicated on the assumption that speech actions are performed by agents just like other actions, in the furtherance of their intentions.

I begin with an historical overview of speech act theory, focusing in particular on attempts to develop formal theories of speech acts, where communications are modelled as actions that alter the mental state of communication participants.

8.1.1 Austin

The theory of speech acts is generally recognized to have begun with the work of the philosopher John Austin (Austin, 1962). He noted that a certain class of natural language utterances – hereafter referred to as *speech acts* – had the characteristics of *actions*, in the sense that they change the state of the world in a way analogous to physical actions. It may seem strange to think of utterances changing the world in the way that physical actions do. If I pick up a block from a table (to use an overworked but traditional example), then the world has changed in an obvious way. But how does speech change the world? Austin gave as paradigm examples declaring war and saying 'I now pronounce you man and wife'. Stated in the appropriate circumstances, these utterances clearly change the state of the world in a very tangible way[1].

Austin identified a number of *performative verbs*, which correspond to various different types of speech acts. Examples of such performative verbs are *request*, *inform*, and *promise*. In addition, Austin distinguished three different aspects of speech acts: the *locutionary act*, or act of making an utterance (e.g. saying 'Please make some tea'), the *illocutionary act*, or action performed in saying something (e.g. 'He requested me to make some tea'), and *perlocution*, or effect of the act (e.g. 'He got me to make tea').

Austin referred to the conditions required for the successful completion of performatives as *felicity conditions*. He recognized three important felicity conditions.

(1) There must be an accepted conventional procedure for the performative, and the circumstances and persons must be as specified in the procedure.

(2) The procedure must be executed correctly and completely.

(3) The act must be sincere, and any *uptake* required must be completed, insofar as is possible.

8.1.2 Searle

Austin's work was extended by John Searle in his 1969 book *Speech Acts* (Searle, 1969). Searle identified several properties that must hold for a speech act performed between a hearer and a speaker to succeed. For example, consider a *request* by SPEAKER to HEARER to perform ACTION.

(1) Normal I/O conditions. Normal I/O conditions state that HEARER is able to hear the request (thus must not be deaf, etc.), the act was performed in normal circumstances (not in a film or play, etc.), etc.

(2) Preparatory conditions. The preparatory conditions state what must be true of the world in order that SPEAKER correctly choose the speech act. In this case, HEARER must be able to perform ACTION, and SPEAKER must believe that HEARER is able to perform ACTION. Also, it must not be obvious that HEARER will do ACTION anyway.

---

[1]Notice that when referring to the effects of communication, I am ignoring 'pathological' cases, such as shouting while on a ski run and causing an avalanche. Similarly, I will ignore 'microscopic' effects (such as the minute changes in pressure or temperature in a room caused by speaking).

(3) **Sincerity conditions.** These conditions distinguish sincere performances of the request; an insincere performance of the act might occur if SPEAKER did not really want ACTION to be performed.

Searle also attempted a systematic classification of possible types of speech acts, identifying the following five key classes.

(1) **Representatives.** A representative act commits the speaker to the truth of an expressed proposition. The paradigm case is *informing*.

(2) **Directives.** A directive is an attempt on the part of the speaker to get the hearer to do something. Paradigm case: *requesting*.

(3) **Commissives.** Commit the speaker to a course of action. Paradigm case: *promising*.

(4) **Expressives.** Express some psychological state (gratitude for example). Paradigm case: *thanking*.

(5) **Declarations.** Effect some changes in an institutional state of affairs. Paradigm case: *declaring war*.

8.1.3   The plan-based theory of speech acts

In the late 1960s and early 1970s, a number of researchers in AI began to build systems that could plan how to autonomously achieve goals (Allen *et al.*, 1990). Clearly, if such a system is required to interact with humans or other autonomous agents, then such plans must include *speech* actions. This introduced the question of how the properties of speech acts could be represented such that planning systems could reason about them. Cohen and Perrault (1979) gave an account of the semantics of speech acts by using techniques developed in AI planning research (Fikes and Nilsson, 1971). The aim of their work was to develop a theory of speech acts

> ...by modelling them in a planning system as operators defined...in terms of speakers' and hearers' beliefs and goals. Thus speech acts are treated in the same way as physical actions.
>
> (Cohen and Perrault, 1979)

The formalism chosen by Cohen and Perrault was the STRIPS notation, in which the properties of an action are characterized via preconditions and postconditions (Fikes and Nilsson, 1971). The idea is very similar to Hoare logic (Hoare, 1969). Cohen and Perrault demonstrated how the preconditions and postconditions of speech acts such as *request* could be represented in a multimodal logic containing operators for describing the *beliefs*, *abilities*, and *wants* of the participants in the speech act.

Consider the *Request* act. The aim of the *Request* act will be for a speaker to get a hearer to perform some action. Figure 8.1 defines the *Request* act. Two preconditions are stated: the 'cando.pr' (can-do preconditions), and 'want.pr' (want preconditions). The cando.pr states that for the successful completion of the *Request*, two conditions must hold. First, the speaker must believe that the hearer of the *Request* is able to perform the action. Second, the speaker must believe that the hearer also believes it has the ability to perform the action. The want.pr states that in order for the *Request* to be successful, the speaker must also believe it actually wants the *Request* to be performed. If the preconditions of the *Request* are fulfilled, then the *Request* will be successful: the result (defined by the 'effect' part of the definition) will be that the hearer believes the speaker believes it wants some action to be performed.

While the successful completion of the *Request* ensures that the hearer is aware of the speaker's desires, it is not enough in itself to guarantee that the desired action is actually performed. This is because the definition of *Request* only models the illocutionary force of the act. It says nothing of the perlocutionary force. What is required is a *mediating act*. Figure 8.1 gives a definition of *CauseToWant*, which is an example of such an act. By this definition, an agent will come to believe it wants to do something if it believes that another agent believes it wants to do it. This definition could clearly be extended by adding more preconditions, perhaps to do with beliefs about social relationships, power structures, etc.

The *Inform* act is as basic as *Request*. The aim of performing an *Inform* will be for a speaker to get a hearer to believe some statement. Like *Request*, the definition of *Inform* requires an associated mediating act to model the perlocutionary force of the act. The cando.pr of *Inform* states that the speaker must believe φ is true. The effect of the act will simply be to make the hearer believe that the speaker believes φ. The cando.pr of *Convince* simply states that the hearer must believe that the speaker believes φ. The effect is simply to make the hearer believe φ.

8.1.4 Speech acts as rational action

While the plan-based theory of speech acts was a major step forward, it was recognized that a theory of speech acts should be rooted in a more general theory of rational action. This observation led Cohen and Levesque to develop a theory in which speech acts were modelled as actions performed by rational agents in the furtherance of their intentions (Cohen and Levesque, 1990b). The foundation upon which they built this model of rational action was their theory of intention, described in Cohen and Levesque (1990a). The formal theory is summarized in Chapter 12, but, for now, here is the Cohen–Levesque definition of *requesting*, paraphrased in English.

> A request is an attempt on the part of *spkr*, by doing *e*, to bring about a state where, ideally (i) *addr* intends α (relative to the *spkr* still having

Figure 8.1   Definitions from Cohen and Perrault's plan-based theory of speech acts

$Request(S, H, \alpha)$		
Preconditions	Cando.pr	$(S\ BELIEVE\ (H\ CANDO\ \alpha)) \wedge$ $(S\ BELIEVE\ (H\ BELIEVE\ (H\ CANDO\ \alpha)))$
	Want.pr	$(S\ BELIEVE\ (S\ WANT\ requestInstance))$
Effect		$(H\ BELIEVE\ (S\ BELIEVE\ (S\ WANT\ \alpha)))$

$CauseToWant(A_1, A_2, \alpha)$		
Preconditions	Cando.pr	$(A_1\ BELIEVE\ (A_2\ BELIEVE\ (A_2\ WANT\ \alpha)))$
	Want.pr	$\times$
Effect		$(A_1\ BELIEVE\ (A_1\ WANT\ \alpha))$

$Inform(S, H, \varphi)$		
Preconditions	Cando.pr	$(S\ BELIEVE\ \varphi)$
	Want.pr	$(S\ BELIEVE\ (S\ WANT\ informInstance))$
Effect		$(H\ BELIEVE\ (S\ BELIEVE\ \varphi))$

$Convince(A_1, A_2, \varphi)$		
Preconditions	Cando.pr	$(A_1\ BELIEVE\ (A_2\ BELIEVE\ \varphi))$
	Want.pr	$\times$
Effect		$(A_1\ BELIEVE\ \varphi)$

that goal, and $addr$ still being helpfully inclined to $spkr$), and (ii) $addr$ actually eventually does α, or at least brings about a state where $addr$ believes it is mutually believed that it wants the ideal situation.

(Cohen and Levesque, 1990b, p. 241)

8.2   Agent Communication Languages

As I noted earlier, speech act theories have directly informed and influenced a number of languages that have been developed specifically for agent communication. In the early 1990s, the US-based DARPA-funded Knowledge Sharing Effort (KSE) was formed, with the remit of [developing] protocols for the exchange of represented knowledge between autonomous information systems.

(Finin *et al.*, 1993)

The KSE generated two main deliverables as follows.

• The *Knowledge Query and Manipulation Language* (KQML). KQML is an 'outer' language for agent communication. It defines an 'envelope' format for messages, using which an agent can explicitly state the intended illocutionary force of a message. KQML is not concerned with the *content* part of messages (Patil *et al.*, 1992; Mayfield *et al.*, 1996).

• The *Knowledge Interchange Format* (KIF). KIF is a language explicitly intended to allow the representation of knowledge about some particular 'domain of discourse'. It was intended primarily (though not uniquely) to form the content parts of KQML messages.

8.2.1 KIF

I will begin by describing the Knowledge Interchange Format – KIF (Genesereth and Fikes, 1992). This language was originally developed with the intent of being a common language for expressing properties of a particular domain. It was *not* intended to be a language in which messages themselves would be expressed, but rather it was envisaged that the KIF would be used to express message *content*. KIF is closely based on first-order logic (Enderton, 1972; Genesereth and Nilsson, 1987). (In fact, KIF looks very like first-order logic recast in a LISP-like notation; to fully understand the details of this section, some understanding of first-order logic is therefore helpful.) Thus, for example, by using KIF, it is possible for agents to express

• properties of things in a domain (e.g. 'Michael is a vegetarian' – Michael has the property of being a vegetarian);

• relationships between things in a domain (e.g. 'Michael and Janine are married' – the relationship of marriage exists between Michael and Janine);

• general properties of a domain (e.g. 'everybody has a mother').

In order to express these things, KIF assumes a basic, fixed logical apparatus, which contains the usual connectives that one finds in first-order logic: the binary Boolean connectives `and`, `or`, `not`, and so on, and the universal and existential quantifiers `forall` and `exists`. In addition, KIF provides a basic vocabulary of objects – in particular, numbers, characters, and strings. Some standard functions and relations for these objects are also provided, for example the 'less than' relationship between numbers, and the 'addition' function. A LISP-like notation is also provided for handling lists of objects. Using this basic apparatus, it is possible to *define* new objects, and the functional and other relationships between these objects. At this point, some examples seem appropriate. The following KIF expression asserts that the temperature of m1 is 83 Celsius:

```
(= (temperature m1) (scalar 83 Celsius))
```

In this expression, = is equality: a relation between two objects in the domain; temperature is a function that takes a single argument, an object in the domain (in this case, m1), and scalar is a function that takes two arguments. The = relation is provided as standard in KIF, but both the temperature and scalar functions must be defined.

The second example shows how definitions can be used to introduced new concepts for the domain, in terms of existing concepts. It says that an object is a bachelor if this object is a man and is not married:

```
(defrelation bachelor (?x) :=
   (and (man ?x)
      (not (married ?x))))
```

In this example, ?x is a variable, rather like a parameter in a programming language. There are two relations: man and married, each of which takes a single argument. The := symbol means 'is, by definition'.

The next example shows how relationships between individuals in the domain can be stated – it says that any individual with the property of being a person also has the property of being a mammal:

```
(defrelation person (?x) :=> (mammal ?x))
```

Here, both person and mammal are relations that take a single argument.

8.2.2   KQML

KQML is a message-based language for agent communication. Thus KQML defines a common format for messages. A KQML message may crudely be thought of as an object (in the sense of object-oriented programming): each message has a *performative* (which may be thought of as the class of the message), and a number of *parameters* (attribute/value pairs, which may be thought of as instance variables).

Here is an example KQML message:

```
(ask-one
   :content  (PRICE IBM ?price)
   :receiver stock-server
   :language LPROLOG
   :ontology NYSE-TICKS
)
```

The intuitive interpretation of this message is that the sender is asking about the price of IBM stock. The performative is ask-one, which an agent will use to

Table 8.1 Parameters for KQML messages.

Parameter	Meaning
`:content`	content of the message
`:force`	whether the sender of the message will ever deny the content of the message
`:reply-with`	whether the sender expects a reply, and, if so, an identifier for the reply
`:in-reply-to`	reference to the `:reply-with` parameter
`:sender`	sender of the message
`:receiver`	intended recipient of the message

ask a question of another agent where exactly one reply is needed. The various other components of this message represent its attributes. The most important of these is the `:content` field, which specifies the message content. In this case, the content simply asks for the price of IBM shares. The `:receiver` attribute specifies the intended recipient of the message, the `:language` attribute specifies that the language in which the content is expressed is called LPROLOG (the recipient is assumed to 'understand' LPROLOG), and the final `:ontology` attribute defines the *terminology* used in the message – we will hear more about ontologies later in this chapter. The main parameters used in KQML messages are summarized in Table 8.1; note that different performatives require different sets of parameters.

Several different versions of KQML were proposed during the 1990s, with different collections of performatives in each. In Table 8.2, I summarize the version of KQML performatives that appeared in Finin *et al.* (1993); this version contains a total of 41 performatives. In this table, S denotes the `:sender` of the messages, R denotes the `:receiver`, and C denotes the content of the message.

To more fully understand these performatives, it is necessary to understand the notion of a *virtual knowledge base* (VKB) as it was used in KQML. The idea was that agents using KQML to communicate may be implemented using different programming languages and paradigms – and, in particular, any information that agents have may be *internally* represented in many different ways. No agent can assume that another agent will use the same internal representation; indeed, no actual 'representation' may be present in an agent at all. Nevertheless, for the purposes of communication, it makes sense for agents to treat other agents *as if* they had some internal representation of knowledge. Thus agents *attribute* knowledge to other agents; this attributed knowledge is known as the virtual knowledge base.

Table 8.2   KQML performatives.

Performative	Meaning
achieve	S wants R to make something true of their environment
advertise	S claims to be suited to processing a performative
ask-about	S wants all relevant sentences in R's VKB
ask-all	S wants all of R's answers to a question C
ask-if	S wants to know whether the answer to C is in R's VKB
ask-one	S wants one of R's answers to question C
break	S wants R to break an established pipe
broadcast	S wants R to send a performative over all connections
broker-all	S wants R to collect all responses to a performative
broker-one	S wants R to get help in responding to a performative
deny	the embedded performative does not apply to S (anymore)
delete-all	S wants R to remove all sentences matching C from its VKB
delete-one	S wants R to remove one sentence matching C from its VKB
discard	S will not want R's remaining responses to a query
eos	end of a stream response to an earlier query
error	S considers R's earlier message to be malformed
evaluate	S wants R to evaluate (simplify) C
forward	S wants R to forward a message to another agent
generator	same as a standby of a stream-all
insert	S asks R to add content to its VKB
monitor	S wants updates to R's response to a stream-all
next	S wants R's next response to a previously streamed performative
pipe	S wants R to route all further performatives to another agent
ready	S is ready to respond to R's previously mentioned performative
recommend-all	S wants all names of agents who can respond to C
recommend-one	S wants the name of an agent who can respond to a C
recruit-all	S wants R to get all suitable agents to respond to C
recruit-one	S wants R to get one suitable agent to respond to C
register	S can deliver performatives to some named agent
reply	communicates an expected reply
rest	S wants R's remaining responses to a previously named performative
sorry	S cannot provide a more informative reply
standby	S wants R to be ready to respond to a performative
stream-about	multiple response version of ask-about
stream-all	multiple response version of ask-all
subscribe	S wants updates to R's response to a performative
tell	S claims to R that C is in S's VKB
transport-address	S associates symbolic name with transport address
unregister	the deny of a register
untell	S claims to R that C is *not* in S's VKB

```
Dialogue (a)
(evaluate
  :sender A :receiver B
  :language KIF :ontology motors
  :reply-with q1 :content (val (torque m1)))
(reply
  :sender B :receiver A
  :language KIF :ontology motors
  :in-reply-to q1 :content (= (torque m1) (scalar 12 kgf)))
Dialogue (b)
(stream-about
  :sender A :receiver B
  :language KIF :ontology motors
  :reply-with q1 :content m1)
(tell
  :sender B :receiver A
  :in-reply-to q1 :content (= (torque m1) (scalar 12 kgf)))
(tell
  :sender B :receiver A
  :in-reply-to q1 :content (= (status m1) normal))
(eos
  :sender B :receiver A
  :in-reply-to q1)
```

Figure 8.2 Example KQML Dialogues.

Example KQML dialogues

To illustrate the use of KQML, we will now consider some example KQML dialogues (these examples are adapted from Finin *et al.* (1993)). In the first dialogue (Figure 8.2(a)), agent A sends to agent B a query, and subsequently gets a response to this query. The query is the value of the torque on m1; agent A gives the query the name q1 so that B can later refer back to this query when it responds. Finally, the :ontology of the query is motors – as might be guessed, this ontology defines a terminology relating to motors. The response that B sends indicates that the torque of m1 is equal to 12 kgf – a scalar value.

The second dialogue (Figure 8.2(b)) illustrates a *stream* of messages: agent A asks agent B for everything it knows about m1. Agent B responds with two tell messages, indicating what it knows about m1, and then sends an eos (end of stream) message, indicating that it will send no more messages about m1. The first tell message indicates that the torque of m1 is 12 kgf (as in dialogue (a)); the second tell message indicates that the status of m1 is normal. Note that there is no content to the eos message; eos is thus a kind of meta-message – a message about messages.

```
Dialogue (c)
(advertise
  :sender A
  :language KQML :ontology K10
  :content
    (subscribe
      :language KQML :ontology K10
      :content
        (stream-about
          :language KIF :ontology motors
          :content m1)))
(subscribe
  :sender B :receiver A
  :reply-with s1
  :content
    (stream-about
      :language KIF :ontology motors
      :content m1))
(tell
  :sender A :receiver B
  :in-reply-to s1 :content (= (torque m1) (scalar 12 kgf)))
(tell
  :sender A :receiver B
  :in-reply-to s1 :content (= (status m1) normal))
(untell
  :sender A :receiver B
  :in-reply-to s1 :content (= (torque m1) (scalar 12 kgf)))
(tell
  :sender A :receiver B
  :in-reply-to s1 :content (= (torque m1) (scalar 15 kgf)))
(eos
  :sender A :receiver B
  :in-reply-to s1)
```

Figure 8.3   Another KQML dialogue.

The third (and most complex) dialogue, shown in Figure 8.3, shows how KQML messages themselves can be the content of KQML messages. The dialogue begins when agent A advertises to agent B that it is willing to accept subscriptions relating to m1. Agent B responds by subscribing to agent A with respect to m1. Agent A then responds with sequence of messages about m1; as well as including tell messages, as we have already seen, the sequence includes an untell message, to the effect that the torque of m1 is no longer 12 kgf, followed by a tell message indicating the new value of torque. The sequence ends with an end of stream message.

The take-up of KQML by the multiagent systems community was significant, and several KQML-based implementations were developed and distributed. Despite this success, KQML was subsequently criticized on a number of grounds as follows.

- The basic KQML performative set was rather fluid – it was never tightly constrained, and so different implementations of KQML were developed that could not, in fact, interoperate.

- Transport mechanisms for KQML messages (i.e. ways of getting a message from agent *A* to agent *B*) were never precisely defined, again making it hard for different KQML-talking agents to interoperate.

- The semantics of KQML were never rigorously defined, in such a way that it was possible to tell whether two agents claiming to be talking KQML were in fact using the language 'properly'. The 'meaning' of KQML performatives was only defined using informal, English language descriptions, open to different interpretations. (I discuss this issue in more detail later on in this chapter.)

- The language was missing an entire class of performatives – *commissives*, by which one agent makes a commitment to another. As Cohen and Levesque point out, it is difficult to see how many multiagent scenarios could be implemented without commissives, which appear to be important if agents are to *coordinate* their actions with one another.

- The performative set for KQML was overly large and, it could be argued, rather *ad hoc*.

These criticisms – amongst others – led to the development of a new, but rather closely related language by the FIPA consortium.

8.2.3 The FIPA agent communication languages

In 1995, the Foundation for Intelligent Physical Agents (FIPA) began its work on developing standards for agent systems. The centerpiece of this initiative was the development of an ACL (FIPA, 1999). This ACL is superficially similar to KQML: it defines an 'outer' language for messages, it defines 20 performatives (such as `inform`) for defining the intended interpretation of messages, and it does not mandate any specific language for message content. In addition, the concrete syntax for FIPA ACL messages closely resembles that of KQML. Here is an example of a FIPA ACL message (from FIPA, 1999, p. 10):

```
(inform
    :sender    agent1
    :receiver  agent2
    :content   (price good2 150)
    :language  sl
    :ontology  hpl-auction
)
```

Table 8.3 Performatives provided by the FIPA communication language.

Performative	Passing information	Requesting information	Negotiation	Performing actions	Error handling
accept-proposal			×		
agree				×	
cancel		×		×	
cfp			×		
confirm	×				
disconfirm	×				
failure					×
inform	×				
inform-if	×				
inform-ref	×				
not-understood					×
propagate				×	
propose			×		
proxy				×	
query-if		×			
query-ref		×			
refuse				×	
reject-proposal			×		
request				×	
request-when				×	
request-whenever				×	
subscribe		×			

As should be clear from this example, the FIPA communication language is similar to KQML: the structure of messages is the same, and the message attribute fields are also very similar. The relationship between the FIPA ACL and KQML is discussed in FIPA (1999, pp. 68, 69). The most important difference between the two languages is in the collection of performatives they provide. The performatives provided by the FIPA communication language are categorized in Table 8.3.

Informally, these performatives have the following meaning.

accept-proposal   The accept-proposal performative allows an agent to state that it accepts a proposal made by another agent.

agree   An accept performative is used by one agent to indicate that it has acquiesced to a request made by another agent. It indicates that the sender of the agree message intends to carry out the requested action.

cancel   A cancel performative is used by an agent to follow up to a previous request message, and indicates that it no longer desires a particular action to be carried out.

cfp   A cfp (call for proposals) performative is used to initiate negotiation between agents. The content attribute of a cfp message contains both an action (e.g. 'sell me a car') and a condition (e.g. 'the price of the car is less than US$10 000'). Essentially, it says 'here is an action that I wish to be carried out, and here are the terms under which I want it to be carried out – send me your proposals'. (We will see in the next chapter that the `cfp` message is a central component of *task-sharing* systems such as the *Contract Net*.)

`confirm`   The `confirm` performative allows the sender of the message to confirm the truth of the content to the recipient, where, before sending the message, the sender believes that the recipient is unsure about the truth or otherwise of the content.

`disconfirm`   Similar to `confirm`, but this performative indicates to a recipient that is unsure as to whether or not the sender believes the content that the content is in fact false.

`failure`   This allows an agent to indicate to another agent that an attempt to perform some action (typically, one that it was previously `requested` to perform) failed.

`inform`   Along with `request`, the `inform` performative is one of the two most important performatives in the FIPA ACL. It is the basic mechanism for communicating information. The content of an `inform` performative is a statement, and the idea is that the sender of the `inform` wants the recipient to believe this content. Intuitively, the sender is also implicitly stating that *it* believes the content of the message.

`inform-if`   An `inform-if` implicitly says either that a particular statement is true or that it is false. Typically, an `inform-if` performative forms the content part of a message. An agent will send a `request` message to another agent, with the content part being an `inform-if` message. The idea is that the sender of the `request` is saying 'tell me if the content of the `inform-if` is either true or false'.

`inform-ref`   The idea of `inform-ref` is somewhat similar to that of `inform-if`: the difference is that rather than asking whether or not an expression is true or false, the agent asks for the *value* of an expression.

`not-understood`   This performative is used by one agent to indicate to another agent that it recognized that it performed some action, but did not understand why this action was performed. The most common use of `not-understood` is for one agent to indicate to another agent that a message that was just received was not understood. The content part of a `not-understood` message consists of both an action (the one whose purpose was not understood) and a statement, which gives some explanation of why it was not understood. This performative is the central error-handling mechanism in the FIPA ACL.

propagate The content attribute of a `propagate` message consists of two things: another message, and an expression that denotes a set of agents. The idea is that the recipient of the `propagate` message should send the embedded message to the agent(s) denoted by this expression.

propose This performative allows an agent to make a proposal to another agent, for example in response to a `cfp` message that was previously sent out.

proxy The `proxy` message type allows the sender of the message to treat the recipient of the message as a proxy for a set of agents. The content of a `proxy` message will contain both an embedded message (one that it wants forwarded to others) and a specification of the agents that it wants the message forwarded to.

query-if This performative allows one agent to ask another whether or not some specific statement is true or not. The content of the message will be the statement that the sender wishes to enquire about.

query-ref This performative is used by one agent to determine a specific value for an expression (cf. the `evaluate` performative in KQML).

refuse A `refuse` performative is used by one agent to state to another agent that it will not perform some action. The message content will contain both the action and a sentence that characterizes why the agent will not perform the action.

reject-proposal Allows an agent to indicate to another that it does not accept a `proposal` that was made as part of a negotiation process. The content specifies both the proposal that is being rejected, and a statement that chacterizes the reasons for this rejection.

request The second fundamental performative allows an agent to request another agent to perform some action.

request-when The content of a `request-when` message will be both an action and a statement; the idea is that the sender wants the recipient to carry out the action when the statement is true (e.g. 'sound the bell when the temperature falls below 20 Celsius').

request-whenever Similar to `request-when`, the idea is that the recipient should perform the action *whenever* the statement is true.

subscribe Essentially as in KQML: the content will be a statement, and the sender wants to be notified whenever something relating to the statement changes.

Given that one of the most frequent and damning criticisms of KQML was the lack of an adequate semantics, it is perhaps not surprising that the developers of the FIPA agent communication language felt it important to give a comprehensive formal semantics to their language. The approach adopted drew heavily on Cohen and Levesque's theory of speech acts as rational action (Cohen and Levesque, 1990b), but in particular on Sadek's enhancements to this work (Bretier and Sadek, 1997). The semantics were given with respect to a formal language called SL. This language allows one to represent *beliefs*, *desires*, and *uncertain beliefs* of agents, as well as the actions that agents perform. The semantics of the FIPA ACL map each ACL message to a formula of SL, which defines a constraint that the sender of the message must satisfy if it is to be considered as conforming to the FIPA ACL standard. FIPA refers to this constraint as the *feasibility* condition. The semantics also map each message to an SL-formula that defines the *rational effect* of the action – the 'purpose' of the message: what an agent will be attempting to achieve in sending the message (cf. perlocutionary act). However, in a society of autonomous agents, the rational effect of a message cannot (and should not) be guaranteed. Hence conformance does not require the recipient of a message to respect the rational effect part of the ACL semantics – only the feasibility condition.

As I noted above, the two most important communication primitives in the FIPA languages are `inform` and `request`. In fact, *all* other performatives in FIPA are defined in terms of these performatives. Here is the semantics for `inform` (FIPA, 1999, p. 25):

$$\langle i, inform(j, \varphi) \rangle$$

feasibility precondition: $B_i \varphi \wedge \neg B_i (Bif_j \varphi \vee Uif_j \varphi)$

rational effect: $B_j \varphi.$ (8.1)

The $B_i \varphi$ means 'agent i believes φ'; $Bif \varphi$ means that 'agent i has a definite opinion one way or the other about the truth or falsity of φ'; and $Uif_i \varphi$ means that agent i is 'uncertain' about φ. φ. Thus an agent i sending an *inform* message with content φ to agent j will be respecting the semantics of the FIPA ACL if it believes φ, and it is not the case that it believes of j either that j believes whether φ is true or false, or that j is uncertain of the truth or falsity of φ. If the agent is *successful* in performing the `inform`, then the recipient of the message – agent j – will believe φ.

The semantics of `request` are as follows[2]:

$$\langle i, request(j, \alpha) \rangle$$

feasibility precondition: $B_i Agent(\alpha, j) \wedge \neg B_i I_j Done(\alpha)$

rational effect: $Done(\alpha).$ (8.2)

The SL expression $Agent(\alpha, j)$ means that the agent of action α is j (i.e. j is the agent who performs α); and $Done(\alpha)$ means that the action α has been done. Thus agent i requesting agent j to perform action α means that agent i believes that the agent of α is j (and so it is sending the message to the right agent), and

---

[2]In the interests of comprehension, I have simplified the semantics a little.

agent *i* believes that agent *j* does not currently intend that α is done. The rational effect – what *i* wants to achieve by this – is that the action is done.

One key issue for this work is that of *semantic conformance testing*. The conformance testing problem can be summarized as follows (Wooldridge, 1998). We are given an agent, and an agent communication language with some well-defined semantics. The aim is to determine whether or not the agent respects the semantics of the language whenever it communicates. *Syntactic* conformance testing is of course easy – the difficult part is to see whether or not a particular agent program respects the *semantics* of the language.

The importance of conformance testing *has* been recognized by the ACL community (FIPA, 1999, p. 1). However, to date, little research has been carried out either on how verifiable communication languages might be developed, or on how existing ACLs might be verified. One exception is (my) Wooldridge (1998), where the issue of conformance testing is discussed from a formal point of view: I point out that ACL semantics are generally developed in such a way as to express *constraints* on the senders of messages. For example, the constraint imposed by the semantics of an 'inform' message might state that the sender believes the message content. This constraint can be viewed as a *specification*. Verifying that an agent respects the semantics of the agent communication language then reduces to a conventional program verification problem: show that the agent sending the message satisfies the specification given by the communication language semantics. But to solve this verification problem, we would have to be able to talk about the mental states of agents – what they believed, intended and so on. Given an agent implemented in (say) Java, it is not clear how this might be done.

8.3 Ontologies for Agent Communication

One issue that I have rather glossed over until now has been that of *ontologies*. The issue of ontologies arises for the following reason. If two agents are to communicate about some domain, then it is necessary for them to agree on the *terminology* that they use to describe this domain. For example, imagine an agent is buying a particular engineering item (nut or bolt) from another agent: the buyer needs to be able to unambiguously specify to the seller the desired properties of the item, such as its size. The agents thus need to be able to agree both on what 'size' means, and also what terms like 'inch' or 'centimetre' mean. An *ontology* is thus a specification of a set of terms as follows.

> An ontology is a formal definition of a body of knowledge. The most typical type of ontology used in building agents involves a structural component. Essentially a taxonomy of class and subclass relations coupled with definitions of the relationships between these things.
>
> (Jim Hendler)

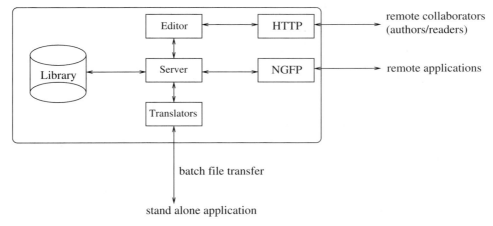

Figure 8.4   Architecture of the Ontolingua server.

In fact, we have already seen an example of a language for defining ontologies: KIF (Genesereth and Fikes, 1992). By using KIF, we can declaratively express the properties of a domain and the relationships between the things in this domain. As KIF was not primarily intended as a language for use by humans, but for processing by computers, software tools were developed that allow a user to develop KIF ontologies – of these, the best known is the Ontolingua server (Farquhar *et al.*, 1997). The Ontolingua server is a Web-based service that is intended to provide a common platform in which ontologies developed by different groups can be shared, and perhaps a common view of these ontologies achieved.

The structure of the Ontolingua server is illustrated in Figure 8.4. The central component is a library of ontologies, expressed in the Ontolingua ontology definition language (based on KIF). A server program provides access to this library. The library may be accessed through the server in several different ways: either by editing it directly (via a Web-based interface), or by programs that contact the server remotely via the NGFP interface. The Ontolingua server was as capable of automatically transforming ontologies expressed in one format to a variety of others (e.g. the CORBA Interface Definition Language – IDL).

As I noted above, KIF is very closely based on first-order logic, which gives it a clean, well-understood semantics, and in addition means that it is extremely expressive (with sufficient ingenuity, pretty much any kind of knowledge can be expressed in first-order logic). However, many other languages and tools have been developed for expressing ontologies. Perhaps the most important of these at the time of writing is the Xtensible Markup Language (XML, 2001) and its close relative, the DARPA Agent Markup Language (DAML, 2001). To understand how XML and DAML came about, it is necessary to look at the history of the Web. The Web essentially comprises two things: a protocol (HTTP), which provides a common set of rules for enabling Web servers and clients to communicate with one another, and a format for documents called (as I am sure you know!) the Hypertext Markup Language (HTML). Now HTML essentially defines a grammar for interspersing documents with *markup commands*. Most of these markup commands relate to document layout, and thus give indications to a Web browser of how to display a document: which parts of the document should be treated as section headers, emphasized text, and so on. Of course, markup is not restricted to layout information: programs, for example in the form of JavaScript code, can also be attached. The grammar of HTML is defined by a *Document Type Declaration* (DTD). A DTD can be thought of as being analogous to the formal grammars used to define the syntax of programming languages. The HTML DTD thus defines what constitutes a syntactically acceptable HTML document. A DTD is in fact itself expressed in a formal language – the Standard Generalized Markup Language (SGML, 2001). SGML is essentially a language for defining other languages.

Now, to all intents and purposes, the HTML standard is fixed, in the sense that you cannot arbitrarily introduce tags and attributes into HTML documents that were not defined in the HTML DTD. But this severely limits the usefulness of the Web. To see what I mean by this, consider the following example. An e-commerce company selling CDs wishes to put details of its prices on its Web page. Using conventional HTML techniques, a Web page designer can only markup the document with layout information (see, for example, Figure 8.5(a)). But this means that a Web browser – or indeed any program that looks at documents on the Web – has no way of knowing which parts of the document refer to the titles of CDs, which refer to their prices, and so on. Using XML it is possible to define *new* markup tags – and so, in essence, to extend HTML. To see the value of this, consider Figure 8.5(b), which shows the same information as Figure 8.5(a), expressed using new tags (`catalogue`, `product`, and so on) that were defined using XML. Note that new tags such as these cannot be arbitrarily introduced into HTML documents: they must be defined. The way they are defined is by writing an XML DTD: thus XML, like SGML, is a language for defining languages. (In fact, XML is a subset of SGML.)

I hope it is clear that a computer program would have a much easier time *understanding the meaning* of Figure 8.5(b) than Figure 8.5(a). In Figure 8.5(a), there is nothing to help a program understand which part of the document refers to the price of the product, which refers to the title of the product, and so on. In contrast, Figure 8.5(b) makes all this explicit.

XML was developed to answer one of the longest standing critiques of the Web: the lack of *semantic markup*. Using languages like XML, it becomes possible to add information to Web pages in such a way that it becomes easy for computers not simply to display it, but to process it in meaningful ways. This idea led Tim Berners-Lee, widely credited as the inventor of the Web, to develop the idea of the *semantic Web*.

```
(a) Plain HTML

<ul>
    <li><em>Music</em>,
        <b>Madonna<b>,
        USD12<br><p>
    <li><em>Get Ready</em>,
        <b>New Order</b>,
        USD14<br><p>
</ul>

(b) XML

<catalogue>
    <product type="CD">
        <title>Music</title>
        <artist>Madonna</artist>
        <price currency="USD">12</price>
    </product>
    <product type="CD">
        <title>Get Ready</title>
        <artist>New Order</artist>
        <price currency="USD">14</price>
    </product>
</catalogue>
```

Figure 8.5 Plain HTML versus XML.

I have a dream for the Web [in which computers] become capable of analysing all the data on the Web – the content, links, and transactions between people and computers. A 'Semantic Web', which should make this possible, has yet to emerge, but when it does, the day-to-day mechanisms of trade, bureaucracy and our daily lives will be handled by machines talking to machines. The 'intelligent agents' people have touted for ages will finally materialise.

(Berners-Lee, 1999, pp. 169, 170)

In an attempt to realize this vision, work has begun on several languages and tools – notably the Darpa Agent Markup Language (DAML, 2001), which is based on XML. A fragment of a DAML ontology and knowledge base (from the DAML version of the CIA world fact book (DAML, 2001)) is shown in Figure 8.6.

8.4 Coordination Languages

One of the most important precursors to the development of multiagent systems was the blackboard model (Engelmore and Morgan, 1988). Initially developed as part of the Hearsay speech understanding project, the blackboard model proposes

```
<rdf:Description rdf:ID="UNITED-KINGDOM">
    <rdf:type rdf:resource="GEOREF"/>
    <HAS-TOTAL-AREA>
        (* 244820 Square-Kilometer)
    </HAS-TOTAL-AREA>
    <HAS-LAND-AREA>
        (* 241590 Square-Kilometer)
    </HAS-LAND-AREA>
    <HAS-COMPARATIVE-AREA-DOC>
        slightly smaller than Oregon
    </HAS-COMPARATIVE-AREA-DOC>
    <HAS-BIRTH-RATE>
        13.18
    </HAS-BIRTH-RATE>
    <HAS-TOTAL-BORDER-LENGTH>
        (* 360 Kilometer)
    </HAS-TOTAL-BORDER-LENGTH>
    <HAS-BUDGET-REVENUES>
        (* 3.255E11 Us-Dollars)
    </HAS-BUDGET-REVENUES>
    <HAS-BUDGET-EXPENDITURES>
        (* 4.009E11 Us-Dollars)
    </HAS-BUDGET-EXPENDITURES>
    <HAS-BUDGET-CAPITAL-EXPENDITURES>
        (* 3.3E10 Us-Dollars)
    </HAS-BUDGET-CAPITAL-EXPENDITURES>
    <HAS-CLIMATE-DOC>
        more than half of the days are overcast
    </HAS-CLIMATE-DOC>
    <HAS-COASTLINE-LENGTH>
        (* 12429 Kilometer)
    </HAS-COASTLINE-LENGTH>
    <HAS-CONSTITUTION-DOC>
        unwritten; partly statutes, partly common law
    </HAS-CONSTITUTION-DOC>
</rdf:Description>
```

Figure 8.6 Some facts about the UK, expressed in DAML.

that group problem solving proceeds by a group of 'knowledge sources' (agents) observing a shared data structure known as a blackboard: problem solving proceeds as these knowledge sources contribute partial solutions to the problem. In the 1980s, an interesting variation on the blackboard model was proposed within the programming language community. This variation was called Linda (Gelernter, 1985; Carriero and Gelernter, 1989).

Strictly speaking, Linda is not a programming language. It is the generic name given to a collection of programming language constructs, which can be used to implement blackboard-like systems. The core of the Linda model – corresponding loosely to a blackboard – is the *tuple space*. A tuple space is a shared data structure, the components of which are *tagged tuples*. Here is an example of a tagged tuple:

$$\langle \text{"person"}, \text{"mjw"}, 35 \rangle.$$

A tuple may be thought of as a list of data elements. The first of these is the *tag* of the tuple, which corresponds loosely to a class in object-oriented programming. In the example above, the tag is 'person', suggesting that this tuple records information about a person. The remainder of the elements in the tuple are data values.

Processes (agents) who can see the tuple space can access it via three instructions (Table 8.4). The out operation is the simplest: the expressions that are parameters to the operation are evaluated in turn, and the tagged tuple that results is deposited into the tuple space. The in and out operations allow a process to access the tuple space. The idea of the in operation is that the parameters to it may either be expressions or parameters of the form ?v, where v is a variable name. When an instruction

```
in("tag", field1, ..., fieldN)
```

is executed, then each of the expressions it contains is evaluated in turn. When this is done, the process that is executing the instruction waits (*blocks*) until a *matching* tuple is in the tuple space. For example, suppose that the tuple space contained the single person tuple above, and that a process attempted to execute the following instruction:

```
in("person", "mjw", ?age).
```

Then this operation would succeed, and the variable age would subsequently have the value 35. If, however, a process attempted to execute the instruction

```
in("person", "sdp", ?age),
```

then the process would block until a tuple whose tag was "person" and whose first data element was "sdp" appeared in the tuple space. (If there is more than one matching tuple in the tuple space, then one is selected at random.)

The rd operation is essentially the same as in except that it does not remove the tuple from the tuple space – it simply copies the data elements into fields.

Despite its simplicity, Linda turns out be a very simple and intuitive language for developing complex distributed applications that must be coordinated with one another.

Notes and Further Reading

The problems associated with communicating concurrent systems have driven a significant fraction of research into theoretical computer science since the early

Table 8.4   Operations for manipulating Linda tuple spaces.

Operation	Meaning
`out("tag", expr1, ..., exprN)`	evaluate `expr1,...,exprN` and deposit resulting tuple in tuple space
`in("tag", field1, ..., fieldN)`	wait until matching tuple occupies tuple space, then remove it, copying its values into fields
`rd("tag", field1, ..., fieldN)`	wait until matching tuple occupies tuple space, then copy its values into fields

1980s. Two of the best-known formalisms developed in this period are Tony Hoare's Communicating Sequential Processes (CSPs) (Hoare, 1978), and Robin Milner's Calculus of Communicating Systems (CCS) (Milner, 1989). Temporal logic has also been widely used for reasoning about concurrent systems – see, for example, Pnueli (1986) for an overview. A good reference, which describes the key problems in concurrent and distributed systems, is Ben-Ari (1990).

The plan-based theory of speech acts developed by Cohen and Perrault made speech act theory accessible and directly usable to the artificial intelligence community (Cohen and Perrault, 1979). In the multiagent systems community, this work is arguably the most influential single publication on the topic of speech act-like communication. Many authors have built on its basic ideas. For example, borrowing a formalism for representing the mental state of agents that was developed by Moore (1990), Douglas Appelt was able to implement a system that was capable of planning to perform speech acts (Appelt, 1982, 1985).

Many other approaches to speech act semantics have appeared in the literature. For example, Perrault (1990) described how Reiter's default logic (Reiter, 1980) could be used to reason about speech acts. Appelt gave a critique of Perrault's work (Appelt and Konolige, 1988, pp. 167, 168), and Konolige proposed a related technique using hierarchic auto-epistemic logic (HAEL) (Konolige, 1988) for reasoning about speech acts. Galliers emphasized the links between speech acts and AMG belief revision (Gärdenfors, 1988): she noted that the changes in a hearer's state caused by a speech act could be understood as analogous to an agent revising its beliefs in the presence of new information (Galliers, 1991). Singh developed a theory of speech acts (Singh, 1991c, 1993) using his formal framework for representing rational agents (Singh, 1990a,b, 1991a,b, 1994, 1998b; Singh and Asher, 1991). He introduced a predicate $comm(i,j,m)$ to represent the fact that agent i communicates message m to agent j, and then used this predicate to define the semantics of assertive, directive, commissive, and permissive speech acts.

Dignum and Greaves (2000) is a collection of papers on agent communication languages. As I mentioned in the main text of the chapter, a number of KQML implementations have been developed: well-known examples are InfoSleuth (Nodine and Unruh, 1998), KAoS (Bradshaw *et al.*, 1997) and JATLite (Jeon *et al.*, 2000)). Several FIPA implementations have also been developed, of which the Java-based Jade system is probably the best known (Poggi and Rimassa, 2001).

A critique of KIF was published as Ginsberg (1991), while a critique of KQML appears in Cohen and Levesque (1995). A good general survey of work on ontologies (up to 1996) is Uschold and Gruninger (1996). There are many good online references to XML, DAML and the like: a readable published reference is Decker *et al.* (2000). The March/April 2001 issue of *IEEE Intelligent Systems* magazine contained a useful collection of articles on the semantic web (Fensel and Musen, 2001), agents in the semantic Web (Hendler, 2001), and the OIL language for ontologies on the semantic Web (Fensel *et al.*, 2001).

Recently, a number of proposals have appeared for communication languages with a verifiable semantics (Singh, 1998a; Pitt and Mamdani, 1999; Wooldridge, 1999). See Labrou *et al.* (1999) for a discussion of the state of the art in agent communication languages as of early 1999.

Coordination languages have been the subject of much interest by the theoretical computer science community: a regular conference is now held on the subject, the proceedings of which were published as Ciancarini and Hankin (1996). Interestingly, the Linda model has been implemented in the JavaSpaces package (Freeman *et al.*, 1999), making it possible to use the model with Java/JINI systems (Oaks and Wong, 2000).

Class discussion: Cohen and Perrault (1979).   A nice introduction to speech acts and the semantics of speech acts, this paper was hugely influential, and although it was written for a natural language understanding audience, it is easy to make sense of.

Exercises

(1) **[Class discussion.]**

What are the potential advantages and disadvantages of the use of agent communication languages such as KQML or FIPA, as compared with (say) method invocation in object-oriented languages? If you are familiar with distributed object systems like the Java RMI paradigm, then compare the benefits of the two.

(2) **[Level 2.]**

Using the ideas of Cohen and Perrault's plan-based theory of speech acts, as well as the semantics of FIPA's `request` and `inform` performatives, try to give a semantics to other FIPA performatives.

9

Working Together

In the three preceding chapters, we have looked at the basic theoretical principles of multiagent encounters and the properties of such encounters. We have also seen how agents might reach agreements in encounters with other agents, and looked at languages that agents might use to communicate with one another. So far, however, we have seen nothing of how agents can *work together*. In this chapter, we rectify this. We will see how agents can be designed so that they can work together effectively. As I noted in Chapter 1, the idea of computer systems working together may not initially appear to be very novel: the term 'cooperation' is frequently used in the concurrent systems literature, to describe systems that must interact with one another in order to carry out their assigned tasks. There are two main distinctions between multiagent systems and 'traditional' distributed systems as follows.

- Agents in a multiagent system may have been designed and implemented by different individuals, with different goals. They therefore may not share common goals, and so the encounters between agents in a multiagent system more closely resemble *games*, where agents must act strategically in order to achieve the outcome they most prefer.

- Because agents are assumed to be acting autonomously (and so making decisions about what to do *at run time*, rather than having all decisions hardwired in at design time), they must be capable of *dynamically* coordinating their activities and cooperating with others. In traditional distributed and concurrent systems, coordination and cooperation are typically hardwired in at design time.

Working together involves several different kinds of activities, that we will investigate in much more detail throughout this chapter, in particular, the sharing both of tasks and of information, and the dynamic (i.e. run-time) coordination of multiagent activities.

9.1   Cooperative Distributed Problem Solving

Work on *cooperative distributed problem solving* began with the work of Lesser and colleagues on systems that contained agent-like entities, each of which with distinct (but interrelated) expertise that they could bring to bear on problems that the entire system is required to solve:

> CDPS studies how a loosely-coupled network of problem solvers can work together to solve problems that are beyond their individual capabilities. Each problem-solving node in the network is capable of sophisticated problem-solving and can work independently, but the problems faced by the nodes cannot be completed without cooperation. Cooperation is necessary because no single node has sufficient expertise, resources, and information to solve a problem, and different nodes might have expertise for solving different parts of the problem.
>
> (Durfee *et al.*, 1989b, p. 63)

Historically, most work on cooperative problem solving has made the *benevolence* assumption: that the agents in a system implicitly share a common goal, and thus that there is no potential for conflict between them. This assumption implies that agents can be designed so as to help out whenever needed, even if it means that one or more agents must suffer in order to do so: intuitively, all that matters is the *overall* system objectives, not those of the individual agents within it. The benevolence assumption is generally acceptable if all the agents in a system are designed or 'owned' by the same organization or individual. It is important to emphasize that the ability to assume benevolence *greatly* simplifies the designer's task. If we can assume that all the agents need to worry about is the overall utility of the system, then we can design the overall system so as to optimize this.

In contrast to work on distributed problem solving, the more general area of multiagent systems has focused on the issues associated with societies of *self-interested* agents. Thus agents in a multiagent system (unlike those in typical distributed problem-solving systems), cannot be assumed to share a common goal, as they will often be designed by different individuals or organizations in order to represent their interests. One agent's interests may therefore conflict with those of others, just as in human societies. Despite the potential for conflicts of interest, the agents in a multiagent system will ultimately need to cooperate in order to achieve their goals; again, just as in human societies.

Multiagent systems research is therefore concerned with the wider problems of designing societies of autonomous agents, such as why and how agents cooperate (Wooldridge and Jennings, 1994); how agents can recognize and resolve conflicts (Adler *et al.*, 1989; Galliers, 1988b; Galliers, 1990; Klein and Baskin, 1991; Lander *et al.*, 1991); how agents can negotiate or compromise in situations where they are apparently at loggerheads (Ephrati and Rosenschein, 1993; Rosenschein and Zlotkin, 1994); and so on.

It is also important to distinguish CDPS from *parallel* problem solving (Bond and Gasser, 1988, p. 3). Parallel problem solving simply involves the exploitation of parallelism in solving problems. Typically, in parallel problem solving, the computational components are simply processors; a single node will be responsible for *decomposing* the overall problem into sub-components, allocating these to processors, and subsequently assembling the solution. The nodes are frequently assumed to be homogeneous in the sense that they do not have distinct expertise – they are simply processors to be exploited in solving the problem. Although parallel problem solving was synonymous with CDPS in the early days of multiagent systems, the two fields are now regarded as quite separate. (However, it goes without saying that a multiagent system will employ parallel architectures and languages: the point is that the concerns of the two areas are rather different.)

Coherence and coordination

Having implemented an artificial agent society in order to solve some problem, how does one assess the success (or otherwise) of the implementation? What criteria can be used? The multiagent systems literature has proposed two types of issues that need to be considered.

Coherence. Refers to 'how well the [multiagent] system behaves as a unit, along some dimension of evaluation' (Bond and Gasser, 1988, p. 19). Coherence may be measured in terms of solution quality, efficiency of resource usage, conceptual clarity of operation, or how well system performance degrades in the presence of uncertainty or failure; a discussion on the subject of when multiple agents can be said to be acting coherently appears as (Wooldridge, 1994).

Coordination. In contrast, is 'the degree...to which [the agents]...can avoid 'extraneous' activity [such as]...synchronizing and aligning their activities' (Bond and Gasser, 1988, p. 19); in a perfectly coordinated system, agents will not accidentally clobber each other's sub-goals while attempting to achieve a common goal; they will not need to explicitly communicate, as they will be mutually predictable, perhaps by maintaining good internal models of each other. The presence of conflict between agents, in the sense of agents destructively interfering with one another (which requires time and effort to resolve), is an indicator of poor coordination.

It is probably true to say that these problems have been the focus of more attention in multiagent systems research than any other issues (Durfee and Lesser,

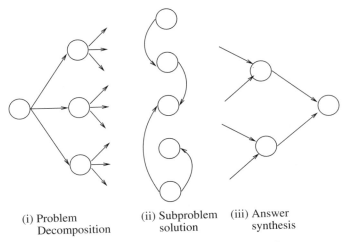

(i) Problem
    Decomposition

(ii) Subproblem
     solution

(iii) Answer
      synthesis

Figure 9.1   The three stages of CDPS.

1987; Durfee, 1988; Gasser and Hill, 1990; Goldman and Rosenschein, 1993; Jennings, 1993a; Weiß, 1993).

The main issues to be addressed in CDPS include the following.

- How can a problem be divided into smaller tasks for distribution among agents?

- How can a problem solution be effectively synthesized from sub-problem results?

- How can the overall problem-solving activities of the agents be optimized so as to produce a solution that maximizes the coherence metric?

- What techniques can be used to coordinate the activity of the agents, so avoiding destructive (and thus unhelpful) interactions, and maximizing effectiveness (by exploiting any positive interactions)?

In the remainder of this chapter, we shall see some techniques developed by the multiagent systems community for addressing these concerns.

9.2   Task Sharing and Result Sharing

How do a group of agents work together to solve problems? Smith and Davis (1980) suggested that the CDPS process can canonically be viewed as a three-stage activity (see Figure 9.1) as follows.

(1) Problem decomposition. In this stage, the overall problem to be solved is decomposed into smaller sub-problems. The decomposition will typically be hierarchical, so that sub-problems are then further decomposed into smaller sub-problems, and so on, until the sub-problems are of an appropriate granularity to be solved by individual agents. The different levels of decomposition will often represent different levels of problem abstraction. For example, consider a (real-world) example of cooperative problem solving, which occurs when a government body asks whether a new hospital is needed in a particular region. In order to answer this question, a number of smaller sub-problems need to be solved, such as whether the existing hospitals can cope, what the likely demand is for hospital beds in the future, and so on. The smallest level of abstraction might involve asking individuals about their day-to-day experiences of the current hospital provision. Each of these different levels in the problem-solving hierarchy represents the problem at a progressively lower level of abstraction.

Notice that the grain size of sub-problems is important: one extreme view of CDPS is that a decomposition continues until the sub-problems represent 'atomic' actions, which cannot be decomposed any further. This is essentially what happens in the ACTOR paradigm, with new agents – ACTORs being spawned for every sub-problem, until ACTORs embody individual program instructions such as addition, subtraction, and so on (Agha, 1986). But this approach introduces a number of problems. In particular, the overheads involved in managing the interactions between the (typically very many) sub-problems outweigh the benefits of a cooperative solution.

Another issue is how to perform the decomposition. One possibility is that the problem is decomposed by one individual agent. However, this assumes that this agent must have the appropriate expertise to do this – it must have knowledge of the *task structure*, that is, how the task is 'put together'. If other agents have knowledge pertaining to the task structure, then they may be able to assist in identifying a better decomposition. The decomposition itself may therefore be better treated as a cooperative activity.

Yet another issue is that task decomposition cannot in general be done without some knowledge of the agents that will eventually solve problems. There is no point in arriving at a particular decomposition that is impossible for a particular collection of agents to solve.

(2) Sub-problem solution. In this stage, the sub-problems identified during problem decomposition are individually solved. This stage typically involves sharing of information between agents: one agent can help another out if it has information that may be useful to the other.

(3) Solution synthesis. In this stage, solutions to individual sub-problems are integrated into an overall solution. As in problem decomposition, this stage may be hierarchical, with partial solutions assembled at different levels of abstraction.

Note that the extent to which these stages are explicitly carried out in a particular problem domain will depend very heavily on the domain itself; in some domains, some of the stages may not be present at all.

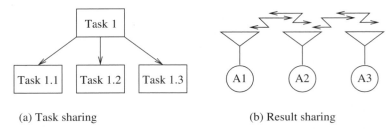

(a) Task sharing   (b) Result sharing

Figure 9.2   (a) Task sharing and (b) result sharing. In task sharing, a task is decomposed into sub-problems that are allocated to agents, while in result sharing, agents supply each other with relevant information, either proactively or on demand.

Given this general framework for CDPS, there are two specific cooperative problem-solving activities that are likely to be present: *task sharing* and *result sharing* (Smith and Davis, 1980) (see Figure 9.2).

Task sharing.   Task sharing takes place when a problem is decomposed to smaller sub-problems and allocated to different agents. Perhaps the key problem to be solved in a task-sharing system is that of how tasks are to be *allocated* to individual agents. If all agents are homogeneous in terms of their capabilities (cf. the discussion on parallel problem solving, above), then task sharing is straightforward: any task can be allocated to any agent. However, in all but the most trivial of cases, agents have very different capabilities. In cases where the agents are really autonomous – and can hence decline to carry out tasks (in systems that do not enjoy the *benevolence* assumption described above), then task allocation will involve agents *reaching agreements* with others, perhaps by using the techniques described in Chapter 7.

Result sharing.   Result sharing involves agents sharing information relevant to their sub-problems. This information may be shared *proactively* (one agent sends another agent some information because it believes the other will be interested in it), or *reactively* (an agent sends another information in response to a request that was previously sent – cf. the subscribe performatives in the agent communication languages discussed earlier).

In the sections that follow, I shall discuss task sharing and result sharing in more detail.

9.2.1   Task sharing in the Contract Net

The Contract Net (CNET) protocol is a high-level protocol for achieving efficient cooperation through task sharing in networks of communicating problem solvers (Smith, 1977, 1980a,b; Smith and Davis, 1980). The basic metaphor used in the CNET is, as the name of the protocol suggests, contracting – Smith took his inspiration from the way that companies organize the process of putting contracts out to tender (see Figure 9.3).

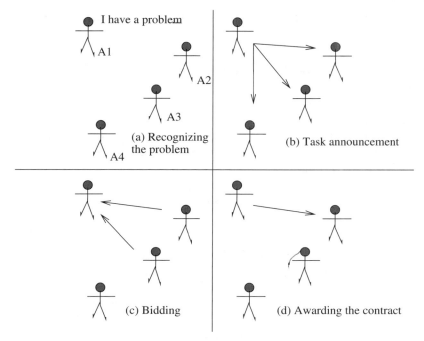

Figure 9.3   The Contract Net (CNET) protocol.

[A] node that generates a task advertises existence of that task to other nodes in the net with a *task announcement*, then acts as the *manager* of that task for its duration. In the absence of any information about the specific capabilities of the other nodes in the net, the manager is forced to issue a *general broadcast* to all other nodes. If, however, the manager possesses some knowledge about which of the other nodes in the net are likely candidates, then it can issue a *limited broadcast* to just those candidates. Finally, if the manager knows exactly which of the other nodes in the net is appropriate, then it can issue a *point-to-point* announcement. As work on the problem progresses, many such task announcements will be made by various managers.

Nodes in the net listen to the task announcements and evaluate them with respect to their own specialized hardware and software resources. When a task to which a node is suited is found, it submits a *bid*. A bid indicates the capabilities of the bidder that are relevant to the execution of the announced task. A manager may receive several such bids in response to a single task announcement; based on the information in the bids, it selects the most appropriate nodes to execute the task. The selection is communicated to the successful bidders through an *award* message. These selected nodes assume responsibility for execution of the task, and each is called a *contractor* for that task.

$$\vdots$$

After the task has been completed, the contractor sends a *report* to the manager. (Smith, 1980b, pp. 60, 61)

[This] normal contract negotiation process can be simplified in some instances, with a resulting enhancement in the efficiency of the protocol. If a manager knows exactly which node is appropriate for the execution of a task, a *directed contract* can be awarded. This differs from the *announced contract* in that no announcement is made and no bids are submitted. Instead, an award is made directly. In such cases, nodes awarded contracts must acknowledge receipt, and have the option of refusal.

$$\vdots$$

Finally, for tasks that amount to simple requests for information, a contract may not be appropriate. In such cases, a request–response sequence can be used without further embellishment. Such messages (that aid in the distribution of data as opposed to control) are implemented as *request* and *information* messages. The request message is used to encode straightforward requests for information when contracting is unnecessary. The information message is used both as a response to a request message and a general data transfer message.

(Smith, 1980b, pp. 62, 63)

In addition to describing the various messages that agents may send, Smith describes the procedures to be carried out on receipt of a message. Briefly, these procedures are as follows (see Smith (1980b, pp. 96–102) for more details).

(1) Task announcement processing. On receipt of a task announcement, an agent decides if it is *eligible* for the task. It does this by looking at the *eligibility specification* contained in the announcement. If it is eligible, then details of the task are stored, and the agent will subsequently bid for the task.

(2) Bid processing. Details of bids from would-be contractors are stored by (would-be) managers until some deadline is reached. The manager then awards the task to a single bidder.

(3) Award processing. Agents that bid for a task, but fail to be awarded it, simply delete details of the task. The successful bidder must attempt to expedite the task (which may mean generating new sub-tasks).

(4) Request and inform processing. These messages are the simplest to handle. A request simply causes an inform message to be sent to the requestor, containing the required information, but only if that information is immediately available. (Otherwise, the requestee informs the requestor that the information is unknown.) An inform message causes its content to be added to the recipient's database. It is assumed that at the conclusion of a task, a contractor will send an information message to the manager, detailing the results of the expedited task[1].

Despite (or perhaps because of) its simplicity, the Contract Net has become the most implemented and best-studied framework for distributed problem solving.

9.3 Result Sharing

In result sharing, problem solving proceeds by agents cooperatively exchanging information as a solution is developed. Typically, these results will progress from being the solution to small problems, which are progressively refined into larger, more abstract solutions. Durfee (1999, p. 131) suggests that problem solvers can improve group performance in result sharing in the following ways.

Confidence: independently derived solutions can be cross-checked, highlighting possible errors, and increasing confidence in the overall solution.

Completeness: agents can share their *local* views to achieve a better overall *global* view.

Precision: agents can share results to ensure that the precision of the overall solution is increased.

Timeliness: even if one agent could solve a problem on its own, by sharing a solution, the result could be derived more quickly.

9.4 Combining Task and Result Sharing

In the everyday cooperative working that we all engage in, we frequently *combine* task sharing and result sharing. In this section, I will briefly give an overview of how this was achieved in the FELINE system (Wooldridge *et al.*, 1991). FELINE was a *cooperating expert system*. The idea was to build an overall problem-solving system as a collection of cooperating experts, each of which had expertise in distinct but related areas. The system worked by these agents cooperating to both *share knowledge* and *distribute subtasks*. Each agent in FELINE was in fact an independent rule-based system: it had a working memory, or database, containing information about the current state of problem solving; in addition, each agent had a collection of rules, which encoded its domain knowledge.

Each agent in FELINE also maintained a data structure representing its beliefs about itself and its environment. This data structure is called the *environment model* (cf. the agents with symbolic representations discussed in Chapter 3). It

---

[1]This is done via a special *report* message type in the original CNET framework.

contained an entry for the modelling agent and each agent that the modelling agent might communicate with (its *acquaintances*). Each entry contained two important attributes as follows.

Skills. This attribute is a set of identifiers denoting hypotheses which the agent has the expertise to establish or deny. The skills of an agent will correspond roughly to root nodes of the inference networks representing the agent's domain expertise.

Interests. This attribute is a set of identifiers denoting hypotheses for which the agent requires the truth value. It may be that an agent actually has the expertise to establish the truth value of its interests, but is nevertheless 'interested' in them. The interests of an agent will correspond roughly to leaf nodes of the inference networks representing the agent's domain expertise.

Messages in FELINE were triples, consisting of a *sender*, *receiver*, and *contents*. The contents field was also a triple, containing *message type*, *attribute*, and *value*. Agents in FELINE communicated using three message types as follows (the system predated the KQML and FIPA languages discussed in Chapter 8).

Request. If an agent sends a request, then the attribute field will contain an identifier denoting a hypothesis. It is assumed that the hypothesis is one which lies within the domain of the intended recipient. A request is assumed to mean that the sender wants the receiver to derive a truth value for the hypothesis.

Response. If an agent receives a request and manages to successfully derive a truth value for the hypothesis, then it will send a response to the originator of the request. The attribute field will contain the identifier denoting the hypothesis; the value field will contain the associated truth value.

Inform. The attribute field of an inform message will contain an identifier denoting a hypothesis. The value field will contain an associated truth value. An inform message will be unsolicited; an agent sends one if it thinks the recipient will be 'interested' in the hypothesis.

To understand how problem solving in FELINE worked, consider goal-driven problem solving in a conventional rule-based system. Typically, goal-driven reasoning proceeds by attempting to establish the truth value of some hypothesis. If the truth value is not known, then a recursive descent of the inference network associated with the hypothesis is performed. Leaf nodes in the inference network typically correspond to questions which are asked of the user, or data that is acquired in some other way. Within FELINE, this scheme was augmented by the following principle. When evaluating a leaf node, if it is not a question, then the environment model was checked to see if any other agent has the node as a 'skill'. If there was some agent that listed the node as a skill, then a request was sent to that agent, requesting the hypothesis. The sender of the request then waited until a response was received; the response indicates the truth value of the node.

Typically, data-driven problem solving proceeds by taking a database of facts (hypotheses and associated truth values), and a set of rules, and repeatedly generating a set of new facts. These new facts are then added to the database, and the process begins again. If a hypothesis follows from a set of facts and a set of rules, then this style of problem solving will eventually generate a result. In FELINE, this scheme was augmented as follows. Whenever a new fact was generated by an agent, the environment model was consulted to see if any agent has the hypothesis as an 'interest'. If it did, then an 'inform' message was sent to the appropriate agent, containing the hypothesis and truth value. Upon receipt of an 'inform' message, the recipient agent added the fact to its database and entered a forward chaining cycle, to determine whether any further information could be derived; this could lead to yet more information being sent to other agents. Similar schemes were implemented in (for example) the CoOpera system (Sommaruga *et al.*, 1989).

9.5 Handling Inconsistency

One of the major problems that arises in cooperative activity is that of *inconsistencies* between different agents in the system. Agents may have inconsistencies with respect to both their *beliefs* (the information they hold about the world), and their *goals/intentions* (the things they want to achieve). As I indicated earlier, inconsistencies between goals generally arise because agents are assumed to be autonomous, and thus not share common objectives. Inconsistencies between the beliefs that agents have can arise from several sources. First, the viewpoint that agents have will typically be limited – no agent will ever be able to obtain a *complete* picture of their environment. Also, the sensors that agents have may be faulty, or the information sources that the agent has access to may in turn be faulty.

In a system of moderate size, inconsistencies are inevitable: the question is how to deal with them. Durfee *et al.* (1989a) suggest a number of possible approaches to the problem as follows.

- Do not allow it to occur – or at least ignore it. This is essentially the approach of the Contract Net: task sharing is always driven by a manager agent, who has the only view of the problem that matters.

- Resolve inconsistencies through negotiation (see Chapter 7). While this may be desirable in theory, the communication and computational overheads incurred suggest that it will rarely be possible in practice.

- Build systems that degrade gracefully in the presence of inconsistency.

The third approach is clearly the most desirable. Lesser and Corkill (1981) refer to systems that can behave robustly in the presence of inconsistency as *functionally accurate/cooperative* (FA/C):

[In FA/C systems]...nodes cooperatively exchange and integrate partial, tentative, high-level results to construct a consistent and complete solution. [An agent's] problem-solving is structured so that its local knowledge bases need not be complete, consistent, and up-to-date in order to make progress on its problem-solving tasks. Nodes do the best they can with their current information, but their solutions to their local sub-problems may be only partial, tentative, and incorrect.

(Durfee *et al.*, 1989a, pp. 117, 118)

Lesser and Corkill (1981) suggested the following characteristics of FA/C systems that tolerate inconsistent/incorrect information.

- Problem solving is not tightly constrained to a particular sequence of events – it progresses opportunistically (i.e. not in a strict predetermined order, but taking advantage of whatever opportunities arise) and incrementally (i.e. by gradually piecing together solutions to sub-problems).

- Agents communicate by exchanging high-level intermediate results, rather than by exchanging raw data.

- Uncertainty and inconsistency is implicitly resolved when partial results are exchanged and compared with other partial solutions. Thus inconsistency and uncertainty is resolved as problem solving progresses, rather than at the beginning or end of problem solving.

- The solution is not constrained to a single solution route: there are many possible ways of arriving at a solution, so that if one fails, there are other ways of achieving the same end. This makes the system robust against localized failures and bottlenecks in problem solving.

9.6 Coordination

Perhaps the defining problem in cooperative working is that of *coordination*. The coordination problem is that of *managing inter-dependencies between the activities of agents*: some coordination mechanism is essential if the activities that agents can engage in can interact in any way. How might two activities interact? Consider the following real-world examples.

- You and I both want to leave the room, and so we independently walk towards the door, which can only fit one of us. I graciously permit you to leave first.

    In this example, our activities need to be coordinated because there is a resource (the door) which we both wish to use, but which can only be used by one person at a time.

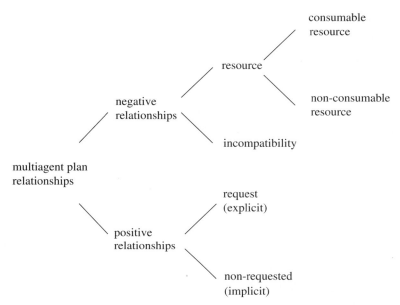

Figure 9.4   Von Martial's typology of coordination relationships.

- I intend to submit a grant proposal, but in order to do this, I need your signature.

  In this case, my activity of sending a grant proposal depends upon your activity of signing it off – I cannot carry out my activity until yours is completed. In other words, my activity *depends* upon yours.

- I obtain a soft copy of a paper from a Web page. I know that this report will be of interest to you as well. Knowing this, I proactively photocopy the report, and give you a copy.

  In this case, our activities do not strictly need to be coordinated – since the report is freely available on a Web page, you could download and print your own copy. But by proactively printing a copy, I save you time and hence, intuitively, increase your utility.

von Martial (1990) suggested a typology for coordination relationships (see Figure 9.4). He suggested that, broadly, relationships between activities could be either *positive* or *negative.*

Positive relationships 'are all those relationships between two plans from which some benefit can be derived, for one or both of the agents plans, by combining them' (von Martial, 1990, p. 111). Such relationships may be *requested* (I *explicitly* ask you for help with my activities) or *non-requested* (it so happens that by working together we can achieve a solution that is better for at least one of us, without making the other any worse off, cf. discussions of pareto optimality in the preceding chapters). von Martial (1990, p. 112) distinguishes three types of non-requested relationship as follows.

The action equality relationship. We both plan to perform an identical action, and by recognizing this, one of us can perform the action alone and so save the other effort.

The consequence relationship. The actions in my plan have the side-effect of achieving one of your goals, thus relieving you of the need to explicitly achieve it.

The favour relationship. Some part of my plan has the side effect of contributing to the achievement of one of your goals, perhaps by making it easier (e.g. by achieving a precondition of one of the actions in it).

Coordination in multiagent systems is assumed to happen *at run time*, that is, the agents themselves must be capable of recognizing these relationships and, where necessary, managing them as part of their activities (von Martial, 1992). This contrasts with the more conventional situation in computer science, where a designer explicitly attempts to anticipate possible interactions in advance, and designs the system so as to avoid negative interactions and exploit potential positive interactions.

In the sections that follow, I present some of the main approaches that have been developed for dynamically coordinating activities.

9.6.1   Coordination through partial global planning

The Distributed Vehicle Monitoring Testbed (DVMT) was one of the earliest and best-known testbeds for multiagent systems. The DVMT was a fully instrumented testbed for developing distributed problem-solving networks (Lesser and Erman, 1980; Lesser and Corkill, 1988). The testbed was based around the domain of distributed vehicle sensing and monitoring: the aim was to successfully track a number of vehicles that pass within the range of a set of distributed sensors. The main purpose of the testbed was to support experimentation into different problem-solving strategies.

The distributed sensing domain is inherently data driven: new data about vehicle movements appears and must be processed by the system. The main problem with the domain was to process information as rapidly as possible, so that the system could come to conclusions about the paths of vehicles in time for them to be useful. To coordinate the activities of agents in the DVMT, Durfee developed an approach known as *partial global planning* (Durfee and Lesser, 1987; Durfee, 1988, 1996).

The main principle of partial global planning is that cooperating agents exchange information in order to reach common conclusions about the problem-solving process. Planning is *partial* because the system does not (indeed *cannot*) generate a plan for the entire problem. It is *global* because agents form non-local plans by exchanging local plans and cooperating to achieve a non-local view of problem solving.

Partial global planning involves three iterated stages.

(1) Each agent decides what its own goals are, and generates short-term plans in order to achieve them.

(2) Agents exchange information to determine where plans and goals interact.

(3) Agents alter local plans in order to better coordinate their own activities.

In order to prevent incoherence during these processes, Durfee proposed the use of a *meta-level structure*, which guided the cooperation process within the system. The meta-level structure dictated which agents an agent should exchange information with, and under what conditions it ought to do so.

The actions and interactions of a group of agents were incorporated into a data structure known as a *partial global plan*. This data structure will be generated cooperatively by agents exchanging information. It contained the following principle attributes.

Objective. The objective is the larger goal that the system is working towards.

Activity maps. An activity map is a representation of what agents are actually doing, and what results will be generated by their activities.

Solution construction graph. A solution construction graph is a representation of how agents ought to interact, what information ought to be exchanged, and when, in order for the system to successfully generate a result.

Keith Decker extended and refined the PGP coordination mechanisms in his TÆMS testbed (Decker, 1996); this led to what he called *generalized partial global planning* (GPGP – pronounced 'gee pee gee pee') (Decker and Lesser, 1995). GPGP makes use of five techniques for coordinating activities as follows.

Updating non-local viewpoints. Agents have only local views of activity, and so sharing information can help them achieve broader views. In his TÆMS system, Decker uses three variations of this policy: communicate no local information, communicate all information, or an intermediate level.

Communicate results. Agents may communicate results in three different ways. A minimal approach is where agents only communicate results that are essential to satisfy obligations. Another approach involves sending all results. A third is to send results to those with an interest in them.

Handling simple redundancy. Redundancy occurs when efforts are duplicated. This may be deliberate – an agent may get more than one agent to work on a task because it wants to ensure the task gets done. However, in general, redundancies indicate wasted resources, and are therefore to be avoided. The solution adopted in GPGP is as follows. When redundancy is detected, in the form of multiple agents working on identical tasks, one agent is selected at random to carry out the task. The results are then broadcast to other interested agents.

Handling hard coordination relationships. 'Hard' coordination relationships are essentially the 'negative' relationships of von Martial, as discussed above. Hard coordination relationships are thus those that threaten to prevent activities being successfully completed. Thus a hard relationship occurs when there is a danger of the agents' actions destructively interfering with one another, or preventing each others actions being carried out. When such relationships are encountered, the activities of agents are rescheduled to resolve the problem.

Handling soft coordination relationships. 'Soft' coordination relationships include the 'positive' relationships of von Martial. Thus these relationships include those that are not 'mission critical', but which may improve overall performance. When these are encountered, then rescheduling takes place, but with a high degree of 'negotiability': if rescheduling is not found possible, then the system does not worry about it too much.

9.6.2 Coordination through joint intentions

The second approach to coordination that I shall discuss is the use of *human teamwork models*. We saw in Chapter 4 how some researchers have built agents around the concept of practical reasoning, and how central intentions are in this practical reasoning process. Intentions also play a critical role in coordination: they provide both the stability and predictability that is necessary for social interaction, and the flexibility and reactivity that is necessary to cope with a changing environment. If you know that I am planning to write a book, for example, then this gives you information that you can use to coordinate your activities with mine. For example, it allows you to rule out the possibility of going on holiday with me, or partying with me all night, because you know I will be working hard on the book.

When humans work together as a team, mental states that are closely related to intentions appear to play a similarly important role (Levesque *et al.*, 1990; Cohen and Levesque, 1991). It is important to be able to distinguish coordinated action that is not cooperative from coordinated cooperative action. As an illustration of this point, consider the following scenario (Searle, 1990).

> A group of people are sitting in a park. As a result of a sudden downpour all of them run to a tree in the middle of the park because it is the only available source of shelter. This may be coordinated behaviour, but it is not cooperative action, as each person has the intention of stopping themselves from becoming wet, and even if they are aware of what others are doing and what their goals are, it does not affect their intended action. This contrasts with the situation in which the people are dancers, and the choreography calls for them to converge

on a common point (the tree). In this case, the individuals are performing exactly the same actions as before, but because they each have the aim of meeting at the central point as a consequence of the overall aim of executing the dance, this is cooperative action.

How does having an individual intention towards a particular goal differ from being part of a team, with some sort of collective intention towards the goal? The distinction was first studied in Levesque *et al.* (1990), where it was observed that being part of a team implies some sort of *responsibility* towards the other members of the team. To illustrate this, suppose that you and I are together lifting a heavy object as part of a team activity. Then clearly we both individually have the intention to lift the object – but is there more to teamwork than this? Well, suppose I come to believe that it is not going to be possible to lift it for some reason. If I just have an *individual* goal to lift the object, then the rational thing for me to do is simply drop the intention (and thus perhaps also the object). But you would hardly be inclined to say I was cooperating with you if I did so. Being part of a team implies that I show some responsibility towards you: that if I discover the team effort is not going to work, then I should at least attempt to make you aware of this.

Building on the work of Levesque *et al.* (1990), Jennings distinguished between the *commitment* that underpins an intention and the associated *convention* (Jennings, 1993a). A *commitment* is a pledge or a promise (for example, to have lifted the object); a *convention* in contrast is a means of monitoring a commitment – it specifies under what circumstances a commitment can be abandoned and how an agent should behave both locally and towards others when one of these conditions arises.

In more detail, one may commit either to a particular course of action, or, more generally, to a state of affairs. Here, we are concerned only with commitments that are *future directed* towards a state of affairs. Commitments have a number of important properties (see Jennings (1993a) and Cohen and Levesque (1990a, pp. 217–219) for a discussion), but the most important is that *commitments persist*: having adopted a commitment, we do not expect an agent to drop it until, for some reason, it becomes redundant. The conditions under which a commitment can become redundant are specified in the associated convention – examples include the motivation for the goal no longer being present, the goal being achieved, and the realization that the goal will never be achieved (Cohen and Levesque, 1990a).

When a group of agents are engaged in a cooperative activity they must have a joint commitment to the overall aim, as well as their individual commitments to the specific tasks that they have been assigned. This joint commitment shares the persistence property of the individual commitment; however, it differs in that its state is distributed amongst the team members. An appropriate social convention must also be in place. This social convention identifies the conditions under which the joint commitment can be dropped, and also describes how an agent should behave towards its fellow team members. For example, if an agent drops its joint commitment because it believes that the goal will never be attained, then it is part of the notion of 'cooperativeness' that is inherent in joint action that it informs all of its fellow team members of its change of state. In this context, social conventions provide general guidelines, and a common frame of reference in which agents can work. By adopting a convention, every agent knows what is expected both of it, and of every other agent, as part of the collective working towards the goal, and knows that every other agent has a similar set of expectations.

We can begin to define this kind of cooperation in the notion of a *joint persistent goal* (JPG), as defined in Levesque *et al.* (1990). In a JPG, a group of agents have a collective commitment to bringing about some goal φ; the *motivation* for this goal, i.e. the reason that the group has the commitment, is represented by ψ. Thus φ might be 'move the heavy object', while ψ might be 'Michael wants the heavy object moved'. The mental state of the team of agents with this JPG might be described as follows:

- initially, every agent does not believe that the goal φ is satisfied, but believes φ is possible;
- every agent i then has a goal of φ until the termination condition is satisfied (see below);
- until the termination condition is satisfied, then
    - if any agent i believes that the goal is achieved, then it will have a goal that this becomes a mutual belief, and will retain this goal until the termination condition is satisfied;
    - if any agent i believes that the goal is impossible, then it will have a goal that this becomes a mutual belief, and will retain this goal until the termination condition is satisfied;
    - if any agent i believes that the motivation ψ for the goal is no longer present, then it will have a goal that this becomes a mutual belief, and will retain this goal until the termination condition is satisfied;
- the termination condition is that it is mutually believed that either
    - the goal φ is satisfied;
    - the goal φ is impossible to achieve;
    - the motivation/justification ψ for the goal is no longer present.

Commitments and conventions in ARCHON

Jennings (1993a, 1995) investigated the use of commitments and such as JPGs in the coordination of an industrial control system called ARCHON (Wittig, 1992; Jennings *et al.*, 1996a; Perriolat *et al.*, 1996). He noted that commitments and conventions could be encoded as *rules* in a rule-based system. This makes it possible to explicitly encode coordination structures in the reasoning mechanism of an agent.

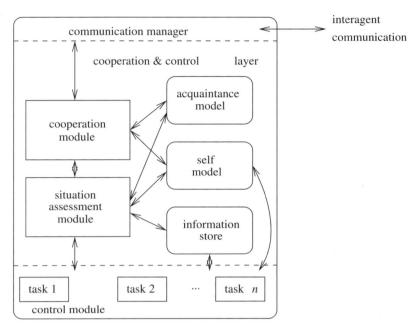

Figure 9.5 ARCHON agent architecture.

The overall architecture of agents in ARCHON is illustrated in Figure 9.5. Agents have three layers. The lowest layer is the *control* layer. This layer contains domain-specific agent capabilities. The idea is that agents in ARCHON *wrap* legacy software in agent-like capabilities. In the ARCHON case, these legacy systems were stand-alone expert systems. The legacy systems were embedded within a control module, which provided access to them via an API. ARCHON agents maintained three different types of information, in the forms of an *acquaintance model* (cf. the acquaintance models of the MACE system described later in this chapter), a *self model* (which contains information about the agent's own skills and interests), and, finally, a general-purpose information store, which contains other information about the agent's environment. The behaviour of the agent was determined by three main control modules: the *cooperation module*, which was responsible for the agent's social ability; the *situation assessment module*, which was responsible for determining when the need for new teamwork arose; and, finally, the *communication manager*, which was responsible for sending/receiving messages.

Some of the rules used for reassessing joint commitments and selecting actions to repair failed teamwork are shown in Figure 9.6 (from Jennings, 1995). The first four rules capture the conditions where the joint goal has been successfully achieved, where the motivation for the joint goal is no longer present, and where the current plan to achieve the joint goal has been invalidated in some way. The following 'select' rules are used to determine a repair action.

Match rules::

R1:   if   *task t has finished executing* and
               t has produced desired outcome of joint action
        then   *joint goal is satisfied.*

R2:   if   *receive information i* and
               i is related to triggering conditions
                   for joint goal G and
               i invalidates beliefs for wanting G
        then   *motivation for G is no longer present.*

R3:   if   *delay task t1* and
               t1 is a component of common recipe R and
               t1 must be synchronized with t2 in R
        then   *R is violated.*

R4:   if   *finished executing common recipe R* and
               expected results of R not produced and
               alternative recipe exists
        then   *R is invalid.*

Select rules:

R1:   if   *joint goal is satisfied*
        then   *abandon all associated local activities* and
               inform cooperation module

R2:   if   *motivation for joint goal no longer present*
        then   *abandon all associated local activities* and
               inform cooperation module

R3:   if   *common recipe R is violated* and
               R can be rescheduled
        then   *suspend local activities associated with R* and
               reset timings and descriptions associated with R and
               inform cooperation module

R4:   if   *common recipe R1 is invalid* and
               alternative recipe R2 exists
        then   *abandon all local activities with R1* and
               inform cooperation module that R1 is invalid and
               propose R2 to cooperation module

Figure 9.6 Joint commitment rules in ARCHON.

Milind Tambe developed a similar framework for teamwork called Steam (Tambe, 1997). Agents in Steam are programmed using the Soar rule-based architecture (Newell *et al.*, 1989, 1990). The cooperation component of Steam is encoded in about 300 domain-independent rules, somewhat similar in principle to Jennings's teamwork rules, as shown above. However, the cooperation rules of Steam are far more complex, allowing for sophisticated hierarchical team structures.

The Steam framework was used in a number of application domains, including military mission simulations, as well as the RoboCup simulated robotic soccer domain.

A teamwork-based model of CDPS

Building on Jennings's teamwork-based coordination model (Jennings, 1995), a four-stage model of CDPS was presented in Wooldridge and Jennings (1994, 1999). The four stages of the model are as follows.

(1) Recognition. CDPS begins when some agent in a multiagent community has a goal, and recognizes the potential for cooperative action with respect to that goal. Recognition may occur for several reasons. The paradigm case is that in which the agent is unable to achieve the goal in isolation, but believes that cooperative action can achieve it. For example, an agent may have a goal which, to achieve, requires information that is only accessible to another agent. Without the cooperation of this other agent, the goal cannot be achieved. More prosaically, an agent with a goal to move a heavy object might simply not have the strength to do this alone.

Alternatively, an agent may be able to achieve the goal on its own, but may not want to. There may be several reasons for this. First, it may believe that in working alone, it will clobber one of its other goals. For example, suppose I have a goal of lifting a heavy object. I may have the capability of lifting the object, but I might believe that in so doing, I would injure my back, thereby clobbering my goal of being healthy. In this case, a cooperative solution – involving no injury to my back – is preferable. More generally, an agent may believe that a cooperative solution will in some way be better than a solution achieved by action in isolation. For example, a solution might be obtained more quickly, or may be more accurate as a result of cooperative action.

Believing that you either cannot achieve your goal in isolation, or that (for whatever reason) you would prefer not to work alone, is part of the potential for cooperation. But it is not enough in itself to initiate the social process. For there to be potential for cooperation with respect to an agent's goal, the agent must also believe there is some group of agents that can actually achieve the goal.

(2) Team formation. During this stage, the agent that recognized the potential for cooperative action at stage (1) solicits assistance. If this stage is successful, then it will end with a group of agents having some kind of nominal commitment to collective action. This stage is essentially a collective deliberation stage (see the discussion on deliberation in Walton and Krabbe's dialogue types, discussed in

Chapter 7). At the conclusion of this stage, the team will have agreed to the *ends* to be achieved (i.e. to the principle of joint action), but not to the means (i.e. the way in which this end will be achieved). Note that the agents are assumed to be rational, in the sense that they will not form a team unless they implicitly believe that the goal is achievable.

(3) Plan formation. We saw above that a group will not form a collective unless they believe they can actually achieve the desired goal. This, in turn, implies there is at least one action known to the group that will take them 'closer' to the goal. However, it is possible that there are many agents that know of actions the group can perform in order to take them closer to the goal. Moreover, some members of the collective may have objections to one or more of these actions. It is therefore necessary for the collective to come to some agreement about exactly which course of action they will follow. Such an agreement is reached via negotiation or argumentation, of exactly the kind discussed in Chapter 7.

(4) Team action. During this stage, the newly agreed plan of joint action is executed by the agents, which maintain a close-knit relationship throughout. This relationship is defined by a convention, which every agent follows. The JPG described above might be one possible convention.

9.6.3   Coordination by mutual modelling

Another approach to coordination, closely related to the models of human teamwork I discussed above, is that of *coordination by mutual modelling*. The idea is as follows. Recall the simple coordination example I gave earlier: you and I are both walking to the door, and there is not enough room for both of us – a collision is imminent. What should we do? One option is for both of us to simply stop walking. This possibility guarantees that no collision will occur, but it is in some sense sub-optimal: while we stand and wait, there is an unused resource (the door), which could fruitfully have been exploited by one of us. Another possibility is for both of us to *put ourselves in the place of the other*: to build a model of other agents – their beliefs, intentions, and the like – and to coordinate our activities around the predictions that this model makes. In this case, you might believe that I am eager to please you, and therefore that I will likely allow you to pass through the door first; on this basis, you can continue to walk to the door.

This approach to coordination was first explicitly articulated in Genesereth *et al.* (1986), where the approach was dubbed 'cooperation without communication'. The models that were proposed were essentially the game-theoretic models that I discussed in Chapter 6. The idea was that if you assume that both you and the other agents with which you interact share a common view of the scenario (in game-theory terms, you all know the payoff matrix), then you can do a game-theoretic analysis to determine what is the rational thing for each player to do.

Note that – as the name of the approach suggests – explicit communication is not necessary in this scenario.

MACE

Les Gasser's MACE system, developed in the mid-1980s, can, with some justification, claim to be the first general experimental testbed for multiagent systems (Gasser *et al.*, 1987a,b). MACE is noteworthy for several reasons, but perhaps most importantly because it brought together most of the components that have subsequently become common in testbeds for developing multiagent systems. I mention it in this section because of one critical component: the *acquaintance models*, which are discussed in more detail below. Acquaintance models are representations of other agents: their abilities, interests, capabilities, and the like.

A MACE system contains five components:

- a collection of *application agents*, which are the basic computational units in a MACE system (see below);

- a collection of predefined *system agents*, which provide service to users (e.g. user interfaces);

- a collection of facilities, available to all agents (e.g. a pattern matcher);

- a *description database*, which maintains agent descriptions, and produces executable agents from those descriptions; and

- a set of *kernels*, one per physical machine, which handle communication and message routing, etc.

Gasser *et al.* identified three aspects of agents: they contain knowledge, they sense their environment, and they perform actions (Gasser *et al.*, 1987b, p. 124). Agents have two kinds of knowledge: specialized, local, domain knowledge, and *acquaintance knowledge* – knowledge about other agents. An agent maintains the following information about its acquaintances (Gasser *et al.*, 1987b, pp. 126, 127).

Class. Agents are organized in structured groups called *classes*, which are identified by a class name.

Name. Each agent is assigned a name, unique to its class – an agent's address is a $\langle class, name \rangle$ pair.

Roles. A role describes the part an agent plays in a class.

Skills. Skills are what an agent knows are the capabilities of the modelled agent.

Goals. Goals are what the agent knows the modelled agent wants to achieve.

Plans. Plans are an agent's view of the way a modelled agent will achieve its goals.

Agents sense their environment primarily through receiving messages. An agent's ability to act is encoded in its *engine*. An engine is a LISP function, evaluated by default once on every scheduling cycle. The only externally visible signs of

```
((NAME plus-ks)
    (IMPORT ENGINE FROM dbb-def)
    (ACQUAINTANCES
        (plus-ks
            ... model for plus-ks ...
        )
        (de-exp
            [ROLE (ORG-MEMBER)]
            [GOALS ( ... goal list ... )]
            [SKILLS ( ... skill list ... )]
            [PLANS ( ... plan list ...)]
        )
        (simple-plus
            ... acquaintance model for simple-plus ...
        )
    )
    (INIT-CODE ( ... LISP code ...))
) ; end of plus-ks
```

Figure 9.7   Structure of MACE agents.

an agent's activity are the messages it sends to other agents. Messages may be directed to a single agent, a group of agents, or all agents; the interpretation of messages is left to the programmer to define.

An example MACE agent is shown in Figure 9.7. The agent modelled in this example is part of a simple calculator system implemented using the black-board model. The agent being modelled here is called PLUS-KS. It is a knowledge source which knows about how to perform the addition operation. The PLUS-KS knowledge source is the 'parent' of two other agents; DE-EXP, an agent which knows how to decompose simple expressions into their primitive components, and SIMPLE-PLUS, an agent which knows how to add two numbers.

The definition frame for the PLUS-KS agent consists of a name for the agent – in this case PLUS-KS – the engine, which defines what actions the agent may perform (in this case the engine is imported, or inherited, from an agent called DBB-DEF), and the acquaintances of the agent.

The acquaintances slot for PLUS-KS defines models for three agents. Firstly, the agent models itself. This defines how the rest of the world will see PLUS-KS. Next, the agents DE-EXP and SIMPLE-PLUS are modelled. Consider the model for the agent DE-EXP. The role slot defines the relationship of the modelled agent to the modeller. In this case, both DE-EXP and SIMPLE-PLUS are members of the class defined by PLUS-KS. The GOALS slot defines what the modelling agent believes the modelled agent wants to achieve. The SKILLS slot defines what resources the modeller believes the modelled agent can provide. The PLANS slot defines how the modeller believes the modelled agent will achieve its goals. The PLANS slot consists of a list of skills, or operations, which the modelled agent will perform in order to achieve its goals.

Gasser *et al.* described how MACE was used to construct blackboard systems, a Contract Net system, and a number of other experimental systems (see Gasser *et al.*, 1987b, 1989, pp. 138–140).

9.6.4 Coordination by norms and social laws

In our everyday lives, we use a range of techniques for coordinating activities. One of the most important is the use of *norms* and *social laws* (Lewis, 1969). A norm is simply an established, expected pattern of behaviour; the term social law carries essentially the same meaning, but it is usually implied that social laws carry with them some authority. Examples of norms in human society abound. For example, in the UK, it is a norm to form a queue when waiting for a bus, and to allow those who arrived first to enter the bus first. This norm is not *enforced* in any way: it is simply expected behaviour: diverging from this norm will (usually) cause nothing more than icy looks from others on the bus. Nevertheless, this norm provides a template that can be used by all those around to regulate their own behaviour.

Conventions play a key role in the social process. They provide agents with a template upon which to structure their action repertoire. They represent a behavioural constraint, striking a balance between individual freedom on the one hand, and the goal of the agent society on the other. As such, they also simplify an agent's decision-making process, by dictating courses of action to be followed in certain situations. It is important to emphasize what a key role conventions play in our everyday lives. As well as formalized conventions, which we all recognize as such (an example being driving on the left- or right-hand side of the road), almost every aspect of our social nature is dependent on convention. After all, language itself is nothing more than a convention, which we use in order to coordinate our activities with others.

One key issue in the understanding of conventions is to decide on the most effective method by which they can come to exist within an agent society. There are two main approaches as follows.

Offline design. In this approach, social laws are designed offline, and hardwired into agents. Examples in the multiagent systems literature include Shoham and Tennenholtz (1992b), Goldman and Rosenschein (1993) and Conte and Castelfranchi (1993).

Emergence from within the system. This possibility is investigated in Shoham and Tennenholtz (1992a), Kittock (1993) and Walker and Wooldridge (1995), who experiment with a number of techniques by which a convention can 'emerge' from within a group of agents.

The first approach will often be simpler to implement, and might present the system designer with a greater degree of control over system functionality. However, there are a number of disadvantages with this approach. First, it is not always the case that *all* the characteristics of a system are known at design time. (This is most obviously true of open systems such as the Internet.) In such systems, the ability of agents to organize themselves would be advantageous. Secondly, in complex systems, the goals of agents (or groups of agents) might be constantly changing. To keep reprogramming agents in such circumstances would be costly and inefficient. Finally, the more complex a system becomes, the less likely it is that system designers will be able to design effective norms or social laws: the dynamics of the system – the possible 'trajectories' that it can take – will be too hard to predict. Here, flexibility within the agent society might result in greater coherence.

Emergent norms and social laws

A key issue, then, is how a norm or social law can emerge in a society of agents. In particular, the question of how agents can come to reach a *global* agreement on the use of social conventions by using only *locally available* information is of critical importance. The convention must be *global* in the sense that all agents use it. But each agent must decide on which convention to adopt based solely on its own experiences, as recorded in its internal state: predefined inter-agent power structures or authority relationships are not allowed.

This problem was perhaps first investigated in Shoham and Tennenholtz (1992a), who considered the following scenario, which I will call the *tee shirt game*.

> Consider a group of agents, each of which has two tee shirts: one red and one blue. The agents – who have never met previously, and who have no prior knowledge of each other – play a game, the goal of which is for *all* the agents to end up wearing the same coloured tee shirt. Initially, each agent wears a red or blue tee shirt selected randomly. The game is played in a series of rounds. On each round, every agent is paired up with exactly one other agent; pairs are selected at random. Each pair gets to see the colour of the tee shirt the other is wearing – no other information or communication between the agents is allowed. After a round is complete, every agent is allowed to either stay wearing the same coloured tee shirt, or to swap to the other colour.

Notice that no global view is possible in this game: an agent can never 'climb the wall' to see what every other agent is wearing. An agent must therefore base its decision about whether to change tee shirts or stick with the one it is currently wearing using only its memory of the agents it has encountered on previous rounds. The key problem is this: to design what Shoham and Tennenholtz (1992b) refer to as a *strategy update function*, which represents an agent's decision-making process. A strategy update function is a function from the history that the agent has observed so far, to a colour (red or blue). Note that the term 'strategy' here may be a bit misleading – it simply refers to the colour of the tee shirt. The goal is to develop a strategy update function such that, when it is used by every agent in the society, will bring the society to a global agreement as efficiently as possible.

In Shoham and Tennenholtz (1992b, 1997) and Walker and Wooldridge (1995), a number of different strategy update functions were evaluated as follows.

Simple majority. This is the simplest form of update function. Agents will change to an alternative strategy if so far they have observed more instances of it in other agents than their present strategy. If more than one strategy has been observed more than that currently adopted, the agent will choose the strategy observed most often.

Simple majority with agent types. As simple majority, except that agents are divided into two types. As well as observing each other's strategies, agents in these experiments can communicate with others whom they can 'see', and who are of the same type. When they communicate, they exchange memories, and each agent treats the other agent's memory as if it were his own, thus being able to take advantage of another agent's experiences. In other words, agents are particular about whom they confide in.

Simple majority with communication on success. This strategy updates a form of communication based on a success threshold. When an individual agent has reached a certain level of success with a particular strategy, he communicates his memory of experiences with this successful strategy to all other agents that he can 'see'. Note, only the memory relating to the successful strategy is broadcast, not the whole memory. The intuition behind this update function is that an agent will only communicate with another agent when it has something *meaningful* to say. This prevents 'noise' communication.

Highest cumulative reward. For this update to work, an agent must be able to see that using a particular strategy gives a particular payoff (cf. the discussion in Chapter 6). The highest cumulative reward update rule then says that an agent uses the strategy that it sees has resulted in the highest cumulative payoff to date.

In addition, the impact of *memory restarts* on these strategies was investigated. Intuitively, a memory restart means that an agent periodically 'forgets' everything it has seen to date – its memory is emptied, and it starts as if from scratch again. The intuition behind memory restarts is that it allows an agent to avoid being over-committed to a particular strategy as a result of history: memory restarts thus make an agent more 'open to new ideas'.

The *efficiency of convergence* was measured by Shoham and Tennenholtz (1992b) primarily by the *time taken to convergence*: how many rounds of the tee shirt game need to be played before all agents converge on a particular strategy. However, it was noted in Walker and Wooldridge (1995) that *changing* from one strategy to another can be expensive. Consider a strategy such as using a particular kind of computer operating system. Changing from one to another has an associated cost, in terms of the time spent to learn it, and so we do not wish to change too frequently. Another issue is that of *stability*. We do not usually want our society to reach agreement on a particular strategy, only for it then to immediately fall apart, with agents reverting to different strategies.

When evaluated in a series of experiments, all of the strategy update functions described above led to the emergence of particular conventions within an agent society. However, the most important results were associated with the highest cumulative reward update function (Shoham and Tennenholtz, 1997, pp. 150, 151). It was shown that, for any value ϵ such that $0 < \epsilon \leqslant 1$, there exists some bounded value n such that a collection of agents using the highest cumulative reward update function will reach agreement on a strategy in n rounds with probability $1 - \epsilon$. Furthermore, it was shown that this strategy update function is stable in the sense that, once reached, the agents would not diverge from the norm. Finally, it was shown that the strategy on which agents reached agreement was 'efficient', in the sense that it guarantees agents a payoff no worse than that they would have received had they stuck with the strategy they initially chose.

Offline design of norms and social laws

The alternative to allowing conventions to emerge within a society is to design them offline, before the multiagent system begins to execute. The offline design of social laws is closely related to that of mechanism design, which I discussed in Chapter 7 in the context of protocols for multiagent systems, and much of the discussion from that chapter applies to the design of social laws.

There have been several studies of offline design of social laws, particularly with respect to the computational complexity of the social law design problem (Shoham and Tennenholtz, 1992b, 1996). To understand the way these problems are formulated, recall the way in which agents were defined in Chapter 2, as functions from runs (which end in environment states) to actions:

$$Ag : \mathcal{R}^E \rightarrow Ac.$$

A *constraint* is then a pair

$$\langle E', \alpha \rangle,$$

where

- $E' \subseteq E$ is a set of environment states; and
- $\alpha \in Ac$ is an action.

The reading of a constraint $\langle E', \alpha \rangle$ is that, if the environment is in some state $e \in E'$, then the action α is forbidden. A *social law* is then defined to be a set sl of such constraints. An agent – or plan, in the terminology of Shoham and Tennenholtz (1992b, p. 279) – is then said to be legal with respect to a social law sl if it never attempts to perform an action that is forbidden by some constraint in sl.

The next question is to define what is meant by a *useful* social law. The answer is to define a set $F \subseteq E$ of *focal states*. The intuition here is that these are the states that are *always legal*, in that an agent should always be able to 'visit' the focal states. To put it another way, whenever the environment is in some focal state $e \in F$, it should be possible for the agent to act so as to be able to guarantee that any other state $e' \in F$ is brought about. A useful social law is then one that does not constrain the actions of agents so as to make this impossible.

The *useful social law problem* can then be understood as follows.

> Given an environment $Env = \langle E, \tau, e_0 \rangle$ and a set of focal states $F \subseteq E$, find a useful social law if one exists, or else announce that none exists.

In Shoham and Tennenholtz (1992b, 1996), it is proved that this problem is NP-complete, and so is unlikely to be soluble by 'normal' computing techniques in reasonable time. Some variations of the problem are discussed in Shoham and Tennenholtz (1992b, 1996), and some cases where the problem becomes tractable are examined. However, these tractable instances do not appear to correspond to useful real-world cases.

Social laws in practice

Before leaving the subject of social laws, I will briefly discuss some examples of social laws that have been evaluated both in theory and practice. These are *traffic laws* (Shoham and Tennenholtz, 1996).

Imagine a two-dimensional grid world – rather like the Tileworld introduced in Chapter 2 – populated by mobile robots. Only one robot is allowed to occupy a grid point at any one time – more than one is a collision. The robots must collect and transport items from one grid point to another. The goal is then to design a social law that prevents collisions. However, to be useful in this setting, the social law must not impede the movement of the robots to such an extent that they are unable to get from a location where they collect an item to the delivery location. As a first cut, consider a law which completely constrains the movements of robots, so that they must all follow a single, completely predetermined path, leaving no possibility of collision. Here is an example of such a social law, from Shoham and Tennenholtz (1996, p. 602).

> Each robot is required to move constantly. The direction of motion is fixed as follows. On even rows each robot must move left, while in odd rows it must move right. It is required to move up when it is in the rightmost column. Finally, it is required to move down when it is on either the leftmost column of even rows or on the second rightmost column of odd rows. The movement is therefore in a 'snake-like' structure, and defines a Hamiltonian cycle on the grid.

It should be clear that, using this social law,

- the next move of an agent is *uniquely* determined: the law does not leave any doubt about the next state to move to;

- an agent will always be able to get from its current location to its desired location,

- to get from the current location to the desired location will require at most $O(n^2)$ moves, where n is the size of the grid (to see this, simply consider the dimensions of the grid).

Although it is effective, this social law is obviously not very efficient: surely there are more 'direct' social laws which do not involve an agent moving around all the points of the grid? Shoham and Tennenholtz (1996) give an example of one, which superimposes a 'road network' on the grid structure, allowing robots to change direction as they enter a road. They show that this social law guarantees to avoid collisions, while permitting agents to achieve their goals much more efficiently than the naive social law described above.

9.7 Multiagent Planning and Synchronization

An obvious issue in multiagent problem solving is that of *planning* the activities of a group of agents. In Chapter 4, we saw how planning could be incorporated as a component of a practical reasoning agent: what extensions or changes might be needed to plan for a team of agents? Although it is broadly similar in nature to 'conventional' planning, of the type seen in Chapter 4, multiagent planning must take into consideration the fact that the activities of agents can interfere with one another – their activities must therefore be coordinated. There are broadly two possibilities for multiagent planning as follows (Durfee, 1999, p. 139).

Centralized planning for distributed plans: a centralized planning system develops a plan for a group of agents, in which the division and ordering of labour is defined. This 'master' agent then distributes the plan to the 'slaves', who then execute their part of the plan.

Distributed planning: a group of agents cooperate to form a centralized plan. Typically, the component agents will be 'specialists' in different aspects of the overall plan, and will contribute to a part of it. However, the agents that form the plan will not be the ones to execute it; their role is merely to generate the plan.

Distributed planning for distributed plans: a group of agents *cooperate* to form individual plans of action, dynamically coordinating their activities along the way. The agents may be self-interested, and so, when potential coordination problems arise, they may need to be resolved by negotiation of the type discussed in Chapter 7.

In general, centralized planning will be simpler than decentralized planning, because the 'master' can take an overall view, and can dictate coordination relationships as required. The most difficult case to consider is the third. In this case, there may never be a 'global' plan. Individual agents may only ever have pieces of the plan which they are interested in.

Plan merging

Georgeff (1983) proposed an algorithm which allows a planner to take a set a plans generated by single agents, and from them generate a conflict free (but not necessarily optimal) multiagent plan. Actions are specified by using a generalization of the STRIPS notation (Chapter 4). In addition to the usual precondition–delete–add lists for actions, Georgeff proposes using a *during* list. This list contains a set of conditions which must hold *while* the action is being carried out. A plan is seen as a set of states; an action is seen as a function which maps the set onto itself. The precondition of an action specifies the domain of the action; the add and delete lists specify the range.

Given a set of single agent plans specified using the modified STRIPS notation, generating a synchronized multiagent plan consists of three stages.

(1) Interaction analysis. Interaction analysis involves generating a description of how single agent plans interact with one another. Some of these interactions will be harmless; others will not. Georgeff used the notions of *satisfiability, commutativity*, and *precedence* to describe goal interactions. Two actions are said to be *satisfiable* if there is some sequence in which they may be executed without invalidating the preconditions of one or both. *Commutativity* is a restricted case of satisfiability: if two actions may be executed in parallel, then they are said to be commutative. It follows that if two actions are commutative, then either they do not interact, or any interactions are harmless. Precedence describes the sequence in which actions may be executed; if action α_1 has precedence over action α_2, then the preconditions of α_2 are met by the postconditions of α_1. That is not to say that α_1 *must* be executed before α_2; it is possible for two actions to have precedence over each other.

Interaction analysis involves searching the plans of the agents to detect any interactions between them.

(2) Safety analysis. Having determined the possible interactions between plans, it now remains to see which of these interactions are *unsafe*. Georgeff defines safeness for pairs of actions in terms of the precedence and commutativity of the pair. Safety analysis involves two stages. First, all actions which are harmless (i.e. where there is no interaction, or the actions commute) are removed from the plan. This is known as simplification. Georgeff shows that the validity of the final plan is not affected by this process, as it is only *boundary* regions that need to be considered. Secondly, the set of all harmful interactions is generated. This stage also involves searching; a rule known as the *commutativity theorem* is applied to reduce the search space. All harmful interactions have then been identified.

(3) Interaction resolution. In order to resolve conflicts in the simplified plan, Georgeff treats unsafe plan interactions as *critical sections*; to resolve the conflicts, mutual exclusion of the critical sections must be guaranteed. To do this, Georgeff used ideas from Hoare's CSP paradigm to enforce mutual exclusion, although simpler mechanisms (e.g. semaphores) may be used to achieve precisely the same result (Ben-Ari, 1993).

Stuart (1985) describes an implemented system which bears a superficial resemblance to Georgeff's algorithm. It takes a set of unsynchronized single agent plans and from them generates a synchronized multiagent plan. Like Georgeff's algorithm, Stuart's system also guarantees a synchronized solution if one exists. Also, the final plan is represented as a sequence of actions interspersed with CSP primitives to guarantee mutual exclusion of critical sections (Hoare, 1978). Actions are also represented using an extended STRIPS notation. There, however, the resemblance ends. The process of determining which interactions are possibly harmful and resolving conflicts is done not by searching the plans, but by representing the plan as a set of formulae of temporal logic, and attempting to derive a synchronized plan using a temporal logic theorem prover. The idea is that temporal logic is a language for describing sequences of states. As a plan is just a description of exactly such a sequence of states, temporal logic could be used to describe plans. Suppose two plans, π_1 and π_2, were represented by temporal logic formulae φ_1 and φ_2, respectively. Then if the conjunction of these two plans is satisfiable – if there is some sequence of events that is compatible with the conjunction of the formulae – then there is some way that the two plans could be concurrently executed. The temporal logic used was very similar to that used in the Concurrent MetateM language discussed in Chapter 3.

The algorithm to generate a synchronized plan consists of three stages.

(1) A set of single agent plans are given as input. They are then translated into a set of formulae in a propositional linear temporal logic (LTL) (Manna and Pnueli, 1992, 1995).

(2) The formulae are conjoined and fed into an LTL theorem prover. If the conjoined formula is satisfiable, then the theorem prover will generate a set of sequences of actions which satisfy these formulae. These sequences are encoded in a graph structure. If the formula is not satisfiable, then the theorem prover will report this.

(3) The graph generated as output encodes all the possible synchronized executions of the plans. A synchronized plan is then 'read off' from the graph structure.

In general, this approach to multiagent synchronization is computationally expensive, because the temporal theorem prover has to solve a PSPACE-complete problem.

Notes and Further Reading

Published in 1988, Bond and Gasser's *Readings in Distributed Artificial Intelligence* brings together most of the early classic papers on CDPS (Bond and Gasser, 1988). Although some of the papers that make up this collection are perhaps now rather dated, the survey article written by the editors as a preface to this collection remains one of the most articulate and insightful introductions to the problems and issues of CDPS to date. Victor Lesser and his group at the University of Massachusetts are credited with more or less inventing the field of CDPS, and most innovations in this field to date have originated from members of this group over the years. Two survey articles that originated from the work of Lesser's group provide overviews of the field: Durfee *et al.* (1989a,b). Another useful survey is Decker *et al.* (1989).

The Contract Net has been hugely influential in the multiagent systems literature. It originally formed the basis of Smith's doctoral thesis (published as Smith (1980b)), and was further described in Smith (1980a) and Smith and Davis (1980). Many variations on the Contract Net theme have been described, including the effectiveness of a Contract Net with 'consultants', which have expertise about the abilities of agents (Tidhar and Rosenschein, 1992), and a sophisticated variation involving marginal cost calculations (Sandholm and Lesser, 1995). Several formal specifications of the Contract Net have been developed, using basic set theoretic/first-order logic constructs (Werner, 1989), temporal belief logics (Wooldridge, 1992), and the Z specification language (d'Inverno and Luck, 1996).

In addition to the model of cooperative action discussed above, a number of other similar formal models of cooperative action have also been developed, the best known of which is probably the Shared Plans model of Barbara Grosz and Sarit Kraus (Grosz and Kraus, 1993, 1999); also worth mentioning is the work of Tuomela and colleagues (Tuomela and Miller, 1988; Tuomela, 1991), Power (1984), and Rao and colleagues (Rao *et al.*, 1992; Kinny *et al.*, 1992).

A number of researchers have considered the development and exploitation of norms and social laws in multiagent systems. Examples of the issues investigated include the control of aggression (Conte and Castelfranchi, 1993), the role of social structure in the emergence of conventions (Kittock, 1993), group behaviour (Findler and Malyankar, 1993), and the reconsideration of commitments (Jennings, 1993a). In addition, researchers working in philosophy, sociology, and economics have considered similar issues. A good example is the work of Lewis (1969), who made some progress towards a (non-formal) theory of normative behaviour.

One issue that I have been forced to omit from this chapter due to space and time limitations is the use of *normative specifications* in multiagent systems, and, in particular, the use of *deontic logic* (Meyer and Wieringa, 1993). Deontic logic is the logic of obligations and permissions. Originally developed within formal philosophy, deontic logic was been taken up by researchers in computer science in order to express the desirable properties of computer systems. Dignum (1999) gives an overview of the use of deontic logic in multiagent systems, and also discusses the general issue of norms and social laws.

Class reading: Durfee (1999).   A detailed and precise introduction to distributed problem solving and distributed planning, with many useful pointers into the literature.

Exercises

(1) **[Level 2.]**

Using the FIPA or KQML languages (see preceding chapter), describe how you would implement the Contract Net protocol.

(2) **[Level 3.]**

Implement the Contract Net protocol using Java (or your programming language of choice). You might implement agents as threads, and have tasks as (for example) factoring numbers. Have an agent that continually generates new tasks and allocates them to an agent, which must distribute them to others.

(3) **[Level 3.]**

Download an FIPA or KQML system (such as Jade or JATLite – see preceding chapter), and use it to re-implement your Contract Net system.

10

Methodologies

As multiagent systems become more established in the collective consciousness of the computer science community, then we might expect to see increasing effort devoted to devising *methodologies* to support the development of agent systems. Such methodologies have been highly successful in the OO community: examples include the methodologies of Booch, and Rumbaugh and colleagues (Booch, 1994; Rumbaugh *et al.*, 1991).

In this chapter I give an overview of work that has been carried out on the development of methodologies for multiagent systems. This work is, at the time of writing, rather tentative – not much experience has yet been gained with them. I begin by considering some of the domain attributes that indicate the appropriateness of an agent-based solution. I then go on to describe various prototypical methodologies, and discuss some of the pitfalls associated with agent-oriented development. I conclude by discussing the technology of *mobile* agents.

10.1 When is an Agent-Based Solution Appropriate?

There are a number of factors which point to the appropriateness of an agent-based approach (cf. Bond and Gasser, 1988; Jennings and Wooldridge, 1998b).

The environment is open, or at least highly dynamic, uncertain, or complex. In such environments, systems capable of flexible autonomous action are often the only solution.

Agents are a natural metaphor. Many environments (including most organizations, and any commercial or competitive environment) are naturally modelled as societies of agents, either cooperating with each other to solve complex problems, or else competing with one another. Sometimes, as in intelligent interfaces, the idea of an agent is seen as a natural metaphor: Maes (1994a) discusses agents as 'expert assistants', cooperating with the user to work on some problem.

Distribution of data, control or expertise. In some environments, the distribution of either data, control, or expertise means that a centralized solution is at best extremely difficult or at worst impossible. For example, distributed database systems in which each database is under separate control do not generally lend themselves to centralized solutions. Such systems may often be conveniently modelled as multiagent systems, in which each database is a semi-autonomous component.

Legacy systems. A problem increasingly faced by software developers is that of *legacy*: software that is technologically obsolete but functionally essential to an organization. Such software cannot generally be discarded, because of the short-term cost of rewriting. And yet it is often required to interact with other software components, which were never imagined by the original designers. One solution to this problem is to *wrap* the legacy components, providing them with an 'agent layer' functionality, enabling them to communicate and cooperate with other software components (Genesereth and Ketchpel, 1994).

10.2   Agent-Oriented Analysis and Design Techniques

An analysis and design methodology is intended to assist first in gaining an understanding of a particular system, and, secondly, in designing it. Methodologies generally consist of a collection of *models*, and associated with these models, a set of guidelines. The models are intended to formalize understanding of a system being considered. Typically, the models start out as being tentative and rather abstract, and as the analysis and design process continues, they become increasingly more concrete, detailed, and closer to implementation.

Methodologies for the analysis and design of agent-based system. These can be broadly divided into two groups:

- those that take their inspiration from object-oriented development, and either extend existing OO methodologies or adapt OO methodologies to the purposes of AOSE (Burmeister, 1996; Kinny *et al.*, 1996; Wooldridge *et al.*, 1999; Odell *et al.*, 2001; Depke *et al.*, 2001; Bauer *et al.*, 2001; Kendall, 2001; Omicini, 2001; Wood and DeLoach, 2001); and

- those that adapt knowledge engineering or other techniques (Brazier *et al.*, 1995; Luck *et al.*, 1997; Iglesias *et al.*, 1998; Collinot *et al.*, 1996).

In the remainder of this section, I review some representative samples of this work. As representatives of the first category, I survey the AAII methodology of Kinny *et al.* (1996), the Gaia methodology of Wooldridge *et al.* (1999), and summarize work on adapting UML (Odell *et al.*, 2001; Depke *et al.*, 2001; Bauer *et al.*, 2001). As representatives of the second category, I survey the Cassiopeia methodology of Collinot *et al.* (1996), the DESIRE framework of Brazier *et al.* (1995), and the use of Z for specifying agent systems (Luck *et al.*, 1997; d'Inverno and Luck, 2001).

Kinny et al.: the AAII methodology

Throughout the 1990s, the Australian AI Institute (AAII) developed a range of agent-based systems using their PRS-based belief–desire–intention technology (Wooldridge, 2000b) and the Distributed Multiagent Reasoning System (DMARS) (Rao and Georgeff, 1995). The AAII methodology for agent-oriented analysis and design was developed as a result of experience gained with these major applications. It draws primarily upon object-oriented methodologies, and enhances them with some agent-based concepts. The methodology itself is aimed at the construction of a set of models which, when fully elaborated, define an agent system specification.

The AAII methodology provides both *internal* and *external* models. The external model presents a system-level view: the main components visible in this model are agents themselves. The external model is thus primarily concerned with agents and the relationships between them. It is not concerned with the internals of agents: how they are constructed or what they do. In contrast, the internal model is entirely concerned with the internals of agents: their beliefs, desires, and intentions.

The external model is intended to define inheritance relationships between agent classes, and to identify the instances of these classes that will appear at run-time. It is itself composed of two further models: the *agent model* and the *interaction model*. The agent model is then further divided into an *agent class model* and an *agent instance model*. These two models define the agents and agent classes that can appear, and relate these classes to one another via inheritance, aggregation, and instantiation relations. Each agent class is assumed to have at least three attributes: for beliefs, desires, and intentions. The analyst is able to define how these attributes are overridden during inheritance. For example, it is assumed that by default, inherited intentions have less priority than those in sub-classes. The analyst may tailor these properties as desired.

Details of the internal model are not given, but it seems clear that developing an internal model corresponds fairly closely to implementing a PRS agent, i.e. designing the agent's belief, desire, and intention structures.

The AAII methodology is aimed at elaborating the models described above. It may be summarized as follows.

(1) Identify the relevant *roles* in the application domain, and, on the basis of these, develop an *agent class hierarchy*. An example role might be a weather monitor, whereby agent i is required to make agent j aware of the prevailing weather conditions every hour.

(2) Identify the responsibilities associated with each role, the services required by and provided by the role, and then determine the *goals* associated with each service. With respect to the above example, the goals would be to find out the current weather, and to make agent j aware of this information.

(3) For each goal, determine the plans that may be used to achieve it, and the context conditions under which each plan is appropriate. With respect to the above example, a plan for the goal of making agent j aware of the weather conditions might involve sending a message to j.

(4) Determine the belief structure of the system – the information requirements for each plan and goal. With respect to the above example, we might propose a unary predicate $windspeed(x)$ to represent the fact that the current wind speed is x. A plan to determine the current weather conditions would need to be able to represent this information.

Note that the analysis process will be iterative, as in more traditional methodologies. The outcome will be a model that closely corresponds to the PRS agent architecture. As a result, the move from end-design to implementation using PRS is relatively simple.

Wooldridge et al.: Gaia

The Gaia[1] methodology is intended to allow an analyst to go systematically from a statement of requirements to a design that is sufficiently detailed that it can be implemented directly. Note that we view the requirements capture phase as being independent of the paradigm used for analysis and design. In applying Gaia, the analyst moves from abstract to increasingly concrete concepts. Each successive move introduces greater implementation bias, and shrinks the space of possible systems that could be implemented to satisfy the original requirements statement. (See Jones (1990, pp. 216–222) for a discussion of implementation bias.)

Gaia borrows some terminology and notation from object-oriented analysis and design (specifically, FUSION (Coleman *et al.*, 1994)). However, it is not simply a naive attempt to apply such methods to agent-oriented development. Rather, it provides an agent-specific set of concepts through which a software engineer can understand and model a complex system. In particular, Gaia encourages a

---

[1]The name comes from the Gaia hypothesis put forward by James Lovelock, to the effect that all the organisms in the Earth's biosphere can be viewed as acting together to regulate the Earth's environment.

Table 10.1   Abstract and concrete concepts in Gaia.

Abstract concepts	Concrete concepts
Roles	Agent types
Permissions	Services
Responsibilities	Acquaintances
Protocols	
Activities	
Liveness properties	
Safety properties	

developer to think of building agent-based systems as a process of *organizational design*.

The main Gaian concepts can be divided into two categories: *abstract* and *concrete* (both of which are summarized in Table 10.1). Abstract entities are those used during analysis to conceptualize the system, but which do not necessarily have any *direct* realization within the system. Concrete entities, in contrast, are used within the design process, and will typically have direct counterparts in the run-time system.

The objective of the analysis stage is to develop an understanding of the system and its structure (without reference to any implementation detail). In the Gaia case, this understanding is captured in the system's *organization*. An organization is viewed as a collection of roles that stand in certain relationships to one another and that take part in systematic, institutionalized patterns of interactions with other roles.

The idea of a system as a society is useful when thinking about the next level in the concept hierarchy: *roles*. It may seem strange to think of a computer system as being defined by a set of roles, but the idea is quite natural when adopting an organizational view of the world. Consider a human organization such as a typical company. The company has roles such as 'president', 'vice president', and so on. Note that in a concrete *realization* of a company, these roles will be *instantiated* with actual individuals: there will be an individual who takes on the role of president, an individual who takes on the role of vice president, and so on. However, the instantiation is not necessarily static. Throughout the company's lifetime, many individuals may take on the role of company president, for example. Also, there is not necessarily a one-to-one mapping between roles and individuals. It is not unusual (particularly in small or informally defined organizations) for one individual to take on many roles. For example, a single individual might take on the role of 'tea maker', 'mail fetcher', and so on. Conversely, there may be many individuals that take on a single role, e.g. 'salesman'.

A role is defined by four attributes: *responsibilities, permissions, activities*, and *protocols. Responsibilities* determine functionality and, as such, are perhaps the key attribute associated with a role. An example responsibility associated with the role of company president might be calling the shareholders meeting every year. Responsibilities are divided into two types: *liveness properties* and *safety properties* (Pnueli, 1986). Liveness properties intuitively state that 'something good happens'. They describe those states of affairs that an agent must bring about, given certain environmental conditions. In contrast, safety properties are *invariants*. Intuitively, a safety property states that 'nothing bad happens' (i.e. that an acceptable state of affairs is maintained across all states of execution). An example might be 'ensure the reactor temperature always remains in the range 0–100'.

In order to realize responsibilities, a role has a set of *permissions*. Permissions are the 'rights' associated with a role. The permissions of a role thus identify the resources that are available to that role in order to realize its responsibilities. Permissions tend to be *information resources*. For example, a role might have associated with it the ability to read a particular item of information, or to modify another piece of information. A role can also have the ability to *generate* information.

The *activities* of a role are computations associated with the role that may be carried out by the agent without interacting with other agents. Activities are thus 'private' actions, in the sense of Shoham (1993).

Finally, a role is also identified with a number of *protocols*, which define the way that it can interact with other roles. For example, a 'seller' role might have the protocols 'Dutch auction' and 'English auction' associated with it; the Contract Net protocol is associated with the roles 'manager' and 'contractor' (Smith, 1980b).

Odell et al.: agent UML

Over the past two decades, many different notations and associated methodologies have been developed within the object-oriented development community (see, for example, Booch, 1994; Rumbaugh *et al.*, 1991; Coleman *et al.*, 1994). Despite many similarities between these notations and methods, there were nevertheless many fundamental inconsistencies and differences. The Unified Modelling Language – UML – is an attempt by three of the main figures behind object-oriented analysis and design (Grady Booch, James Rumbaugh and Ivar Jacobson) to develop a single notation for modelling object-oriented systems (Booch *et al.*, 1998). It is important to note that UML is *not* a methodology; it is, as its name suggests, a language for documenting models of systems; associated with UML is a methodology known as the Rational Unified Process (Booch *et al.*, 1998, pp. 449–456).

The fact that UML is a de facto standard for object-oriented modelling promoted its rapid take-up. When looking for agent-oriented modelling languages and tools, many researchers felt that UML was the obvious place to start (Odell *et al.*, 2001; Depke *et al.*, 2001; Bauer *et al.*, 2001). The result has been a number of attempts to adapt the UML notation for modelling agent systems. Odell and colleagues have discussed several ways in which the UML notation might usefully be extended to enable the modelling of agent systems (Odell *et al.*, 2001; Bauer *et al.*, 2001). The proposed modifications include:

- support for expressing concurrent threads of interaction (e.g. broadcast messages), thus enabling UML to model such well-known agent protocols as the Contract Net (Chapter 9);

- a notion of 'role' that extends that provided in UML, and, in particular, allows the modelling of an agent playing many roles.

Both the Object Management Group (OMG, 2001), and FIPA (see Chapter 8) are currently supporting the development of UML-based notations for modelling agent systems, and there is therefore likely to be considerable work in this area.

Treur et al.: DESIRE

In an extensive series of papers (see, for example, Brazier *et al.*, 1995; Dunin-Keplicz and Treur, 1995), Treur and colleagues have described the DESIRE framework. DESIRE is a framework for the design and formal specification of compositional systems. As well as providing a graphical notation for specifying such compositional systems, DESIRE has associated with it a graphical editor and other tools to support the development of agent systems.

Collinot et al.: Cassiopeia

In contrast to Gaia and the AAII methodology, the Cassiopeia method proposed by Collinot *et al.* is essentially *bottom up* in nature (Collinot *et al.*, 1996). Essentially, with the Cassiopeia method, one starts from the *behaviours* required to carry out some task; this is rather similar to the behavioural view of agents put forward by Brooks and colleagues (Brooks, 1999). Essentially, the methodology proposes three steps:

(1) identify the *elementary behaviours* that are implied by the overall system task;

(2) identify the *relationships* between elementary behaviours;

(3) identify the *organizational behaviours* of the system, for example, the way in which agents form themselves into groups.

Collinot *et al.* illustrate the methodology by way of the design of a RoboCup soccer team (see RoboCup, 2001).

Luck and d'Inverno: agents in Z

Luck and d'Inverno have developed an agent specification framework in the Z language (Spivey, 1992), although the types of agents considered in this framework are somewhat different from those discussed throughout most of this book (Luck and d'Inverno, 1995; Luck *et al.*, 1997; d'Inverno and Luck, 2001). They define a four-tiered hierarchy of the entities that can exist in an agent-based system. They start with *entities*, which are inanimate objects – they have attributes (colour, weight, position) but nothing else. They then define *objects* to be entities that have capabilities (e.g. tables are entities that are capable of supporting things). *Agents* are then defined to be objects that have goals, and are thus in some sense active; finally, *autonomous agents* are defined to be agents with motivations. The idea is that a chair could be viewed as taking on my goal of supporting me when I am using it, and can hence be viewed as an agent for me. But we would not view a chair as an *autonomous* agent, since it has no motivations (and cannot easily be attributed them). Starting from this basic framework, Luck and d'Inverno go on to examine the various relationships that might exist between agents of different types. In Luck *et al.* (1997), they examine how an agent-based system specified in their framework might be implemented. They found that there was a natural relationship between their hierarchical agent specification framework and object-oriented systems.

> The formal definitions of agents and autonomous agents rely on inheriting the properties of lower-level components. In the Z notation, this is achieved through schema inclusion. ... This is easily modelled in C++ by deriving one class from another. ... Thus we move from a principled but abstract theoretical framework through a more detailed, yet still formal, model of the system, down to an object-oriented implementation, preserving the hierarchical structure at each stage.
>
> (Luck *et al.*, 1997)

The Luck–d'Inverno formalism is attractive, particularly in the way that it captures the relationships that can exist between agents. The emphasis is placed on the notion of agents acting for another, rather than on agents as rational systems, as we discussed above. The types of agents that the approach allows us to develop are thus inherently different from the 'rational' agents discussed above. So, for example, the approach does not help us to construct agents that can interleave proactive and reactive behaviour. This is largely a result of the chosen specification language: Z. This language is inherently geared towards the specification of operation-based, functional systems. The basic language has no mechanisms that allow us to easily specify the ongoing behaviour of an agent-based system. There are of course extensions to Z designed for this purpose.

Discussion

The predominant approach to developing methodologies for multiagent systems is to adapt those developed for object-oriented analysis and design (Booch, 1994). There are several disadvantages with such approaches. First, the kinds of *decomposition* that object-oriented methods encourage is at odds with the kind of decomposition that *agent-oriented* design encourages. I discussed the relationship between agents and objects in Chapter 2: it should be clear from this discussion that agents and objects are very different beasts. While agent systems implemented using object-oriented programming languages will typically contain many objects, they will contain far fewer agents. A good agent-oriented design methodology would encourage developers to achieve the correct decomposition of entities into either agents or objects.

Another problem is that object-oriented methodologies simply do not allow us to capture many aspects of agent systems; for example, it is hard to capture in object models such notions as an agent proactively generating actions or dynamically reacting to changes in their environment, still less how to effectively cooperate and negotiate with other self-interested agents. The extensions to UML proposed in Odell *et al.* (2001), Depke *et al.* (2001) and Bauer *et al.* (2001) address some, but by no means all of these deficiencies. At the heart of the problem is the problem of the relationship between agents and objects, which has not yet been satisfactorily resolved.

10.3   Pitfalls of Agent Development

In this section (summarized from Wooldridge and Jennings (1998)), I give an overview of some of the main pitfalls awaiting the unwary multiagent system developer.

You oversell agent solutions, or fail to understand where agents may usefully be applied. Agent technology is currently the subject of considerable attention in the computer science and AI communities, and many predictions have been made about its long-term potential. However, one of the greatest current sources of perceived failure in agent-development initiatives is simply the fact that developers overestimate the potential of agent systems. While agent technology represents a potentially novel and important new way of conceptualizing and implementing software, it is important to understand its limitations. Agents are ultimately just software, and agent solutions are subject to the same fundamental limitations as more conventional software solutions. In particular, agent technology has not somehow solved the (very many) problems that have dogged AI since its inception. This is not the case. Agent systems typically make use of AI techniques. In this sense, they are an application of AI technology. But their 'intelligent' capabilities are limited by the state of the art in this field. Artificial intelligence as a field has suffered from over-optimistic claims about its potential. It seems essential that agent technology does not fall prey to this same problem: realistic expectations of what agent technology can provide are thus important.

You get religious or dogmatic about agents. Although agents have been used in a wide range of applications (see Chapter 11), they are not a universal solution. There are many applications for which conventional software development paradigms (such as object-oriented programming) are more appropriate.

Indeed, given the relative immaturity of agent technology and the small number of deployed agent applications, there should be clear advantages to an agent-based solution before such an approach is even contemplated.

You do not know why you want agents. This is a common problem for any new technology that has been hyped as much as agents. Managers read optimistic financial forecasts of the potential for agent technology and, not surprisingly, they want part of this revenue. However, in many cases, managers who propose an agent project do not actually have a clear idea about what 'having agents' will buy them. In short, they have no business model for agents – they have no understanding of how agents can be used to enhance their existing products, how they can enable them to generate new product lines, and so on.

You want to build generic solutions to one-off problems. This is a pitfall to which many software projects fall victim, but it seems especially prevalent in the agent community. It typically manifests itself in the devising of an architecture or testbed that supposedly enables a whole range of potential types of system to be built, when what is really required is a bespoke design to tackle a single problem. In such situations, a custom-built solution will be easier to develop and far more likely to satisfy the requirements of the application.

You believe that agents are a silver bullet. The holy grail of software engineering is a 'silver bullet': a technique that will provide an order of magnitude improvement in software development. Agent technology is a newly emerged, and as yet essentially untested, software paradigm: but it is only a matter of time before someone claims agents are a silver bullet. This would be dangerously naive. As we pointed out above, there are good arguments in favour of the view that agent technology will lead to improvements in the development of complex distributed software systems. But, as yet, these arguments are largely untested in practice.

You forget you are developing software. At the time of writing, the development of any agent system – however trivial – is essentially a process of experimentation. Although I discussed a number of methodologies above, there are no tried and trusted methodologies available. Unfortunately, because the process is experimental, it encourages developers to forget that they are actually developing software. The result is a foregone conclusion: the project flounders, not because of agent-specific problems, but because basic software engineering good practice was ignored.

You forget you are developing multi-threaded software. Multi-threaded systems have long been recognized as one of the most complex classes of computer system to design and implement. By their very nature, multiagent systems tend to be multi-threaded (both within an agent and certainly within the society of agents). So, in building a multiagent system, it is vital not to ignore the lessons learned from the concurrent and distributed systems community – the problems inherent in multi-threaded systems do not go away, just because you adopt an agent-based approach.

Your design does not exploit concurrency. One of the most obvious features of a poor multiagent design is that the amount of concurrent problem solving is comparatively small or even in extreme cases non-existent. If there is only ever a need for a single thread of control in a system, then the appropriateness of an agent-based solution must seriously be questioned.

You decide you want your own agent architecture. Agent architectures are essentially templates for building agents. When first attempting an agent project, there is a great temptation to imagine that no existing agent architecture meets the requirements of your problem, and that it is therefore necessary to design one from first principles. But designing an agent architecture from scratch in this way is often a mistake: my recommendation is therefore to study the various architectures described in the literature, and either license one or else implement an 'off-the-shelf' design.

Your agents use too much AI. When one builds an agent application, there is an understandable temptation to focus exclusively on the agent-specific, 'intelligence' aspects of the application. The result is often an agent framework that is too overburdened with experimental techniques (natural language interfaces, planners, theorem provers, reason maintenance systems, etc.) to be usable.

You see agents everywhere. When one learns about multiagent systems for the first time, there is a tendency to view everything as an agent. This is perceived to be in some way conceptually pure. But if one adopts this viewpoint, then one ends up with agents for everything, including agents for addition and subtraction. It is not difficult to see that naively viewing everything as an agent in this way will be extremely inefficient: the overheads of managing agents and inter-agent communication will rapidly outweigh the benefits of an agent-based solution. Moreover, we do not believe it is useful to refer to very fine-grained computational entities as agents.

You have too few agents. While some designers imagine a separate agent for every possible task, others appear not to recognize the value of a multiagent approach at all. They create a system that completely fails to exploit the power offered by the agent paradigm, and develop a solution with a very small number of agents doing all the work. Such solutions tend to fail the standard software engineering test of cohesion, which requires that a software module should have a single, coherent function. The result is rather as if one were to write an object-oriented program by bundling all the functionality into a single class. It can be done, but the result is not pretty.

You spend all your time implementing infrastructure. One of the greatest obstacles to the wider use of agent technology is that there are no widely used software platforms for developing multiagent systems. Such platforms would provide all the basic infrastructure (for message handling, tracing and monitoring, run-time management, and so on) required to create a multiagent system. As a result, almost every multiagent system project that we have come across has had a significant portion of available resources devoted to implementing this infrastructure from scratch. During this implementation stage, valuable time (and hence money) is often spent implementing libraries and software tools that, in the end, do little more than exchange messages across a network. By the time these libraries and tools have been implemented, there is frequently little time, energy, or enthusiasm left to work either on the agents themselves, or on the cooperative/social aspects of the system.

Your agents interact too freely or in an disorganized way. The dynamics of multiagent systems are complex, and can be chaotic. Often, the only way to find out what is likely to happen is to run the system repeatedly. If a system contains many agents, then the dynamics can become too complex to manage effectively. Another common misconception is that agent-based systems require no real structure. While this may be true in certain cases, most agent systems require considerably more system-level engineering than this. Some way of structuring the society is typically needed to reduce the system's complexity, to increase the system's efficiency, and to more accurately model the problem being tackled.

10.4   Mobile Agents

So far in this book I have avoided mention of an entire species of agent, which has aroused much interest, particularly in the programming-language and object-oriented-development community. *Mobile* agents are agents that are capable of transmitting themselves – their program *and* their state – across a computer network, and recommencing execution at a remote site. Mobile agents became known largely through the pioneering work of General Magic, Inc., on their Telescript programming language, although there are now mobile agent platforms available for many languages and platforms (see Appendix A for some notes on the history of mobile agents).

The original motivation behind mobile agents is simple enough. The idea was that mobile agents would replace *remote procedure calls* as a way for processes to communicate over a network – see Figure 10.1. With remote procedure calls, the idea is that one process can invoke a procedure (method) on another process which is remotely located. Suppose one process A invokes a method m on process B with arguments args; the value returned by process B is to be assigned to a variable v. Using a Java-like notation, A executes an instruction somewhat like the following:

```
v=B.m(args)
```

Crucially, in remote procedure calls, communication is *synchronous*. That is, process A *blocks* from the time that it starts executing the instruction until the time that B returns a value. If B *never* returns a value – because the network fails, for example – then A may remain indefinitely suspended, waiting for a reply that will never come. The network connection between A and B may well also remain open, and even though it is largely unused (no data is being sent for most of the time), this may be costly.

The idea of mobile agents (Figure 10.1(b)) is to replace the remote procedure call by sending out an agent to do the computation. Thus instead of invoking a method, process A sends out a program – a *mobile agent* – to process B. This program then interacts with process B. Since the agent shares the same address space as B, these interactions can be carried out much more efficiently than if the same interactions were carried out over a network. When the agent has completed its interactions, it returns to A with the required result. During the entire operation, the only network time required is that to send the agent to B, and that required to return the agent to A when it has completed its task. This is potentially a much more efficient use of network resources than the remote procedure call alternative described above. One of the original visions for Telescript was that it might provide an efficient way of managing network resources on devices such as hand-held/palmtop computers, which might be equipped with expensive, limited-bandwidth Internet connections.

There are a number of technical issues that arise when considering mobile agents.

Serialization. How is the agent serialized (i.e. encoded in a form suitable to be sent across the network), and, in particular, what aspects of the agent are serialized – the program, the data, or the program and its data?

Hosting and remote execution. When the agent arrives at its destination, how is it executed, for example if the original host of the agent employs a different operating system or processor to the destination host?

Security. When the agent from A is sent to the computer that hosts process B, there is obvious potential for the agent to cause trouble. It could potentially do this in a number of ways:

- it might obtain sensitive information by reading filestore or RAM directly;

- it might deny service to other processes on the host machine, by either occupying too much of the available processing resource (processor cycles or memory) or else by causing the host machine to malfunction (for example by writing over the machine's RAM); and, finally,

- it might simply cause irritation and annoyance, for example by causing many windows to pop up on the user's GUI.

Many different answers have been developed to address these issues. With respect to the first issue – that of how to serialize and transmit an agent – there are several possibilities.

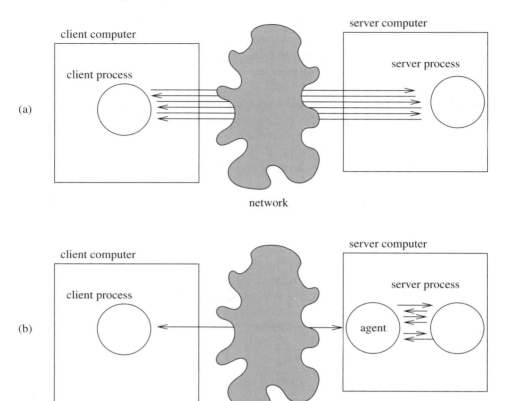

Figure 10.1   Remote procedure calls (a) versus mobile agents (b).

- Both the agent and its state are transmitted, and the state includes the program counter, i.e. the agent 'remembers' where it was before it was transmitted across the network, and when it reaches its destination, it recommences execution at the program instruction following that which caused it to be transmitted. This is the kind of mobility employed in the Telescript language (White, 1994, 1997).

- The agent contains both a program and the values of variables, but not the 'program counter', so the agent can remember the values of all variables, but not where it was when it transmitted itself across the network. This is how Danny Lange's Java-based Aglets framework works (Lange and Oshima, 1999).

- The agent to be transmitted is essentially a script, without any associated state (although state might be downloaded from the original host once the agent has arrived at its destination).

The issue of security dominates discussions about mobile agents. The key difficulty is that, in order for an agent to be able to do anything useful when it arrives at a remote location, it must access and make use of the resources supplied by the remote host. But providing access to these resources is inherently dangerous: it lays open the possibility that the host will be abused in some way. Languages like Java go some way to addressing these issues. For example, unlike languages such as C or C++, the Java language does not have pointers. It is thus inherently difficult (though not impossible) for a Java process to access the memory of the machine on which it is running. Java virtual machines also have a built in `SecurityManager`, which defines the extent to which processes running on the virtual machine can access various resources. However, it is very hard to ensure that (for example) a process does not use more than a certain number of processor cycles.

Telescript

Telescript was a language-based environment for constructing multiagent systems developed in the early 1990s by General Magic, Inc. It was a commercial product, developed with the then very new palm-top computing market in mind (White, 1994, 1997).

There are two key concepts in Telescript technology: places and agents. Places are virtual locations that are occupied by agents – a place may correspond to a single machine, or a family of machines. Agents are the providers and consumers of goods in the *electronic marketplace* applications that Telescript was developed to support. Agents in Telescript are interpreted programs; the idea is rather similar to the way that Java bytecodes are interpreted by the Java virtual machine.

Telescript agents are able to move from one place to another, in which case their program and state are encoded and transmitted across a network to another place, where execution recommences. In order to travel across the network, an agent uses a *ticket*, which specifies the parameters of its journey:

- the agent's destination;
- the time at which the journey will be completed.

Telescript agents communicate with one another in several different ways:

- if they occupy different places, then they can connect across a network;
- if they occupy the same location, then they can *meet* one another.

Telescript agents have an associated *permit*, which specifies what the agent can do (e.g. limitations on travel), and what resources the agent can use. The most important resources are

- 'money', measured in 'teleclicks' (which correspond to real money);
- lifetime (measured in seconds);
- size (measured in bytes).

Both Telescript agents and places are executed by an *engine*, which is essentially a virtual machine in the style of Java. Just as operating systems can limit the access provided to a process (e.g. in Unix, via access rights), so an engine limits the way an agent can access its environment. Engines continually monitor agent's resource consumption, and kill agents that exceed their limit. In addition, engines provide (C/C++) links to other applications via APIs.

Agents and places are programmed using the Telescript language. The Telescript language has the following characteristics.

- It is a pure object oriented language – everything is an object (somewhat based on Smalltalk).

- It is interpreted, rather than compiled.

- It comes in two levels – *high* (the 'visible' language for programmers) and *low* (a semi-compiled language for efficient execution, rather like Java bytecodes).

- It contains a 'process' class, of which 'agent' and 'place' are sub-classes.

- It is persistent, meaning that, for example, if a host computer was switched off and then on again, the state of the Telescript processes running on the host would have been automatically recorded, and execution would recommence automatically.

As noted in Appendix A, although Telescript was a pioneering language, which attracted a lot of attention, it was rapidly overtaken by Java, and throughout the late 1990s, a number of Java-based mobile agent frameworks appeared. The best known of these was Danny Lange's Aglets system.

Aglets – mobile agents in Java

Aglets is probably the best-known Java-based mobile agent platform. The core of Aglets lies in Java's ability to dynamically load and make instances of classes at run-time. An Aglet is an instance of a Java class that extends the `Aglet` class. When implementing such a class, the user can override a number of important methods provided by the `Aglet` class. The most important of these are

- the `onCreation()` method, which allows an Aglet to initialize itself; and

- the `run()` method, which is executed when an Aglet arrives at a new destination.

The core of an Aglet – the bit that does the work – is the `run()` method. This defines the behaviour of the Aglet. Inside a `run()` method, an Aglet can execute the `dispatch()` method, in order to transmit itself to a remote destination. An example of the use of the `dispatch()` method might be:

```
this.dispatch(new URL("atp://some.host.com/context1"));
```

This instruction causes the Aglet executing it to be serialized (i.e. for its state to be recorded), and then sent to the 'context' called `context1` on the host `some.host.com`. A context plays the role of a host in Telescript; a single host machine can support many different Aglet contexts. In this instruction, `atp` is the name of the protocol via which the agent is transferred (in fact, `atp` stands for Agent Transfer Protocol). When the agent is received at the remote host, an instance of the agent is created, the agent is initialized, its state is reconstructed from the serialized state sent with the agent, and, finally, the `run()` method is invoked. Notice that this is *not* the same as Telescript, where the agent recommences execution at the program instruction following the `go` instruction that caused the agent to be transmitted. This information is lost in Aglets (although the user can record this information 'manually' in the state of the Aglet if required).

Agent Tcl and other scripting languages

The Tool Control Language (Tcl – pronounced 'tickle') and its companion Tk are sometimes mentioned in connection with mobile agent systems. Tcl was primarily intended as a standard *command language* (Ousterhout, 1994). The idea is that many applications provide control languages (databases, spreadsheets, etc.), but every time a new application is developed, a new command language must be as well. Tcl provides the facilities to easily implement your own command language. Tk is an X Window based widget toolkit – it provides facilities for making GUI features such as buttons, labels, text and graphic windows (much like other X widget sets). Tk also provides powerful facilities for interprocess communication, via the exchange of Tcl scripts. Tcl/Tk combined make an attractive and simple to use GUI development tool; however, they have features that make them much more interesting:

- Tcl it is an *interpreted language*;
- Tcl is *extendable* – it provides a core set of primitives, implemented in C/C++, and allows the user to build on these as required;
- Tcl/Tk can be *embedded* – the interpreter itself is available as C++ code, which can be embedded in an application, and can itself be extended.

Tcl programs are called *scripts*. These scripts have many of the properties that Unix shell scripts have:

- they are plain text programs, that contain control structures (iteration, sequence, selection) and data structures (e.g. variables, lists, and arrays) just like a normal programming language;
- they can be executed by a shell program (`tclsh` or `wish`);
- they can call up various other programs and obtain results from these programs (cf. procedure calls).

As Tcl programs are interpreted, they are very much easier to prototype and debug than compiled languages like C/C++ – they also provide more powerful control constructs. The idea of a mobile agent comes in because it is easy to build applications where Tcl scripts are exchanged across a network, and executed on remote machines. The *Safe Tcl* language provides mechanisms for limiting the access provided to a script. As an example, Safe Tcl controls the access that a script has to the GUI, by placing limits on the number of times a window can be modified by a script.

In summary, Tcl/Tk provide a rich environment for building language-based applications, particularly GUI-based ones. But they are not/were not intended as agent programming environments. The core primitives may be used for building agent programming environments – the source code is free, stable, well-designed, and easily modified. The Agent Tcl framework is one attempt to do this (Gray, 1996; Kotz *et al.*, 1997).

Notes and Further Reading

Two collections of papers on the subject of agent-oriented software engineering are Ciancarini and Wooldridge (2001) and Wooldridge *et al.* (2002). Huhns (2001) and Lind (2001) give motivations for agent-oriented software engineering. A survey of methodologies for agent-oriented software engineering can be found in Iglesias *et al.* (1999).

A number of issues remain outstanding for the developer of agent-oriented methodologies.

Sorting out the relationship of agents to other software paradigms – objects in particular. It is not yet clear how the development of agent systems will coexist with other software paradigms, such as object-oriented development.

Agent-oriented methodologies. Although a number of preliminary agent-oriented analysis and design methodologies have been proposed, there is comparatively little consensus between these. In most cases, there is not even agreement on the kinds of concepts the methodology should support. The waters are muddied by the presence of UML as the predominant modelling language for object-oriented systems (Booch *et al.*, 1998): the kinds of concepts and notations supported by UML are not necessarily those best suited to the development of agent systems. Finding common ground between them – fitting agents into 'conventional' approaches to software development – needs some work.

Engineering for open systems. In open systems, it is essential to be capable of reacting to unforeseen events, exploiting opportunities where these arise, and dynamically reaching agreements with system components whose presence could not be predicted at design time. However, it is difficult to know how to *specify* such systems; still less how to implement them. In short, we need a better understanding of how to engineer open systems.

Engineering for scalability. Finally, we need a better understanding of how to safely and predictably engineer systems that comprise massive numbers of agents dynamically interacting with one another in order to achieve their goals. Such systems seem prone to problems such as unstable/chaotic behaviours, feedback, and so on, and may fall prey to malicious behaviour such as viruses.

See Wooldridge and Jennings (1998) for a more detailed discussion of the pitfalls that await the agent developer, and Webster (1995) for the book that inspired this article.

There is a substantial literature on mobile agents; see, for example, Rothermel and Popescu-Zeletin (1997) for a collection of papers on the subject; also worth looking at are Knabe (1995), Merz *et al.* (1997), Kiniry and Zimmerman (1997), Oshuga *et al.* (1997), Pham and Karmouch (1998), Breugst *et al.* (1999) and Brewington *et al.* (1999). Security for mobile agent systems is discussed in Tschudin (1999) and Yoshioka *et al.* (2001)

Class reading: Kinny and Georgeff (1997). This article describes arguably the first agent-specific methodology. For a class familiar with OO methodologies, it may be worth discussing the similarities, differences, and what changes might be required to make this methodology really usable in practice.

Exercises

(1) **[Class discussion.]**

For classes with some familiarity with object-oriented development: decomposition is perhaps the critical issue in an analysis and design methodology. Discuss the differences in the decomposition achieved with OO techniques to those of an agent system. What is the right 'grain size' for an agent? When we do analysis and design for agent systems, what are the key attributes that we need to characterize an agent in terms of?

(2) **[Class discussion.]**

With respect to mobile agent systems, discuss those circumstances where a mobile agent solution is *essential* – where you cannot imagine how it could be done without mobility.

(3) **[Level 2/3.]**

Use GAIA or the AAII methodology to do an analysis and design of a system with which you are familiar (if you are stuck for one, read about the ADEPT system described in Chapter 11). Compare it with an OO analysis and design approach.

(4) **[Level 4.]**

Extend the UML notation to incorporate agent facilities (such as communication in an agent communication languages). How might you capture the fact that agents are self-interested?

11

Applications

Agents have found application in many domains: in this chapter, I will describe some of the most notable. Broadly speaking, applications of agents can be divided into two main groups.

Distributed systems. In which agents become processing nodes in a distributed system. The emphasis in such systems is on the 'multi' aspect of multiagent systems.

Personal software assistants. In which agents play the role of proactive assistants to users working with some application. The emphasis here is on 'individual' agents.

In this chapter, I will discuss a range of such applications.

11.1 Agents for Workflow and Business Process Management

Workflow and business process control systems are an area of increasing importance in computer science. Workflow systems aim to automate the processes of a business, ensuring that different business tasks are expedited by the appropriate people at the right time, typically ensuring that a particular document flow is maintained and managed within an organization. The ADEPT system is a current example of an agent-based business process management system (Jennings *et al.*, 1996b). In ADEPT, a business organization is modelled as a society of negotiating, service providing agents.

More specifically, the process was providing customers with a quote for installing a network to deliver a particular type of telecommunications service.

This activity involves the following British Telecom (BT) departments: the Customer Service Division (CSD), the Design Division (DD), the Surveyor Department (SD), the Legal Division (LD), and the various organizations which provide the outsourced service of vetting customers (VCs). The process is initiated by a customer contacting the CSD with a set of requirements. In parallel to capturing the requirements, the CSD gets the customer vetted. If the customer fails the vetting procedure, the quote process terminates. Assuming the customer is satisfactory, their requirements are mapped against the service portfolio. If they can be met by an off-the-shelf item, then an immediate quote can be offered. In the case of bespoke services, however, the process is more complex. CSD further analyses the customer's requirements and whilst this is occurring LD checks the legality of the proposed service. If the desired service is illegal, the quote process terminates. If the requested service is legal, the design phase can start. To prepare a network design it is usually necessary to dispatch a surveyor to the customer's premises so that a detailed plan of the existing equipment can be produced. On completion of the network design and costing, DD informs CSD of the quote. CSD, in turn, informs the customer. The business process then terminates.

From this high-level system description, a number of autonomous problem-solving entities were identified. Thus, each department became an agent, and each individual within a department became an agent. To achieve their individual objectives, agents needed to interact with one another. In this case, all interactions took the form of negotiations about which services the agents would provide to one another and under what terms and conditions. The nature of these negotiations varied, depending on the context and the prevailing circumstances: interactions between BT internal agents were more cooperative than those involving external organizations, and negotiations where time is plentiful differed from those where time is short. In this context, negotiation involved generating a series of proposals and counter-proposals. If negotiation was successful, it resulted in a mutually agreeable contract. The agents were arranged in various organizational structures: collections of agents were grouped together as a single conceptual unit (e.g. the individual designers and lawyers in DD and LD, respectively), authority relationships (e.g. the DD agent is the manager of the SD agent), peers within the same organization (e.g. the CSD, LD, and DD agents) and customer–subcontractor relationships (e.g. the CSD agent and the various VCs).

The ADEPT application had a clear rationale for adopting an agent-based solution. Centralized workflow systems are simply too unresponsive and are unable to cope with unpredictable events. It was decided, therefore, to devolve responsibility for managing the business process to software entities that could respond more rapidly to changing circumstances. Since there will inevitably be inter-dependencies between the various devolved functions, these software entities must interact to resolve their conflicts. Such a method of approach leaves autonomous agents as the most natural means of modelling the solution. Further arguments in favour of an agent-based solution are that agents provide a software model that is ideally suited to the devolved nature of the proposed business management system. Thus, the project's goal was to devise an agent framework that could be used to build agents for business process management. Note that ADEPT was neither conceived nor implemented as a general-purpose agent framework.

Rather than reimplementing communications from first principles, ADEPT was built on top of a commercial CORBA platform (OMG, 2001). This platform provided the basis of handling distribution and heterogeneity in the ADEPT system. ADEPT agents also required the ability to undertake context-dependent reasoning and so a widely used expert system shell was incorporated into the agent architecture for this purpose. Development of either of these components from scratch would have consumed large amounts of project resources and would probably have resulted in a less robust and reliable solution. On the negative side, ADEPT failed to exploit any of the available standards for agent communication languages. This is a shortcoming that restricts the interoperation of the ADEPT system. In the same way that ADEPT exploited an off-the-shelf communications framework, so it used an architecture that had been developed in two previous projects (GRATE* (Jennings, 1993b) and ARCHON (Jennings *et al.*, 1996a)). This meant the analysis and design phases could be shortened since an architecture (together with its specification) had already been devised.

The business process domain has a large number of legacy components (especially databases and scheduling software). In this case, these were generally wrapped up as resources or tasks within particular agents.

ADEPT agents embodied comparatively small amounts of AI technology. For example, planning was handled by having partial plans stored in a plan library (in the style of the Procedural Reasoning System (Georgeff and Lansky, 1987)). The main areas in which AI techniques were used was in the way agents negotiated with one another and the way that agents responded to their environment. In the former case, each agent had a rich set of rules governing which negotiation strategy it should adopt in which circumstances, how it should respond to incoming negotiation proposals, and when it should change its negotiation strategy. In the latter case, agents were required to respond to unanticipated events in a dynamic and uncertain environment. To achieve their goals in such circumstances they needed to be flexible about their individual and their social behaviour.

ADEPT agents were relatively coarse grained in nature. They represented organizations, departments or individuals. Each such agent had a number of resources under its control, and was capable of a range of problem-solving behaviours. This led to a system design in which there were typically less than 10 agents at each level of abstraction and in which primitive agents were still capable of fulfilling some high-level goals.

11.2   Agents for Distributed Sensing

The classic application of multiagent technology was in distributed sensing (Lesser and Erman, 1980; Durfee, 1988). The broad idea is to have a system constructed as a network of spatially distributed sensors. The sensors may, for example, be acoustic sensors on a battlefield, or radars distributed across some airspace. The global goal of the system is to monitor and track all vehicles that pass within range of the sensors. This task can be made simpler if the sensor nodes in the network *cooperate* with one another, for example by exchanging predictions about when a vehicle will pass from the region of one sensor to the region of another. This apparently simple domain has yielded surprising richness as an environment for experimentation into multiagent systems: Lesser's well-known *Distributed Vehicle Monitoring Testbed* (DVMT) provided the proving ground for many of today's multiagent system development techniques (Lesser and Erman, 1980).

11.3   Agents for Information Retrieval and Management

The widespread provision of distributed, semi-structured information resources such as the World Wide Web obviously presents enormous potential; but it also presents a number of difficulties (such as 'information overload'). Agents have widely been proposed as a solution to these problems. An *information agent* is an agent that has access to at least one and potentially many information sources, and is able to collate and manipulate information obtained from these sources in order to answer queries posed by users and other information agents (the network of interoperating information sources are often referred to as intelligent and cooperative information systems (Papazoglou *et al.*, 1992)). The information sources may be of many types, including, for example, traditional databases as well as other information agents. Finding a solution to a query might involve an agent accessing information sources over a network. A typical scenario is that of a user who has heard about somebody at Stanford who has proposed something called agent-oriented programming. The agent is asked to investigate, and, after a careful search of various Web sites, returns with an appropriate technical report, as well as the name and contact details of the researcher involved.

To see how agents can help in this task, consider the Web. What makes the Web so effective is that

- it allows access to networked, widely distributed information resources;

- it provides a uniform interface to multi-media resources including text, images, sound, video, and so on;

- it is hypertext based, making it possible to link documents together in novel or interesting ways; and

- perhaps most importantly, it has an extraordinarily simple and intuitive user interface, which can be understood and used in seconds.

The reality of Web use at the beginning of the 21st century is, however, still somewhat beset by problems. These problems may be divided into two categories: *human* and *organizational*.

Human factors

The most obvious difficulty from the point of view of human users of the World-Wide Web is the 'information overload' problem (Maes, 1994a). People get overwhelmed by the sheer amount of information available, making it hard for them to filter out the junk and irrelevancies and focus on what is important, and also to actively search for the right information. Search engines such as Google and Yahoo attempt to alleviate this problem by indexing largely unstructured and unmanaged information on the Web. While these tools are useful, they tend to lack functionality: most search engines provide only simple search features, not tailored to a user's particular demands. In addition, current search engine functionality is directed at textual (typically HTML) content – despite the fact that one of the main selling features of the Web is its support for heterogeneous, multi-media content. Finally, it is not at all certain that the brute-force indexing techniques used by current search engines will scale to the size of the Internet in the next century. So *finding* and *managing* information on the Internet is, despite tools such as Google, still a problem.

In addition, people easily get bored or confused while browsing the Web. The hypertext nature of the Web, while making it easy to link related documents together, can also be disorienting – the 'back' and 'forward' buttons provided by most browsers are better suited to linear structures than the highly connected graph-like structures that underpin the Web. This can make it hard to understand the topology of a collection of linked Web pages; indeed, such structures are inherently difficult for humans to visualize and comprehend. In short, it is all too easy to become lost in cyberspace. When searching for a particular item of information, it is also easy for people to either miss or misunderstand things.

Finally, the Web was not really designed to be used in a methodical way. Most Web pages attempt to be attractive and highly animated, in the hope that people will find them interesting. But there is some tension between the goal of making a Web page animated and diverting and the goal of conveying information. Of course, it *is* possible for a well-designed Web page to effectively convey information, but, sadly, most Web pages emphasize appearance, rather than content. It is telling that the process of using the Web is known as 'browsing' rather than 'reading'. Browsing is a useful activity in many circumstances, but is not generally appropriate when attempting to answer a complex, important query.

Organizational factors

In addition, there are many organizational factors that make the Web difficult to use. Perhaps most importantly, apart from the (very broad) HTML standard, there are no standards for how a Web page should look.

Another problem is the cost of providing online content. Unless significant information owners can see that they are making money from the provision of their content, they will simply cease to provide it. How this money is to be made is probably the dominant issue in the development of the Web today. I stress that these are not criticisms of the Web – its designers could hardly have anticipated the uses to which it would be put, nor that they were developing one of the most important computer systems to date. But these are all obstacles that need to be overcome if the potential of the Internet/Web is to be realized. The obvious question is then: what more do we need?

In order to realize the potential of the Internet, and overcome the limitations discussed above, it has been argued that we need tools that (Durfee *et al.*, 1997)

- give a single coherent view of distributed, heterogeneous information resources;
- give rich, *personalized*, user-oriented services, in order to overcome the 'information overload' problem – they must enable users to find information they really want to find, and shield them from information they do not want;
- are scalable, distributed, and modular, to support the expected growth of the Internet and Web;
- are adaptive and self-optimizing, to ensure that services are flexible and efficient.

Personal information agents

Many researchers have argued that agents provide such a tool. Pattie Maes from the MIT media lab is perhaps the best-known advocate of this work. She developed a number of prototypical systems that could carry out some of these tasks. I will here describe MAXIMS, an email assistant developed by Maes.

> [MAXIMS] learns to prioritize, delete, forward, sort, and archive mail messages on behalf of a user.
>
> (Maes, 1994a)

MAXIMS works by 'looking over the shoulder' of a user, and learning about how they deal with email. Each time a new event occurs (e.g. email arrives), MAXIMS records the event in the form of

$$\text{situation} \longrightarrow \text{action}$$

pairs. A situation is characterized by the following attributes of an event:

- sender of email;

- recipients;

- subject line;

- keywords in message body and so on.

When a new situation occurs, MAXIMS matches it against previously recorded rules. Using these rules, it then tries to predict what the user will do, and generates a *confidence level*: a real number indicating how confident the agent is in its decision. The confidence level is matched against two preset real number thresholds: a 'tell me' threshold and a 'do it' threshold. If the confidence of the agent in its decision is less than the 'tell me' threshold, then the agent gets feedback from the user on what to do. If the confidence of the agent in its decision is between the 'tell me' and 'do it' thresholds, then the agent makes a suggestion to the user about what to do. Finally, if the agent's confidence is greater than the 'do it' threshold, then the agent takes the initiative, and acts.

Rules can also be hard coded by users (e.g. 'always delete mails from person *X*'). MAXIMS has a simple 'personality' (an animated face on the user's GUI), which communicates its 'mental state' to the user: thus the icon smiles when it has made a correct guess, frowns when it has made a mistake, and so on.

The NewT system is a Usenet news filter (Maes, 1994a, pp. 38, 39). A NewT agent is trained by giving it a series of examples, illustrating articles that the user would and would not choose to read. The agent then begins to make suggestions to the user, and is given feedback on its suggestions. NewT agents are not intended to remove human choice, but to represent an extension of the human's wishes: the aim is for the agent to be able to bring to the attention of the user articles of the type that the user has shown a consistent interest in. Similar ideas have been proposed by McGregor, who imagines *prescient agents* – intelligent administrative assistants, that predict our actions, and carry out routine or repetitive administrative procedures on our behalf (McGregor, 1992).

Web agents

Etzioni and Weld (1995) identify the following specific types of Web-based agent they believe are likely to emerge in the near future.

Tour guides. The idea here is to have agents that help to answer the question 'where do I go next' when browsing the Web. Such agents can learn about the user's preferences in the same way that MAXIMS does, and, rather than just providing a single, uniform type of hyperlink, they actually indicate the likely interest of a link.

Indexing agents. Indexing agents will provide an extra layer of abstraction on top of the services provided by search/indexing agents such as Google and *InfoSeek*. The idea is to use the raw information provided by such engines, together

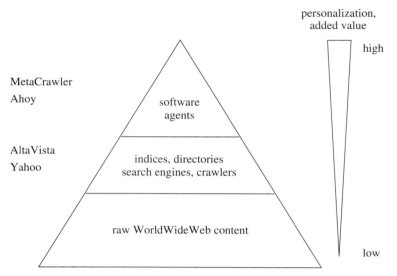

Figure 11.1   The Web information food chain.

with knowledge of the user's goals, preferences, etc., to provide a *personalized* service.

FAQ-finders. The idea here is to direct users to 'Frequently Asked Questions' (FAQs) documents in order to answer specific questions. Since FAQs tend to be knowledge-intensive, structured documents, there is a lot of potential for automated FAQ finders.

Expertise finders. Suppose I want to know about people interested in temporal belief logics. Current Web search tools would simply take the three words 'temporal', 'belief', 'logic', and search on them. This is not ideal: Google has no model of what you *mean* by this search, or what you really *want*. Expertise finders 'try to understand the user's wants and the contents of information services' in order to provide a better information provision service.

Etzioni (1996) put forward a model of information agents that *add value* to the underlying information infrastructure of the Web – the *information food chain* (see Figure 11.1). At the lowest level in the Web information food chain is raw content: the home pages of individuals and companies. The next level up the food chain is the services that 'consume' this raw content. These services include search engines such as Google, Lycos, and Yahoo.

These search engines maintain large databases of Web pages, indexed by content. Apart from the technical difficulties associated with storing such large databases and being able to process and retrieve their contents sufficiently quickly to provide a useful online service, the search engines must also *obtain* and *index* new or changed Web pages on a regular basis. Currently, this is done in one of two ways. The simplest is to have humans search for pages and classify them manually. This has the advantage that the classifications obtained in this way are likely to be meaningful and useful. But it has the very obvious disadvantage that it is not necessarily thorough, and is costly in terms of human resources. The second approach is to use simple software agents, often called *spiders*, to systematically search the Web, following all links, and automatically classifying content. The classification of content is typically done by removing 'noise' words from the page ('the', 'and', etc.), and then attempting to find those words that have the most meaning.

All current search engines, however, suffer from the disadvantage that their coverage is partial. Etzioni (1996) suggested that one way around this is to use a *meta* search engine. This search engine works not by directly maintaining a database of pages, but by querying a number of search engines in parallel. The results from these search engines can then be collated and presented to the user. The meta search engine thus 'feeds' off the other search engines. By allowing the engine to run on the user's machine, it becomes possible to personalize services – to tailor them to the needs of individual users.

Multiagent information retrieval systems

The information resources – Web sites – in the kinds of applications I discussed above are essentially *passive*. They simply deliver specific pages when requested. A common approach is thus to make information resources more 'intelligent' by *wrapping* them with agent capabilities. The structure of such a system is illustrated in Figure 11.2.

In this figure, there are a number of information repositories; these repositories may be Web sites, databases, or any other form of store. Access to these repositories is provided by information agents. These agents, which typically communicate using an agent communication language, are 'experts' about their associated repository. As well as being able to provide access to the repository, they are able to answer 'meta-level' queries about the content ('do you know about *X*'?). The agents will communicate with the repository using whatever native API the repository provides – HTTP, in the case of Web repositories.

To address the issue of finding agents in an open environment like the Internet, *middle agents* or *brokers* are used (Wiederhold, 1992; Kuokka and Harada, 1996). Each agent typically *advertises* its capabilities to some broker. Brokers come in several different types. They may be simply *matchmakers* or *yellow page* agents, which match advertisements to requests for advertised capabilities. Alternatively, they may be *blackboard* agents, which simply collect and make available requests. Or they may do both of these (Decker *et al.*, 1997). Different brokers may be specialized in different areas of expertise. For example, in Figure 11.2, one broker 'knows about' repositories 1, 2, and 3; the other knows about 2, 3, and 4.

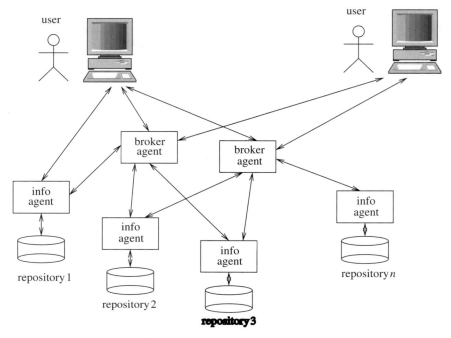

Figure 11.2   Typical architecture of a multiagent information system.

Brokered systems are able to cope more quickly with a rapidly fluctuating agent population. Middle agents allow a system to operate robustly in the face of intermittent communications and agent appearance and disappearance.

The overall behaviour of a system such as that in Figure 11.2 is that a user issues a query to an agent on their local machine. This agent may then contact information agents directly, or it may go to a broker, which is skilled at the appropriate type of request. The broker may then contact a number of information agents, asking first whether they have the correct skills, and then issuing specific queries. This kind of approach has been successfully used in *digital library* applications (Wellman *et al.*, 1996).

11.4   Agents for Electronic Commerce

The boom in interest in the Internet throughout the late 1990s went hand-in-hand with an explosion of interest in electronic commerce (e-commerce) (Ovum, 1994; Guilfoyle *et al.*, 1997). As it currently stands, the Web has a number of features that limit its use as an 'information market'. Many of these stem from the fact that the Web has academic origins, and as such, it was designed for free, open access. The Web was thus not designed to be used for commercial purposes, and a number of issues limit its use for this purpose.

Trust: in an online global marketplace, it is difficult for consumers to know which vendors are reliable/secure and which are not, as they are faced with vendor brands that they have not previously encountered.

Privacy and security: consumers (still) have major worries about the security of their personal information when using e-commerce systems – mechanisms such as secure HTTP (`https`) go some way to alleviating this problem, but it remains a major issue.

Billing/revenue: no built-in billing mechanisms are provided by the Web – they must be implemented over the basic Web structure; in addition, the Web was not designed with any particular revenue model in mind.

Reliability: the Internet – and hence the Web – is unreliable, in that data and connections are frequently lost, and it thus has unpredictable performance. These limitations may be accepted by academic or home/hobby users, but they represent a very real obstacle in the way of the wider commercial use of the Web.

'First-generation' e-commerce systems (of which `amazon.com` was perhaps the best known example) allowed a user to browse an online catalogue of products, choose some, and then purchase these selected products using a credit card. However, agents make it possible for *second-generation* e-commerce systems, in which many aspects of a consumer's buying behaviour is automated.

There are many models that attempt to describe consumer buying behaviour. Of these, one of the most popular postulates that consumers tend to engage in the following six steps (Guttman *et al.*, 1998, pp. 148, 149).

(1) Need identification. This stage characterizes the consumer becoming aware of some need that is not satisfied.

(2) Product brokering. In this stage, a would-be consumer obtains information relating to available products, in order to determine *what* product to buy.

(3) Merchant brokering. In this stage, the consumer decides *who* to buy from. This stage will typically involve examining offers from a range of different merchants.

(4) Negotiation. In this stage, the terms of the transaction are agreed between the would-be consumer and the would-be merchant. In some markets (e.g. regular retail markets), the negotiation stage is empty – the terms of agreement are fixed and not negotiable. In other markets (e.g. the used car market), the terms are negotiable.

(5) Purchase and delivery. In this stage, the transaction is actually carried out, and the good delivered.

(6) Product service and evaluation. The post-purchase stage involves product service, customer service, etc.

Table 11.1 Current agents for electronic commerce.

	Persona Logic	Firefly	Bargain Finder	Jango	Kasbah	Auction Bot	Tête-à-tête
Need identification	×	×		×			×
Product brokering	×			×			×
Merchant brokering			×	×	×	×	×
Negotiation					×	×	×
Purchase & delivery							
Service & evaluation							

Agents have been widely promoted as being able to automate (or at least partially automate) some of these stages, and hence assist the consumer to reach the best deal possible (Noriega and Sierra, 1999). Table 11.1 (from Guttman *et al.*, 1998) summarizes the extent to which currently developed agents can help in each stage.

Comparison shopping agents

The simplest type of agent for e-commerce is the *comparison shopping* agent. The idea is very similar to the meta search engines discussed above. Suppose you want to purchase the CD 'Music' by Madonna. Then a comparison shopping agent will search a number of online shops to find the best deal possible.

Such agents work well when the agent is required to compare goods with respect to a single attribute – typically price. The obvious examples of such situations are 'shrink wrapped' goods such as CDs and books. However, they work less well when there is more than one attribute to consider. An example might be the used-car market, where in addition to considering price, the putative consumer would want to consider the reputation of the merchant, the length and type of any guarantee, and many other attributes.

The Jango system (Doorenbos *et al.*, 1997) is a good example of a first-generation e-commerce agent. The long-term goals of the Jango project were to

- help the user decide what to buy;

- find specifications and reviews of products;

- make recommendations to the user;

- perform comparison shopping for the best buy;

- monitor 'what's new' lists; and

- watch for special offers and discounts.

A key obstacle that the developers of Jango encountered was simply that Web pages are all different. Jango exploited several *regularities* in vendor Web sites in order to make 'intelligent guesses' about their content.

Navigation regularity. Web sites are designed by vendors so that products are easy to find.

Corporate regularity. Web sites are usually designed so that pages have a similar 'look'n'feel';

Vertical separation. Merchants use white space to separate products.

Internally, Jango has two key components:

- a component to *learn vendor descriptions* (i.e. learn about the structure of vendor Web pages); and

- a *comparison shopping* component, capable of comparing products across different vendor sites.

In 'second-generation' agent mediated electronic commerce systems, it is proposed that agents will be able to assist with the fourth stage of the purchasing model set out above: negotiation. The idea is that a would-be consumer delegates the authority to negotiate terms to a software agent. This agent then negotiates with another agent (which may be a software agent or a person) in order to reach an agreement.

There are many obvious hurdles to overcome with respect to this model: The most important of these is *trust*. Consumers will not delegate the authority to negotiate transactions to a software agent unless they trust the agent. In particular, they will need to trust that the agent (i) really understands what they want, and (ii) that the agent is not going to be exploited ('ripped off') by another agent, and end up with a poor agreement.

Comparison shopping agents are particularly interesting because it would seem that, if the user is able to search the entire marketplace for goods at the best price, then the overall effect is to force vendors to push prices as low as possible. Their profit margins are inevitably squeezed, because otherwise potential purchasers would go elsewhere to find their goods.

Auction bots

A highly active related area of work is *auction bots*: agents that can run, and participate in, online auctions for goods. Auction bots make use of the kinds of auction techniques discussed in Chapter 7. A well-known example is the Kasbah system (Chavez and Maes, 1996). The aim of Kasbah was to develop a Web-based system in which users could create agents to buy and sell goods on their behalf. In Kasbah, a user can set three parameters for selling agents:

- desired date to sell the good by;

- desired price to sell at; and

- minimum price to sell at.

Selling agents in Kasbah start by offering the good at the desired price, and as the deadline approaches, this price is systematically reduced to the minimum price fixed by the seller. The user can specify the 'decay' function used to determine the current offer price. Initially, three choices of decay function were offered: linear, quadratic, and cubic decay. The user was always asked to confirm sales, giving them the ultimate right of veto over the behaviour of the agent.

As with selling agents, various parameters could be fixed for buying agents: the date to buy the item by, the desired price, and the maximum price. Again, the user could specify the 'growth' function of price over time.

Agents in Kasbah operate in a *marketplace*. The marketplace manages a number of ongoing auctions. When a buyer or seller enters the marketplace, Kasbah matches up requests for goods against goods on sale, and puts buyers and sellers in touch with one another.

The *Spanish Fishmarket* is another example of an online auction system (Rodríguez *et al.*, 1997). Based on a real fishmarket that takes place in the town of Blanes in northern Spain, the FM system provides similar facilities to Kasbah, but is specifically modelled on the auction protocol used in Blanes.

11.5 Agents for Human–Computer Interfaces

Currently, when we interact with a computer via a user interface, we are making use of an interaction paradigm known as *direct manipulation*. Put simply, this means that a computer program (a word processor, for example) will only do something if we explicitly tell it to, for example by clicking on an icon or selecting an item from a menu. When we work with humans on a task, however, the interaction is more two-way: we work with them as peers, each of us carrying out parts of the task and proactively helping each other as problem-solving progresses. In essence, the idea behind interface agents is to make computer systems more like proactive assistants. Thus, the goal is to have computer programs that in certain circumstances could *take the initiative*, rather than wait for the user to spell out exactly what they wanted to do. This leads to the view of computer programs as *cooperating* with a user to achieve a task, rather than acting simply as servants. A program capable of taking the initiative in this way would in effect be operating as a semi-autonomous agent. Such agents are sometimes referred to as *expert assistants* or *interface agents*. Maes (1994b, p. 71) defines interface agents as

> [C]omputer programs that employ artificial intelligence techniques in order to provide assistance to a user dealing with a particular application. . . . The metaphor is that of a *personal assistant* who is *collaborating with the user* in the same work environment.

One of the key figures in the development of agent-based interfaces has been Nicholas Negroponte (director of MIT's influential Media Lab). His vision of agents at the interface was set out in his 1995 book *Being Digital* (Negroponte, 1995):

The agent answers the phone, recognizes the callers, disturbs you when appropriate, and may even tell a white lie on your behalf. The same agent is well trained in timing, versed in finding opportune moments, and respectful of idiosyncrasies. .... If you have somebody who knows you well and shares much of your information, that person can act on your behalf very effectively. If your secretary falls ill, it would make no difference if the temping agency could send you Albert Einstein. This issue is not about IQ. It is shared knowledge and the practice of using it in your best interests. .... Like an army commander sending a scout ahead...you will dispatch agents to collect information on your behalf. Agents will dispatch agents. The process multiplies. But [this process] started at the interface where you delegated your desires.

11.6 Agents for Virtual Environments

There is obvious potential for marrying agent technology with that of the cinema, computer games, and virtual reality. The OZ project was initiated to develop:

> ...artistically interesting, highly interactive, simulated worlds...to give users the experience of living in (not merely watching) dramatically rich worlds that include moderately competent, emotional agents.

> (Bates *et al.*, 1992b, p. 1)

In order to construct such simulated worlds, one must first develop *believable agents*: agents that 'provide the illusion of life, thus permitting the audience's suspension of disbelief' (Bates, 1994, p. 122). A key component of such agents is *emotion*: agents should not be represented in a computer game or animated film as the flat, featureless characters that appear in current computer games. They need to show emotions; to act and react in a way that resonates in tune with our empathy and understanding of human behaviour. The OZ group investigated various architectures for emotion (Bates *et al.*, 1992a), and have developed at least one prototype implementation of their ideas (Bates, 1994).

11.7 Agents for Social Simulation

I noted in Chapter 1 that one of the visions behind multiagent systems technology is that of using agents as an experimental tool in the social sciences (Gilbert and Doran, 1994; Gilbert, 1995; Moss and Davidsson, 2001). Put crudely, the idea is that agents can be used to simulate the behaviour of human societies. At its simplest, individual agents can be used to represent individual people; alternatively, individual agents can be used to represent organizations and similar such entities.

Conte and Gilbert (1995, p. 4) suggest that multiagent simulation of social processes can have the following benefits:

- computer simulation allows the observation of properties of a model that may *in principle* be analytically derivable but have not yet been established;

- possible alternatives to a phenomenon observed in nature may be found;

- properties that are difficult/awkward to observe in nature may be studied at leisure in isolation, recorded, and then 'replayed' if necessary;

- 'sociality' can be modelled explicitly – agents can be built that have representations of other agents, and the properties and implications of these representations can be investigated.

Moss and Davidsson (2001, p. 1) succinctly states a case for multiagent simulation:

> [For many systems,] behaviour cannot be predicted by statistical or qualitative analysis. ... Analysing and designing...such systems requires a different approach to software engineering and mechanism design.

Moss goes on to give a general critique of approaches that focus on formal analysis at the expense of accepting and attempting to deal with the 'messiness' that is inherent in most multiagent systems of any complexity. It is probably fair to say that his critique might be applied to many of the techniques described in Chapter 7, particularly those that depend upon a 'pure' logical or game-theoretic foundation. There is undoubtedly some strength to these arguments, which echo cautionary comments made by some of the most vocal proponents of game theory (Binmore, 1992, p. 196). In the remainder of this section, I will review one major project in the area of social simulation, and point to some others.

The EOS project

The EOS project, undertaken at the University of Essex in the UK, is a good example of a social simulation system (Doran, 1987; Doran *et al.*, 1992; Doran and Palmer, 1995). The aim of the EOS project was to investigate the causes of the emergence of social complexity in Upper Palaeolithic France. Between 15 000 and 30 000 years ago, at the height of the last ice age, there was a relatively rapid growth in the complexity of societies that existed at this time. The evidence of this social complexity came in the form of Doran and Palmer (1995)

- larger and more abundant archaeological sites;

- increased wealth, density, and stratigraphic complexity of archaeological material in sites;

- more abundant and sophisticated cave art (the well-known caves at Lascaux are an example);

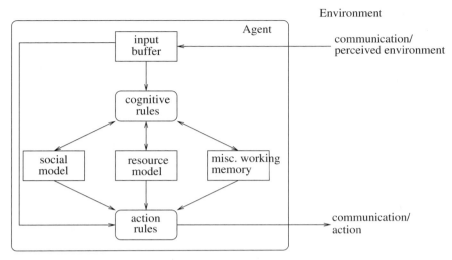

Figure 11.3   Agents in EOS.

- increased stone, bone, and antler technology;
- abundance of 'trade' objects.

A key open question for archaeologists is what exactly *caused* this emergence of complexity. In 1985, the archaeologist Paul Mellars proposed a model that attempted to explain this complexity. The main points of Mellar's model were that the key factors leading to this growth in complexity were an exceptional wealth and diversity of food resources, and a strong, stable, predictable concentration of these resources.

In order to investigate this model, a multiagent experimental platform – the EOS testbed – was developed. This testbed, implemented in the Prolog language (Clocksin and Mellish, 1981), allows agents to be programmed as rule-based systems. The structure of an EOS agent is shown in Figure 11.3.

Each agent in EOS is endowed with a symbolic representation of its environment – its beliefs. Beliefs are composed of beliefs about other agents (the *social model*), beliefs about resources in the environment (the *resource model*), and miscellaneous other beliefs. To update its beliefs, an agent has a set of *cognitive rules*, which map old beliefs to new ones. To decide what action to perform, agents have *action rules*: action rules map beliefs to actions. (Compare with Shoham's Agent0 system described in Chapter 3.) Both cognitive rules and action rules are executed in a forward-chaining manner.

Agents in the EOS testbed inhabit a simulated two-dimensional environment, some $10\,000 \times 10\,000$ cells in size (cf. the Tileworld described in Chapter 2.) Each agent occupies a single cell, initially allocated at random. Agents have associated with them *skills* (cf. the MACE system described in Chapter 9.) The idea is that an agent will attempt to obtain resources ('food') which are situated in the environment; resources come in different types, and only agents of certain types are able to obtain certain resources. Agents have a number of 'energy stores', and for each of these a 'hunger level'. If the energy store associated with a particular hunger level falls below the value of the hunger level, then the agent will attempt to replenish it by consuming appropriate resources. Agents travel about the EOS world in order to obtain resources, which are scattered about the world. Recall that the Mellars model suggested that the availability of resources at predictable locations and times was a key factor in the growth of the social complexity in the Palaeolithic period. To reflect this, resources (intuitively corresponding to things like a Reindeer herd or a fruit tree) were clustered, and the rules governing the emergence and disappearance of resources reflects this.

The basic form of social structure that emerges in EOS does so because certain resources have associated with them a *skill profile*. This profile defines, for every type of skill or capability that agents may possess, how many agents with this skill are required to obtain the resource. For example, a 'fish' resource might require two 'boat' capabilities; and a 'deer' resource might require a single 'spear' capability.

In each experiment, a user may specify a number of parameters:

- the number of resource locations of each type and their distribution;
- the number of resource instances that each resource location comprises;
- the type of energy that each resource location can supply;
- the quantity of energy an instance of a particular resource can supply;
- the skill profiles for each resource; and
- the 'renewal' period, which elapses between a resource being consumed and being replaced.

To form collaborations in order to obtain resources, agents use a variation of Smith's Contract Net protocol (see Chapter 9): thus, when an agent finds a resource, it can advertise this fact by sending out a broadcast announcement. Agents can then bid to collaborate on obtaining a resource, and the successful bidders then work together to obtain the resource.

A number of social phenomena were observed in running the EOS testbed, for example: 'overcrowding', when too many agents attempt to obtain resources in some locale; 'clobbering', when agents accidentally interfere with each other's goals; and semi-permanent groups arising. With respect to the emergence of deep hierarchies of agents, it was determined that the growth of hierarchies depended to a great extent on the perceptual capabilities of the group. If the group is not equipped with adequate perceptual ability, then there is insufficient information to cause a group to form. A second key aspect in the emergence of social structure is the complexity of resources – how many skills it requires in order to obtain and exploit a resource. If resources are too complex, then groups will not be able to form to exploit them before they expire.

An interesting aspect of the EOS project was that it highlighted the *cognitive* aspects of multiagent social simulation. That is, by using EOS, it was possible to see how the beliefs and aspirations of individuals in a society can influence the possible trajectories of this society. One of the arguments in favour of this style of multiagent societal simulation is that this kind of property is very hard to model or understand using analytical techniques such as game or economic theory (cf. the quote from Moss, above).

Policy modelling by multiagent simulation

Another application area for agents in social simulation is that of *policy modelling and development* (Downing *et al.*, 2001). Regulatory and other similar bodies put forward policies, which are designed – or at least intended – to have some desired effect. An example might be related to the issue of potential climate change caused by the release of greenhouse gases (cf. Downing *et al.*, 2001). A national government, or an international body such as the EU, might desire to reduce the potentially damaging effects of climate change, and put forward a policy designed to limit it. A typical first-cut at such a policy might be to increase fuel taxes, the idea being that this reduces overall fuel consumption, in turn reducing the release of greenhouse gases. But policy makers must generally form their policies in ignorance of what the *actual* effect of their policies will be, and, in particular, the actual effect may be something quite different to that intended. In the greenhouse gas example, the effect of increasing fuel taxes might be to cause consumers to switch to cheaper – dirtier – fuel types, at best causing no overall reduction in the release of greenhouse gases, and potentially even leading to an increase. So, it is proposed, multiagent simulation models might fruitfully be used to gain an understanding of the effect of their nascent policies.

An example of such a system is the Freshwater Integrated Resource Management with Agents (FIRMA) project (Downing *et al.*, 2001). This project is specifically intended to understand the impact of governments exhorting water consumers to exercise care and caution in water use during times of drought (Downing *et al.*, 2001, p. 206). (In case you were wondering, yes, droughts *do* happen in the UK!) Downing *et al.* (2001) developed a multiagent simulation model in which water consumers were represented by agents, and a 'policy' agent issued exhortations to consume less at times of drought. The authors were able to develop a simulation model that fairly closely resembled the observed behaviour in human societies in similar circumstances; developing this model was an iterative process of model reformulation followed by a review of the observed results of the model with water utilities.

11.8 Agents for *X*

Agents have been proposed for many more application areas than I have the space to discuss here. In this section, I will give a flavour of some of these.

Agents for industrial systems management. Perhaps the largest and probably best-known European multiagent system development project to date was ARCHON (Wittig, 1992; Jennings and Wittig, 1992; Jennings *et al.*, 1995). This project developed and deployed multiagent technology in several industrial domains. The most significant of these domains was a power distribution system, which was installed and is currently operational in northern Spain. Agents in ARCHON have two main parts: a *domain* component, which realizes the domain-specific functionality of the agent; and a *wrapper* component, which provides the agent functionality, enabling the system to plan its actions, and to represent and communicate with other agents. The ARCHON technology has subsequently been deployed in several other domains, including particle accelerator control. (ARCHON was the platform through which Jennings's joint intention model of cooperation (Jennings, 1995), discussed in Chapter 9, was developed.)

Agents for Spacecraft Control. It is difficult to imagine a domain with harder real-time constraints than that of in-flight diagnosis of faults on a spacecraft. Yet one of the earliest applications of the PRS architecture was precisely this (Georgeff and Lansky, 1987). In brief, the procedures that an astronaut would use to diagnose faults in the Space Shuttle's reaction control systems were directly coded as PRS plans, and the PRS architecture was used to interpret these plans, and provide real-time advice to astronauts in the event of failure or malfunction in this system.

Agents for Air-Traffic Control. Air-traffic control systems are among the oldest application areas in multiagent systems (Steeb *et al.*, 1988; Findler and Lo, 1986). A recent example is OASIS (*O*ptimal *A*ircraft *S*equencing using *I*ntelligent *S*cheduling), a system that is currently undergoing field trials at Sydney airport in Australia (Ljunberg and Lucas, 1992). The specific aim of OASIS is to assist an air-traffic controller in managing the flow of aircraft at an airport: it offers estimates of aircraft arrival times, monitors aircraft progress against previously derived estimates, informs the air-traffic controller of any errors, and perhaps most importantly finds the optimal sequence in which to land aircraft. OASIS contains two types of agents: *global* agents, which perform generic domain functions (for example, there is a 'sequencer agent', which is responsible for arranging aircraft into a least-cost sequence); and *aircraft agents*, one for each aircraft in the system airspace. The OASIS system was implemented using the PRS agent architecture.

Notes and Further Reading

Jennings and Wooldridge (1998a) is a collection of papers on applications of agent systems. Parunak (1999) gives a more recent overview of industrial applications.

Hayzelden and Bigham (1999) is a collection of articles loosely based around the theme of agents for computer network applications; Klusch (1999) is a similar collection centred around the topic of information agents.

Van Dyke Parunak (1987) describes the use of the Contract Net protocol (Chapter 8) for manufacturing control in the YAMS (*Y*et *A*nother *M*anufacturing *S*ystem). Mori *et al.* have used a multiagent approach to controlling a steel coil processing plant (Mori *et al.*, 1988), and Wooldridge *et al.* have described how the process of determining an optimal production sequence for some factory can naturally be viewed as a problem of negotiation between the various production cells within the factory (Wooldridge *et al.*, 1996).

A number of studies have been made of information agents, including a theoretical study of how agents are able to incorporate information from different sources (Levy *et al.*, 1994; Gruber, 1991), as well as a prototype system called IRA (information retrieval agent) that is able to search for loosely specified articles from a range of document repositories (Voorhees, 1994). Another important system in this area was Carnot (Huhns *et al.*, 1992), which allows preexisting and heterogeneous database systems to work together to answer queries that are outside the scope of any of the individual databases.

There is much related work being done by the computer supported cooperative work (CSCW) community. CSCW is informally defined by Baecker to be 'computer assisted coordinated activity such as problem solving and communication carried out by a group of collaborating individuals' (Baecker, 1993, p. 1). The primary emphasis of CSCW is on the development of (hardware and) software tools to support collaborative human work – the term *groupware* has been coined to describe such tools. Various authors have proposed the use of agent technology in groupware. For example, in his *participant systems* proposal, Chang suggests systems in which humans collaborate with not only other humans, but also with artificial agents (Chang, 1987). We refer the interested reader to the collection of papers edited by Baecker (1993) and the article by Greif (1994) for more details on CSCW.

Noriega and Sierra (1999) is a collection of paper on agent-mediated electronic commerce. Kephart and Greenwald (1999) investigates the dynamics of systems in which buyers and sellers are agents.

Gilbert and Doran (1994), Gilbert and Conte (1995) and Moss and Davidsson (2001) are collections of papers on the subject of simulating societies by means of multiagent systems. Davidsson (2001) discusses the relationship between multiagent simulation and other types of simulation (e.g. object-oriented simulation and discrete event models).

Class reading: Parunak (1999).   This paper gives an overview of the use of agents in industry from one of the pioneers of agent applications.

Exercises

(1) **[Level 1/Class Discussion.]**

Many of the systems discussed in this chapter (e.g. MAXIMS, NewT, Jango) do not perhaps match up too well to the notion of an agent as I discussed it in Chapter 2 (i.e. reactive, proactive, social). Does this matter? Do they still deserve to be called agents?

(2) **[Level 4.]**

Take an agent programming environment off the shelf (e.g. Jam (Huber, 1999), Jack (Busetta *et al.*, 2000), Jade (Poggi and Rimassa, 2001) or JATLite (Jeon *et al.*, 2000)) and, using one of the methodologies described in the preceding chapter, use it to implement a major multiagent system. Document your experiences, and contrast them with the experiences you would expect with conventional approaches to system development. Weigh up the pros and cons, and use them to feed back into the multiagent research and development literature.

12

Logics for Multiagent Systems

Computer science is, as much as it is about anything, about developing formal theories to specify and reason about computer systems. Many formalisms have been developed in mainstream computer science to do this, and it comes as no surprise to discover that the agents community has also developed many such formalisms. In this chapter, I give an overview of some of the logics that have been developed for reasoning about multiagent systems. The predominant approach has been to use what are called *modal* logics to do this. The idea is to develop logics that can be used to characterize the *mental states* of agents as they act and interact. (See Chapter 2 for a discussion on the use of mental states for reasoning about agents.)

Following an introduction to the need for modal logics for reasoning about agents, I introduce the paradigm of *normal modal logics with Kripke semantics*, as this approach is almost universally used. I then go on to discuss how these logics can be used to reason about the *knowledge* that agents possess, and then *integrated theories of agency*. I conclude by speculating on the way that these formalisms might be used in the development of agent systems.

> *Please note*: this chapter presupposes some understanding of the use of logic and formal methods for specification and verification. It is probably best avoided by those without such a background.

12.1   Why Modal Logic?

Suppose one wishes to reason about mental states – beliefs and the like – in a logical framework. Consider the following statement (after Genesereth and Nilsson, 1987, pp. 210, 211):

Janine believes Cronos is the father of Zeus.   (12.1)

The best-known and most widely used logic in computer science is first-order logic. So, can we represent this statement in first-order logic? A naive attempt to translate (12.1) into first-order logic might result in the following:

$$Bel(Janine, Father(Zeus, Cronos)).   \text{(12.2)}$$

Unfortunately, this naive translation does not work, for at least two reasons. The first is syntactic: the second argument to the *Bel* predicate is a *formula* of first-order logic, and is not, therefore, a term. So (12.2) is not a well-formed formula of classical first-order logic.

The second problem is semantic. The constants *Zeus* and *Jupiter*, by any reasonable interpretation, denote the same individual: the supreme deity of the classical world. It is therefore acceptable to write, in first-order logic,

$$(Zeus = Jupiter).   \text{(12.3)}$$

Given (12.2) and (12.3), the standard rules of first-order logic would allow the derivation of the following:

$$Bel(Janine, Father(Jupiter, Cronos)).   \text{(12.4)}$$

But intuition rejects this derivation as invalid: believing that the father of Zeus is Cronos is *not* the same as believing that the father of Jupiter is Cronos.

So what is the problem? Why does first-order logic fail here? The problem is that the intentional notions – such as belief and desire – are *referentially opaque*, in that they set up *opaque contexts*, in which the standard substitution rules of first-order logic do not apply. In classical (propositional or first-order) logic, the denotation, or semantic value, of an expression is dependent solely on the denotations of its sub-expressions. For example, the denotation of the propositional logic formula $p \wedge q$ is a function of the truth-values of p and q. The operators of classical logic are thus said to be *truth functional*.

In contrast, intentional notions such as belief are *not* truth functional. It is surely not the case that the truth value of the sentence:

Janine believes p (12.5)

is dependent solely on the truth-value of p[1]. So substituting equivalents into opaque contexts is not going to preserve meaning. This is what is meant by referential opacity. The existence of referentially opaque contexts has been known

---

[1]Note, however, that the sentence (12.5) is itself a proposition, in that its denotation is the value true or false.

since the time of Frege. He suggested a distinction between *sense* and *reference*. In ordinary formulae, the 'reference' of a term/formula (i.e. its denotation) is needed, whereas in opaque contexts, the 'sense' of a formula is needed (see also Seel, 1989, p. 3).

Clearly, classical logics are not suitable in their standard form for reasoning about intentional notions: alternative formalisms are required. A vast enterprise has sprung up devoted to developing such formalisms.

The field of formal methods for reasoning about intentional notions is widely reckoned to have begun with the publication, in 1962, of Jaakko Hintikka's book *Knowledge and Belief: An Introduction to the Logic of the Two Notions* (Hintikka, 1962). At that time, the subject was considered fairly esoteric, of interest to comparatively few researchers in logic and the philosophy of mind. Since then, however, it has become an important research area in its own right, with contributions from researchers in AI, formal philosophy, linguistics and economics. There is now an enormous literature on the subject, and with a major biannual international conference devoted solely to theoretical aspects of reasoning about knowledge, as well as the input from numerous other, less specialized conferences, this literature is growing ever larger.

Despite the diversity of interests and applications, the number of basic techniques in use is quite small. Recall, from the discussion above, that there are two problems to be addressed in developing a logical formalism for intentional notions: a syntactic one, and a semantic one. It follows that any formalism can be characterized in terms of two independent attributes: its *language of formulation*, and *semantic model* (Konolige, 1986, p. 83).

There are two fundamental approaches to the syntactic problem. The first is to use a *modal* language, which contains non-truth-functional *modal operators*, which are applied to formulae. An alternative approach involves the use of a *meta-language*: a many-sorted first-order language containing terms which denote formulae of some other *object-language*. Intentional notions can be represented using a meta-language predicate, and given whatever axiomatization is deemed appropriate. Both of these approaches have their advantages and disadvantages, and will be discussed at length in the sequel.

As with the syntactic problem, there are two basic approaches to the semantic problem. The first, best-known, and probably most widely used approach is to adopt a *possible-worlds* semantics, where an agent's beliefs, knowledge, goals, etc., are characterized as a set of so-called *possible worlds*, with an *accessibility relation* holding between them. Possible-worlds semantics have an associated *correspondence theory* which makes them an attractive mathematical tool to work with (Chellas, 1980). However, they also have many associated difficulties, notably the well-known logical omniscience problem, which implies that agents are perfect reasoners. A number of minor variations on the possible-worlds theme have been proposed, in an attempt to retain the correspondence theory, but without logical omniscience.

The most common alternative to the possible-worlds model for belief is to use a *sentential* or *interpreted symbolic structures* approach. In this scheme, beliefs are viewed as symbolic formulae explicitly represented in a data structure associated with an agent. An agent then believes φ if φ is present in the agent's belief structure. Despite its simplicity, the sentential model works well under certain circumstances (Konolige, 1986).

The next part of this chapter contains detailed reviews of some of these formalisms. First, the idea of possible-worlds semantics is discussed, and then a detailed analysis of normal modal logics is presented, along with some variants on the possible-worlds theme.

12.2   Possible-Worlds Semantics for Modal Logics

The possible-worlds model for epistemic logics was originally proposed by Hintikka (1962), and is now most commonly formulated in a normal modal logic using the techniques developed by Kripke (1963). Hintikka's insight was to see that an agent's beliefs could be characterized in terms of a set of *possible worlds*, in the following way. Consider an agent playing the card game Gin Rummy (this example was adapted from Halpern (1987)). In this game, the more one knows about the cards possessed by one's opponents, the better one is able to play. And yet complete knowledge of an opponent's cards is generally impossible (if one excludes cheating). The ability to play Gin Rummy well thus depends, at least in part, on the ability to deduce what cards are held by an opponent, given the limited information available. Now suppose our agent possessed the ace of spades. Assuming the agent's sensory equipment was functioning normally, it would be rational of her to believe that she possessed this card. Now suppose she were to try to deduce what cards were held by her opponents. This could be done by first calculating all the various different ways that the cards in the pack could possibly have been distributed among the various players. (This is not being proposed as an actual card-playing strategy, but for illustration!) For argument's sake, suppose that each possible configuration is described on a separate piece of paper. Once the process was complete, our agent could then begin to systematically eliminate from this large pile of paper all those configurations which were *not possible, given what she knows*. For example, any configuration in which she did not possess the ace of spades could be rejected immediately as impossible. Call each piece of paper remaining after this process a *world*. Each world represents one state of affairs considered possible, given what she knows. Hintikka coined the term *epistemic alternatives* to describe the worlds possible given one's beliefs. Something true in *all* our agent's epistemic alternatives could be said to be believed by the agent. For example, it will be true in all our agent's epistemic alternatives that she has the ace of spades.

On a first reading, this technique seems a peculiarly roundabout way of characterizing belief, but it has two advantages. First, it remains neutral on the subject of the cognitive structure of agents. It certainly does not posit any internalized collection of possible worlds. It is just a convenient way of characterizing belief. Second, the mathematical theory associated with the formalization of possible worlds is extremely appealing (see below).

The next step is to show how possible worlds may be incorporated into the semantic framework of a logic. This is the subject of the next section.

12.3 Normal Modal Logics

Epistemic logics are usually formulated as *normal modal logics* using the semantics developed by Kripke (1963). Before moving on to explicitly epistemic logics, this section describes normal modal logics in general.

Modal logics were originally developed by philosophers interested in the distinction between *necessary* truths and mere *contingent* truths. Intuitively, a necessary truth is something that is true *because it could not have been otherwise*, whereas a contingent truth is something that could, plausibly, have been otherwise. For example, it is a fact that as I write, the Labour Party of Great Britain holds a majority in the House of Commons. But although this is true, it is *not* a necessary truth; it could quite easily have turned out that the Conservative Party won a majority at the last general election. This fact is thus only a contingent truth.

Contrast this with the following statement: *the square root of 2 is not a rational number*. There seems no earthly way that this could be anything *but* true (given the standard reading of the sentence). This latter fact is an example of a necessary truth. Necessary truth is usually defined as something true in *all possible worlds*. It is actually quite difficult to think of any necessary truths other than mathematical laws.

To illustrate the principles of modal epistemic logics, I will define a simple normal propositional modal logic. This logic is essentially classical propositional logic, extended by the addition of two operators: '$\Box$' (necessarily), and '$\Diamond$' (possibly).

First, its syntax. Let $Prop = \{p, q, \dots\}$ be a countable set of *atomic propositions*. The syntax of normal propositional modal logic is defined by the following rules.

(1) If $p \in Prop$, then p is a formula.

(2) If φ, ψ are formulae, then so are

$$\text{true} \quad \neg\varphi \quad \varphi \vee \psi.$$

(3) If φ is a formula, then so are

$$\Box\varphi \quad \Diamond\varphi.$$

The operators '$\neg$' (not) and '$\vee$' (or) have their standard meaning; true is a logical constant (sometimes called *verum*) that is always true. The remaining connectives

$\langle M, w \rangle$	$\models$	true	
$\langle M, w \rangle$	$\models$	p	where $p \in Prop$, if and only if $p \in \pi(w)$
$\langle M, w \rangle$	$\models$	$\neg \varphi$	if and only if $\langle M, w \rangle \not\models \varphi$
$\langle M, w \rangle$	$\models$	$\varphi \vee \psi$	if and only if $\langle M, w \rangle \models \varphi$ or $\langle M, w \rangle \models \psi$
$\langle M, w \rangle$	$\models$	$\Box \varphi$	if and only if $\forall w' \in W \cdot$ if $(w, w') \in R$ then $\langle M, w' \rangle \models \varphi$
$\langle M, w \rangle$	$\models$	$\Diamond \varphi$	if and only if $\exists w' \in W \cdot (w, w') \in R$ and $\langle M, w' \rangle \models \varphi$

Figure 12.1   The semantics of normal modal logic.

of propositional logic can be defined as abbreviations in the usual way. The formula $\Box \varphi$ is read 'necessarily φ', and the formula $\Diamond \varphi$ is read 'possibly φ'. Now to the semantics of the language.

Normal modal logics are concerned with truth at worlds; models for such logics therefore contain a set of worlds, W, and a binary relation, R, on W, saying which worlds are considered possible relative to other worlds. Additionally, a valuation function π is required, saying what propositions are true at each world.

A model for a normal propositional modal logic is a triple $\langle W, R, \pi \rangle$, where W is a non-empty set of worlds, $R \subseteq W \times W$, and

$$\pi : W \rightarrow \wp(Prop)$$

is a valuation function, which says for each world $w \in W$ which atomic propositions are true in w. An alternative, equivalent technique would have been to define π as follows:

$$\pi : W \times Prop \rightarrow \{\text{true}, \text{false}\},$$

though the rules defining the semantics of the language would then have to be changed slightly.

The semantics of the language are given via the satisfaction relation, '$\models$', which holds between pairs of the form $\langle M, w \rangle$ (where M is a model, and w is a reference world), and formulae of the language. The semantic rules defining this relation are given in Figure 12.1.

The definition of satisfaction for atomic propositions thus captures the idea of truth in the 'current' world (which appears on the left of '$\models$'). The semantic rules for 'true', '$\neg$', and '$\vee$' are standard. The rule for '$\Box$' captures the idea of truth in all accessible worlds, and the rule for '$\Diamond$' captures the idea of truth in at least one possible world.

Note that the two modal operators are *duals* of each other, in the sense that the universal and existential quantifiers of first-order logic are duals:

$$\Box \varphi \Leftrightarrow \neg \Diamond \neg \varphi.$$

It would thus have been possible to take either one as primitive, and introduce the other as a derived operator.

Correspondence theory

To understand the extraordinary properties of this simple logic, it is first necessary to introduce *validity* and *satisfiability*. A formula is

- *satisfiable* if it is satisfied for some model/world pair;
- *unsatisfiable* if it is not satisfied by any model/world pair;
- *true in a model* if it is satisfied for every world in the model;
- *valid in a class of models* if it true in every model in the class;
- *valid* if it is true in the class of all models.

If φ is valid, we indicate this by writing $\vDash \varphi$. Notice that validity is essentially the same as the notion of 'tautology' in classical propositional logic – all tautologies are valid.

The two basic properties of this logic are as follows. First, the following axiom schema is valid:

$$\vDash \Box(\varphi \Rightarrow \psi) \Rightarrow (\Box\varphi \Rightarrow \Box\psi).$$

This axiom is called K, in honour of Kripke. The second property is as follows.

$$\text{If } \vDash \varphi, \text{ then } \vDash \Box\varphi.$$

Proofs of these properties are trivial, and are left as an exercise for the reader. Now, since K is valid, it will be a theorem of any complete axiomatization of normal modal logic. Similarly, the second property will appear as a rule of inference in any axiomatization of normal modal logic; it is generally called the *necessitation* rule. These two properties turn out to be the most problematic features of normal modal logics when they are used as logics of knowledge/belief (this point will be examined later).

The most intriguing properties of normal modal logics follow from the properties of the accessibility relation, R, in models. To illustrate these properties, consider the following axiom schema:

$$\Box\varphi \Rightarrow \varphi.$$

It turns out that this axiom is *characteristic* of the class of models with a *reflexive* accessibility relation. (By characteristic, we mean that it is true in all and only those models in the class.) There are a host of axioms which correspond to certain properties of R: the study of the way that properties of R correspond to axioms is called *correspondence theory*. In Table 12.1, I list some axioms along with their characteristic property on R, and a first-order formula describing the property.

A *system of logic* can be thought of as a set of formulae valid in some class of models; a member of the set is called a *theorem* of the logic (if φ is a theorem, this is usually denoted by $\vdash \varphi$). The notation $K\Sigma_1 \ldots \Sigma_n$ is often used to denote the smallest normal modal logic containing axioms $\Sigma_1, \ldots, \Sigma_n$ (recall that any normal modal logic will contain K; cf. Goldblatt (1987, p. 25)).

Table 12.1 Some correspondence theory.

Name	Axiom	Condition on R	First-order characterization
T	$\Box\varphi \Rightarrow \varphi$	Reflexive	$\forall w \in W \cdot (w,w) \in R$
D	$\Box\varphi \Rightarrow \Diamond\varphi$	Serial	$\forall w \in W \cdot \exists w' \in W \cdot (w,w') \in R$
4	$\Box\varphi \Rightarrow \Box\Box\varphi$	Transitive	$\forall w, w', w'' \in W \cdot (w,w') \in R \wedge$ $(w',w'') \in R \Rightarrow (w,w'') \in R$
5	$\Diamond\varphi \Rightarrow \Box\Diamond\varphi$	Euclidean	$\forall w, w', w'' \in W \cdot (w,w') \in R \wedge$ $(w,w'') \in R \Rightarrow (w',w'') \in R$

For the axioms *T*, *D*, *4*, and *5*, it would seem that there ought to be 16 distinct systems of logic (since $2^4 = 16$). However, some of these systems turn out to be equivalent (in that they contain the same theorems), and as a result there are only 11 distinct systems. The relationships between these systems are described in Figure 12.2 (after Konolige (1986, p. 99) and Chellas (1980, p. 132)). In this diagram, an arc from *A* to *B* means that *B* is a strict superset of *A*: every theorem of *A* is a theorem of *B*, but not vice versa; *A* = *B* means that *A* and *B* contain precisely the same theorems.

Because some modal systems are so widely used, they have been given names:

$$
\begin{aligned}
&KT   &&\text{is known as} &&\text{T,} \\
&KT4   &&\text{is known as} &&\text{S4,} \\
&KD45 &&\text{is known as} &&\text{weak-S5,} \\
&KT5   &&\text{is known as} &&\text{S5.}
\end{aligned}
$$

Normal modal logics as epistemic logics

To use the logic developed above as an epistemic logic, the formula $\Box\varphi$ is read as 'it is known that φ'. The worlds in the model are interpreted as epistemic alternatives, the accessibility relation defines what the alternatives are from any given world. The logic deals with the knowledge of a single agent. To deal with multi-agent knowledge, one adds to a model structure an indexed set of accessibility relations, one for each agent. A model is then a structure

$$\langle W, R_1, \ldots, R_n, \pi \rangle,$$

where R_i is the knowledge accessibility relation of agent i. The simple language defined above is extended by replacing the single modal operator '$\Box$' by an indexed set of unary modal operators $\{K_i\}$, where $i \in \{1, \ldots, n\}$. The formula

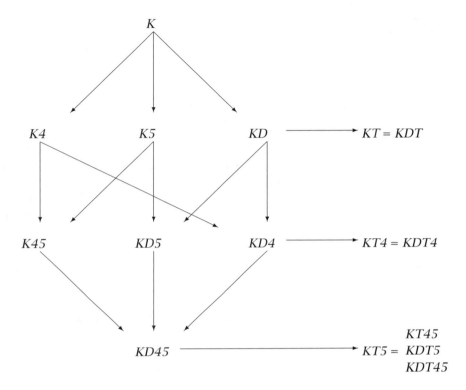

Figure 12.2   The modal systems based on axioms *T*, *D*, *4* and *5*.

$K_i \varphi$ is read '*i* knows that φ'. The semantic rule for '$\square$' is replaced by the following rule:

$$\langle M, w \rangle \vDash K_i \varphi \text{ if and only if } \forall w' \in W \cdot \text{ if } (w, w') \in R_i \text{ then } \langle M, w' \rangle \vDash \varphi.$$

Each operator K_i thus has exactly the same properties as '$\square$'. Corresponding to each of the modal systems Σ, above, a corresponding system Σ_n is defined, for the multiagent logic. Thus K_n is the smallest multiagent epistemic logic and $S5_n$ is the largest.

The next step is to consider how well normal modal logic serves as a logic of knowledge/belief. Consider first the necessitation rule and axiom *K*, since any normal modal system is committed to these.

The necessitation rule tells us that an agent knows all valid formulae. Amongst other things, this means an agent knows all propositional tautologies. Since there are an infinite number of these, an agent will have an infinite number of items of knowledge: immediately, one is faced with a counterintuitive property of the knowledge operator.

Now consider the axiom K, which says that an agent's knowledge is closed under implication. Suppose φ is a logical consequence of the set $\Phi = \{\varphi_1, \ldots, \varphi_n\}$, then in every world where all of Φ are true, φ must also be true, and hence

$$\varphi_1 \wedge \cdots \wedge \varphi_n \Rightarrow \varphi$$

must be valid. By necessitation, this formula will also be believed. Since an agent's beliefs are closed under implication, whenever it believes each of Φ, it must also believe φ. Hence an agent's knowledge is closed under logical consequence. This also seems counterintuitive. For example, suppose, like every good logician, our agent knows Peano's axioms. It may well be that Fermat's last theorem follows from Peano's axioms – although, it took the labour of centuries to prove it. Yet if our agent's beliefs are closed under logical consequence, then our agent must know it. So consequential closure, implied by necessitation and the K axiom, seems an overstrong property for resource-bounded reasoners.

Logical omniscience

These two problems – that of knowing all valid formulae, and that of knowledge/belief being closed under logical consequence – together constitute the famous *logical omniscience* problem. This problem has some damaging corollaries.

The first concerns consistency. Human believers are rarely consistent in the logical sense of the word; they will often have beliefs φ and ψ, where $\varphi \vdash \neg\psi$, without being aware of the implicit inconsistency. However, the ideal reasoners implied by possible-worlds semantics cannot have such inconsistent beliefs without believing *every* formula of the logical language (because the consequential closure of an inconsistent set of formulae is the set of all formulae). Konolige has argued that logical consistency is much too strong a property for resource-bounded reasoners: he argues that a lesser property, that of being *non-contradictory*, is the most one can reasonably demand (Konolige, 1986). Non-contradiction means that an agent would not simultaneously believe φ and $\neg\varphi$, although the agent might have logically inconsistent beliefs.

The second corollary is more subtle. Consider the following propositions (this example is from Konolige (1986, p. 88)).

(1) Hamlet's favourite colour is black.

(2) Hamlet's favourite colour is black *and* every planar map can be four coloured.

The second conjunct of (2) is valid, and will thus be believed. This means that (1) and (2) are logically equivalent; (2) is true just when (1) is. Since agents are ideal reasoners, they will believe that the two propositions are logically equivalent. This is yet another counterintuitive property implied by possible-worlds semantics, as 'equivalent propositions are *not* equivalent as beliefs' (Konolige, 1986, p. 88). Yet this is just what possible-worlds semantics implies. It has been suggested that propositions are thus too *coarse grained* to serve as the objects of belief in this way.

Axioms for knowledge and belief

Let us now consider the appropriateness of the axioms D_n, T_n, 4_n, and 5_n for logics of knowledge/belief.

The axiom D_n says that an agent's beliefs are non-contradictory; it can be rewritten in the following form:

$$K_i\varphi \Rightarrow \neg K_i\neg\varphi,$$

which is read 'if i knows φ, then i does not know $\neg\varphi$'. This axiom seems a reasonable property of knowledge/belief.

The axiom T_n is often called the *knowledge* axiom, since it says that what is known is true. It is usually accepted as the axiom that distinguishes knowledge from belief: it seems reasonable that one could believe something that is false, but one would hesitate to say that one could *know* something false. Knowledge is thus often defined as true belief: i knows φ if i believes φ and φ is true. So defined, knowledge satisfies T_n.

Axiom 4_n is called the *positive introspection axiom*. Introspection is the process of examining one's own beliefs, and is discussed in detail in Konolige (1986, Chapter 5). The positive introspection axiom says that an agent knows what it knows. Similarly, axiom 5_n is the *negative introspection axiom*, which says that an agent is aware of what it does not know. Positive and negative introspection together imply that an agent has perfect knowledge about what it does and does not know (cf. Konolige, 1986, Equation (5.11), p. 79). Whether or not the two types of introspection are appropriate properties for knowledge/belief is the subject of some debate. However, it is generally accepted that positive introspection is a less demanding property than negative introspection, and is thus a more reasonable property for resource-bounded reasoners.

Given the comments above, the modal system $S5_n$ is often chosen as a logic of *knowledge*, and weak-$S5_n$ is often chosen as a logic of *belief*.

Discussion

To sum up, the basic possible-worlds approach described above has the following disadvantages as a multiagent epistemic logic:

- agents believe all valid formulae;
- agents' beliefs are closed under logical consequence;
- equivalent propositions are identical beliefs; and
- if agents are inconsistent, then they believe everything.

To which many people would add the following:

> [T]he ontology of possible worlds and accessibility relations...is frankly mysterious to most practically minded people, and in particular has nothing to say about agent architecture.
>
> (Seel, 1989)

Despite these serious disadvantages, possible worlds are still the semantics of choice for many researchers, and a number of variations on the basic possible-worlds theme have been proposed to get around some of the difficulties – see Wooldridge and Jennings (1995) for a survey.

12.4   Epistemic Logic for Multiagent Systems

Most people, confronted with possible-worlds semantics for the first time, are – initially at least – uncomfortable with the idea:

> [The notion] of one possible world being accessible to another has at first sight a certain air of fantasy or science fiction about it.
>
> (Hughes and Cresswell, 1968, p. 77)

The problem seems to be with the ontological status of possible worlds: do they really exist? If so, where are they? How do they map onto an agent's physical architecture? If these questions cannot be answered, then one would be reluctant to treat epistemic alternatives as anything other than a theoretical nicety.

Some researchers have proposed *grounding* epistemic alternatives: giving them a precise meaning in the real world, thus overcoming any confusion about their status. This section describes grounded possible worlds, and will focus on the distributed systems approach; the formal treatment is adapted from Fagin *et al.* (1995).

Using a logic of knowledge to analyse a distributed system may seem strange. However, as Halpern points out, when informally reasoning about a distributed system, one often makes statements such as: 'processor 1 cannot send a packet to processor 2 until it knows that processor 2 received the previous one' (Halpern, 1987). A logic of knowledge formalizes such reasoning.

The starting point for our study is to define a simple model of distributed systems. A system contains an *environment*, which may be in any of a set E of environment states, and a set of n processes $\{1, \ldots, n\}$, each of which may be in any of a set L of 'local' states. At any time, a system may therefore be in any of a set G of global states:

$$G = E \times \underbrace{L \times \cdots \times L}_{n \text{ times}}.$$

Next, a *run* of a system is a function which assigns to each time point a global state: time points are isomorphic to the natural numbers (and time is thus discrete, bounded in the past, and infinite in the future). Note that this is essentially the same notion of runs that was introduced in Chapter 2, but I have formulated it slightly differently. A run r is thus a function

$$r : \mathbb{N} \rightarrow G.$$

A *point* is a run together with a time:

$$Point = Run \times \mathbb{N}.$$

A point implicitly identifies a global state. Points will serve as worlds in the logic of knowledge to be developed. A *system* is a set of runs.

Now, suppose s and s' are two global states.

$$s = \langle e, l_1, \ldots, l_n \rangle,$$
$$s' = \langle e', l'_1, \ldots, l'_n \rangle.$$

We now define a relation $\sim_i$ on states, for each process i,

$$s \sim_i s' \quad \text{if and only if } (l_i = l'_i).$$

Note that $\sim_i$ will be an equivalence relation. The terminology is that if $s \sim_i s'$, then s and s' are *indistinguishable* to i, since the local state of i is the same in each global state. Intuitively, the local state of a process represents the information that the process has, and if two global states are indistinguishable, then it has the same information in each.

> The crucial point here is that since a processes [sic] [choice of] actions…are a function of its local state, if two points are indistinguishable to processor i, then processor i will perform the same actions in each state.
>
> (Halpern, 1987, pp. 46, 47)

(Again, this is the same notion of indistinguishability that I introduced in Chapter 2, except that there it was with respect to the notion of percepts.)

The next step is to define a language for reasoning about such systems. The language is that of the multiagent epistemic logic defined earlier (i.e. classical propositional logic enriched by the addition of a set of unary modal operators K_i, for $i \in \{1, \ldots, n\}$). The semantics of the language are presented via the satisfaction relation, '$\models$', which holds between triples of the form

$$\langle M, r, u \rangle$$

and formulae of the language. Here, $\langle r, u \rangle$ is a point, and M is a structure

$$\langle \mathcal{R}, \pi \rangle,$$

where $\mathcal{R}$ is a system (cf. the set of runs discussed in Chapter 2), and

$$\pi : Point \rightarrow \wp(Prop)$$

returns the set of atomic propositions true at a point. The structure $\langle \mathcal{R}, \pi \rangle$ is called an *interpreted system*. The only non-standard semantic rules are for propositions and modal formulae:

$$\langle M, r, u \rangle \vDash p \qquad \text{where } p \in Prop, \text{ if and only if } p \in \pi(\langle r, u \rangle),$$

$$\langle M, r, u \rangle \vDash K_i \varphi \quad \text{if and only if } \langle M, r', u' \rangle \vDash \varphi \text{ for all } r' \in \mathcal{R}$$
$$\text{and } u' \in \mathbb{N} \text{ such that } r(u) \sim_i r'(u').$$

Note that since $\sim_i$ is an equivalence relation (i.e. it is reflexive, symmetric, and transitive), this logic will have the properties of the system $S5_n$, discussed above. In what sense does the second rule capture the idea of a processes knowledge? The idea is that if $r(u) \sim_i r'(u')$, then *for all i knows*, it could be in either run r, time u, or run r', time u'; the process does not have enough information to be able to distinguish the two states. The information/knowledge it *does* have are the things true in all its indistinguishable states.

> In this model, knowledge is an *external* notion. We do not imagine a processor scratching its head wondering whether or not it knows a fact φ. Rather, a programmer reasoning about a particular protocol would say, from the outside, that the processor knew φ because in all global states [indistinguishable] from its current state (intuitively, all the states the processor could be in, for all it knows), φ is true.
>
> (Halpern, 1986, p. 6)

12.5   Pro-attitudes: goals and desires

An obvious approach to developing a logic of goals or desires is to adapt possible-worlds semantics – see, for example, Cohen and Levesque (1990a) and Wooldridge (1994). In this view, each goal-accessible world represents one way the world might be if the agent's goals were realized. However, this approach falls prey to the *side effect* problem, in that it predicts that agents have a goal of the logical consequences of their goals (cf. the logical omniscience problem, discussed above). This is not a desirable property: one might have a goal of going to the dentist, with the necessary consequence of suffering pain, without having a goal of suffering pain. The problem is discussed (in the context of intentions) in Bratman (1990). The basic possible-worlds model has been adapted by some researchers in an attempt to overcome this problem (Wainer, 1994). Other, related semantics for goals have been proposed (Doyle *et al.*, 1991; Kiss and Reichgelt, 1992; Rao and Georgeff, 1991b).

12.6 Common and distributed knowledge

In addition to reasoning about what one agent knows or believes, it is often useful to be able to reason about 'cultural' knowledge: the things that everyone knows, and that everyone knows that everyone knows, etc. This kind of knowledge is called *common knowledge*. The famous 'muddy children' puzzle – a classic problem in epistemic reasoning – is an example of the kind of problem that is efficiently dealt with via reasoning about common knowledge (see Fagin *et al.* (1995) for a statement of the problem).

The starting point for common knowledge is to develop an operator for things that 'everyone knows'. A unary modal operator E is added to the modal language discussed above; the formulae $E\varphi$ is read 'everyone knows φ'. It can be defined as an abbreviation:

$$E\varphi \mathrel{\hat{=}} K_1\varphi \wedge \cdots \wedge K_n\varphi.$$

The E operator does not satisfactorily capture the idea of common knowledge. For this, another derived operator C is required; C is defined, ultimately, in terms of E. It is first necessary to introduce the derived operator E^k; the formula $E^k\varphi$ is read 'everyone knows φ to degree k'. It is defined as follows:

$$E^1\varphi \mathrel{\hat{=}} E\varphi,$$
$$E^{k+1}\varphi \mathrel{\hat{=}} E(E^k\varphi).$$

The common knowledge operator can then be defined as an abbreviation:

$$C\varphi \mathrel{\hat{=}} E\varphi \wedge E^2\varphi \wedge \cdots \wedge E^k\varphi \wedge \cdots.$$

Thus common knowledge is the infinite conjunction: everyone knows, and everyone knows that everyone knows, and so on.

It is interesting to ask when common knowledge can arise in a system. A classic problem in distributed systems folklore is the *coordinated attack problem*.

> Two divisions of an army, each commanded by a general, are camped on two hilltops overlooking a valley. In the valley awaits the enemy. It is clear that if both divisions attack the enemy simultaneously they will win the battle, while if only one division attacks, it will be defeated. As a result, neither general will attack unless he is absolutely sure that the other will attack with him. In particular, a general will not attack if he receives no messages. The commanding general of the first division wishes to coordinate a simultaneous attack (at some time the next day). The generals can communicate only by means of messengers. Normally, it takes a messenger one hour to get from one encampment to the other. However, it is possible that he will get lost in the dark or, worse yet, be captured by the enemy. Fortunately, on this particular night, everything goes smoothly. How long will it take them to coordinate an attack?

Suppose a messenger sent by general A reaches General B with a message saying "attack at dawn." Should General B attack? Although the message was in fact delivered, General A has no way of knowing that it was delivered. A must therefore consider it possible that B did not receive the message (in which case B would definitely not attack). Hence A will not attack given his current state of knowledge. Knowing this, and not willing to risk attacking alone, B cannot attack solely based on receiving A's message. Of course, B can try to improve matters by sending the messenger back to A with an acknowledgment. When A receives this acknowledgment, can he then attack? A here is in a similar position to the one B was in when he received the original message. This time B does not know that the acknowledgment was delivered.

(Fagin *et al.*, 1995, p. 176).

Intuitively, the two generals are trying to bring about a state where it is common knowledge between them that the message to attack was delivered. Each successive round of communication, even if successful, only adds one level to the depth of nested belief. *No* amount of communication is sufficient to bring about the infinite nesting that common knowledge requires. As it turns out, if communication delivery is not guaranteed, then common knowledge can *never* arise in such a scenario. Ultimately, this is because, no matter how many messages and acknowledgments are sent, at least one of the generals will always be uncertain about whether or not the last message was received.

One might ask about whether *infinite* nesting of common knowledge is required. Could the two generals agree between themselves beforehand to attack after, say, only two acknowledgments? Assuming that they could meet beforehand to come to such an agreement, then this would be feasible. But the point is that whoever sent the last acknowledgment would be uncertain as to whether this was received, and would hence be attacking while unsure as to whether it was a coordinated attack or a doomed solo effort.

A related issue to common knowledge is that of distributed, or implicit, knowledge. Suppose there is an omniscient observer of some group of agents, with the ability to 'read' each agent's beliefs/knowledge. Then this agent would be able to pool the collective knowledge of the group of agents, and would generally be able to deduce more than any one agent in the group. For example, suppose, in a group of two agents, agent 1 only knew φ, and agent 2 only knew $\varphi \Rightarrow \psi$. Then there would be *distributed* knowledge of ψ, even though no agent explicitly knew ψ. Distributed knowledge cannot be reduced to any of the operators introduced so far: it must be given its own definition. The distributed knowledge operator D has the following semantic rule:

$$\langle M, w \rangle \vDash D\varphi \text{ if and only if } \langle M, w' \rangle \vDash \varphi \text{ for all } w'$$
$$\text{such that } (w, w') \in (R_1 \cap \cdots \cap R_n).$$

This rule might seem strange at first, since it uses set intersection rather than set union, which is at odds with a naive perception of how distributed knowledge works. However, a *restriction* on possible worlds generally means an *increase* in knowledge.

Distributed knowledge is potentially a useful concept in cooperative problem-solving systems, where knowledge about a problem is distributed among a group of problem-solving agents, which must try to deduce a solution through cooperative interaction.

The various group knowledge operators form a hierarchy:

$$C\varphi \Rightarrow E^k\varphi \Rightarrow \cdots \Rightarrow E\varphi \Rightarrow K_i\varphi \Rightarrow D\varphi.$$

See Fagin *et al.* (1995) for further discussion of these operators and their properties.

12.7 Integrated Theories of Agency

All of the formalisms considered so far have focused on just one aspect of agency. However, it is to be expected that a realistic agent theory will be represented in a logical framework that *combines* these various components. Additionally, we expect an agent logic to be capable of representing the *dynamic* aspects of agency. A complete agent theory, expressed in a logic with these properties, must define how the attributes of agency are related. For example, it will need to show how an agent's information and pro-attitudes are related; how an agent's cognitive state changes over time; how the environment affects an agent's cognitive state; and how an agent's information and pro-attitudes lead it to perform actions. Giving a good account of these relationships is the most significant problem faced by agent theorists.

An all-embracing agent theory is some time off, and yet significant steps have been taken towards it. In the following subsection, I survey the work of Cohen and Levesque on intention logics – one of the most influential agent theories developed to date.

Cohen and Levesque's intention logic

One of the best known, and most sophisticated, attempts to show how the various components of an agent's cognitive make-up could be combined to form a logic of rational agency is due to Cohen and Levesque (1990a). Cohen and Levesque's formalism was originally used to develop a theory of intention (as in 'I intended to...'), which the authors required as a prerequisite for a theory of speech acts (see the next chapter for a summary, and Cohen and Levesque (1990b) for full details). However, the logic has subsequently proved to be so useful for specifying and reasoning about the properties of agents that it has been used in an analysis of conflict and cooperation in multiagent dialogue (Galliers, 1988a,b), as well as several studies in the theoretical foundations of cooperative problem solving (Levesque *et al.*, 1990; Jennings, 1992a,b). This section will focus on the use of the logic in developing a theory of intention. The first step is to lay out the criteria that a theory of intention must satisfy.

When building intelligent agents – particularly agents that must interact with humans – it is important that a *rational balance* is achieved between the beliefs, goals, and intentions of the agents.

> For example, the following are desirable properties of intention: an autonomous agent should act on its intentions, not in spite of them; adopt intentions it believes are feasible and forego those believed to be infeasible; keep (or commit to) intentions, but not forever; discharge those intentions believed to have been satisfied; alter intentions when relevant beliefs change; and adopt subsidiary intentions during plan formation.
>
> (Cohen and Levesque, 1990a, p. 214)

Recall the properties of intentions, as discussed in Chapter 4.

(1) Intentions pose problems for agents, who need to determine ways of achieving them.

(2) Intentions provide a 'filter' for adopting other intentions, which must not conflict.

(3) Agents track the success of their intentions, and are inclined to try again if their attempts fail.

(4) Agents believe their intentions are possible.

(5) Agents do not believe they will not bring about their intentions.

(6) Under certain circumstances, agents believe they will bring about their intentions.

(7) Agents need not intend all the expected side effects of their intentions.

Given these criteria, Cohen and Levesque adopt a two-tiered approach to the problem of formalizing a theory of intention. First, they construct the logic of rational agency, 'being careful to sort out the relationships among the basic modal operators' (Cohen and Levesque, 1990a, p. 221). On top of this framework, they introduce a number of derived constructs, which constitute a 'partial theory of rational action' (Cohen and Levesque, 1990a, p. 221); intention is one of these constructs.

Syntactically, the logic of rational agency is a many-sorted, first-order, multi-modal logic with equality, containing four primary modalities (see Table 12.2).

The semantics of Bel and Goal are given via possible worlds, in the usual way: each agent is assigned a belief accessibility relation, and a goal accessibility relation. The belief accessibility relation is Euclidean, transitive, and serial, giving a belief logic of KD45. The goal relation is serial, giving a conative logic KD. It is assumed that each agent's goal relation is a subset of its belief relation, implying that an agent will not have a goal of something it believes will not happen. Worlds in the formalism are a discrete sequence of events, stretching infinitely into past and future.

Table 12.2　Atomic modalities in Cohen and Levesque's logic.

Operator	Meaning
(Bel i φ)	agent i believes φ
(Goal i φ)	agent i has goal of φ
(Happens α)	action α will happen next
(Done α)	action α has just happened

The two basic temporal operators, Happens and Done, are augmented by some operators for describing the structure of event sequences, in the style of dynamic logic (Harel, 1979). The two most important of these constructors are ';' and '?':

$$\alpha; \alpha' \text{ denotes } \alpha \text{ followed by } \alpha',$$

$$\varphi? \text{ denotes a 'test action' } \varphi.$$

The standard future time operators of temporal logic, '$\square$' (always), and '$\lozenge$' (sometime), can be defined as abbreviations, along with a 'strict' sometime operator, Later:

$$\lozenge \alpha \mathrel{\hat{=}} \exists x \cdot (\text{Happens } x; \alpha?),$$

$$\square \alpha \mathrel{\hat{=}} \neg \lozenge \neg \alpha,$$

$$(\text{Later } p) \mathrel{\hat{=}} \neg p \wedge \lozenge p.$$

A temporal precedence operator, (Before p q) can also be derived, and holds if p holds before q. An important assumption is that *all* goals are eventually dropped:

$$\lozenge \neg (\text{Goal } x \text{ (Later } p)).$$

The first major derived construct is a *persistent* goal:

$$
(\text{P-Goal } i \ p) \quad \mathrel{\hat{=}} \quad
\begin{array}{ll}
(\text{Goal } i \text{ (Later } p)) & \wedge \\
(\text{Bel } i \ \neg p) & \wedge \\
\left[
\begin{array}{l}
\text{Before} \\
\quad ((\text{Bel } i \ p) \vee (\text{Bel } i \ \square \neg p)) \\
\quad \neg(\text{Goal } i \text{ (Later } p))
\end{array}
\right] &
\end{array}
$$

So, an agent has a persistent goal of p if

(1) it has a goal that p eventually becomes true, and believes that p is not currently true; and

(2) before it drops the goal, one of the following conditions must hold:

    (a) the agent believes the goal has been satisfied;

    (b) the agent believes the goal will never be satisfied.

It is a small step from persistent goals to a first definition of intention, as in 'intending to act'. Note that 'intending that something becomes true' is similar, but requires a slightly different definition (see Cohen and Levesque, 1990a). An agent i intends to perform action α if it has a persistent goal to have brought about a state where it had just believed it was about to perform α, and then did α:

$$(\text{Int } i \ \alpha) \ \hat{=} \ (\text{P-Goal } i$$
$$[\text{Done } i \ (\text{Bel } i \ (\text{Happens } \alpha))?; \alpha]$$
$$)$$

Cohen and Levesque go on to show how such a definition meets many of Bratman's criteria for a theory of intention (outlined above). In particular, by basing the definition of intention on the notion of a *persistent goal*, Cohen and Levesque are able to avoid overcommitment or undercommitment. An agent will only drop an intention if it believes that the intention has either been achieved, or is unachievable.

Modelling speech acts

We saw in Chapter 8 how speech acts form the basis of communication in most multiagent systems. Using their logic of intention, Cohen and Levesque developed a theory which arguably represents the state of the art in the logical analysis of speech acts (Cohen and Levesque, 1990b). Their work proceeds from two basic premises.

(1) Illocutionary force recognition is unnecessary.

> What speakers and hearers have to do is only recognize each other's intentions (based on mutual beliefs). [W]e do not require that those intentions include intentions that the hearer recognize precisely what illocutionary act(s) were being performed.
>
> (Cohen and Levesque, 1990b, p. 223)

(2) Illocutionary acts are *complex event types*, and not primitives.

Given this latter point, one must find some way of describing the actions that are performed. Cohen and Levesque's solution is to use their logic of rational action, which provides a number of primitive event types, which can be put together into more complex event types, using dynamic-logic-style constructions. Illocutionary acts are then defined as complex event types.

Their approach is perhaps best illustrated by giving their definition of a request. Some preliminary definitions are required. First, *alternating belief*:

$$(\text{A-Bel } n \ x \ y \ p) \ \hat{=} \ \underbrace{(\text{Bel } x \ (\text{Bel } y \ (\text{Bel } x \ \cdots (\text{Bel } x}_{n \text{ times}} \ p \underbrace{) \cdots)}_{n \text{ times}}.$$

And the related concept of *mutual belief*:

$$(\text{M-Bel } x \ y \ p) \ \hat{=} \ \forall n \cdot (\text{A-Bel } n \ x \ y \ p).$$

Next, an *attempt* is defined as a complex action expression – hence the use of curly brackets, to distinguish it from a predicate or modal operator:

$$\{\text{Attempt } x \ e \ p \ q\} \quad \hat{=} \left[\begin{array}{ll} (\text{Bel } x \ \neg p) & \wedge \\ (\text{Goal } x \ (\text{Happens } x \ e; p?)) & \wedge \\ (\text{Int } x \ e; q?) & \end{array} \right] ?; e$$

In English:

> An attempt is a complex action that agents perform when they do something (*e*) desiring to bring about some effect (*p*) but with intent to produce at least some result (*q*).

> (Cohen and Levesque, 1990b, p. 240)

The idea is that *p* represents the ultimate goal that the agent is aiming for by doing *e*; the proposition *q* represents what it takes to at least make an 'honest effort' to achieve *p*. A definition of *helpfulness* is now presented:

$$(\text{Helpful } x \ y) \quad \hat{=} \forall e \cdot \left[\begin{array}{l} (\text{Bel } x \ (\text{Goal } y \ \Diamond(\text{Done } x \ e))) \quad \wedge \\ \neg(\text{Goal } x \ \Box\neg(\text{Done } x \ e)) \end{array} \right] \\ \Rightarrow (\text{Goal } x \ \Diamond(\text{Done } x \ e)).$$

In English:

> [C]onsider an agent [*x*] to be helpful to another agent [*y*] if, for any action [*e*] he adopts the other agent's goal that he eventually do that action, whenever such a goal would not conflict with his own.

> (Cohen and Levesque, 1990b, p. 230)

The definition of requests can now be given (note again the use of curly brackets: requests are complex event types, not predicates or operators):

$$\{\text{Request } spkr \ addr \ e \ \alpha\} \ \hat{=} \ \{\text{Attempt } spkr \ e \ \varphi$$
$$(\text{M-Bel } addr \ spkr \ (\text{Goal } spkr \ \varphi))$$
$$\}$$

where φ is

$$\Diamond(\text{Done } addr \ \alpha) \ \wedge$$
$$(\text{Int } addr \ \alpha$$
$$\left[\begin{array}{l} (\text{Goal } spkr \ \Diamond(\text{Done } addr \ \alpha)) \ \wedge \\ (\text{Helpful } addr \ spkr) \end{array} \right]$$
$$).$$

In English:

> A request is an attempt on the part of *spkr*, by doing *e*, to bring about a state where, ideally (i) *addr* intends α (relative to the *spkr* still having that goal, and *addr* still being helpfully inclined to *spkr*), and (ii) *addr* actually eventually does α, or at least brings about a state where *addr* believes it is mutually believed that it wants the ideal situation.

By this definition, there is no primitive request act:

> [A] speaker is viewed as having performed a request if he executes any sequence of actions that produces the needed effects.
>
> (Cohen and Levesque, 1990b, p. 246)

In short, any event, of whatever complexity, that satisfies this definition, can be counted a request. Cohen and Levesque show that if a request takes place, it is possible to infer that many of Searle's preconditions for the act must have held (Cohen and Levesque, 1990b, pp. 246–251).

Using Cohen and Levesque's work as a starting point, Galliers has developed a more general framework for multiagent dialogue, which acknowledges the possibility for conflict (Galliers, 1988b).

12.8   Formal Methods in Agent-Oriented Software Engineering

The next question to address is what role logics of agency might actually play in the development of agent systems. Broadly speaking, formal methods play three roles in software engineering:

- in the *specification* of systems;
- for *directly programming* systems; and
- in the *verification* of systems.

In the subsections that follow, we consider each of these roles in turn. Note that these subsections presuppose some familiarity with formal methods, and logic in particular.

12.8.1   Formal methods in specification

In this section, we consider the problem of *specifying* an agent system. What are the requirements for an agent specification framework? What sort of properties must it be capable of representing?

Comparatively few serious attempts have been made to specify real agent systems using such logics – see, for example, Fisher and Wooldridge (1997) for one such attempt.

A specification expressed in such a logic would be a formula φ. The idea is that such a specification would express the desirable behaviour of a system. To see how this might work, consider the following, intended to form part of a specification of a process control system:

> if
>> i believes valve 32 is open
> then
>> i should intend that j should believe valve 32 is open.

Expressed in a Cohen–Levesque type logic, this statement becomes the formula:

$$(\text{Bel } i \; Open(valve32)) \Rightarrow (\text{Int } i \; (\text{Bel } j \; Open(valve32))).$$

It should be intuitively clear how a system specification might be constructed using such formulae, to define the intended behaviour of a system.

One of the main desirable features of a software specification language is that it should not dictate *how* a specification will be satisfied by an implementation. The specification above has exactly this property: it does not dictate how agent i should go about making j aware that valve 32 is open. We simply expect i to behave as a rational agent given such an intention (Wooldridge, 2000b).

There are a number of problems with the use of languages such as for specification. The most worrying of these is with respect to their semantics. The semantics for the modal connectives (for beliefs, desires, and intentions) are given in the normal modal logic tradition of possible worlds (Chellas, 1980). So, for example, an agent's beliefs in some state are characterized by a set of different states, each of which represents one possibility for how the world could actually be, given the information available to the agent. In much the same way, an agent's desires in some state are characterized by a set of states that are consistent with the agent's desires. Intentions are represented similarly. There are several advantages to the possible-worlds model: it is well studied and well understood, and the associated mathematics of correspondence theory is extremely elegant. These attractive features make possible worlds the semantics of choice for almost every researcher in formal agent theory. However, there are also a number of serious drawbacks to possible-worlds semantics. First, possible-worlds semantics imply that agents are logically perfect reasoners (in that their deductive capabilities are sound and complete), and they have infinite resources available for reasoning. No real agent, artificial or otherwise, has these properties.

Second, possible-worlds semantics are generally *ungrounded*. That is, there is usually no precise relationship between the abstract accessibility relations that are used to characterize an agent's state, and any concrete computational model. As we shall see in later sections, this makes it difficult to go from a formal specification of a system in terms of beliefs, desires, and so on, to a concrete computational system. Similarly, given a concrete computational system, there is generally no way to determine what the beliefs, desires, and intentions of that system are.

If temporal modal logics such as these are to be taken seriously as *specification* languages, then this is a significant problem.

12.8.2   Formal methods in implementation

Specification is not (usually!) the end of the story in software development. Once given a specification, we must implement a system that is correct with respect to this specification. The next issue we consider is this move from abstract specification to concrete computational model. There are at least three possibilities for achieving this transformation:

(1)   manually refine the specification into an executable form via some principled but informal refinement process (as is the norm in most current software development);

(2)   directly execute or animate the abstract specification; or

(3)   translate or compile the specification into a concrete computational form using an automatic translation technique (cf. the synthesis of agents, discussed in Chapter 2).

In the subsections that follow, we shall investigate each of these possibilities in turn.

Refinement

At the time of writing, most software developers use structured but informal techniques to transform specifications into concrete implementations. Probably the most common techniques in widespread use are based on the idea of top-down refinement. In this approach, an abstract system specification is *refined* into a number of smaller, less abstract subsystem specifications, which together satisfy the original specification. If these subsystems are still too abstract to be implemented directly, then they are also refined. The process recurses until the derived subsystems are simple enough to be directly implemented. Throughout, we are obliged to demonstrate that each step represents a true refinement of the more abstract specification that preceded it. This demonstration may take the form of a formal proof, if our specification is presented in, say, Z (Spivey, 1992) or VDM (Jones, 1990). More usually, justification is by informal argument. Object-oriented analysis and design techniques, which also tend to be structured but informal, are also increasingly playing a role in the development of systems (see, for example, Booch, 1994).

For *functional* systems, which simply compute a function of some input and then terminate, the refinement process is well understood, and comparatively straightforward. Such systems can be specified in terms of preconditions and postconditions (e.g. using Hoare logic (Hoare, 1969)). Refinement calculi exist, which enable the system developer to take a precondition and postcondition specification, and from it systematically derive an implementation through the use of proof rules (Morgan, 1994). Part of the reason for this comparative simplicity is that there is often an easily understandable relationship between the preconditions and postconditions that characterize an operation and the program structures required to implement it.

For agent systems, which fall into the category of Pnuelian reactive systems (see the discussion in Chapter 2), refinement is not so straightforward. This is because such systems must be specified in terms of their *ongoing* behaviour – they cannot be specified simply in terms of preconditions and postconditions. In contrast to precondition and postcondition formalisms, it is not so easy to determine what program structures are required to realize such specifications. As a consequence, researchers have only just begun to investigate refinement and design technique for agent-based systems.

Directly executing agent specifications

One major disadvantage with manual refinement methods is that they introduce the possibility of error. If no proofs are provided, to demonstrate that each refinement step is indeed a true refinement, then the correctness of the implementation process depends upon little more than the intuitions of the developer. This is clearly an undesirable state of affairs for applications in which correctness is a major issue. One possible way of circumventing this problem, which has been widely investigated in mainstream computer science, is to get rid of the refinement process altogether, and *directly execute* the specification.

It might seem that suggesting the direct execution of complex agent specification languages is naive – it is exactly the kind of suggestion that detractors of logic-based AI hate. One should therefore be very careful about what claims or proposals one makes. However, in certain circumstances, the direct execution of agent specification languages *is* possible.

What does it mean, to execute a formula φ of logic L? It means generating a logical model, M, for φ, such that $M \models \varphi$ (Fisher, 1996). If this could be done without interference from the environment – if the agent had complete control over its environment – then execution would reduce to constructive theorem-proving, where we show that φ is satisfiable by building a model for φ. In reality, of course, agents are *not* interference free: they must iteratively construct a model in the presence of input from the environment. Execution can then be seen as a two-way iterative process:

- environment makes something true;
- agent responds by doing something, i.e. making something else true in the model;
- environment responds, making something else true;
- etc.

Execution of logical languages and theorem-proving are thus closely related. This tells us that the execution of sufficiently rich (quantified) languages is not possible (since any language equal in expressive power to first-order logic is undecidable).

A useful way to think about execution is as if the agent is *playing a game* against the environment. The specification represents the goal of the game: the agent must keep the goal satisfied, while the environment tries to prevent the agent from doing so. The game is played by agent and environment taking turns to build a little more of the model. If the specification ever becomes false in the (partial) model, then the agent loses. In real reactive systems, the game is never over: the agent must continue to play forever. Of course, some specifications (logically inconsistent ones) cannot ever be satisfied. A *winning strategy* for building models from (satisfiable) agent specifications in the presence of arbitrary input from the environment is an execution algorithm for the logic.

Automatic synthesis from agent specifications

An alternative to direct execution is *compilation*. In this scheme, we take our abstract specification, and transform it into a concrete computational model via some automatic synthesis process. The main perceived advantages of compilation over direct execution are in run-time efficiency. Direct execution of an agent specification, as in Concurrent MetateM, above, typically involves manipulating a symbolic representation of the specification at run time. This manipulation generally corresponds to reasoning of some form, which is computationally costly (and, in many cases, simply impracticable for systems that must operate in anything like real time). In contrast, compilation approaches aim to reduce abstract symbolic specifications to a much simpler computational model, which requires no symbolic representation. The 'reasoning' work is thus done offline, at compile-time; execution of the compiled system can then be done with little or no run-time symbolic reasoning. As a result, execution is much faster. The advantages of compilation over direct execution are thus those of compilation over interpretation in mainstream programming.

Compilation approaches usually depend upon the close relationship between models for temporal/modal logic (which are typically labelled graphs of some kind) and automata-like finite-state machines. Crudely, the idea is to take a specification φ, and do a *constructive proof* of the implementability of φ, wherein we show that the specification is satisfiable by systematically attempting to build a model for it. If the construction process succeeds, then the specification is satisfiable, and we have a model to prove it. Otherwise, the specification is unsatisfiable. If we have a model, then we 'read off' the automaton that implements φ from its corresponding model. The most common approach to constructive proof is the *semantic tableaux* method of Smullyan (1968).

In mainstream computer science, the compilation approach to automatic program synthesis has been investigated by a number of researchers. Perhaps the closest to our view is the work of Pnueli and Rosner (1989) on the automatic synthesis of reactive systems from branching time temporal logic specifications. The goal of their work is to generate reactive systems, which share many of the properties of our agents (the main difference being that reactive systems are not generally required to be capable of rational decision making in the way we described above). To do this, they specify a reactive system in terms of a first-order branching time temporal logic formula $\forall x\ \exists y\ A\varphi(x, y)$: the predicate φ characterizes the relationship between inputs to the system (x) and outputs (y). Inputs may be thought of as sequences of environment states, and outputs as corresponding sequences of actions. The A is the universal path quantifier. The specification is intended to express the fact that in all possible futures, the desired relationship φ holds between the inputs to the system, x, and its outputs, y. The synthesis process itself is rather complex: it involves generating a Rabin tree automaton, and then checking this automaton for emptiness. Pnueli and Rosner show that the time complexity of the synthesis process is double exponential in the size of the specification, i.e. $O(2^{2^{c \cdot n}})$, where c is a constant and $n = |\varphi|$ is the size of the specification φ. The size of the synthesized program (the number of states it contains) is of the same complexity.

The Pnueli–Rosner technique is rather similar to (and in fact depends upon) techniques developed by Wolper, Vardi, and colleagues for synthesizing Büchi automata from linear temporal logic specifications (Vardi and Wolper, 1994). Büchi automata are those that can recognize *ω-regular expressions*: regular expressions that may contain infinite repetition. A standard result in temporal logic theory is that a formula φ of linear time temporal logic is satisfiable if and only if there exists a Büchi automaton that accepts just the sequences that satisfy φ. Intuitively, this is because the sequences over which linear time temporal logic is interpreted can be viewed as ω-regular expressions. This result yields a decision procedure for linear time temporal logic: to determine whether a formula φ is satisfiable, construct an automaton that accepts just the (infinite) sequences that correspond to models of φ; if the set of such sequences is empty, then φ is unsatisfiable.

Similar automatic synthesis techniques have also been deployed to develop concurrent system skeletons from temporal logic specifications. Manna and Wolper present an algorithm that takes as input a linear time temporal logic specification of the *synchronization* part of a concurrent system, and generates as output a program skeleton (based upon Hoare's CSP formalism (Hoare, 1978)) that realizes the specification (Manna and Wolper, 1984). The idea is that the functionality of a concurrent system can generally be divided into two parts: a functional part, which actually performs the required computation in the program, and a synchronization part, which ensures that the system components cooperate in the correct way. For example, the synchronization part will be responsible for any mutual exclusion that is required. The synthesis algorithm (like the synthesis algorithm for Büchi automata, above) is based on Wolper's tableau proof method for temporal logic (Wolper, 1985). Very similar work is reported by Clarke and Emerson (1981): they synthesize synchronization skeletons from branching time temporal logic (CTL) specifications.

Perhaps the best-known example of this approach to agent development is the *situated automata* paradigm of Rosenschein and Kaelbling (1996), discussed in Chapter 5.

12.8.3   Verification

Once we have developed a concrete system, we need to show that this system is correct with respect to our original specification. This process is known as *verification*, and it is particularly important if we have introduced any informality into the development process. For example, any manual refinement, done without a formal proof of refinement correctness, creates the possibility of a faulty transformation from specification to implementation. Verification is the process of convincing ourselves that the transformation was sound. We can divide approaches to the verification of systems into two broad classes: (1) *axiomatic*, and (2) *semantic* (model checking). In the subsections that follow, we shall look at the way in which these two approaches have evidenced themselves in agent-based systems.

Deductive verification

Axiomatic approaches to program verification were the first to enter the main-stream of computer science, with the work of Hoare in the late 1960s (Hoare, 1969). Axiomatic verification requires that we can take our concrete program, and from this program systematically derive a logical theory that represents the behaviour of the program. Call this the program theory. If the program theory is expressed in the same logical language as the original specification, then verification reduces to a proof problem: show that the specification is a theorem of (equivalently, is a logical consequence of) the program theory.

The development of a program theory is made feasible by *axiomatizing* the programming language in which the system is implemented. For example, Hoare logic gives us more or less an axiom for every statement type in a simple Pascal-like language. Once given the axiomatization, the program theory can be derived from the program text in a systematic way.

Perhaps the most relevant work from mainstream computer science is the specification and verification of reactive systems using temporal logic, in the way pioneered by Pnueli, Manna, and colleagues (see, for example, Manna and Pnueli, 1995). The idea is that the computations of reactive systems are infinite sequences, which correspond to models for linear temporal logic. Temporal logic can be used both to develop a system specification, and to axiomatize a programming language. This axiomatization can then be used to systematically derive the theory of a program from the program text. Both the specification and the program theory will then be encoded in temporal logic, and verification hence becomes a proof problem in temporal logic.

Comparatively little work has been carried out within the agent-based systems community on axiomatizing multiagent environments. I shall review just one approach.

In Wooldridge (1992), an axiomatic approach to the verification of multiagent systems was proposed. Essentially, the idea was to use a temporal belief logic to axiomatize the properties of two multiagent programming languages. Given such an axiomatization, a program theory representing the properties of the system could be systematically derived in the way indicated above.

A temporal belief logic was used for two reasons. First, a temporal component was required because, as we observed above, we need to capture the ongoing behaviour of a multiagent system. A belief component was used because the agents we wish to verify are each symbolic AI systems in their own right. That is, each agent is a symbolic reasoning system, which includes a representation of its environment and desired behaviour. A belief component in the logic allows us to capture the symbolic representations present within each agent.

The two multiagent programming languages that were axiomatized in the temporal belief logic were Shoham's AGENT0 (Shoham, 1993), and Fisher's Concurrent MetateM (see above). The basic approach was as follows.

(1) First, a simple abstract model was developed of symbolic AI agents. This model captures the fact that agents are symbolic reasoning systems, capable of communication. The model gives an account of how agents might change state, and what a computation of such a system might look like.

(2) The histories traced out in the execution of such a system were used as the semantic basis for a temporal belief logic. This logic allows us to express properties of agents modelled at stage (1).

(3) The temporal belief logic was used to axiomatize the properties of a multiagent programming language. This axiomatization was then used to develop the program theory of a multiagent system.

(4) The proof theory of the temporal belief logic was used to verify properties of the system (cf. Fagin *et al.*, 1995).

Note that this approach relies on the operation of agents being sufficiently simple that their properties can be axiomatized in the logic. It works for Shoham's AGENT0 and Fisher's Concurrent MetateM largely because these languages have a simple semantics, closely related to rule-based systems, which in turn have a simple logical semantics. For more complex agents, an axiomatization is not so straightforward. Also, capturing the semantics of concurrent execution of agents is not easy (it is, of course, an area of ongoing research in computer science generally).

Model checking

Ultimately, axiomatic verification reduces to a proof problem. Axiomatic approaches to verification are thus inherently limited by the difficulty of this proof problem. Proofs are hard enough, even in classical logic; the addition of temporal and modal connectives to a logic makes the problem considerably harder. For this reason, more efficient approaches to verification have been sought. One particularly successful approach is that of *model checking* (Clarke *et al.*, 2000). As the name suggests, whereas axiomatic approaches generally rely on syntactic proof, model-checking approaches are based on the semantics of the specification language.

The model-checking problem, in abstract, is quite simple: given a formula φ of language L, and a model M for L, determine whether or not φ is valid in M, i.e. whether or not $M \vDash_L \varphi$. Verification by model checking has been studied in connection with temporal logic (Clarke *et al.*, 2000). The technique once again relies upon the close relationship between models for temporal logic and finite-state machines. Suppose that φ is the specification for some system, and π is a program that claims to implement φ. Then, to determine whether or not π truly implements φ, we proceed as follows:

- take π, and from it generate a model M_π that corresponds to π, in the sense that M_π encodes all the possible computations of π;

- determine whether or not $M_\pi \vDash \varphi$, i.e. whether the specification formula φ is valid in M_π; the program π satisfies the specification φ just in case the answer is 'yes'.

The main advantage of model checking over axiomatic verification is in complexity: model checking using the branching time temporal logic CTL (Clarke and Emerson, 1981) can be done in time $O(|\varphi| \times |M|)$, where $|\varphi|$ is the size of the formula to be checked, and $|M|$ is the size of the model against which φ is to be checked – the number of states it contains.

In Rao and Georgeff (1993), the authors present an algorithm for model-checking BDI systems. More precisely, they give an algorithm for taking a logical model for their (propositional) BDI logic, and a formula of the language, and determining whether the formula is valid in the model. The technique is closely based on model-checking algorithms for normal modal logics (Clarke *et al.*, 2000). They show that despite the inclusion of three extra modalities (for beliefs, desires, and intentions) into the CTL branching time framework, the algorithm is still quite efficient, running in polynomial time. So the second step of the two-stage model-checking process described above can still be done efficiently. Similar algorithms have been reported for BDI-like logics in Benerecetti *et al.* (1999).

The main problem with model-checking approaches for BDI is that it is not clear how the first step might be realized for BDI logics. Where does the logical model characterizing an agent actually come from? Can it be derived from an arbitrary program π, as in mainstream computer science? To do this, we would need to take a program implemented in, say, Pascal, and from it derive the belief-, desire-, and intention-accessibility relations that are used to give a semantics to the BDI component of the logic. Because, as we noted earlier, there is no clear relationship between the BDI logic and the concrete computational models used to implement agents, it is not clear how such a model could be derived.

Notes and Further Reading

The definitive modern reference to modal logic is Blackburn *et al.* (2001). Written by three of the best people in the field, this is an astonishingly thorough and authoritative work, unlikely to be surpassed for some time to come. The only caveat is that it is emphatically not for the mathematically faint-hearted. For an older (but very readable) introduction to modal logic, see Chellas (1980); an even older, though more wide-ranging introduction, may be found in Hughes and Cresswell (1968).

As for the use of modal logics to model knowledge and belief, the definitive work is Fagin *et al.* (1995). This book, written by the 'gang of four', is a joy to read. Clear, detailed, and rigorous, it is (for my money) one of the most important books in the multiagent systems canon. Another useful book, which has perhaps been overshadowed slightly by Fagin *et al.* (1995) is Meyer and van der Hoek (1995).

Another useful reference to logics of knowledge and belief is Halpern and Moses (1992), which includes complexity results and proof procedures. Related work on modelling knowledge has been done by the distributed systems community, who give the worlds in possible-worlds semantics a precise interpretation; for an introduction and further references, see Halpern (1987) and Fagin *et al.* (1992). Overviews of formalisms for modelling belief and knowledge may be found in Halpern (1986), Konolige (1986), Reichgelt (1989), Wooldridge (1992) and Fagin *et al.* (1995). A variant on the possible-worlds framework, called the *recursive modelling method*, is described in Gmytrasiewicz and Durfee (1993). *Situation semantics*, developed in the early 1980s, represent a fundamentally new approach to modelling the world and cognitive systems (Barwise and Perry, 1983; Devlin, 1991).

Logics which integrate time with mental states are discussed in Kraus and Lehmann (1988), Halpern and Vardi (1989), Wooldridge and Fisher (1994), Wooldridge *et al.* (1998) and Dixon *et al.* (1998); the last of these presents a tableau-based proof method for a temporal belief logic. Two other important references for temporal aspects are Shoham (1988) and Shoham (1989). Thomas developed some logics for representing agent theories as part of her framework for agent programming languages; see Thomas *et al.* (1991) and Thomas (1993). For an introduction to temporal logics and related topics, see Goldblatt (1987) and Emerson (1990).

An informal discussion of intention may be found in Bratman (1987), or more briefly in Bratman (1990). Further work on modelling intention may be found in Grosz and Sidner (1990), Sadek (1992), Goldman and Lang (1991), Konolige and

Pollack (1993), Bell (1995) and Dongha (1995). A critique of Cohen and Levesque's theory of intention is presented in Singh (1992). Related works, focusing less on single-agent attitudes, and more on social aspects, are Levesque *et al.* (1990), Jennings (1993a), Wooldridge (1994) and Wooldridge and Jennings (1994).

Although I have not discussed formalisms for reasoning about action here, we suggested above that an agent logic would need to incorporate some mechanism for representing agent's actions. Our reason for avoiding the topic is simply that the field is so big, it deserves a whole review in its own right. Good starting points for AI treatments of action are Allen (1984) and Allen *et al.* (1990, 1991). Other treatments of action in agent logics are based on formalisms borrowed from mainstream computer science, notably dynamic logic (originally developed to reason about computer programs) (Harel, 1984; Harel *et al.*, 2000). The logic of *seeing to it that* has been discussed in the formal philosophy literature, but has yet to impact on multiagent systems (Belnap and Perloff, 1988; Perloff, 1991; Belnap, 1991; Segerberg, 1989).

See Wooldridge (1997) for a discussion on the possibility of using logic to engineer agent-based systems. Since this article was published, several other authors have proposed the use of agents in software engineering (see, for example, Jennings, 1999).

With respect to the possibility of directly executing agent specifications, a number of problems suggest themselves. The first is that of finding a concrete computational interpretation for the agent specification language in question. To see what we mean by this, consider models for the agent specification language in Concurrent MetateM. These are very simple: essentially just linear discrete sequences of states. Temporal logic is (among other things) simply a language for expressing *constraints* that must hold between successive states. Execution in Concurrent MetateM is thus a process of generating constraints as past-time antecedents are satisfied, and then trying to build a next state that satisfies these constraints. Constraints are expressed in temporal logic, which implies that they may only be in certain, regular forms. Because of this, it is possible to devise an algorithm that is guaranteed to build a next state if it is possible to do so. Such an algorithm is described in Barringer *et al.* (1989). The agent specification language upon which Concurrent MetateM is based thus has a concrete computational model, and a comparatively simple execution algorithm. Contrast this state of affairs with languages like that of Cohen and Levesque (1990a), where we have not only a temporal dimension to the logic, but also modalities for referring to beliefs, desires, and so on. In general, models for these logics have *ungrounded* semantics. That is, the semantic structures that underpin these logics (typically accessibility relations for each of the modal operators) have no concrete computational interpretation. As a result, it is not clear how such agent specification languages might be executed. Another obvious problem is that execution techniques based on theorem-proving are inherently limited when applied to sufficiently expressive (first-order) languages, as first-order logic is undecidable. However, complexity is a problem even in the propositional case. For 'vanilla' propositional logic, the decision problem for satisfiability is NP-complete (Fagin *et al.*, 1995, p. 72); richer logics, or course, have more complex decision problems.

Despite these problems, the undoubted attractions of direct execution have led to a number of attempts to devise executable logic-based agent languages. Rao proposed an executable subset of BDI logic in his AgentSpeak(L) language (Rao, 1996a). Building on this work, Hindriks and colleagues developed the 3APL agent programming language (Hindriks *et al.*, 1998; Hindriks *et al.*, 1999). Lespérance, Reiter, Levesque, and colleagues developed the Golog language throughout the latter half of the 1990s as an executable subset of the situation calculus (Lésperance *et al.*, 1996; Levesque *et al.*, 1996). Fagin and colleagues have proposed *knowledge-based programs* as a paradigm for executing logical formulae which contain epistemic modalities (Fagin *et al.*, 1995, 1997). Although considerable work has been carried out on the properties of knowledge-based programs, comparatively little research to date has addressed the problem of how such programs might be actually executed.

Turning to automatic synthesis, the techniques described above have been developed primarily for propositional specification languages. If we attempt to extend these techniques to more expressive, first-order specification languages, then we again find ourselves coming up against the undecidability of quantified logic. Even in the propositional case, the theoretical complexity of theorem-proving for modal and temporal logics is likely to limit the effectiveness of compilation techniques: given an agent specification of size 1000, a synthesis algorithm that runs in exponential time when used offline is no more useful than an execution algorithm that runs in exponential time on-line. Kupferman and Vardi (1997) is a recent article on automatic synthesis from temporal logic specifications.

Another problem with respect to synthesis techniques is that they typically result in finite-state, automata-like machines, which are less powerful than Turing machines. In particular, the systems generated by the processes outlined above cannot modify their behaviour at run-time. In short, they cannot learn. While for many applications this is acceptable – even desirable – for equally many others, it is not. In expert assistant agents, of the type described in Maes (1994a), learning is pretty much the *raison d'être*. Attempts to address this issue are described in Kaelbling (1993).

Turning to verification, axiomatic approaches suffer from two main problems. First, the temporal verification of reactive systems relies upon a simple model of concurrency, where the actions that programs perform are assumed to be atomic. We cannot make this assumption when we move from programs to agents. The actions we think of agents as performing will generally be much more coarse-grained. As a result, we need a more realistic model of concurrency. One possibility, investigated in Wooldridge (1995), is to model agent execution cycles as intervals over the real numbers, in the style of the temporal logic of reals (Barringer *et al.*, 1986). The second problem is the difficulty of the proof problem for agent specification languages. The theoretical complexity of proof for many of these logics is quite daunting.

Hindriks and colleagues have used Plotkin's structured operational semantics to axiomatize their 3APL language (Hindriks *et al.*, 1998, 1999).

With respect to model-checking approaches, the main problem, as we indicated above, is again the issue of ungrounded semantics for agent specification languages. If we cannot take an arbitrary program and say, for this program, what its beliefs, desires, and intentions are, then it is not clear how we might verify that this program satisfied a specification expressed in terms of such constructs.

Formalisms for reasoning about agents have come a long way since Hintikka's pioneering work on logics of knowledge and belief (Hintikka, 1962). Within AI, perhaps the main emphasis of subsequent work has been on attempting to develop formalisms that capture the relationship between the various elements that comprise an agent's cognitive state; the paradigm example of this work is the well-known theory of intention developed by Cohen and Levesque (1990a). Despite the very real progress that has been made, there still remain many fairly fundamental problems and issues outstanding.

On a technical level, we can identify a number of issues that remain open. First, the problems associated with possible-worlds semantics (notably, logical omniscience) cannot be regarded as solved. As we observed above, possible worlds remain the semantics of choice for many researchers, and yet they do not in general represent a realistic model of agents with limited resources – and of course all real agents are resource-bounded. One solution is to *ground* possible-worlds semantics, giving them a precise interpretation in terms of the world. This was the approach taken in Rosenschein and Kaelbling's situated automata paradigm, and can be very successful. However, it is not clear how such a grounding could be given to pro-attitudes such as desires or intentions (although some attempts have been made (Singh, 1990a; Wooldridge, 1992; Werner, 1990)). There is obviously much work remaining to be done on formalisms for knowledge and belief, in particular in the area of modelling resource-bounded reasoners.

With respect to logics that combine different attitudes, perhaps the most important problems still outstanding relate to intention. In particular, the relationship between intention and action has not been formally represented in a satisfactory way. The problem seems to be that having an intention to act makes it more likely that an agent will act, but does not generally guarantee it. While it seems straightforward to build systems that appear to have intentions (Wooldridge, 1995), it seems much harder to capture this relationship formally. Other problems that have not yet really been addressed in the literature include the management of multiple, possibly conflicting intentions, and the formation, scheduling, and reconsideration of intentions.

The question of exactly *which combination* of attitudes is required to characterize an agent is also the subject of some debate. As we observed above, a currently popular approach is to use a combination of beliefs, desires, and intentions (hence BDI architectures (Rao and Georgeff, 1991b)). However, there are alternatives: Shoham, for example, suggests that the notion of choice is more fundamental (Shoham, 1990). Comparatively little work has yet been done on formally comparing the suitability of these various combinations. One might draw a parallel with the use of temporal logics in mainstream computer science, where the expressiveness of specification languages is by now a well-understood research area (Emerson and Halpern, 1986). Perhaps the obvious requirement for the short term is experimentation with real agent specifications, in order to gain a better understanding of the relative merits of different formalisms.

More generally, the kinds of logics used in agent theory tend to be rather elaborate, typically containing many modalities which interact with each other in subtle ways. Very little work has yet been carried out on the theory underlying such logics (perhaps the only notable exception is Catach (1988)). Until the general principles and limitations of such multi-modal logics become understood, we might expect that progress with using such logics will be slow. One area in which work is likely to be done in the near future is theorem-proving techniques for multi-modal logics.

Finally, there is often some confusion about the role played by a theory of agency. The view we take is that such theories represent *specifications* for agents. The advantage of treating agent theories as specifications, and agent logics as specification languages, is that the problems and issues we then face are familiar from the discipline of software engineering. How useful or expressive is the specification language? How concise are agent specifications? How does one refine or otherwise transform a specification into an implementation? However, the view of agent theories as specifications is not shared by all researchers. Some intend their agent theories to be used as knowledge representation formalisms, which raises the difficult problem of algorithms to reason with such theories. Still others intend their work to formalize a concept of interest in cognitive science or philosophy (this is, of course, what Hintikka intended in his early work on logics of knowledge of belief). What *is* clear is that it is important to be precise about the role one expects an agent theory to play.

Class reading: Rao and Georgeff (1992). This paper is not too formal, but is focused on the issue of when a particular agent implementation can be said to implement a particular theory of agency.

Exercises

(1) **[Level 1.]**

Consider the attitudes of believing, desiring, intending, hoping, and fearing. For each of the following.

(a) Discuss the appropriateness of the axioms K, T, D, 4, and 5 for these attitudes.

(b) Discuss the *interrelationships* between these attitudes. For example, if $B_i\varphi$ means '*i* believes φ' and $I_i\varphi$ means '*i* intends φ', then should $I_i\varphi \Rightarrow B_i\varphi$ hold? What about $I_i\varphi \Rightarrow B_i\neg\varphi$ or $I_i\varphi \Rightarrow \neg B_i\neg\varphi$ and so on? Systematically draw up a table of these possible relationships, and informally argue for/against them – discuss the circumstances under which they might be acceptable.

(c) Add temporal modalities into the framework (as in Cohen and Levesque's formalism), and carry out the same exercise.

(2) **[Level 2.]**

Formally, prove the correspondences in Table 12.1.

(3) **[Level 3.]**

I argued that formalisms such as Cohen and Levesque's might be used as specification languages. Using their formalism (or that in Wooldridge (2000b)), develop a specification of a system with which you are familiar (in case you are stuck, look at the ADEPT system in the preceding chapter).

Appendix A
A History Lesson

We often naively assume that technologies and academic disciplines somehow spontaneously emerge from nowhere, fully formed and well-defined. Of course, nothing could be further from the truth. They tend to emerge in a rather haphazard fashion, and are shaped as much as anything by the personalities, prejudices, and fashions of the time. The multiagent systems field is no exception to this rule. Indeed, the number of other disciplines that have contributed to the multiagent systems field is so large that the story is even murkier than is normally the case. In this section, therefore, I will attempt to give a potted history of the field, identifying some of the milestones and key players.

> *Please note*: more than any other part of the book, this appendix is subjective. The interpretation of events is my own, and as I was not personally present for many of the events described, I have sometimes had to construct a (semi)coherent history from the literature. It follows that not everyone will agree with my version of events. I welcome comments and suggestions, which I will endeavour to take into account if there is ever a second edition.

A history of intelligent agent research

We could spend a month debating exactly when the multiagent systems field was born; as with the computing and artificial intelligence fields, we could identify many agent related ideas that emerged prior to the 20th century. But we can say with some certainty that the agents field (although not necessarily the *multiagent* systems field) was alive following the now famous 1956 Dartmouth workshop at which John McCarthy coined the term 'artificial intelligence'. The notion of an 'agent' is clearly evident in the early AI literature. For example, consider the Turing test, put forward by Alan Turing as a way of settling the argument about whether machines could ever be considered to be intelligent. The idea of the test is that a person interrogates some entity via a monitor. The person is free to put forward any questions or statements whatsoever, and after five minutes is required to decide whether or not the entity at the other end is either another person or a machine. If such a test cannot distinguish a particular program from a person, then, Turing argued, the program must be considered intelligent to all intents and purposes. Clearly, we can think of the program at the other end of the teletype as an agent – the program is required to respond, in real time, to statements made by the person, and the rules of the test prohibit interference with the program. It exhibits some autonomy, in other words.

Although the idea of an agent was clearly present in the early days of AI, there was comparatively little development in the idea of agents as *holistic* entities (i.e. integrated systems capable of independent autonomous action) until the mid-1980s; below, we will see why this happened.

Between about 1969 and 1985, research into systems capable of independent action was carried out primarily within the AI planning community, and was dominated by what I will call the 'reasoning and planning' paradigm. AI planning (see Chapter 3) is essentially automatic programming: a planning algorithm takes as input a description of a goal to be achieved, a description of how the world currently is, and a description of a number of available actions and their effects. The algorithm then outputs a plan – essentially, a program – which describes how the available actions can be executed so as to bring about the desired goal. The best-known, and most influential, planning algorithm was the STRIPS system (Fikes and Nilsson, 1971). STRIPS was so influential for several reasons. First, it developed a particular notation for describing actions and their effects that remains to this day the foundation for most action representation notations. Second, it emphasized the use of formal, logic-based notations for representing both the properties of the world and the actions available. Finally, STRIPS was actually used in an autonomous robot called Shakey at Stanford Research Institute.

The period between the development of STRIPS and the mid-1980s might be thought of as the 'classic' period in AI planning. There was a great deal of progress in developing planning algorithms, and understanding the requirements for representation formalisms for the world and actions. At the risk of over generalizing, this work can be characterized by two features, both of which were pioneered in the STRIPS system:

- the use of explicit, symbolic representations of the world;

- an increasing emphasis on the use of *formal*, typically logic-based representations, and, associated with this work, an increasing emphasis on *deductive* decision making (i.e. decision making as logical proof).

Rodney Brooks recalls the title of a seminar series in the early 1980s: *From Pixels to Predicates*, which for him neatly summed up the spirit of the age (Brooks, 1999, p. ix). By the mid-1980s, however, some researchers were having doubts about the assumptions on which this work was based, and were beginning to voice concerns about the direction in which research on the design of agents was going.

I noted above that the idea of 'integrated' or 'whole' agents, as opposed to agent behaviours (such as learning and planning) did not greatly evolve between the emergence of AI and the mid-1980s. The reason for this lack of progress is as follows. In the early days of AI, there was a great deal of scepticism about computers being able to exhibit 'intelligent' behaviour. A common form of argument was that 'computers will never be able to X', where X = solve problems, learn, communicate in natural language, and so on (see Russell and Norvig (1995, p. 823) for a discussion). A natural response to these kinds of arguments by those interested in AI was to build systems that could exhibit behaviour X. These early systems that could plan, learn, communicate in natural language, and so on, led to the emergence of a number of sub-disciplines in AI: the planning, learning, and natural language communication communities, for example, all have their own conferences, workshops, and literature. And all these communities evolved from the groundbreaking work done on these types of behaviour in the early days of AI.

But critically, there were few attempts to actually *integrate* these kinds of behaviours into whole systems – agents. Instead, researchers focused on building better planning algorithms, better learning algorithms, and so on. By and large, they did not address the problem of how such algorithms might be placed in the context of a 'whole' agent. As a consequence, by the mid-1980s (as we will see below), significant progress had been made in each of these component disciplines, but there was a dearth of experience with respect to building agents from these components. Worse, some researchers began to argue that, because no consideration had been given to how these components might be integrated to build an agent, the component technologies had evolved in such a way that the integration and use of these components in realistic systems was, for all practical purposes, impossible: most component techniques had been evaluated on problems that were some distance from being as complex as real-world problems.

The upshot of all this was that, some researchers argued, 'vertical decomposition' of an agent into the different functional components was based on the flawed assumption that the components could be easily integrated to produce an agent.

In addition, it was argued that 'Artificial intelligence research has foundered on the issue of representation' (Brooks, 1991b)[1]. The problems associated with building an agent that decides what to do by manipulating a symbolic (particularly logic-based) representation of the world were simply too deep to make the approach viable. The conclusion that many researchers came to was that a completely new approach was required.

The result was an entirely new approach to building agents, variously referred to as 'behavioural AI', 'reactive AI', or simply 'the new AI'. Rodney Brooks was perhaps the most vocal member of this community, and came to be seen as the champion of the movement. The workers in this area were not united by any com-

---

[1] To many researchers who do 'good old fashioned AI', the title of this paper – *Intelligence without representation* – is provocative, if not actually heretical.

mon approaches, but certain themes did recur in this work. Recurring themes were the rejection of architectures based on symbolic representations, an emphasis on a closer coupling between the agent's environment and the action it performs, and the idea that intelligent behaviour can be seen to emerge from the interaction of a number of much simpler behaviours.

The term 'furore' might reasonably be used to describe the response from the symbolic and logical reasoning communities to the emergence of behavioural AI. Some researchers seemed to feel that behavioural AI was a direct challenge to the beliefs and assumptions that had shaped their entire academic careers. Not surprisingly, they were not predisposed simply to abandon their ideas and research programs.

I do not believe there was (or is) a clear cut 'right' or 'wrong' in this debate. With the benefit of hindsight, it seems clear that much symbolic AI research had wandered into the realms of abstract theory, and did not connect in any realistic way with the reality of building and deploying agents in realistic scenarios. It also seems clear that the decomposition of AI into components such as planning and learning, without any emphasis on synthesizing these components into an integrated architecture, was perhaps not the best strategy for AI as a discipline. But it also seems that some claims made by members of the behavioural community were extreme, and in many cases suffered from the over-optimism that AI itself suffered from in its early days.

The practical implications of all this were threefold.

- The first was that the behavioural AI community to a certain extent split off from the mainstream AI community. Taking inspiration from biological metaphors, many of the researchers in behavioural AI began working in a community that is today known as 'artificial life' (alife).

- The second was that mainstream AI began to recognize the importance of integrating the components of intelligent behaviour into agents, and, from the mid-1980s to the present day, the area of agent architectures has grown steadily in importance.

- The third was that within AI, the value of testing and deploying agents in *realistic* scenarios (as opposed to simple, contrived, obviously unrealistic scenarios) was recognized. This led to the emergence of such scenarios as the RoboCup robotic soccer challenge, in which the aim is to build agents that can actually play a game of soccer against a team of robotic opponents (RoboCup, 2001).

So, by the mid-1980s, the area of *agent architectures* was becoming established as a specific research area within AI itself.

Most researchers in the agent community accept that neither a purely logicist or reasoning approach nor a purely behavioural approach is the best route to building agents capable of intelligent autonomous action. Intelligent autonomous action seems to imply the capability for *both* reasoning and reactive behaviour. As Innes Ferguson succinctly put it (Ferguson, 1992a, p. 31):

> It is both desirable and feasible to combine suitably designed deliberative and non-deliberative control functions to obtain effective, robust, and flexible behaviour from autonomous, task-achieving agents operating in complex environments.

This recognition led to the development of a range of *hybrid* architectures, which attempt to combine elements of both behavioural and deliberative systems. At the time of writing, hybrid approaches dominate in the literature.

A *history of multiagent systems research*

Research in *multiagent* systems progressed quite independently of research into individual agents until about the early 1990s. It is interesting to note that although the notion of an agent as an isolated system was evident in the early AI literature, the notion of a *multiagent system* did not begin to gain prominence until the early 1980s. Some attention was certainly given to interaction between artificial agents and humans, in the form of research on natural language understanding and generation. (The Turing test, after all, is predicated on the development of other computer systems with such abilities.) But almost no consideration was given to interactions among artificial agents.

To understand how multiagent systems research emerged, it is necessary to go back to the work of Alan Newell and Herb Simon on *production systems* (Russell and Norvig, 1995, pp. 297, 298). A production system is essentially a collection of 'pattern ⟶ action' rules, together with a *working memory* of facts. The production system works by *forward chaining* through the rules: continually matching the left-hand side of rules against working memory, and performing the action of a rule that fires. The action may involve adding or removing facts from working memory. A key problem with standard production systems is that the system's knowledge is *unstructured*: all the rules are collected together into a single amorphous set. This can make it hard to understand and structure the behaviour of the production system. The need for structured knowledge led to the earliest work that was recognizably multiagent systems: *blackboard systems* (Engelmore and Morgan, 1988). A blackboard system is characterized by two main attributes (see Figure A.1):

- a collection of independent entities known as *knowledge sources*, each of which has some specialized knowledge, typically encoded in the form of rules; and

- a shared data structure known as a *blackboard*, which knowledge sources use to communicate.

Knowledge sources in blackboard systems are capable of reading and writing to the blackboard data structure, and problem solving proceeds by the knowledge

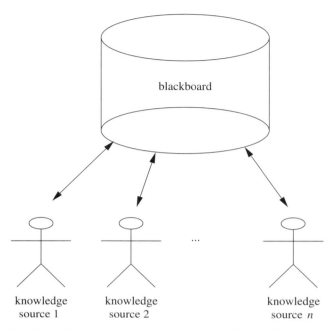

Figure A.1   A blackboard architecture: a number of knowledge sources encapsulate knowledge about a problem, and communicate by reading and writing on a shared data structure known as a blackboard.

sources each monitoring the blackboard and writing to it when they can contribute partial problem solutions. The blackboard metaphor was neatly described by Alan Newell long before the blackboard model became widely known:

> Metaphorically we can think of a set of workers, all looking at the same blackboard: each is able to read everything that is on it, and to judge when he has something worthwhile to add to it. This conception is...a set of demons, each independently looking at the total situation and shrieking in proportion to what they see fits their natures

(Newell, 1962)

(quoted from Engelmore and Morgan (1988, p. 16)).

The first, and probably best-known, blackboard system was the Hearsay system for speech understanding, developed in the early 1970s under the supervision of Reddy *et al.* (1973). One of Reddy's co-workers on the Hearsay project was Victor ('Vic') Lesser, who moved to the University of Massachusetts at Amherst in 1977. Lesser had worked on multiprocessing computer systems in the 1960s, and was well aware of the potential value of *parallelism*. He recognized that the blackboard model, with its multiple knowledge sources each contributing partial solutions to the overall problem, provided a natural metaphor for problem solving that exploited parallelism (Fennell and Lesser, 1977). But the blackboard model is essentially a shared data structure architecture; in order for knowledge sources to communicate in a classical blackboard architecture, they need to write to this shared data structure, which implies that there can only ever be a single thread of control writing to the blackboard at any given time. This limits the parallelism possible in the classical blackboard model, as the shared data structure (and the need to synchronize access to this data structure) introduces a bottleneck in problem solving. The next step was to introduce 'true' parallelism into the architecture, by allowing *multiple* blackboard systems to communicate by message passing: Lesser and Erman did this in the late 1970s, still working within the Hearsay problem domain of speech understanding (Lesser and Erman, 1980).

Blackboard systems were highly influential in the early days of multiagent systems, but are no longer a major area of research activity. The definitive reference is Engelmore and Morgan (1988), and other useful references include Erman *et al.* (1980), Hayes-Roth (1985) and Corkill *et al.* (1987).

At about the same time as Lesser and colleagues were beginning to build parallel blackboard systems, Doug Lenat proposed the BEINGS model of problem solving (Lenat, 1975). This model of problem solving is very similar to the blackboard model, the metaphor being that of a number of experts cooperating to solve problems by asking and answering questions. The beings in Lenat's system were not autonomous agents – they were more closely related to knowledge sources in the blackboard model – but the metaphors of cooperation and distribution are clearly evident.

Throughout the 1970s, several other researchers developed prototypical multiagent systems. The first was Carl Hewitt, who proposed the ACTOR model of computation. Hewitt obtained his PhD from MIT in 1971 for his work on a system called PLANNER (Hewitt, 1971). This system made use of data structures called schemata, which somewhat resemble the knowledge sources in blackboard architectures. After his PhD work, Hewitt was made aware of work on the Smalltalk system underway at Xerox Palo Alto Research Center (Xerox PARC) (Goldberg, 1984). Smalltalk is widely recognized as the first real object-oriented programming language. Smalltalk made liberal use of the metaphor of *message passing* to describe how objects communicated with one another[2]. Taking inspiration from Smalltalk, Hewitt proposed the ACTOR model, in which computation itself is viewed primarily as message passing. The ACTOR model was described as early as 1973 (Hewitt, 1973), but the best-known and most widely cited expression of the ACTOR model was a 1977 article published in *Artificial Intelligence* journal (Hewitt, 1977). The ACTOR model was Hewitt's expression of some radical views about the future direction of computation, and with the benefit of hindsight, it is remarkable just how far ahead of his time Hewitt was. He recognized that the future of computing itself was inexorably tied to distributed, *open* systems (Hewitt, 1985), and that

---

[2] The notion of objects communicating by message passing was a key idea in early object-oriented programming systems, but has been somewhat obscured in languages such as C++ and Java. Message passing in Smalltalk was essentially method invocation.

traditional models of computation were not well suited for modelling or understanding such distributed computation. The ACTOR paradigm was his attempt to develop a model of computation that more accurately reflected the direction in which computer science was going.

An ACTOR is a computational system with the following properties.

- ACTORs are social – they are able to send messages to other ACTORs.

- ACTORs are reactive – they carry out computation in response to a message received from another ACTOR. (ACTORs are thus *message driven*.)

Intuitively, an actor can be considered as consisting of

- a *mail address* which names the ACTOR;

- a *behaviour*, which specifies what the ACTOR will do upon receipt of a message.

The possible components of an ACTOR's behaviour are

- sending messages to itself or other ACTORs;

- creating more actors;

- specifying a *replacement behaviour*.

Intuitively, the way an ACTOR works is quite simple:

- upon receipt of a message, the message is matched against the ACTOR's behaviour (script);

- upon a match, the corresponding action is executed, which may involve sending more messages, creating more ACTORs, or replacing the ACTOR by another.

An example ACTOR, which computes the factorial of its argument, is shown in Figure A.2 (from Agha, 1986). Receipt of a message containing a non-zero integer n by `Factorial` will result in the following behaviour:

- create an ACTOR whose behaviour will be to multiply n by an integer it receives and send the reply to the mail address to which the factorial of n was to be sent;

- send itself the 'request' to evaluate the factorial of n−1 and send the value to the customer it created.

The creation of ACTORs in this example mirrors the recursive procedures for computing factorials in more conventional programming languages.

The ACTOR paradigm greatly influenced work on concurrent object languages (Agha *et al.*, 1993). Particularly strong communities working on concurrent object languages emerged in France (led by Jacques Ferber and colleagues (Ferber and Carle, 1991)) and Japan (led by Akinora Yonezawa, Mario Tokoro and colleagues (Yonezawa and Tokoro, 1997; Yonezawa, 1990; Sueyoshi and Tokoro, 1991)).

```
1.  Rec-Factorial with acquaintances self
2.  let communication be an integer n and a customer u
3.  become Rec-Factorial
4.  if n=0
5.      then
6.          send [1] to customer
7.      else
8.          let c=Rec-Customer with acquaintances n and u
9.          {send [n-1, mail address of c] to self}
10. Rec-Customer with acquaintances integer n and customer u
12. let communication be an integer k
13. {send [n * k] to u}
```

Figure A.2   An ACTOR for computing factorials.

In the late 1970s at Stanford University in California, a doctoral student called Reid Smith was completing his PhD on a system called the Contract Net, in which a number of agents ('problem solving nodes' in Smith's parlance) solved problems by delegating sub-problems to other agents (Smith, 1977, 1980a,b). As the name suggests, the key metaphor is that of sub-contracting in human organizations. The Contract Net remains to this day one of the most influential multiagent systems developed. It introduced several key concepts into the multiagent systems literature, including the economics metaphor and the negotiation metaphor.

Smith's thesis was published in 1980, a year also notable for the emergence of the first academic forum for research specifically devoted to the new paradigm of multiagent systems. Randy Davis from MIT organized the first workshop on what was then called 'Distributed Artificial Intelligence' (DAI) (Davis, 1980). Throughout the 1980s, the DAI workshops, held more or less annually in the USA, became the main focus of activity for the new community. The 1985 workshop, organized by Michael Genesereth and Matt Ginsberg of Stanford University, was particularly important as the proceedings were published as the first real book on the field: the 'green book', edited by Michael Huhns (Huhns, 1987). The proceedings of the 1988 workshop, held at Lake Arrowhead in California, were published two years later as the 'second green book' (Gasser and Huhns, 1989). Another key publication at this time was Bond and Gasser's 1988 collection *Readings in Distributed Artificial Intelligence* (Bond and Gasser, 1988). This volume brought together many of the key papers of the field. It was prefaced with a detailed and insightful survey article, which attempted to summarize the key problems and issues facing the field; the survey remains relevant even at the time of writing.

Until about the mid-1980s the emphasis was on 'parallelism in problem solving', or *distributed problem solving* as it became known. In other words, the main type of issue being addressed was 'given a problem, how can we exploit multiple processor architectures to solve this problem'. In the mid-1980s, a Stanford University PhD student called Jeff Rosenschein fundamentally changed the emphasis of the field, by recognizing that distributed problem-solving systems implicitly assumed 'common interest' among the agents in the system. He realized that while such systems are undoubtedly important, they represent a special case of a much more general class of systems, in which agents are assumed to be *self-interested*. In his 1985 paper *Deals Among Rational Agents*, he coined the term 'benevolent agent' to describe agents that could be assumed to help out wherever asked (Rosenschein and Genesereth, 1985). As well as making the critically important distinction between self-interested and benevolent agents, this paper is also significant for a second reason: it was the first paper to make use of techniques from *game theory* to analyse interactions among artificial agents.

The mid-1980s also saw the development of the first general-purpose testbed for experimentation with agent systems. The MACE system (an acronym of 'multia-gent computing environment') was developed under the supervision of Les Gasser at the University of Southern California (Gasser *et al.*, 1987a,b). MACE provided many features that have subsequently become standard in multiagent systems; for example, it pioneered the provision of *acquaintance models* by which agents could have representations of the capabilities and plans of their peers.

Somewhat surprisingly, those active in the field at the time report that interest in DAI actually *waned* throughout the latter half of the 1980s. The reasons for this are unclear; it may well be that this reduction of interest was simply a result of some of the key figures from the early days of the field moving into new jobs and new areas of work. But the seeds sown with the establishment of a regular workshop and the publication of three key books led to an international flowering of interest in DAI. In the late 1980s, the European Commission funded a research project entitled ARCHON ('Architecture for Cooperating Heterogeneous Online Systems'), which was originally focused on the problem of getting a number of distinct 'expert systems' to pool their expertise in solving problems and diagnosing faults in several industrial domains (Wittig, 1992; Jennings *et al.*, 1996a; Perriolat *et al.*, 1996). ARCHON was a *large* project (14 partners across 9 European countries!), and subsequently became recognized as one of the first real industrial applications of agent systems.

At about the same time, the European Commission also funded the MAGMA project (loosely derived from 'Modelling an Autonomous Agent in a Multiagent World'). As part of this project, the participants decided to organize a workshop with the same name; it was held in Cambridge, UK, in 1989, and was so successful that the MAAMAW workshops became an annual event. Through the early 1990s, led by Yves Demazeau, MAAMAW was the main European forum for agent research (Demazeau and Müller, 1990). In Japan, the MACC workshops were also established as a regional forum for agent research.

Interest in agent systems grew very rapidly in the first half of the 1990s. There were several reasons for this. The first, and probably most important reason was the spread of the Internet, which through the 1990s changed from being a tool unknown outside academia to something in everyday use for commerce and leisure across the globe. In many ways, 1994 seems to have been a milestone year for agents. The first is that 1994 was the year that the Web emerged; the Mosaic browser only began to reach a truly wide audience in 1994 (Berners-Lee, 1999). The Web provided an easy-to-use front end for the Internet, enabling people with very limited IT training to productively use the Internet for the first time. The explosive growth of the Internet was perhaps the most vivid illustration possible that the future of computing lay in distributed, networked systems, and that in order to exploit the potential of such distributed systems, new models of computation were required. By the summer of 1994 it was becoming clear that the Internet would be a major proving ground for agent technology (perhaps even the 'killer application'), although the full extent of this interest was not yet apparent.

As well as the emergence of the Web, 1994 saw the publication in July of a special issue of *Communications of the ACM* that was devoted to intelligent agents. CACM is one of the best-known publications in the computing world, and ACM is arguably its foremost professional body; the publication of a special issue of CACM on agents was therefore some kind of recognition by the computing world that agents were worth knowing about. Many of the articles in this special issue described a new type of agent system, that acted as a kind of 'expert assistant' to a user working with a particular class of application. The vision of agents as intelligent assistants was perhaps articulated most clearly by Pattie Maes from MIT's Media Lab, who described a number of prototype systems to realize the vision (Maes, 1994a). Such user interface agents rapidly caught the imagination of a wider community, and, in particular, the commercial possibilities of such technologies was self-evident. A number of agent startup companies were founded to commercialize this technology, including Pattie Maes's company FireFly (subsequently sold to Microsoft), and Oren Etzioni's company NetBot (subsequently sold to the Web portal company Excite).

With the growth of the Internet in the late 1990s came electronic commerce (e-commerce), and the rapid international expansion of 'dot com' companies. It was quickly realized that e-commerce represents a natural – and potentially very lucrative – application domain for multiagent systems. The idea is that agents can partially automate many of the stages of electronic commerce, from finding a product to buy, through to actually negotiating the terms of agreement (Noriega and Sierra, 1999). This area of *agent-mediated electronic commerce* became perhaps the largest single application area for agent technology by the turn of the century, and gave an enormous impetus (commercial, as well as scientific) to the areas of *negotiation* and *auctions* in agent systems. Researchers such as Sarit Kraus, Carles Sierra, Tuomas Sandholm, Moshe Tennenholtz, and Makoto Yokoo investigated the theoretical foundations of agent-mediated electronic commerce (building to a great extent on the pioneering work of Jeff Rosenschein and colleagues on game-theoretic models) and began to investigate how such techniques could be applied in real systems.

The emergence of agents on and for the Internet gave rise to a new, associated software technology, somewhat distinct from the 'mainstream' of agent research and development. In the summer of 1994, a California-based company called General Magic was creating intense interest in the idea of *mobile agents* – programs that could transmit themselves across an electronic network and recommence execution at a remote site (White, 1997). At the time, General Magic were distributing a widely read white paper that described Telescript – a programming language intended to realize the vision of mobile agents (White, 1994). In the event, it was not Telescript, but another programming language that caught the imagination of the Internet community: Java. When Netscape incorporated a Java virtual machine into their Navigator browser, they made it possible for browsers to download and execute small programs called *applets*. Applets transformed the Web from being a large but essentially static collection of linked documents to being an active and dynamic system of inter-working components. The potential to the computer science community was obvious, and this gave Java an enormous impetus, both as a way of animating the Internet, but also as a powerful, well-designed object-oriented programming language in its own right. Although they are not agents in the sense that I use the term in this book, applets give a hint of what might be possible in the future.

A number of mobile agent frameworks were rapidly developed and released as Java packages, and interest in Telescript waned. As I write this history in the summer of 2000, Java is the programming language of choice not just for agent systems, but also, it seems, for most other applications in computing. Java was never intended to be an 'agent programming language' (although it can of course be used for programming agents), but since it was first released, the language has been progressively extended to give it ever more agent-like features. A good example is the JINI framework, which allows objects to advertise their services and, in a simple way, to cooperate with one another in a similar way to that proposed by the agent community (Oaks and Wong, 2000).

By the mid-1990s, the level of industrial interest in agent systems was such that *standardization* became a major issue, and some researchers began to suspect that the lack of recognized international standards was an impediment to the wider take-up of agent technology. The early 1990s had already seen some activity in this area, in the form of the US-based Knowledge Sharing Effort, within which two influential languages for agent communication were developed: KQML and KIF (Patil *et al.*, 1992). However, these languages were never formally standardized, which led to great difficulties for agent developers that actually wanted to use them in open settings. As a result, in 1995, the FIPA movement began its work on standards for agent systems (FIPA, 2001). The centrepiece of the FIPA initiative was a language for agent communication. By the end of the decade, many major IT and telecommunications companies had become involved in the FIPA movement, and a set of prototypical standards had been developed. At the time of writing, the major initiative underway is to *deploy* these languages in real settings, and – hopefully – demonstrate their value to agent developers.

Another body of work that arose in the mid-1990s, led by Rosaria Conte, Jim Doran, and Nigel Gilbert, was the use of multiagent systems for modelling natural societies (Gilbert and Doran, 1994; Gilbert and Conte, 1995). The Simulating Societies (SimSoc) workshop, first held in 1993, brought together researchers who were interested in using multiagent systems to gain insights into the behaviour of human societies.

Finally, in the late 1990s, researchers in multiagent systems began to seek increasingly realistic domains in which to develop systems. This led, perhaps indirectly, to the *RoboCup* initiative (RoboCup, 2001; Kitano, 1998). The RoboCup challenge is simple: to demonstrate, within 50 years, a team of soccer-playing robots that can beat a World Cup-strength team of human soccer players. The rationale for RoboCup is that successfully playing soccer demands a range of different skills, such as real-time dynamic coordination using limited communication bandwidth. (From a robotics point of view, RoboCup also presents profound challenges – today's autonomous robots come nowhere near the dexterity or flexibility of human soccer players.) Interest in RoboCup had exploded by the turn of the century, with hundreds of teams from across the world attending the regular RoboCup tournaments. In 2000, RoboCup launched a new initiative, entitled *RoboCup Rescue*. In RoboCup rescue, the goal is to build robots that can cooperate to carry out search and rescue missions in a scenario based on the earthquake that hit the city of Kobe, Japan, in the mid-1990s. Miniature robots designed by a team working on the RoboCup Rescue scenario were used to search in the ruins of the World Trade Center in New York, following the devastating terrorist attacks of 11 September 2001.

Afterword

I began this book by pointing to some trends that have so far marked the short history of computer science: ubiquity, interconnection, intelligence, delegation, and human-orientation. I claimed that these trends naturally led to the emergence of the multiagent systems paradigm. I hope that after reading this book, you will agree with this claim.

After opening this book by talking about the history of computing, you may expect me to close it by talking about its future. But prediction, as Nils Bohr famously remarked, is hard – particularly predicting the future. Rather than making specific predictions about the future of computing, I will therefore restrict my observations to some hopefully rather uncontentious (and safe) points. The most important of these is simply that these trends will continue. Computer systems will continue to be ever more ubiquitous and interconnected; we will continue to delegate ever more tasks to computers, and these tasks will be increasingly complex, requiring ever more intelligence to successfully carry them out; and, finally, the way in which we interact with computers will increasingly resemble the way in which we interact with each other.

Douglas Adams, author of the well-known *Hitch Hiker's Guide to the Galaxy* books, was also, in the final years of his life, a commentator on the computer industry. In a radio programme broadcast by the BBC shortly before his death, he predicted that, eventually, computers and processor power will become as cheap and common as grains of sand. Imagine such a world: in which every device created by humans is equipped with processor power, and is capable of interacting with any other device, or any person, anywhere in the world. Outlandish – preposterous – as it may seem, this future follows directly from the trends that I discussed above. Now imagine the *potential* in this vision. Those of us old enough to have worked with computers before 1993 will recall the sense of awe as we realized what might be possible with the Web. But this pales into insignificance next to the possibilities of this, as yet distant future Internet.

Note that the *plumbing* for this future – the processors and the network connections to link them – is the easy part. The difficult part – the real challenge – is the software to *realize its potential*. I do not know exactly what software technologies will be deployed to make this future happen. But it seems to me – and to many other researchers – that multiagent systems are the best candidate we currently have. It does not matter whether we call them agents or not; in 20 years, the term may not be used. The key thing is that the problems being addressed by the agent community are exactly the problems that I believe will need to be solved to realize the potential.

References

Adler, M. R. *et al.* (1989) Conflict resolution strategies for nonhierarchical distributed agents. In *Distributed Artificial Intelligence* (eds L. Gasser and M. Huhns), Volume 2, pp. 139–162. Pitman, London and Morgan Kaufmann, San Mateo, CA.

Agha, G. (1986) *ACTORS: a Model of Concurrent Computation in Distributed Systems.* MIT Press, Cambridge, MA.

Agha, G., Wegner, P. and Yonezawa, A. (eds) (1993) *Research Directions in Concurrent Object-Oriented Programming.* MIT Press, Cambridge, MA.

Agre, P. and Chapman, D. (1987) PENGI: an implementation of a theory of activity. In *Proceedings of the 6th National Conference on Artificial Intelligence (AAAI-87), Seattle, WA*, pp. 268–272.

Agre, P. E. and Rosenschein, S. J. (eds) (1996) *Computational Theories of Interaction and Agency.* MIT Press, Cambridge, MA.

Allen, J. F. (1984) Towards a general theory of action and time. *Artificial Intelligence*, **23**(2), 123–154.

Allen, J. F., Hendler, J. and Tate, A. (eds) (1990) *Readings in Planning.* Morgan Kaufmann, San Mateo, CA.

Allen, J. F., Kautz, H., Pelavin, R. and Tenenberg, J. (1991) *Reasoning about Plans.* Morgan Kaufmann, San Mateo, CA.

Amgoud, L. (1999) *Contribution à l'intégration des préferences dans le raisonnement argumentatif.* PhD thesis, l'Université Paul Sabatier, Toulouse. (In French.)

Amgoud, L., Maudet, N. and Parsons, S. (2000) Modelling dialogues using argumentation. In *Proceedings of the 4th International Conference on Multi-Agent Systems (ICMAS-2000), Boston, MA*, pp. 31–38.

Appelt, D. E. (1982) Planning natural language utterances. In *Proceedings of the 2nd National Conference on Artificial Intelligence (AAAI-82), Pittsburgh, PA*, pp. 59–62.

Appelt, D. E. (1985) *Planning English Sentences.* Cambridge University Press, Cambridge.

Appelt, D. E. and Konolige, K. (1988) A nonmonotonic logic for reasoning about speech acts and belief revision. In *Nonmonotonic Reasoning. Proceedings of the 2nd International Workshop* (eds M. Reinfrank, J. de Kleer, M. L. Ginsberg and E. Sandewall), LNAI Volume 346, pp. 164–175. Springer, Berlin.

Austin, J. L. (1962) *How To Do Things With Words.* Oxford University Press, Oxford.

Axelrod, R. (1984) *The Evolution of Cooperation.* Basic Books, New York.

Axelrod, R. (1997) *The Complexity of Cooperation.* Princeton University Press, Princeton, NJ.

Baecker, R. M. (ed.) (1993) *Readings in Groupware and Computer-Supported Cooperative Work.* Morgan Kaufmann, San Mateo, CA.

Barringer, H. *et al.* (1989) METATEM: a framework for programming in temporal logic. In *REX Workshop on Stepwise Refinement of Distributed Systems: Models, Formalisms, Correctness,* LNCS Volume 430, pp. 94–129. Springer, Berlin.

Barringer, H., Kuiper, R. and Pnueli, A. (1986) A really abstract concurrent model and its temporal logic. In *Proceedings of the 13th ACM Symposium on the Principles of Programming Languages,* pp. 173–183.

Barwise, J. and Perry, J. (1983) *Situations and Attitudes.* MIT Press, Cambridge, MA.

Bates, J. (1994) The role of emotion in believable agents. *Communications of the ACM,* **37**(7), 122–125.

Bates, J., Bryan Loyall, A. and Scott Reilly, W. (1992a) An architecture for action, emotion and social behaviour. Technical report CMU-CS-92-144, School of Computer Science, Carnegie-Mellon University, Pittsburgh, PA.

Bates, J., Bryan Loyall, A. and Scott Reilly, W. (1992b) Integrating reactivity, goals and emotion in a broad agent. Technical report CMU-CS-92-142, School of Computer Science, Carnegie-Mellon University, Pittsburgh, PA.

Bauer, B., Müller, J. P. and Odell, J. (2001) Agent UML: a formalism for specifying multiagent software systems. In *Agent-Oriented Software Engineering. Proceedings of the First International Workshop AOSE-2000* (eds P. Ciancarini and M. Wooldridge), LNCS Volume 1957, pp. 91–104. Springer, Berlin.

Bell, J. (1995) Changing attitudes. In *Intelligent Agents: Theories, Architectures and Languages* (eds M. Wooldridge and N. R. Jennings), LNAI Volume 890, pp. 40–55. Springer, Berlin.

Belnap, N. (1991) Backwards and forwards in the modal logic of agency. *Philosophy and Phenomenological Research,* **51**(4), 777–807.

Belnap, N. and Perloff, M. (1988) Seeing to it that: a canonical form for agentives. *Theoria,* **54**, 175–199.

Ben-Ari, M. (1990) *Principles of Concurrent and Distributed Programming.* Prentice-Hall, Englewood Cliffs, NJ.

Ben-Ari, M. (1993) *Mathematical Logic for Computer Science.* Prentice-Hall, Englewood Cliffs, NJ.

Benerecetti, M., Giunchiglia, F. and Serafini, L. (1999) A model checking algorithm for multiagent systems. In *Intelligent Agents, V* (eds J. P. Müller, M. P. Singh and A. S. Rao), LNAI Volume 1555. Springer, Berlin.

Berners-Lee, T. (1999) *Weaving the Web.* Orion Business, London.

Binmore, K. (1992) *Fun and Games: a Text on Game Theory.* D. C. Heath and Company, Lexington, MA.

Blackburn, P., de Rijke, M. and Venema, Y. (2001) *Modal Logic.* Cambridge University Press, Cambridge.

Blythe, J. (1999) An overview of planning under uncertainty. In *Artificial Intelligence Today* (eds M. Wooldridge and M. Veloso), LNAI Volume 1600, pp. 85–110. Springer, Berlin.

Bonasso, R. P., Kortenkamp, D., Miller, D. P. and Slack, M. (1996) Experiences with an architecture for intelligent, reactive agents. In *Intelligent Agents, II* (eds M. Wooldridge, J. P. Müller and M. Tambe), LNAI Volume 1037, pp. 187–202. Springer, Berlin.

Bond, A. H. and Gasser, L. (eds) (1988) *Readings in Distributed Artificial Intelligence.* Morgan Kaufmann, San Mateo, CA.

Booch, G. (1994) *Object-Oriented Analysis and Design,* 2nd edition. Addison-Wesley, Reading, MA.

Booch, G., Rumbaugh, J. and Jacobson, I. (1998) *The Unified Modeling Language User Guide.* Addison-Wesley, Reading, MA.

Bradshaw, J. (ed.) (1997) *Software Agents.* MIT Press, Cambridge, MA.

Bradshaw, J., Dutfield, S., Benoit, P. and Wooley, J. D. (1997) KAoS: towards an industrial strength open agent architecture. In *Software Agents* (ed. J. Bradshaw), pp. 375–418. MIT Press, Cambridge, MA.

Bratman, M. E. (1987) *Intention, Plans and Practical Reason*. Harvard University Press, Cambridge, MA.

Bratman, M. E. (1990) What is intention? In *Intentions in Communication* (eds P. R. Cohen, J. L. Morgan and M. E. Pollack), pp. 15–32. MIT Press, Cambridge, MA.

Bratman, M. E., Israel, D. J. and Pollack, M. E. (1988) Plans and resource-bounded practical reasoning. *Computational Intelligence*, **4**, 349–355.

Brazier, F. *et al.* (1995) Formal specification of multi-agent systems: a real-world case. In *Proceedings of the 1st International Conference on Multi-Agent Systems (ICMAS-95), San Francisco, CA*, pp. 25–32.

Bretier, P. and Sadek, D. (1997) A rational agent as the kernel of a cooperative spoken dialogue system: implementing a logical theory of interaction. In *Intelligent Agents, III* (eds J. P. Müller, M. Wooldridge and N. R. Jennings), LNAI Volume 1193, pp. 189–204. Springer, Berlin.

Breugst, M. *et al.* (1999) Grasshopper: an agent platform for mobile agent-based services in fixed and mobile telecommunications environments. In *Software Agents for Future Communication Systems* (eds A. L. G. Hayzelden and J. Bigham), pp. 326–357. Springer, Berlin.

Brewington, B. *et al.* (1999) Mobile agents for distributed information retrieval. In *Intelligent Information Agents* (ed. M. Klusch), pp. 355–395. Springer, Berlin.

Brooks, R. A. (1986) A robust layered control system for a mobile robot. *IEEE Journal of Robotics and Automation*, **2**(1), 14–23.

Brooks, R. A. (1990) Elephants don't play chess. In *Designing Autonomous Agents* (ed. P. Maes), pp. 3–15. MIT Press, Cambridge, MA.

Brooks, R. A. (1991a) Intelligence without reason. In *Proceedings of the 12th International Joint Conference on Artificial Intelligence (IJCAI-91), Sydney, Australia*, pp. 569–595.

Brooks, R. A. (1991b) Intelligence without representation. *Artificial Intelligence*, **47**, 139–159.

Brooks, R. A. (1999) *Cambrian Intelligence*. MIT Press, Cambridge, MA.

Burmeister, B. (1996) Models and methodologies for agent-oriented analysis and design. In *Working Notes of the KI'96 Workshop on Agent-Oriented Programming and Distributed Systems* (ed. K. Fischer), DFKI Document D-96-06. DFKI.

Busetta, P. *et al.* (2000) Structuring BDI agents in functional clusters. In *Intelligent Agents, VI. Proceedings of the 6th International Workshop on Agent Theories, Architectures and Languages, ATAL-99* (eds N. Jennings and Y. Lespérance), LNAI Volume 1757. Lecture notes in Artificial Intelligence, pp. 277–289. Springer, Berlin.

Bylander, T. (1994) The computational complexity of propositional STRIPS planning. *Artificial Intelligence*, **69**(1–2), 165–204.

Cammarata, S., McArthur, D. and Steeb, R. (1983) Strategies of cooperation in distributed problem solving. In *Proceedings of the 8th International Joint Conference on Artificial Intelligence (IJCAI-83), Karlsruhe, Federal Republic of Germany*, pp. 767–770.

Carriero, N. and Gelernter, D. (1989) Linda in context. *Communications of the ACM*, **32**(4), 444–458.

Castelfranchi, C. (1990) Social power. In *Decentralized AI – Proceedings of the 1st European Workshop on Modelling Autonomous Agents in a Multi-Agent World (MAAMAW-89)* (eds Y. Demazeau and J.-P. Müller), pp. 49–62. Elsevier, Amsterdam.

Castelfranchi, C., Miceli, M. and Cesta, A. (1992) Dependence relations among autonomous agents. In *Decentralized AI 3- Proceedings of the 3rd European Workshop on Modelling Autonomous Agents in a Multi-Agent World (MAAMAW-91)* (eds E. Werner and Y. Demazeau), pp. 215–231. Elsevier, Amsterdam.

Catach, L. (1988) Normal multimodal logics. In *Proceedings of the 7th National Conference on Artificial Intelligence (AAAI-88) St. Paul, MN*, pp. 491–495.

Chang, E. (1987) Participant systems. In *Distributed Artificial Intelligence* (ed. M. Huhns), pp. 311–340. Pitman, London and Morgan Kaufmann, San Mateo, CA.

Chapman, D. and Agre, P. (1986) Abstract reasoning as emergent from concrete activity. In *Reasoning About Actions and Plans – Proceedings of the 1986 Workshop* (eds M. P. Georgeff and A. L. Lansky), pp. 411–424. Morgan Kaufmann, San Mateo, CA.

Chavez, A. and Maes, P. (1996) Kasbah: an agent marketplace for buying and selling goods. In *Proceedings of the 1st International Conference on the Practical Application of Intelligent Agents and Multi-Agent Technology (PAAM-96), London, UK*, pp. 75–90.

Chellas, B. (1980) *Modal Logic: an Introduction.* Cambridge University Press, Cambridge.

Ciancarini, P. and Hankin, C. (eds) (1996) *Coordination Languages and Models – Proceedings of Coordination '96*, LNCS Volume 1061. Springer, Berlin.

Ciancarini, P. and Wooldridge, M. (eds) (2001) *Agent-Oriented Software Engineering – Proceedings of the 1st International Workshop AOSE-2000*, LNCS Volume 1957. Springer, Berlin.

Clarke, E. M. and Emerson, E. A. (1981) Design and synthesis of synchronization skeletons using branching time temporal logic. In *Logics of Programs – Proceedings 1981*, LNCS Volume 131 (ed. D. Kozen), pp. 52–71. Springer, Berlin.

Clarke, E. M., Grumberg, O. and Peled, D. A. (2000) *Model Checking.* MIT Press, Cambridge, MA.

Clocksin, W. F. and Mellish, C. S. (1981) *Programming in Prolog.* Springer, Berlin.

Cohen, P. R. and Levesque, H. J. (1990a) Intention is choice with commitment. *Artificial Intelligence*, **42**, 213–261.

Cohen, P. R. and Levesque, H. J. (1990b) Rational interaction as the basis for communication. In *Intentions in Communication* (eds P. R. Cohen, J. Morgan and M. E. Pollack), pp. 221–256. MIT Press, Cambridge, MA.

Cohen, P. R. and Levesque, H. J. (1991) Teamwork. *Nous*, **25**(4), 487–512.

Cohen, P. R. and Levesque, H. J. (1995) Communicative actions for artificial agents. In *Proceedings of the 1st International Conference on Multi-Agent Systems (ICMAS-95), San Francisco, CA*, pp. 65–72.

Cohen, P. R. and Perrault, C. R. (1979) Elements of a plan based theory of speech acts. *Cognitive Science*, **3**, 177–212.

Coleman, D. *et al.* (1994) *Object-Oriented Development: the* FUSION *Method.* Prentice-Hall International, Hemel Hempstead, UK.

Collinot, A., Drogoul, A. and Benhamou, P. (1996) Agent oriented design of a soccer robot team. In *Proceedings of the 2nd International Conference on Multi-Agent Systems (ICMAS-96)*, pp. 41–47, Kyoto, Japan.

Connah, D. and Wavish, P. (1990) An experiment in cooperation. In *Decentralized AI – Proceedings of the 1st European Workshop on Modelling Autonomous Agents in a Multi-Agent World (MAAMAW-89)* (eds Y. Demazeau and J.-P. Müller), pp. 197–214. Elsevier, Amsterdam.

Conte, R. and Castelfranchi, C. (1993) Simulative understanding of norm functionalities in social groups. In *Simulating Societies-93: Pre-proceedings of the 1993 International Symposium on Approaches to Simulating Social Phenomena and Social Processes, Certosa di Pontignano, Siena, Italy*.

Conte, R. and Gilbert, N. (1995) Computer simulation for social theory. In *Artificial Societies: The Computer Simulation of Social Life* (eds N. Gilbert and R. Conte), pp. 1–15. UCL Press, London.

Corkill, D. D., Gallagher, K. Q. and Johnson, P. M. (1987) Achieving flexibility, efficiency and generality in blackboard architectures. In *Proceedings of the 6th National Conference on Artificial Intelligence (AAAI-87)*, pp. 18–23. Seattle, WA.

DAML (2001) The DARPA agent markup language. See http://www.daml.org/.

Davidsson, P. (2001) Multi agent based simulation: beyond social simulation. In *Multi-Agent-Based Simulation*, LNAI Volume 1979, pp. 97–107. Springer, Berlin.

Davis, R. (1980) Report on the workshop on Distributed AI. *ACM SIGART Newsletter*, **73**, 42–52.

Decker, K. S. (1996) TÆMS: A framework for environment centred analysis and design of coordination algorithms. In *Foundations of Distributed Artificial Intelligence* (eds G. M. P. O'Hare and N. R. Jennings), pp. 429–447. John Wiley and Sons, Chichester.

Decker, K. and Lesser, V. (1995) Designing a family of coordination algorithms. In *Proceedings of the 1st International Conference on Multi-Agent Systems (ICMAS-95)*, pp. 73–80. San Francisco, CA.

Decker, K. S., Durfee, E. H. and Lesser, V. R. (1989) Evaluating research in cooperative distributed problem solving. In *Distributed Artificial Intelligence* (eds L. Gasser and M. Huhns), Volume II, pp. 487–519. Pitman, London and Morgan Kaufmann, San Mateo, CA.

Decker, K., Sycara, K. and Williamson, M. (1997) Middle-agents for the Internet. In *Proceedings of the 15th International Joint Conference on Artificial Intelligence (IJCAI-97)*, Nagoya, Japan.

Decker, S., (2000) The semantic Web: the roles of XML and RDF. *IEEE Internet Computing*, **4**(5), 63–74.

Demazeau, Y. and Müller, J.-P. (eds) (1990) *Decentralized AI – Proceedings of the 1st European Workshop on Modelling Autonomous Agents in a Multi-Agent World (MAAMAW-89)*. Elsevier, Amsterdam.

Dennett, D. C. (1978) *Brainstorms*. MIT Press, Cambridge, MA.

Dennett, D. C. (1987) *The Intentional Stance*. MIT Press, Cambridge, MA.

Dennett, D. C. (1996) *Kinds of Minds*. London: Phoenix.

Depke, R., Heckel, R. and Kuester, J. M. (2001) Requirement specification and design of agent-based systems with graph transformation, roles and uml. In *Agent-Oriented Software Engineering – Proceedings of the 1st International Workshop AOSE-2000* (eds P. Ciancarini and M. Wooldridge), LNCS Volume 1957, pp. 105–120. Springer, Berlin.

Devlin, K. (1991) *Logic and Information*. Cambridge University Press, Cambridge.

Dignum, F. (1999) Autonomous agents with norms. *Artificial Intelligence and Law*, **7**, 69–79.

Dignum, F. and Greaves, M. (eds) (2000) *Issues in Agent Communication*, LNAI Volume 1916. Springer, Berlin.

Dimpoulos, Y., Nebel, B. and Toni, F. (1999) Preferred arguments are harder to compute than stable extensions. In *Proceedings of the 16th International Joint Conference on Artificial Intelligence (IJCAI-99)*, pp. 36–41. Stockholm, Sweden.

d'Inverno, M. and Luck, M. (1996) Formalising the contract net as a goal-directed system. In *Agents Breaking Away – Proceedings of the 7th European Workshop on Modelling Autonomous Agents in a Multi-Agent World, MAAMAW-96 (LNAI 1038)* (eds J. van de Velde and W. Perram), pp. 72–85. Springer, Berlin.

d'Inverno, M. and Luck, M. (2001) *Understanding Agent Systems*. Springer, Berlin.

d'Inverno, M. *et al.* (1997) A formal specification of dMARS. In *Intelligent Agents, IV* (eds A. Rao, M. P. Singh and M. J. Wooldridge), LNAI Volume 1365, pp. 155–176. Springer, Berlin.

Dixon, C., Fisher, M. and Wooldridge, M. (1998) Resolution for temporal logics of knowledge. *Journal of Logic and Computation*, **8**(3), 345–372.

Dongha, P. (1995) Toward a formal model of commitment for resource-bounded agents. In *Intelligent Agents: Theories, Architectures and Languages* (eds M. Wooldridge and N. R. Jennings), LNAI Volume 890, pp. 86–101. Springer, Berlin.

Doorenbos, R., Etzioni, O. and Weld, D. (1997) A scaleable comparison-shopping agent for the world wide web. In *Proceedings of the 1st International Conference on Autonomous Agents (Agents 97), Marina del Rey, CA*, pp. 39–48.

Doran, J. (1987) Distributed artificial intelligence and the modelling of socio-cultural systems. In *Intelligent Systems in a Human Context* (eds L. A. Murray and J. T. E. Richardson), pp. 71–91. Oxford University Press, Oxford.

Doran, J. and Palmer, M. (1995) The EOS project: integrating two models of paeleolithic social change. In *Artificial Societies: the Computer Simulation of Social Life* (eds N. Gilbert and R. Conte), pp. 103–125. UCL Press, London.

Doran, J. *et al.* (1992) The EOS project. In *Simulating Societies-92: Pre-proceedings of the 1992 International Symposium on Approaches to Simulating Social Phenomena and Social Processes, Department of Sociology, University of Surrey.*

Downing, T. E., Moss, S. and Pahl-Wostl, C. (2001) Understanding climate policy using participatory agent-based social simulation. In *Multi-Agent-Based Simulation*, LNAI Volume 1979, pp. 198–213. Springer, Berlin.

Doyle, J., Shoham, Y. and Wellman, M. P. (1991) A logic of relative desire. In *Methodologies for Intelligent Systems – Sixth International Symposium, ISMIS-91* (eds Z. W. Ras and M. Zemankova), LNAI Volume 542, pp. 16–31. Springer, Berlin.

Dung, P. M. (1995) On the acceptability of arguments and its fundamental role in non-monotonic reasoning, logic programming and n-person games. *Artificial Intelligence*, **77**, 321–357.

Dunin-Keplicz, B. and Treur, J. (1995) Compositional formal specification of multi-agent systems. In *Intelligent Agents: Theories, Architectures and Languages* (eds M. Wooldridge and N. R. Jennings), LNAI Volume 890, pp. 102–117. Springer, Berlin.

Durfee, E. H. (1988) *Coordination of Distributed Problem Solvers.* Kluwer Academic, Boston, MA.

Durfee, E. H. (1996) Planning in distributed artificial intelligence. In *Foundations of Distributed Artificial Intelligence* (eds G. M. P. O'Hare and N. R. Jennings), pp. 231–245. John Wiley and Sons, Chichester.

Durfee, E. H. (1999) Distributed problem solving and planning. In *Multiagent Systems* (ed. G. Weiß), pp. 121–164. MIT Press, Cambridge, MA.

Durfee, E. H. and Lesser, V. R. (1987) Using partial global plans to coordinate distributed problem solvers. In *Proceedings of the 10th International Joint Conference on Artificial Intelligence (IJCAI-87), Milan, Italy*, pp. 875–883.

Durfee, E. H., Kiskis, D. L. and Birmingham, W. P. (1997) The agent architecture of the University of Michigan digital library. *IEEE Proceedings on Software Engineering*, **144**(1), 61–71.

Durfee, E. H., Lesser, V. R. and Corkill, D. D. (1989a) Cooperative distributed problem solving. In *Handbook of Artificial Intelligence* (eds E. A. Feigenbaum, A. Barr and P. R. Cohen), Volume IV, pp. 83–147. Addison-Wesley, Reading, MA.

Durfee, E. H., Lesser, V. R. and Corkill, D. D. (1989b) Trends in cooperative distributed problem solving. *IEEE Transactions on Knowledge and Data Engineering*, **1**(1), 63–83.

EBAY (2001) The eBay online marketplace. See `http://www.ebay.com/`.

Eliasmith, C. (1999) Dictionary of the philosophy of mind. Online at `http://www.artsci.wustl.edu/~philos/MindDict/`

Emerson, E. A. (1990) Temporal and modal logic. In *Handbook of Theoretical Computer Science. Volume B: Formal Models and Semantics* (ed. J. van Leeuwen), pp. 996–1072. Elsevier, Amsterdam.

Emerson, E. A. and Halpern, J. Y. (1986) 'Sometimes' and 'not never' revisited: on branching time versus linear time temporal logic. *Journal of the ACM*, **33**(1), 151–178.

Enderton, H. B. (1972) *A Mathematical Introduction to Logic*. Academic Press, London.

Engelmore, R. and Morgan, T. (eds) (1988) *Blackboard Systems*. Addison-Wesley, Reading, MA.

Ephrati, E. and Rosenschein, J. S. (1993) Multi-agent planning as a dynamic search for social consensus. In *Proceedings of the 13th International Joint Conference on Artificial Intelligence (IJCAI-93), Chambéry, France*, pp. 423–429.

Erman, L. D. *et al.* (1980) The Hearsay-II speech-understanding system: integrating knowledge to resolve uncertainty. *Computing Surveys*, **12**(2), 213–253.

Etzioni, O. (1993) Intelligence without robots. *AI Magazine*, **14**(4).

Etzioni, O. (1996) Moving up the information food chain: deploying softbots on the World Wide Web. In *Proceedings of the 13th National Conference on Artificial Intelligence (AAAI-96), Portland, OR*, pp. 4–8.

Etzioni, O. and Weld, D. S. (1995) Intelligent agents on the Internet: fact, fiction and forecast. *IEEE Expert*, **10**(4), 44–49.

Fagin, R. *et al.* (1995) *Reasoning About Knowledge*. MIT Press, Cambridge, MA.

Fagin, R. *et al.* (1997) Knowledge-based programs. *Distributed Computing*, **10**(4), 199–225.

Fagin, R., Halpern, J. Y. and Vardi, M. Y. (1992) What can machines know? On the properties of knowledge in distributed systems. *Journal of the ACM*, **39**(2), 328–376.

Farquhar, A., Fikes, R. and Rice, J. (1997) The Ontolingua server: a tool for collaborative ontology construction. *International Journal of Human-Computer Studies*, **46**, 707–727.

Fennell, R. D. and Lesser, V. R. (1977) Parallelism in Artificial Intelligence problem solving: a case study of Hearsay II. *IEEE Transactions on Computers*, C **26**(2), 98–111. (Also published in *Readings in Distributed Artificial Intelligence* (eds A. H. Bond and L. Gasser), pp. 106–119. Morgan Kaufmann, 1988.)

Fensel, D. and Musen, M. A. (2001) The semantic Web. *IEEE Intelligent Systems*, **16**(2), 24–25.

Fensel, D. *et al.* (2001) The semantic Web. *IEEE Intelligent Systems*, **16**(2), 24–25.

Ferber, J. (1996) Reactive distributed artificial intelligence. In *Foundations of Distributed Artificial Intelligence* (eds G. M. P. O'Hare and N. R. Jennings), pp. 287–317. John Wiley and Sons, Chichester.

Ferber, J. (1999) *Multi-Agent Systems*. Addison-Wesley, Reading, MA.

Ferber, J. and Carle, P. (1991) Actors and agents as reflective concurrent objects: a MERING IV perspective. *IEEE Transactions on Systems, Man and Cybernetics*.

Ferguson, I. A. (1992a) *TouringMachines: an Architecture for Dynamic, Rational, Mobile Agents*. PhD thesis, Clare Hall, University of Cambridge, UK. (Also available as technical report no. 273, University of Cambridge Computer Laboratory.)

Ferguson, I. A. (1992b) Towards an architecture for adaptive, rational, mobile agents. In *Decentralized AI 3 – Proceedings of the 3rd European Workshop on Modelling Autonomous Agents in a Multi-Agent World (MAAMAW-91)* (eds E. Werner and Y. Demazeau), pp. 249–262. Elsevier, Amsterdam.

Ferguson, I. A. (1995) Integrated control and coordinated behaviour: a case for agent models. In *Intelligent Agents: Theories, Architectures and Languages* (eds M. Wooldridge and N. R. Jennings), LNAI Volume 890, pp. 203–218. Springer, Berlin.

Fikes, R. E. and Nilsson, N. (1971) STRIPS: a new approach to the application of theorem proving to problem solving. *Artificial Intelligence*, **2**, 189–208.

Findler, N. V. and Lo, R. (1986) An examination of Distributed Planning in the world of air traffic control. *Journal of Parallel and Distributed Computing*, **3**.

Findler, N. and Malyankar, R. (1993) Alliances and social norms in societies of non-homogenous, interacting agents. In *Simulating Societies–93: Pre-proceedings of the 1993 International Symposium on Approaches to Simulating Social Phenomena and Social Processes, Certosa di Pontignano, Siena, Italy.*

Finin, T. *et al.* (1993) Specification of the KQML agent communication language. DARPA knowledge sharing initiative external interfaces working group.

FIPA (1999) Specification part 2 – agent communication language. The text refers to the specification dated 16 April 1999.

FIPA (2001) The foundation for intelligent physical agents. See `http://www.fipa.org/`.

Firby, J. A. (1987) An investigation into reactive planning in complex domains. In *Proceedings of the 10th International Joint Conference on Artificial Intelligence (IJCAI-87), Milan, Italy*, pp. 202–206.

Fischer, K., Müller, J. P. and Pischel, M. (1996) A pragmatic BDI architecture. In *Intelligent Agents, II* (eds M. Wooldridge, J. P. Müller and M. Tambe), LNAI Volume 1037, pp. 203–218. Springer, Berlin.

Fisher, M. (1994) A survey of Concurrent MetateM–the language and its applications. In *Temporal Logic – Proceedings of the 1st International Conference* (eds D. M. Gabbay and H. J. Ohlbach), LNAI Volume 827, pp. 480–505. Springer, Berlin.

Fisher, M. (1995) Representing and executing agent-based systems. In *Intelligent Agents: Theories, Architectures and Languages* (eds M. Wooldridge and N. R. Jennings), LNAI Volume 890, pp. 307–323. Springer, Berlin.

Fisher, M. (1996) An introduction to executable temporal logic. *The Knowledge Engineering Review*, **11**(1), 43–56.

Fisher, M. and Wooldridge, M. (1997) On the formal specification and verification of multi-agent systems. *International Journal of Cooperative Information Systems*, **6**(1), 37–65.

Fox, J., Krause, P. and Ambler, S. (1992) Arguments, contradictions and practical reasoning. In *Proceedings of the 10th European Conference on Artificial Intelligence (ECAI-92), Vienna, Austria*, pp. 623–627.

Francez, N. (1986) *Fairness*. Springer, Berlin.

Franklin, S. and Graesser, A. (1997) Is it an agent, or just a program? In *Intelligent Agents, III* (eds J. P. Müller, M. Wooldridge and N. R. Jennings), LNAI Volume 1193, pp. 21–36. Springer, Berlin.

Freeman, E., Hupfer, S. and Arnold, K. (1999) *JavaSpaces Principles, Patterns and Practice*. Addison-Wesley, Reading, MA.

Gabbay, D. (1989) Declarative past and imperative future. In *Proceedings of the Colloquium on Temporal Logic in Specification* (eds B. Banieqbal, H. Barringer and A. Pnueli), LNCS Volume 398, pp. 402–450. Springer, Berlin.

Galliers, J. R. (1988a) A strategic framework for multi-agent cooperative dialogue. In *Proceedings of the 8th European Conference on Artificial Intelligence (ECAI-88)*, pp. 415–420. Munich, Germany.

Galliers, J. R. (1988b) *A Theoretical Framework for Computer Models of Cooperative Dialogue, Acknowledging Multi-Agent Conflict*. PhD thesis, The Open University, UK.

Galliers, J. R. (1990) The positive role of conflict in cooperative multi-agent systems. In *Decentralized AI – Proceedings of the First European Workshop on Modelling Autonomous Agents in a Multi-Agent World (MAAMAW-89)* (eds Y. Demazeau and J.-P. Müller), pp. 33–48. Elsevier, Amsterdam.

Galliers, J. R. (1991) Cooperative interaction as strategic belief revision. In *CKBS-90 – Proceedings of the International Working Conference on Cooperating Knowledge Based Systems* (ed. S. M. Deen), pp. 148–163. Springer, Berlin.

Gärdenfors, P. (1988) *Knowledge in Flux.* MIT Press, Cambridge, MA.

Garey, M. R. and Johnson, D. S. (1979) *Computers and Intractability: a Guide to the Theory of* NP-*Completeness.* W. H. Freeman, New York.

Gasser, L. and Briot, J. P. (1992) Object-based concurrent programming and DAI. In *Distributed Artificial Intelligence: Theory and Praxis* (eds N. M. Avouris and L. Gasser), pp. 81–108. Kluwer Academic, Boston, MA.

Gasser, L. and Hill Jr, R. W. 1990 Coordinated problem solvers. *Annual Review of Computer Science*, **4**, 203–253.

Gasser, L. and Huhns, M. (eds) (1989) *Distributed Artificial Intelligence*, Volume II. Pitman, London and Morgan Kaufmann, San Mateo, CA.

Gasser, L., Braganza, C. and Herman, N. (1987a) Implementing distributed AI systems using MACE. In *Proceedings of the 3rd IEEE Conference on AI Applications*, pp. 315–320.

Gasser, L., Braganza, C. and Hermann, N. (1987b) MACE: a flexible testbed for distributed AI research. In *Distributed Artificial Intelligence* (ed. M. Huhns), pp. 119–152. Pitman, London and Morgan Kaufmann, San Mateo, CA.

Gasser, L. *et al.* (1989) Representing and using organizational knowledge in DAI systems. In *Distributed Artificial Intelligence* (eds L. Gasser and M. Huhns), Volume II, pp. 55–78. Pitman, London and Morgan Kaufmann, San Mateo, CA.

Gelernter, D. (1985) Generative communication in Linda. *ACM Transactions on Programming Languages and Systems*, **7**(1), 80–112.

Genesereth, M. R. and Fikes, R. E. (1992) Knowledge Interchange Format, Version 3.0 Reference Manual. Technical report logic-92-1, Computer Science Department, Stanford University.

Genesereth, M. R. and Ketchpel, S. P. (1994) Software agents. *Communications of the ACM*, **37**(7), 48–53.

Genesereth, M. R. and Nilsson, N. (1987) *Logical Foundations of Artificial Intelligence.* Morgan Kaufmann, San Mateo, CA.

Genesereth, M. R., Ginsberg, M. and Rosenschein, J. S. (1986) Cooperation without communication. In *Proceedings of the 5th National Conference on Artificial Intelligence (AAAI-86), Philadelphia, PA*, pp. 51–57.

Georgeff, M. P. (1983) Communication and interaction in multi-agent planning. In *Proceedings of the 3rd National Conference on Artificial Intelligence (AAAI-83), Washington, DC*, pp. 125–129.

Georgeff, M. P. and Ingrand, F. F. (1989) Decision-making in an embedded reasoning system. In *Proceedings of the 11th International Joint Conference on Artificial Intelligence (IJCAI-89), Detroit, MI*, pp. 972–978.

Georgeff, M. P. and Lansky, A. L. (1987) Reactive reasoning and planning. In *Proceedings of the 6th National Conference on Artificial Intelligence (AAAI-87), Seattle, WA*, pp. 677–682.

Georgeff, M. P. and Rao, A. S. (1996) A profile of the Australian AI Institute. *IEEE Expert*, **11**(6), 89–92.

Georgeff, M. *et al.* (1999) The belief-desire-intention model of agency. In *Intelligent Agents, V* (eds J. P. Müller, M. P. Singh and A. S. Rao), LNAI Volume 1555, pp. 1–10. Springer, Berlin.

Gilbert, M. (1994) Multi-modal argumentation. *Philosophy of the Social Sciences*, **24**(2), 159–177.

Gilbert, N. (1995) Emergence in social simulation. In *Artificial Societies: the Computer Simulation of Social Life* (eds N. Gilbert and R. Conte), pp. 144–156. UCL Press, London.

Gilbert, N. and Conte, R. (eds) (1995) *Artificial Societies: the Computer Simulation of Social Life*. UCL Press, London.

Gilbert, N. and Doran, J. (eds) (1994) *Simulating Societies*. UCL Press, London.

Gilkinson, H., Paulson, S. F. and Sikkink, D. E. (1954) Effects of order and authority in argumentative speech. *Quarterly Journal of Speech*, **40**, 183–192.

Ginsberg, M. L. (1989) Universal planning: an (almost) universally bad idea. *AI Magazine*, **10**(4), 40–44.

Ginsberg, M. L. (1991) Knowledge interchange format: the KIF of death. *AI Magazine*, **12**(3), 57–63.

Gmytrasiewicz, P. and Durfee, E. H. (1993) Elements of a utilitarian theory of knowledge and action. In *Proceedings of the 13th International Joint Conference on Artificial Intelligence (IJCAI-93), Chambéry, France*, pp. 396–402.

Goldberg, A. (1984) SMALLTALK-80: *the Interactive Programming Language*. Addison-Wesley, Reading, MA.

Goldblatt, R. (1987) *Logics of Time and Computation* (CSLI Lecture Notes number 7). Center for the Study of Language and Information, Ventura Hall, Stanford, CA 94305. (Distributed by Chicago University Press.)

Goldman, C. V. and Rosenschein, J. S. (1993) Emergent coordination through the use of cooperative state-changing rules. In *Proceedings of the 12th International Workshop on Distributed Artificial Intelligence (IWDAI-93), Hidden Valley, PA*, pp. 171–186.

Goldman, R. P. and Lang, R. R. (1991) Intentions in time. Technical report TUTR 93-101, Tulane University.

Gray, R. S. (1996) Agent Tcl: a flexible and secure mobile agent system. In *Proceedings of the 4th Annual Tcl/Tk Workshop, Monterrey, CA*, pp. 9–23.

Greif, I. (1994) Desktop agents in group-enabled products. *Communications of the ACM*, **37**(7), 100–105.

Grosz, B. and Kraus, S. (1993) Collaborative plans for group activities. In *Proceedings of the 13th International Joint Conference on Artificial Intelligence (IJCAI-93), Chambéry, France*, pp. 367–373.

Grosz, B. J. and Kraus, S. (1999) The evolution of SharedPlans. In *Foundations of Rational Agency* (eds M. Wooldridge and A. Rao), pp. 227–262. Kluwer Academic, Boston, MA.

Grosz, B. J. and Sidner, C. L. (1990) Plans for discourse. In *Intentions in Communication* (eds P. R. Cohen, J. Morgan and M. E. Pollack), pp. 417–444. MIT Press, Cambridge, MA.

Gruber, T. R. (1991) The role of common ontology in achieving sharable, reusable knowledge bases. In *Proceedings of Knowledge Representation and Reasoning (KR & R-91)* (eds R. Fikes and E. Sandewall). Morgan Kaufmann, San Mateo, CA.

Guilfoyle, C., Jeffcoate, J. and Stark, H. (1997) *Agents on the Web: Catalyst for E-Commerce*. Ovum Ltd, London.

Guttman, R. H., Moukas, A. G. and Maes, P. (1998) Agent-mediated electronic commerce: a survey. *The Knowledge Engineering Review*, **13**(2), 147–159.

Haddadi, A. (1996) *Communication and Cooperation in Agent Systems*, LNAI Volume 1056. Springer, Berlin.

Halpern, J. Y. (1986) Reasoning about knowledge: an overview. In *Proceedings of the 1986 Conference on Theoretical Aspects of Reasoning About Knowledge* (ed. J. Y. Halpern), pp. 1–18. Morgan Kaufmann, San Mateo, CA.

Halpern, J. Y. (1987) Using reasoning about knowledge to analyze distributed systems. *Annual Review of Computer Science*, **2**, 37–68.

Halpern, J. Y. and Moses, Y. (1992) A guide to completeness and complexity for modal logics of knowledge and belief. *Artificial Intelligence*, **54**, 319–379.

Halpern, J. Y. and Vardi, M. Y. (1989) The complexity of reasoning about knowledge and time. I. Lower bounds. *Journal of Computer and System Sciences*, **38**, 195–237.

Harel, D. (1979) *First-Order Dynamic Logic*, LNCS Volume 68. Springer, Berlin.

Harel, D. (1984) Dynamic logic. In *Handbook of Philosophical Logic. II. Extensions of Classical Logic* (eds D. Gabbay and F. Guenther), pp. 497–604. D. Reidel, Dordrecht. (Synthese Library, Volume 164.)

Harel, D., Kozen, D. and Tiuryn, J. (2000) *Dynamic Logic*. MIT Press, Cambridge, MA.

Haugeneder, H., Steiner, D. and McCabe, F. G. (1994) IMAGINE: a framework for building multi-agent systems. In *Proceedings of the 1994 International Working Conference on Cooperating Knowledge Based Systems (CKBS-94), DAKE Centre, University of Keele, UK* (ed. S. M. Deen), pp. 31–64.

Hayes-Roth, B. (1985) A blackboard architecture for control. *Artificial Intelligence*, **26**, 251–321.

Hayes-Roth, F., Waterman, D. A. and Lenat, D. B. (eds) (1983) *Building Expert Systems*. Addison-Wesley, Reading, MA.

Hayzelden, A. L. G. and Bigham, J. (eds) (1999) *Software Agents for Future Communication Systems*. Springer, Berlin.

Hendler, J. (2001) Agents and the semantic Web. *IEEE Intelligent Systems*, **16**(2), 30–37.

Hewitt, C. (1971) *Description and Theoretical Analysis (Using Schemata) of PLANNER: a Language for Proving Theorems and Manipulating Models in a Robot*. PhD thesis, Artificial Intelligence Laboratory, Massachusetts Institute of Technology.

Hewitt, C. (1973) A universal modular ACTOR formalism for AI. In *Proceedings of the 3rd International Joint Conference on Artificial Intelligence (IJCAI-73), Stanford, CA*, pp. 235–245.

Hewitt, C. (1977) Viewing control structures as patterns of passing messages. *Artificial Intelligence*, **8**(3), 323–364.

Hewitt, C. (1985) The challenge of open systems. *Byte*, **10**(4), 223–242.

Hewitt, C. E. (1986) Offices are open systems. *ACM Transactions on Office Information Systems*, **4**(3), 271–287.

Hindriks, K. V., de Boer, F. S., van der Hoek, W. and Meyer, J.-J. C. (1998) Formal semantics for an abstract agent programming language. In *Intelligent Agents, IV* (eds M. P. Singh, A. Rao and M. J. Wooldridge), LNAI Volume 1365, pp. 215–230. Springer, Berlin.

Hindriks, K. V. *et al.* (1999) Control structures of rule-based agent languages. In *Intelligent Agents, V* (eds J. P. Müller, M. P. Singh and A. S. Rao), LNAI Volume 1555. Springer, Berlin.

Hintikka, J. (1962) *Knowledge and Belief*. Cornell University Press, Ithaca, NY.

Hoare, C. A. R. (1969) An axiomatic basis for computer programming. *Communications of the ACM*, **12**(10), 576–583.

Hoare, C. A. R. (1978) Communicating sequential processes. *Communications of the ACM*, **21**, 666–677.

Holzmann, G. (1991) *Design and Validation of Computer Protocols*. Prentice-Hall International, Hemel Hempstead, UK.

Huber, M. (1999) Jam: a BDI-theoretic mobile agent architecture. In *Proceedings of the 3rd International Conference on Autonomous Agents (Agents 99), Seattle, WA*, pp. 236–243.

Hughes, G. E. and Cresswell, M. J. (1968) *Introduction to Modal Logic*. Methuen and Co., Ltd.

Huhns, M. (ed.) (1987) *Distributed Artificial Intelligence*. Pitman, London and Morgan Kaufmann, San Mateo, CA.

Huhns, M. N. (2001) Interaction-oriented programming. In *Agent-Oriented Software Engineering – Proceedings of the 1st International Workshop AOSE-2000* (eds P. Ciancarini and M. Wooldridge), LNCS Volume 1957, pp. 29–44. Springer, Berlin.

Huhns, M. and Singh, M. P. (eds) (1998) *Readings in Agents*. Morgan Kaufmann, San Mateo, CA.

Huhns, M. N. *et al.* (1992) Integrating enterprise information models in Carnot. In *Proceedings of the International Conference on Intelligent and Cooperative Information Systems, Rotterdam*, pp. 32–42.

Iglesias, C. *et al.* (1998) Analysis and design of multiagent systems using MAS-CommonKADS. In *Intelligent Agents, IV* (eds M. P. Singh, A. Rao and M. J. Wooldridge), LNAI Volume 1365, pp. 313–326. Springer, Berlin.

Iglesias, C. A., Garijo, M. and Gonzalez, J. C. (1999) A survey of agent-oriented methodologies. In *Intelligent Agents, V* (eds J. P. Müller, M. P. Singh and A. S. Rao), LNAI Volume 1555. Springer, Berlin.

Jackson, P. (1986) *Introduction to Expert Systems*. Addison-Wesley, Reading, MA.

Jennings, N. R. (1992a) On being responsible. In *Decentralized AI 3 – Proceedings of the 3rd European Workshop on Modelling Autonomous Agents in a Multi-Agent World (MAAMAW-91)* (eds E. Werner and Y. Demazeau), pp. 93–102. Elsevier, Amsterdam.

Jennings, N. R. (1992b) Towards a cooperation knowledge level for collaborative problem solving. In *Proceedings of the 10th European Conference on Artificial Intelligence (ECAI-92), Vienna, Austria*, pp. 224–228.

Jennings, N. R. (1993a) Commitments and conventions: the foundation of coordination in multi-agent systems. *The Knowledge Engineering Review*, **8**(3), 223–250.

Jennings, N. R. (1993b) Specification and implementation of a belief desire joint-intention architecture for collaborative problem solving. *Journal of Intelligent and Cooperative Information Systems*, **2**(3), 289–318.

Jennings, N. R. (1995) Controlling cooperative problem solving in industrial multi-agent systems using joint intentions. *Artificial Intelligence*, **75**(2), 195–240.

Jennings, N. R. (1999) Agent-based computing: promise and perils. In *Proceedings of the 16th International Joint Conference on Artificial Intelligence (IJCAI-99), Stockholm, Sweden*, pp. 1429–1436.

Jennings, N. R. (2000) On agent-base software engineering. *Artificial Intelligence*, **117**, 277–296.

Jennings, N. R. and Wittig, T. (1992) ARCHON: theory and practice. In *Distributed Artificial Intelligence: Theory and Praxis* (eds N. Avouris and L. Gasser), pp. 179–195. ECSC, EEC, EAEC.

Jennings, N. R. and Wooldridge, M. (eds) (1998a) *Agent Technology: Foundations, Applications and Markets*. Springer, Berlin.

Jennings, N. R. and Wooldridge, M. (1998b) Applications of intelligent agents. In *Agent Technology: Foundations, Applications and Markets* (eds N. R. Jennings and M. Wooldridge), pp. 3–28. Springer, Berlin.

Jennings, N. R., Corera, J. M. and Laresgoiti, I. (1995) Developing industrial multi-agent systems. In *Proceedings of the 1st International Conference on Multi-Agent Systems (ICMAS-95), San Francisco, CA*, pp. 423–430.

Jennings, N. R. *et al.* (1996a) Using ARCHON to develop real-world DAI applications for electricity transportation management and particle acceleration control. *IEEE Expert*, **11**(6), 60–88.

Jennings, N. R. *et al.* (1996b) Agent-based business process management. *International Journal of Cooperative Information Systems*, **5**(2–3), 105–130.

Jennings, N. R., Sycara, K. and Wooldridge, M. (1998) A roadmap of agent research and development. *Autonomous Agents and Multi-Agent Systems*, **1**(1), 7–38.

Jennings, N. R. *et al.* (2001) Automated negotiation: prospects, methods and challenges. *International Journal of Group Decision and Negotiation*, **10**(2), 199–215.

Jeon, H., Petrie, C. and Cutkosky, M. R. (2000) JATLite: a Java agent infrastructure with message routing. *IEEE Internet Computing*, **4**(2), 87–96.

Jones, C. B. (1990) *Systematic Software Development using VDM*, 2nd edition. Prentice-Hall, Englewood Cliffs, NJ.

Jowett, B. (1875) *The Dialogues of Plato*, 2nd edition. Oxford University Press, Oxford.

Jung, C. G. (1999) Emergent mental attitudes in layered agents. In *Intelligent Agents, V* (eds J. P. Müller, M. P. Singh and A. S. Rao), LNAI Volume 1555. Springer, Berlin.

Kaelbling, L. P. (1986) An architecture for intelligent reactive systems. In *Reasoning About Actions and Plans – Proceedings of the 1986 Workshop* (eds M. P. Georgeff and A. L. Lansky), pp. 395–410. Morgan Kaufmann, San Mateo, CA.

Kaelbling, L. P. (1991) A situated automata approach to the design of embedded agents. *SIGART Bulletin*, **2**(4), 85–88.

Kaelbling, L. P. (1993) *Learning in Embedded Systems*. MIT Press, Cambridge, MA.

Kaelbling, L. P. and Rosenschein, S. J. (1990) Action and planning in embedded agents. In *Designing Autonomous Agents* (ed. P. Maes), pp. 35–48. MIT Press, Cambridge, MA.

Kaelbling, L. P., Littman, M. L. and Cassandra, A. R. (1998) Planning and acting in partially observable stochastic domains. *Artificial Intelligence*, **101**, 99–134.

Kendall, E. A. (2001) Agent software engineering with role modelling. In *Agent-Oriented Software Engineering – Proceedings of the 1st International Workshop AOSE-2000* (eds P. Ciancarini and M. Wooldridge), LNCS Volume 1957, pp. 163–170. Springer, Berlin.

Kephart, J. O. and Greenwald, A. R. (1999) Shopbot economics. In *Proceedings of the 1st Workshop on Game Theoretic and Decision Theoretic Agents* (eds S. Parsons and M. J. Wooldridge), pp. 43–55.

Kiniry, J. and Zimmerman, D. (1997) A hands-on look at Java mobile agents. *IEEE Internet Computing*, **1**(4), 21–33.

Kinny, D. and Georgeff, M. (1991) Commitment and effectiveness of situated agents. In *Proceedings of the 12th International Joint Conference on Artificial Intelligence (IJCAI-91), Sydney, Australia*, pp. 82–88.

Kinny, D. and Georgeff, M. (1997) Modelling and design of multi-agent systems. In *Intelligent Agents, III* (eds J. P. Müller, M. Wooldridge and N. R. Jennings), LNAI Volume 1193, pp. 1–20. Springer, Berlin.

Kinny, D., Georgeff, M. and Rao, A. (1996) A methodology and modelling technique for systems of BDI agents. In *Agents Breaking Away: Proceedings of the 7th European Workshop on Modelling Autonomous Agents in a Multi-Agent World* (eds W. Van de Velde and J. W. Perram), LNAI Volume 1038, pp. 56–71. Springer, Berlin.

Kinny, D., Ljungberg, M., Rao, A. S., Sonenberg, E., Tidhar, G. and Werner, E. (1992) Planned team activity. In *Artificial Social Systems – Selected Papers from the 4th European Workshop on Modelling Autonomous Agents in a Multi-Agent World, MAAMAW-92* (eds C. Castelfranchi and E. Werner), LNAI Volume 830, pp. 226–256. Springer, Berlin.

Kiss, G. and Reichgelt, H. (1992) Towards a semantics of desires. In *Decentralized AI 3 – Proceedings of the 3rd European Workshop on Modelling Autonomous Agents in a Multi-Agent World (MAAMAW-91)* (eds E. Werner and Y. Demazeau), pp. 115–128. Elsevier, Amsterdam.

Kitano, H. (ed.) (1998) *RoboCup-97: Robot Soccer World Cup I*, LNAI Volume 1395. Springer, Berlin.

Kittock, J. E. (1993) Emergent conventions and the structure of multi-agent systems. In *Proceedings of the 1993 Santa Fe Institute Complex Systems Summer School*.

Klein, M. and Baskin, A. B. (1991) A computational model for conflict resolution in cooperative design systems. In *CKBS-90 – Proceedings of the International Working Conference on Cooperating Knowledge Based Systems* (ed. S. M. Deen), pp. 201–222. Springer, Berlin.

Klusch, M. (ed.) (1999) *Intelligent Information Agents*. Springer, Berlin.

Knabe, F. C. (1995) *Language Support for Mobile Agents*. PhD thesis, School of Computer Science, Carnegie-Mellon University, Pittsburgh, PA. (Also published at technical report CMU-CS-95-223.)

Konolige, K. (1986) *A Deduction Model of Belief*. Pitman, London and Morgan Kaufmann, San Mateo, CA.

Konolige, K. (1988) Hierarchic autoepistemic theories for nonmonotonic reasoning: preliminary report. In *Nonmonotonic Reasoning – Proceedings of the Second International Workshop* (eds M. Reinfrank *et al.*), LNAI Volume 346, pp. 42–59. Springer, Berlin.

Konolige, K. and Pollack, M. E. (1993) A representationalist theory of intention. In *Proceedings of the 13th International Joint Conference on Artificial Intelligence (IJCAI-93)*, pp. 390–395, Chambéry, France.

Kotz, D. *et al.* (1997) Agent Tcl: targeting the needs of mobile computers. *IEEE Internet Computing*, **1**(4), 58–67.

Kraus, S. (1997) Negotiation and cooperation in multi-agent environments. *Artificial Intelligence*, **94**(1-2), 79–98.

Kraus, S. (2001) *Strategic Negotiation in Multiagent Environments*. MIT Press, Cambridge, MA.

Kraus, S. and Lehmann, D. (1988) Knowledge, belief and time. *Theoretical Computer Science*, **58**, 155–174.

Kraus, S., Sycara, K. and Evenchik, A. (1998) Reaching agreements through argumentation: a logical model and implementation. *Artificial Intelligence*, **104**, 1–69.

Krause, P. *et al.* (1995) A logic of argumentation for reasoning under uncertainty. *Computational Intelligence*, **11**, 113–131.

Kripke, S. (1963) Semantical analysis of modal logic. *Zeitschrift für Mathematische Logik und Grundlagen der Mathematik*, **9**, 67–96.

Kuokka, D. R. and Harada, L. P. (1996) Issues and extensions for information matchmaking protocols. *International Journal of Cooperative Information Systems*, **5**(2-3), 251–274.

Kupferman, O. and Vardi, M. Y. (1997) Synthesis with incomplete informatio. In *Proceedings of the 2nd International Conference on Temporal Logic, Manchester, UK*, pp. 91–106.

Labrou, Y., Finin, T. and Peng, Y. (1999) Agent communication languages: the current landscape. *IEEE Intelligent Systems*, **14**(2), 45–52.

Lander, S., Lesser, V. R. and Connell, M. E. (1991) Conflict resolution strategies for cooperating expert agents. In *CKBS-90 – Proceedings of the International Working Conference on Cooperating Knowledge Based Systems* (ed. S. M. Deen), pp. 183–200. Springer, Berlin.

Lange, D. B. and Oshima, M. (1999) *Programming and Deploying Java Mobile Agents with Aglets*. Addison-Wesley, Reading, MA.

Langton, C. (ed.) (1989) *Artificial Life*. Santa Fe Institute Studies in the Sciences of Complexity. Addison-Wesley, Reading, MA.

Lenat, D. B. (1975) BEINGS: knowledge as interacting experts. In *Proceedings of the 4th International Joint Conference on Artificial Intelligence (IJCAI-75), Stanford, CA*, pp. 126–133.

Lésperance, Y. *et al.* (1996) Foundations of a logical approach to agent programming. In *Intelligent Agents, II* (eds M. Wooldridge, J. P. Müller and M. Tambe), LNAI Volume 1037, pp. 331–346. Springer, Berlin.

Lesser, V. R. and Corkill, D. D. (1981) Functionally accurate, cooperative distributed systems. *IEEE Transactions on Systems, Man and Cybernetics*, **11**(1), 81–96.

Lesser, V. R. and Corkill, D. D. (1988) The distributed vehicle monitoring testbed: a tool for investigating distributed problem solving networks. In *Blackboard Systems* (eds R. Engelmore and T. Morgan), pp. 353–386. Addison-Wesley, Reading, MA.

Lesser, V. R. and Erman, L. D. (1980) Distributed interpretation: a model and experiment. *IEEE Transactions on Computers*, C **29**(12), 1144–1163.

Levesque, H. J., Cohen, P. R. and Nunes, J. H. T. (1990) On acting together. In *Proceedings of the 8th National Conference on Artificial Intelligence (AAAI-90), Boston, MA*, pp. 94–99.

Levesque, H. *et al.* (1996) Golog: a logic programming language for dynamic domains. *Journal of Logic Programming*, **31**, 59–84.

Levy, A. Y., Sagiv, Y. and Srivastava, D. (1994) Towards efficient information gathering agents. In *Software Agents – Papers from the 1994 Spring Symposium* (ed. O. Etzioni), technical report SS-94-03, pp. 64–70. AAAI Press.

Lewis, D. (1969) *Convention – a Philosophical Study*. Harvard University Press, Cambridge, MA.

Lifschitz, V. (1986) On the semantics of STRIPS. In *Reasoning About Actions and Plans – Proceedings of the 1986 Workshop* (eds M. P. Georgeff and A. L. Lansky), pp. 1–10. Morgan Kaufmann, San Mateo, CA.

Lind, J. (2001) Issues in agent-oriented software engineering. In *Agent-Oriented Software Engineering – Proceedings of the 1st International Workshop AOSE-2000* (eds P. Ciancarini and M. Wooldridge), LNCS Volume 1957, pp. 45–58. Springer, Berlin.

Ljunberg, M. and Lucas, A. (1992) The OASIS air traffic management system. In *Proceedings of the 2nd Pacific Rim International Conference on AI (PRICAI-92), Seoul, Korea*.

Loui, R. (1987) Defeat among arguments: a system of defeasible inference. *Computational Intelligence*, **3**(2), 100–106.

Luck, M. and d'Inverno, M. (1995) A formal framework for agency and autonomy. In *Proceedings of the 1st International Conference on Multi-Agent Systems (ICMAS-95), San Francisco, CA*, pp. 254–260.

Luck, M., Griffiths, N. and d'Inverno, M. (1997) From agent theory to agent construction: a case study. In *Intelligent Agents, III* (eds J. P. Müller, M. Wooldridge and N. R. Jennings), LNAI Volume 1193, pp. 49–64. Springer, Berlin.

McCarthy, J. (1978) Ascribing mental qualities to machines. Technical report, Stanford University AI Lab., Stanford, CA 94305.

McCarthy, J. and Hayes, P. J. (1969) Some philosophical problems from the standpoint of artificial intelligence. In *Machine Intelligence 4* (eds B. Meltzer and D. Michie), pp. 463–502. Edinburgh University Press, Edinburgh.

McGregor, S. L. (1992) Prescient agents. In *Proceedings of Groupware-92* (ed. D. Coleman), pp. 228–230.

Maes, P. (1989) The dynamics of action selection. In *Proceedings of the 11th International Joint Conference on Artificial Intelligence (IJCAI-89), Detroit, MI*, pp. 991–997.

Maes, P. (ed.) (1990a) *Designing Autonomous Agents*. MIT Press, Cambridge, MA.

Maes, P. (1990b) Situated agents can have goals. In *Designing Autonomous Agents* (ed. P. Maes), pp. 49–70. MIT Press, Cambridge, MA.

Maes, P. (1991) The agent network architecture (ANA). *SIGART Bulletin*, **2**(4), 115–120.

Maes, P. (1994a) Agents that reduce work and information overload. *Communications of the ACM*, **37**(7), 31–40.

Maes, P. (1994b) Social interface agents: acquiring competence by learning from users and other agents. In *Software Agents – Papers from the 1994 Spring Symposium* (ed. O. Etzioni), technical report SS-94-03, pp. 71–78. AAAI Press.

Magee, J. and Kramer, J. (1999) *Concurrency*. John Wiley and Sons, Chichester.

Manna, Z. and Pnueli, A. (1992) *The Temporal Logic of Reactive and Concurrent Systems*. Springer, Berlin.

Manna, Z. and Pnueli, A. (1995) *Temporal Verification of Reactive Systems – Safety*. Springer, Berlin.

Manna, Z. and Wolper, P. (1984) Synthesis of communicating processes from temporal logic specifications. *ACM Transactions on Programming Languages and Systems*, **6**(1), 68–93.

Mayfield, J., Labrou, Y. and Finin, T. (1996) Evaluating KQML as an agent communication language. In *Intelligent Agents, II* (eds M. Wooldridge, J. P. Müller and M. Tambe), LNAI Volume 1037, pp. 347–360. Springer, Berlin.

Merz, M., Lieberman, B. and Lamersdorf, W. (1997) Using mobile agents to support inter-organizational workflow management. *Applied Artificial Intelligence*, **11**(6), 551–572.

Meyer, J.-J. C. and van der Hoek, W. (1995) *Epistemic Logic for AI and Computer Science.* Cambridge University Press, Cambridge.

Meyer, J.-J. C. and Wieringa, R. J. (eds) (1993) *Deontic Logic in Computer Science – Normative System Specification.* John Wiley and Sons, Chichester.

Milner, R. (1989) *Communication and Concurrency.* Prentice-Hall, Englewood Cliffs, NJ.

Mitchell, M. (1996) *An Introduction to Genetic Algorithms.* MIT Press, Cambridge, MA.

Moore, R. C. (1990) A formal theory of knowledge and action. In *Readings in Planning* (eds J. F. Allen, J. Hendler and A. Tate), pp. 480–519. Morgan Kaufmann, San Mateo, CA.

Mor, Y. and Rosenschein, J. S. (1995) Time and the prisoner's dilemma. In *Proceedings of the 1st International Conference on Multi-Agent Systems (ICMAS-95), San Francisco, CA*, pp. 276–282.

Móra, M. *et al.* (1999) BDI models and systems: reducing the gap. In *Intelligent Agents, V* (eds J. P. Müller, M. P. Singh and A. S. Rao), LNAI Volume 1555. Springer, Berlin.

Morgan, C. (1994) *Programming from Specifications* (2nd edition). Prentice-Hall International, Hemel Hempstead, UK.

Mori, K., Torikoshi, H., Nakai, K. and Masuda, T. (1988) Computer control system for iron and steel plants. *Hitachi Review*, **37**(4), 251–258.

Moss, S. and Davidsson, P. (eds) (2001) *Multi-Agent-Based Simulation*, LNAI Volume 1979. Springer, Berlin.

Mullen, T. and Wellman, M. P. (1995) A simple computational market for network information services. In *Proceedings of the 1st International Conference on Multi-Agent Systems (ICMAS-95), San Francisco, CA*, pp. 283–289.

Mullen, T. and Wellman, M. P. (1996) Some issues in the design of market-oriented agents. In *Intelligent Agents, II* (eds M. Wooldridge, J. P. Müller and M. Tambe), LNAI Volume 1037, pp. 283–298. Springer, Berlin.

Müller, J. (1997) A cooperation model for autonomous agents. In *Intelligent Agents, III* (eds J. P. Müller, M. Wooldridge and N. R. Jennings), LNAI Volume 1193, pp. 245–260. Springer, Berlin.

Müller, J. P. (1999) The right agent (architecture) to do the right thing. In *Intelligent Agents, V* (eds J. P. Müller, M. P. Singh and A. S. Rao), LNAI Volume 1555. Springer, Berlin.

Müller, J. P., Pischel, M. and Thiel, M. (1995) Modelling reactive behaviour in vertically layered agent architectures. In *Intelligent Agents: Theories, Architectures and Languages* (eds M. Wooldridge and N. R. Jennings), LNAI Volume 890, pp. 261–276. Springer, Berlin.

Müller, J. P., Wooldridge, M. and Jennings, N. R. (eds) (1997) *Intelligent Agents, III*, LNAI Volume 1193. Springer, Berlin.

Muscettola, N. *et al.* (1998) Remote agents: to boldly go where no AI system has gone before. *Artificial Intelligence*, **103**, 5–47.

NEC (2001) Citeseer: The NECI scientific literature digital library. See `http://citeseer.nj.nec.com/`.

Negroponte, N. (1995) *Being Digital.* Hodder and Stoughton, London.

Neumann, J. V. and Morgenstern, O. (1944) *Theory of Games and Economic Behaviour.* Princeton University Press, Princeton, NJ.

Newell, A. (1962) Some problems of the basic organisation in problem solving programs. In *Proceedings of the 2nd Conference on Self-Organizing Systems* (eds M. C. Yovits, G. T. Jacobi and G. D. Goldstein), pp. 393–423. Spartan Books, Washington, DC.

Newell, A. (1982) The knowledge level. *Artificial Intelligence*, **18**(1), 87–127.

Newell, A. (1990) *Unified Theories of Cognition.* Harvard University Press, Cambridge, MA.

Newell, A., Rosenbloom, P. J. and Laird, J. E. (1989) Symbolic architectures for cognition. In *Foundations of Cognitive Science* (ed. M. I. Posner). MIT Press, Cambridge, MA.

NeXT Computer Inc. (1993) *Object-Oriented Programming and the Objective C Language.* Addison-Wesley, Reading, MA.

Nilsson, N. J. (1992) Towards agent programs with circuit semantics. Technical report STAN-CS-92-1412, Computer Science Department, Stanford University, Stanford, CA 94305.

Nodine, M. and Unruh, A. (1998) Facilitating open communication in agent systems: the InfoSleuth infrastructure. In *Intelligent Agents, IV* (eds M. P. Singh, A. Rao and M. J. Wooldridge), LNAI Volume 1365, pp. 281–296. Springer, Berlin.

Noriega, P. and Sierra, C. (eds) (1999) *Agent Mediated Electronic Commerce,* LNAI Volume 1571. Springer, Berlin.

Norman, T. J. and Long, D. (1995) Goal creation in motivated agents. In *Intelligent Agents: Theories, Architectures and Languages* (eds M. Wooldridge and N. R. Jennings), LNAI Volume 890, pp. 277–290. Springer, Berlin.

Oaks, S. and Wong, H. (2000) *Jini in a Nutshell.* O'Reilly and Associates, Inc.

Odell, J., Parunak, H. V. D. and Bauer, B. (2001) Representing agent interaction protocols in UML. In *Agent-Oriented Software Engineering – Proceedings of the First International Workshop AOSE-2000* (eds P. Ciancarini and M. Wooldridge), LNCS Volume 1957, pp. 121–140. Springer, Berlin.

OMG (2001) The Object Management Group. See `http://www.omg.org/`.

Omicini, A. (2001) SODA: societies and infrastructures in the analysis and design of agent-based systems. In *Agent-Oriented Software Engineering – Proceedings of the First International Workshop AOSE-2000* (eds P. Ciancarini and M. Wooldridge), LNCS Volume 1957, pp. 185–194. Springer, Berlin.

Oshuga, A. *et al.* (1997) Plangent: an approach to making mobile agents intelligent. *IEEE Internet Computing,* **1**(4), 50–57.

Ousterhout, J. K. (1994) *Tcl and the Tk Toolkit.* Addison-Wesley, Reading, MA.

Ovum (1994) Intelligent agents: the new revolution in software.

Papadimitriou, C. H. (1994) *Computational Complexity.* Addison-Wesley, Reading, MA.

Papazoglou, M. P., Laufman, S. C. and Sellis, T. K. (1992) An organizational framework for cooperating intelligent information systems. *Journal of Intelligent and Cooperative Information Systems,* **1**(1), 169–202.

Parsons, S. and Jennings, N. R. (1996) Negotiation through argumentation – a preliminary report. In *Proceedings of the 2nd International Conference on Multi-Agent Systems (ICMAS-96), Kyoto, Japan,* pp. 267–274.

Parsons, S., Sierra, C. A. and Jennings, N. R. (1998) Agents that reason and negotiate by arguing. *Journal of Logic and Computation,* **8**(3), 261–292.

Parunak, H. V. D. (1999) Industrial and practical applications of DAI. In *Multi-Agent Systems* (ed. G. Weiß), pp. 377–421. MIT Press, Cambridge, MA.

Patil, R. S. *et al.* (1992) The DARPA knowledge sharing effort: progress report. In *Proceedings of Knowledge Representation and Reasoning (KR&R-92)* (eds C. Rich, W. Swartout and B. Nebel), pp. 777–788.

Perloff, M. (1991) *STIT* and the language of agency. *Synthese,* **86**, 379–408.

Perrault, C. R. (1990) An application of default logic to speech acts theory. In *Intentions in Communication* (eds P. R. Cohen, J. Morgan and M. E. Pollack), pp. 161–186. MIT Press, Cambridge, MA.

Perriolat, F., Skarek, P., Varga, L. Z. and Jennings, N. R. (1996) Using archon: particle accelerator control. *IEEE Expert,* **11**(6), 80–86.

Pham, V. A. and Karmouch, A. (1998) Mobile software agents: an overview. *IEEE Communications Magazine*, pp. 26–37.

Pitt, J. and Mamdani, E. H. (1999) A protocol-based semantics for an agent communication language. In *Proceedings of the 16th International Joint Conference on Artificial Intelligence (IJCAI-99), Stockholm, Sweden.*

Pnueli, A. (1986) Specification and development of reactive systems. In *Information Processing 86*, pp. 845–858. Elsevier, Amsterdam.

Pnueli, A. and Rosner, R. (1989) On the synthesis of a reactive module. In *Proceedings of the 16th ACM Symposium on the Principles of Programming Languages (POPL)*, pp. 179–190.

Poggi, A. and Rimassa, G. (2001) Adding extensible synchronization capabilities to the agent model of a FIPA-compliant agent platform. In *Agent-Oriented Software Engineering – Proceedings of the First International Workshop AOSE-2000* (eds P. Ciancarini and M. Wooldridge), LNCS Volume 1957, pp. 307–322. Springer, Berlin.

Pollack, M. E. (1990) Plans as complex mental attitudes. In *Intentions in Communication* (eds P. R. Cohen, J. Morgan and M. E. Pollack), pp. 77–104. MIT Press, Cambridge, MA.

Pollack, M. E. (1992) The uses of plans. *Artificial Intelligence*, **57**(1), 43–68.

Pollack, M. E. and Ringuette, M. (1990) Introducing the Tileworld: experimentally evaluating agent architectures. In *Proceedings of the 8th National Conference on Artificial Intelligence (AAAI-90), Boston, MA*, pp. 183–189.

Pollock, J. L. (1992) How to reason defeasibly. *Artificial Intelligence*, **57**, 1–42.

Pollock, J. L. (1994) Justification and defeat. *Artificial Intelligence*, **67**, 377–407.

Poundstone, W. (1992) *Prisoner's Dilemma.* Oxford University Press, Oxford.

Power, R. (1984) Mutual intention. *Journal for the Theory of Social Behaviour*, **14**, 85–102.

Prakken, H. and Vreeswijk, G. (2001) Logics for defeasible argumentation. In *Handbook of Philosophical Logic* (eds D. Gabbay and F. Guenther), 2nd edition. Kluwer Academic, Boston, MA.

Rao, A. S. (1996a) AgentSpeak(L): BDI agents speak out in a logical computable language. In *Agents Breaking Away: Proceedings of the 7th European Workshop on Modelling Autonomous Agents in a Multi-Agent World* (eds W. Van de Velde and J. W. Perram), LNAI Volume 1038, pp. 42–55. Springer, Berlin.

Rao, A. S. (1996b) Decision procedures for propositional linear-time Belief–Desire–Intention logics. In *Intelligent Agents, II* (eds M. Wooldridge, J. P. Müller and M. Tambe), LNAI Volume 1037, pp. 33–48. Springer, Berlin.

Rao, A. S. and Georgeff, M. P. (1991a) Asymmetry thesis and side-effect problems in linear time and branching time intention logics. In *Proceedings of the 12th International Joint Conference on Artificial Intelligence (IJCAI-91), Sydney, Australia*, pp. 498–504.

Rao, A. S. and Georgeff, M. P. (1991b) Modeling rational agents within a BDI-architecture. In *Proceedings of Knowledge Representation and Reasoning (KR&R-91)* (eds R. Fikes and E. Sandewall), pp. 473–484. Morgan Kaufmann, San Mateo, CA.

Rao, A. S. and Georgeff, M. P. (1992) An abstract architecture for rational agents. In *Proceedings of Knowledge Representation and Reasoning (KR&R-92)* (eds C. Rich, W. Swartout and B. Nebel), pp. 439–449.

Rao, A. S. and Georgeff, M. P. (1993) A model-theoretic approach to the verification of situated reasoning systems. In *Proceedings of the 13th International Joint Conference on Artificial Intelligence (IJCAI-93), Chambéry, France*, pp. 318–324.

Rao, A. S. and Georgeff, M. P. (1995) Formal models and decision procedures for multiagent systems. Technical note 61, Australian AI Institute, level 6, 171 La Trobe Street, Melbourne, Australia.

Rao, A. S., Georgeff, M. P. and Sonenberg, E. A. (1992) Social plans: a preliminary report. In *Decentralized AI 3 – Proceedings of the 3rd European Workshop on Modelling Autonomous Agents in a Multi-Agent World (MAAMAW-91)* (eds E. Werner and Y. Demazeau), pp. 57–76. Elsevier, Amsterdam.

Reddy, D. R. *et al.* (1973) The Hearsay speech understanding system: and example of the recognition process. In *Proceedings of the 3rd International Joint Conference on Artificial Intelligence (IJCAI-73), Stanford, CA*, pp. 185–193.

Reed, C. (1998) Dialogue frames in agent communication. In *Proceedings of the 3rd International Conference on Multi-Agent Systems (ICMAS-98), Paris, France*, pp. 246–253.

Reichgelt, H. (1989) A comparison of first-order and modal logics of time. In *Logic Based Knowledge Representation* (eds P. Jackson, H. Reichgelt and F. van Harmelen), pp. 143–176. MIT Press, Cambridge, MA.

Reiter, R. (1980) A logic for default reasoning. *Artificial Intelligence*, **13**, 81–132.

RoboCup (2001) The robot world cup initiative. See http://www.RoboCup.org/.

Rodríguez, J. *et al.* (1997) FM96.5: A Java-based electronic marketplace. In *Proceedings of the 2nd International Conference on the Practical Application of Intelligent Agents and Multi-Agent Technology (PAAM-97), London, UK*, pp. 207–224.

Rosenschein, J. S. and Genesereth, M. R. (1985) Deals among rational agents. In *Proceedings of the 9th International Joint Conference on Artificial Intelligence (IJCAI-85), Los Angeles, CA*, pp. 91–99.

Rosenschein, J. S. and Zlotkin, G. (1994) *Rules of Encounter: Designing Conventions for Automated Negotiation among Computers.* MIT Press, Cambridge, MA.

Rosenschein, S. (1985) Formal theories of knowledge in AI and robotics. *New Generation Computing*, **3**(4), 345–357.

Rosenschein, S. and Kaelbling, L. P. (1986) The synthesis of digital machines with provable epistemic properties. In *Proceedings of the 1986 Conference on Theoretical Aspects of Reasoning About Knowledge* (ed. J. Y. Halpern), pp. 83–98. Morgan Kaufmann, San Mateo, CA.

Rosenschein, S. J. and Kaelbling, L. P. (1996) A situated view of representation and control. In *Computational Theories of Interaction and Agency* (eds P. E. Agre and S. J. Rosenschein), pp. 515–540. MIT Press, Cambridge, MA.

Rothermel, K. and Popescu-Zeletin, R. (eds) (1997) *Mobile Agents*, LNCS Volume 1219. Springer, Berlin.

Rumbaugh, J. *et al.* (1991) *Object-Oriented Modeling and Design.* Prentice-Hall, Englewood Cliifs, NJ.

Russell, S. and Norvig, P. (1995) *Artificial Intelligence: a Modern Approach.* Prentice-Hall, Englewood Cliffs, NJ.

Russell, S. and Subramanian, D. (1995) Provably bounded-optimal agents. *Journal of AI Research*, **2**, 575–609.

Russell, S. J. and Wefald, E. (1991) *Do the Right Thing–Studies in Limited Rationality.* MIT Press, Cambridge, MA.

Sadek, M. D. (1992) A study in the logic of intention. In *Proceedings of Knowledge Representation and Reasoning (KR&R-92)*, pp. 462–473.

Sandholm, T. (1999) Distributed rational decision making. In *Multiagent Systems* (ed. G. Weiß), pp. 201–258. MIT Press, Cambridge, MA.

Sandholm, T. and Lesser, V. (1995) Issues in automated negotiation and electronic commerce: Extending the contract net framework. In *Proceedings of the 1st International Conference on Multi-Agent Systems (ICMAS-95), San Francisco, CA*, pp. 328–335.

Schoppers, M. J. (1987) Universal plans for reactive robots in unpredictable environments. In *Proceedings of the 10th International Joint Conference on Artificial Intelligence (IJCAI-87), Milan, Italy*, pp. 1039–1046.

Schut, M. and Wooldridge, M. (2000) Intention reconsideration in complex environments. In *Proceedings of the 4th International Conference on Autonomous Agents (Agents 2000), Barcelona, Spain*, pp. 209–216.

Searle, J. R. (1969) *Speech Acts: an Essay in the Philosophy of Language*. Cambridge University Press, Cambridge.

Searle, J. R. (1990) Collective intentions and actions. In *Intentions in Communication* (eds P. R. Cohen, J. Morgan and M. E. Pollack), pp. 401–416. MIT Press, Cambridge, MA.

Seel, N. (1989) *Agent Theories and Architectures*. PhD thesis, Surrey University, Guildford, UK.

Segerberg, K. (1989) Bringing it about. *Journal of Philosophical Logic*, **18**, 327–347.

SGML (2001) The standard generalised markup language. See `http://www.sgml.org/`.

Shoham, Y. (1988) *Reasoning About Change: Time and Causation from the Standpoint of Artificial Intelligence*. MIT Press, Cambridge, MA.

Shoham, Y. (1989) Time for action: on the relation between time, knowledge and action. In *Proceedings of the 11th International Joint Conference on Artificial Intelligence (IJCAI-89), Detroit, MI*, pp. 954–959.

Shoham, Y. (1990) Agent-oriented programming. Technical report STAN-CS-1335-90, Computer Science Department, Stanford University, Stanford, CA 94305.

Shoham, Y. (1993) Agent-oriented programming. *Artificial Intelligence*, **60**(1), 51–92.

Shoham, Y. and Tennenholtz, M. (1992a) Emergent conventions in multi-agent systems. In *Proceedings of Knowledge Representation and Reasoning (KR&R-92)* (eds C. Rich, W. Swartout and B. Nebel), pp. 225–231.

Shoham, Y. and Tennenholtz, M. (1992b) On the synthesis of useful social laws for artificial agent societies. In *Proceedings of the 10th National Conference on Artificial Intelligence (AAAI-92), San Diego, CA*.

Shoham, Y. and Tennenholtz, M. (1996) On social laws for artificial agent societies: off-line design. In *Computational Theories of Interaction and Agency* (eds P. E. Agre and S. J. Rosenschein), pp. 597–618. MIT Press, Cambridge, MA.

Shoham, Y. and Tennenholtz, M. (1997) On the emergence of social conventions: modelling, analysis and simulations. *Artificial Intelligence*, **94**(1–2), 139–166.

Sichman, J. and Demazeau, Y. (1995) Exploiting social reasoning to deal with agency level inconsistency. In *Proceedings of the 1st International Conference on Multi-Agent Systems (ICMAS-95), San Francisco, CA*, pp. 352–359.

Sichman, J. S. *et al.* (1994) A social reasoning mechanism based on dependence networks. In *Proceedings of the 11th European Conference on Artificial Intelligence (ECAI-94), Amsterdam*, pp. 188–192.

Simon, H. A. (1981) *The Sciences of the Artificial*, 2nd edition. MIT Press, Cambridge, MA.

Singh, M. P. (1990a) Group intentions. In *Proceedings of the 10th International Workshop on Distributed Artificial Intelligence (IWDAI-90)*.

Singh, M. P. (1990b) Towards a theory of situated know-how. In *Proceedings of the 9th European Conference on Artificial Intelligence (ECAI-90), Stockholm, Sweden*, pp. 604–609.

Singh, M. P. (1991a) Group ability and structure. In *Decentralized AI 2 – Proceedings of the Second European Workshop on Modelling Autonomous Agents in a Multi-Agent World (MAAMAW-90)* (eds Y. Demazeau and J.-P. Müller), pp. 127–146. Elsevier, Amsterdam.

Singh, M. P. (1991b) Social and psychological commitments in multiagent systems. In *AAAI Fall Symposium on Knowledge and Action at Social and Organizational Levels*, pp. 104–106.

Singh, M. P. (1991c) Towards a formal theory of communication for multi-agent systems. In *Proceedings of the 12th International Joint Conference on Artificial Intelligence (IJCAI-91), Sydney, Australia*, pp. 69–74.

Singh, M. P. (1992) A critical examination of the Cohen–Levesque theory of intention. In *Proceedings of the 10th European Conference on Artificial Intelligence (ECAI-92), Vienna, Austria*, pp. 364–368.

Singh, M. P. (1993) A semantics for speech acts. *Annals of Mathematics and Artificial Intelligence*, **8**(I–II), 47–71.

Singh, M. P. (1994) *Multiagent Systems: a Theoretical Framework for Intentions, Know-How and Communications*, LNAI Volume 799. Springer, Berlin.

Singh, M. (1998a) Agent communication languages: rethinking the principles. *IEEE Computer*, pp. 40–49.

Singh, M. P. (1998b) The intentions of teams: team structure, endodeixis and exodeixis. In *Proceedings of the 13th European Conference on Artificial Intelligence (ECAI-98), Brighton, UK*, pp. 303–307.

Singh, M. P. and Asher, N. M. (1991) Towards a formal theory of intentions. In *Logics in AI – Proceedings of the European Workshop JELIA-90* (ed J. van Eijck), LNAI Volume 478, pp. 472–486. Springer, Berlin.

Smith, R. G. (1977) The CONTRACT NET: a formalism for the control of distributed problem solving. In *Proceedings of the 5th International Joint Conference on Artificial Intelligence (IJCAI-77), Cambridge, MA*.

Smith, R. G. (1980a) The contract net protocol. *IEEE Transactions on Computers*, C **29**(12).

Smith, R. G. (1980b) *A Framework for Distributed Problem Solving*. UMI Research Press.

Smith, R. G. and Davis, R. (1980) Frameworks for cooperation in distributed problem solving. *IEEE Transactions on Systems, Man and Cybernetics*, **11**(1).

Smullyan, R. M. (1968) *First-Order Logic*. Springer, Berlin.

Sommaruga, L., Avouris, N. and Van Liedekerke, M. (1989) The evolution of the CooperA platform. In *Foundations of Distributed Artificial Intelligence* (eds G. M. P. O'Hare and N. R. Jennings), pp. 365–400. John Wiley and Sons, Chichester.

Spivey, M. (1992) *The Z Notation*, 2nd edition. Prentice-Hall International, Hemel Hempstead, UK.

Steeb, R. *et al.* (1988) Distributed intelligence for air fleet control. In *Readings in Distributed Artificial Intelligence* (eds A. H. Bond and L. Gasser), pp. 90–101. Morgan Kaufmann, San Mateo, CA.

Steels, L. (1990) Cooperation between distributed agents through self organization. In *Decentralized AI – Proceedings of the 1st European Workshop on Modelling Autonomous Agents in a Multi-Agent World (MAAMAW-89)* (eds Y. Demazeau and J.-P. Müller), pp. 175–196. Elsevier, Amsterdam.

Stich, S. P. (1983) *From Folk Psychology to Cognitive Science*. MIT Press, Cambridge, MA.

Stone, P. (2000) *Layered Learning in Multiagent Systems: a Winning Approach to Robotic Soccer*. MIT Press, Cambridge, MA.

Stuart, C. J. (1985) An implementation of a multi-agent plan synchroniser using a temporal logic theorem prover. In *Proceedings of the 9th International Joint Conference on Artificial Intelligence (IJCAI-85), Los Angeles, CA*, pp. 1031–1033.

Sueyoshi, T. and Tokoro, M. (1991) Dynamic modelling of agents for coordination. In *Decentralized AI 2 – Proceedings of the 2nd European Workshop on Modelling Autonomous Agents in a Multi-Agent World (MAAMAW-90)* (eds Y. Demazeau and J.-P. Müller), pp. 161–180. Elsevier, Amsterdam.

Sycara, K. P. (1989a) Argumentation: planning other agents' plans. In *Proceedings of the 11th International Joint Conference on Artificial Intelligence (IJCAI-89), Detroit, MI*, pp. 517–523.

Sycara, K. P. (1989b) Multiagent compromise via negotiation. In *Distributed Artificial Intelligence* (eds L. Gasser and M. Huhns), Volume II, pp. 119–138. Pitman, London and Morgan Kaufmann, San Mateo, CA.

Sycara, K. P. (1990) Persuasive argumentation in negotiation. *Theory and Decision*, **28**, 203–242.

Tambe, M. (1997) Towards flexible teamwork. *Journal of AI Research*, **7**, 83–124.

Thomas, S. R. (1993) *PLACA, an Agent Oriented Programming Language*. PhD thesis, Computer Science Department, Stanford University, Stanford, CA 94305. (Available as technical report STAN-CS-93-1487.)

Thomas, S. R. (1995) The PLACA agent programming language. In *Intelligent Agents: Theories, Architectures and Languages* (eds M. Wooldridge and N. R. Jennings), LNAI Volume 890, pp. 355–369. Springer, Berlin.

Thomas, S. R. *et al.* (1991) Preliminary thoughts on an agent description language. *International Journal of Intelligent Systems*, **6**, 497–508.

Tidhar, G. and Rosenschein, J. (1992) A contract net with consultants. In *Proceedings of the 10th European Conference on Artificial Intelligence (ECAI-92), Vienna, Austria*, pp. 219–223.

Tschudin, C. F. (1999) Mobile agent security. In *Intelligent Information Agents* (ed. M. Klusch), pp. 431–445. Springer, Berlin.

Tuomela, R. (1991) We will do it: an analysis of group intentions. *Philosophy and Phenomenological Research*, **51**(2), 249–277.

Tuomela, R. and Miller, K. (1988) We-intentions. *Philosophical Studies*, **53**, 367–389.

Turing, A. M. (1963) Computing machinery and intelligence. In *Computers and Thought* (ed. E. A. Feigenbaum). McGraw-Hill.

Uschold, M. and Gruninger, M. (1996) Ontologies: principles, methods and applications. *Knowledge Engineering Review*, **11**(2), 93–136.

Van Dyke Parunak, H. (1987) Manufacturing experience with the contract net. In *Distributed Artificial Intelligence* (ed. M. Huhns), pp. 285–310. Pitman, London and Morgan Kaufmann, San Mateo, CA.

van Eemeren, F. H. *et al.* (1996) *Fundamentals of Argumentation Theory: a Handbook of Historical Backgrounds and Contemporary Developments*. Lawrence Erlbaum Associates, Mahwah, NJ.

Vardi, M. Y. and Wolper, P. (1994) Reasoning about infinite computations. *Information and Computation*, **115**(1), 1–37.

Vere, S. and Bickmore, T. (1990) A basic agent. *Computational Intelligence*, **6**, 41–60.

von Martial, F. (1990) Interactions among autonomous planning agents. In *Decentralized AI – Proceedings of the First European Workshop on Modelling Autonomous Agents in a Multi-Agent World (MAAMAW-89)* (eds Y. Demazeau and J.-P. Müller), pp. 105–120. Elsevier, Amsterdam.

von Martial, F. (1992) *Coordinating Plans of Autonomous Agents*, LNAI Volume 610. Springer, Berlin.

Voorhees, E. M. (1994) Software agents for information retrieval. In *Software Agents – Papers from the 1994 Spring Symposium* (ed. O. Etzioni), technical report SS-94-03, pp. 126–129. AAAI Press.

Vreeswijk, G. A. W. and Prakken, H. (2000) Credulous and sceptical argument games for preferred semantics. In *Logics in Artificial Intelligence – Proceedings of the 7th European Workshop, JELIA 2000* (eds M. Ojeda-Aciego *et al.*), LNAI Volume 1919, pp. 239–253. Springer, Berlin.

Wainer, J. (1994) Yet another semantics of goals and goal priorities. In *Proceedings of the 11th European Conference on Artificial Intelligence (ECAI-94), Amsterdam*, pp. 269–273.

Walker, A. and Wooldridge, M. (1995) Understanding the emergence of conventions in multi-agent systems. In *Proceedings of the 1st International Conference on Multi-Agent Systems (ICMAS-95), San Francisco, CA*, pp. 384–390.

Walton, D. N. and Krabbe, E. C. W. (1995) *Commitment in Dialogue: Basic Concepts of Interpersonal Reasoning.* State University of New York Press, Albany, NY.

Webster, B. F. (1995) *Pitfalls of Object-Oriented Development.* M & T Books, New York.

Weiß, G. (1993) Learning to coordinate actions in multi-agent systems. In *Proceedings of the 13th International Joint Conference on Artificial Intelligence (IJCAI-93), Chambéry, France*, pp. 311–316.

Weiß, G. (ed.) (1997) *Distributed Artificial Intelligence Meets Machine Learning*, LNAI Volume 1221. Springer, Berlin.

Weiß, G. (ed.) (1999) *Multi-Agent Systems.* MIT Press, Cambridge, MA.

Weiß, G. and Sen, S. (eds) (1996) *Adaption and Learning in Multi-Agent Systems*, LNAI Volume 1042. Springer, Berlin.

Wellman, M. P. (1993) A market-oriented programming environment and its applications to multicommodity flow problems. *Journal of AI Research*, **1**, 1–22.

Wellman, M. P., Birmingham, W. P. and Durfee, E. H. (1996) The digital library as a community of information agents. *IEEE Expert*, **11**(3), 10–11.

Werner, E. (1989) Cooperating agents: a unified theory of communication and social structure. In *Distributed Artificial Intelligence* (eds L. Gasser and M. Huhns), Volume II, pp. 3–36. Pitman, London and Morgan Kaufmann, San Mateo, CA.

Werner, E. (1990) What can agents do together: a semantics of co-operative ability. In *Proceedings of the 9th European Conference on Artificial Intelligence (ECAI-90), Stockholm, Sweden*, pp. 694–701.

White, J. E. (1994) Telescript technology: the foundation for the electronic marketplace. White paper, General Magic, Inc., 2465 Latham Street, Mountain View, CA 94040.

White, J. E. (1997) Mobile agents. In *Software Agents* (ed. J. Bradshaw), pp. 437–473. MIT Press, Cambridge, MA.

Wiederhold, G. (1992) Mediators in the architecture of future information systems. *IEEE Transactions on Computers*, **25**(3), 38–49.

Wittig, T. (ed.) (1992) *ARCHON: an Architecture for Multi-Agent Systems.* Ellis Horwood, Chichester.

Wolper, P. (1985) The tableau method for temporal logic: an overview. *Logique et Analyse*, 110–111.

Wood, M. and DeLoach, S. A. (2001) An overview of the multiagent systems engineering methodology. In *Agent-Oriented Software Engineering – Proceedings of the 1st International Workshop AOSE-2000* (eds P. Ciancarini and M. Wooldridge), LNCS Volume 1957, pp. 207–222. Springer, Berlin.

Wooldridge, M. (1992) *The Logical Modelling of Computational Multi-Agent Systems.* PhD thesis, Department of Computation, UMIST, Manchester, UK.

Wooldridge, M. (1994) Coherent social action. In *Proceedings of the 11th European Conference on Artificial Intelligence (ECAI-94), Amsterdam*, pp. 279–283.

Wooldridge, M. (1995) This is MYWORLD: the logic of an agent-oriented testbed for DAI. In *Intelligent Agents: Theories, Architectures and Languages* (eds M. Wooldridge and N. R. Jennings), LNAI Volume 890, pp. 160–178. Springer, Berlin.

Wooldridge, M. (1997) Agent-based software engineering. *IEEE Proceedings on Software Engineering*, **144**(1), 26–37.

Wooldridge, M. (1998) Verifiable semantics for agent communication languages. In *Proceedings of the 3rd International Conference on Multi-Agent Systems (ICMAS-98), Paris, France*, pp. 349–365.

Wooldridge, M. (1999) Verifying that agents implement a communication language. In *Proceedings of the 16th National Conference on Artificial Intelligence (AAAI-99), Orlando, FL*, pp. 52–57.

Wooldridge, M. (2000a) The computational complexity of agent design problems. In *Proceedings of the 4th International Conference on Multi-Agent Systems (ICMAS-2000), Boston, MA*, pp. 341–348.

Wooldridge, M. (2000b) *Reasoning about Rational Agents*. MIT Press, Cambridge, MA.

Wooldridge, M. and Dunne, P. E. (2000) Optimistic and disjunctive agent design problems. In *Intelligent Agents, VII: Proceedings of the Seventh International Workshop on Agent Theories, Architectures and Languages, ATAL-2000* (eds C. Castelfranchi and Y. Lespérance), LNAI Volume 1986, pp. 1–14. Springer, Berlin.

Wooldridge, M. and Fisher, M. (1994) A decision procedure for a temporal belief logic. In *Temporal Logic – Proceedings of the 1st International Conference* (eds D. M. Gabbay and H. J. Ohlbach), LNAI Volume 827, pp. 317–331. Springer, Berlin.

Wooldridge, M. and Jennings, N. R. (1994) Formalizing the cooperative problem solving process. In *Proceedings of the 13th International Workshop on Distributed Artificial Intelligence (IWDAI-94), Lake Quinalt, WA*, pp. 403–417. Reprinted in Huhns and Singh (1998).

Wooldridge, M. and Jennings, N. R. (1995) Intelligent agents: theory and practice. *The Knowledge Engineering Review*, **10**(2), 115–152.

Wooldridge, M. and Jennings, N. R. (1998) Pitfalls of agent-oriented development. In *Proceedings of the 2nd International Conference on Autonomous Agents (Agents 98), Minneapolis/St. Paul, MN*, pp. 385–391.

Wooldridge, M. and Jennings, N. R. (1999) The cooperative problem solving process. *Journal of Logic and Computation*, **9**(4), 563–592.

Wooldridge, M. and Parsons, S. D. (1999) Intention reconsideration reconsidered. In *Intelligent Agents, V* (eds J. P. Müller, M. P. Singh and A. S. Rao), LNAI Volume 1555, pp. 63–80. Springer, Berlin.

Wooldridge, M., Bussmann, S. and Klosterberg, M. (1996) Production sequencing as negotiation. In *Proceedings of the 1st International Conference on the Practical Application of Intelligent Agents and Multi-Agent Technology (PAAM-96), London, UK*, pp. 709–726.

Wooldridge, M., Dixon, C. and Fisher, M. (1998) A tableau-based proof method for temporal logics of knowledge and belief. *Journal of Applied Non-Classical Logics*, **8**(3), 225–258.

Wooldridge, M., Jennings, N. R. and Kinny, D. (1999) A methodology for agent-oriented analysis and design. In *Proceedings of the 3rd International Conference on Autonomous Agents (Agents 99), Seattle, WA*, pp. 69–76.

Wooldridge, M., O'Hare, G. M. P. and Elks, R. (1991) FELINE – a case study in the design and implementation of a co-operating expert system. In *Proceedings of the 11th European Conference on Expert Systems and Their Applications, Avignon, France*.

Wooldridge, M., Weiß, G. and Ciancarini, P. (eds) (2002) *Agent-Oriented Software Engineering II – Proceedings of the 2nd International Workshop, AOSE-2001*, LNCS Volume 2222. Springer, Berlin.

XML (2001) The Xtensible Markup Language. See http://www.xml.org/.

Yonezawa, A. (ed.) (1990) *ABCL – an Object-Oriented Concurrent System*. MIT Press, Cambridge, MA.

Yonezawa, A. and Tokoro, M. (eds) (1997) *Object-Oriented Concurrent Programming*. MIT Press, Cambridge, MA.

Yoshioka, N. *et al.* (2001) Safety and security in mobile agents. In *Agent-Oriented Software Engineering – Proceedings of the First International Workshop AOSE-2000* (eds P. Ciancarini and M. Wooldridge), LNCS Volume 1957, pp. 223–235. Springer, Berlin.

Zagare, F. C. (1984) *Game Theory: Concepts and Applications*. Sage Publications, Beverly Hills, CA.

Index

SENTENCING AND PUNISHMENT